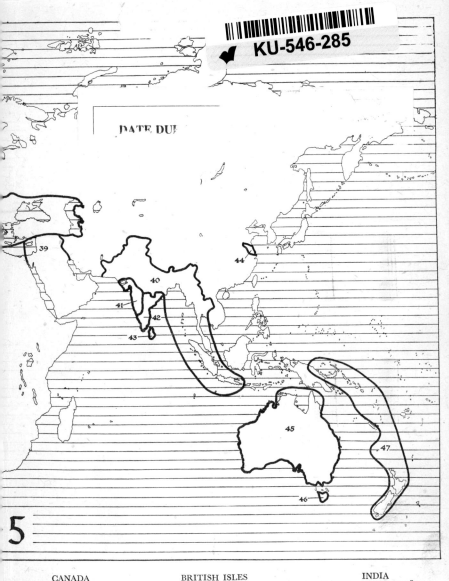

5

CANADA			BRITISH ISLES		INDIA	
9 Nova Scotia	1787				40 Calcutta	1814
0 Fredericton	1845		(Forty-nine Dioceses)		41 Bombay	1837
1 Toronto	1839				42 Madras	1835
2 Quebec	1793				43 Colombo	1845
3 Newfoundland	1839					

WEST INDIES					FAR EAST	
			38 Gibraltar	1842		
4 Jamaica	1824				44 Shanghai	1844
5 Antigua	1842				45 Australia	1836
6 Barbados	1824				46 Tasmania	1842
7 Guiana	1842		39 Jerusalem	1841	47 New Zealand	1841

With grateful good wishes
to the Rev. Dr. Hanson from
R.P. Greene

Christian History in the Making

By

J. McLEOD CAMPBELL

Chaplain to the King.   Hon. Canon of Canterbury.
Formerly Fellow and Chaplain of Hertford College,
Oxford, and Principal of Trinity College, Kandy.
General Secretary of the Missionary
Council of the Church
Assembly

INTRODUCTION
BY THE
ARCHBISHOP
OF YORK

"*History is the essence of innumerable biographies*"
THOMAS CARLYLE

LONDON: THE PRESS & PUBLICATIONS
BOARD OF THE CHURCH ASSEMBLY,
2 GREAT PETER ST., WESTMINSTER

By the Same Author :

MAN-POWER
BRIDGE BUILDERS

AUTHOR'S ACKNOWLEDGEMENTS

I WISH to thank Miss Few of the Missionary Council office for her heavy work in type-writing my manuscript and in correcting the proofs : also my colleague the Rev. F. W. T. Craske for seeing the book through the Press in my absence. I am under great obligation to Miss Pulling, Librarian of the S.P.G. for generous loans of books : the C.M.S. has also lent me books that could not be obtained elsewhere. I am grateful to the Missionary Council for commissioning this book and for allowing me unfettered freedom to write it in a personal capacity. Individuals to whom I am indebted for advice are too numerous to mention, but I must acknowledge the help and encouragement of the writer of the Introduction when Chairman of the Missionary Council. Readers will agree that the interest of the book is greatly enhanced by the maps which have been so skilfully drawn by Miss Freda Hands.

October, 1945.   J. McL. C.

Introduction by the Archbishop of York

THIS book may easily prove to be the most important which has yet been written on the missionary work of the Anglican Communion. What Professor Latourette has been doing for Missions in general, Canon Campbell has done here for the Church of England. It would be hard, if not impossible, to have found anyone with greater qualifications for this work. Canon Campbell has done distinguished work overseas as Principal of Trinity College, Kandy, and for the last ten years he has been Secretary of the Missionary Council of the Church Assembly. In this position he has been in touch with missionary work and problems in all parts of the world.

This book is an inspiring and encouraging account of the awakening of the Church of England to its evangelistic responsibilities. It is strange to read how, little over a century ago, Sidney Smith mocked at proposals to send missionaries overseas. He was not then a solitary voice crying in the wilderness, but was expressing the criticisms and lukewarmness of the great mass of the Churchpeople of his day. Since then there has been nothing less than a revolution in their outlook. Clergy and laity have become convinced that the Church must be missionary-minded. The response that the Church of England makes to-day to the call for missionary support is far from adequate, both in the number of men and women it sends overseas and in the money it contributes year by year for the missionary cause. But it has become missionary conscious, and Canon Campbell describes how the Church, which once was both spiritually and geographically insular, has become the mother of a family of Churches spread throughout the world—and these in their turn are now active in the work of evangelization. In chapter after chapter Canon Campbell gives us a well-documented account of devoted work, noble self-sacrifice and wise statesmanship, in building up and expanding the Anglican Communion.

This book is not only a history of the past. It faces also some of the perplexing problems which have arisen through expansion. In the closing chapters, two of the most difficult of these problems are discussed, under the headings of *Acclimatization* and *Consolidation*. " Acclimatization " is defined as " becoming habituated or inured to a new climate, or one not natural." To acclimatize the Church is a task as delicate as it is essential. It is delicate, for the acceptance of Christianity must mean the expulsion of many rites and customs to which the converts have long been accustomed. But it also means that the people should learn to worship God in the manner most natural to them. If Christianity comes simply under a western guise to the people of Asia or Africa, it will seem an alien religion, and will be regarded with hostility or suspicion among peoples who are becoming nationally conscious. Much has already been done to acclimatize the Church. The architecture of the country and the ceremonial and music which the converts find most natural have been introduced into its worship. But acclimatization means much more than this. It means that eventually what was a missionary church, largely staffed by those sent from a distant land, will become a church governing itself without being controlled from the home base, and ordaining its own Bishops and clergy.

The missionary work of our church was inaugurated and for many generations has been carried on by the various Missionary Societies, for these are the agents of the Church in its work overseas. At first it was inevitable that this work should be inaugurated and carried on by groups of Christians who were anxious, among widespread indifference and hostility, to obey the Lord's command to " make disciples of all nations ". Their work has been magnificent. But for them, the Church might still be confined to English-speaking people. To their enthusiasm Canon Campbell pays a high tribute of praise. With justice he says, " The Anglican Communion owes its expansion, humanly speaking, to the men of faith and vision who founded these voluntary associations, and to all who, at great personal sacrifice, financed their ventures. They hold between them the title-deeds of all the Anglican Churches throughout the world." But he asks if this position is to be perpetuated for ever ? Many with him often ask the question, if the Church of England itself should not initiate and control more definitely its missionary work ? No concrete proposal is made to meet this problem, but Canon Campbell asks that the Church should review its present organization for overseas work, and asks whether, under changed conditions, some new policy might be agreed upon which gives the Church, as a whole, greater responsibility.

This book will be of special value in view of the approach of the Lambeth Conference. It should be found in every parish church library, and should be widely read and studied. For many years to come it will be a comprehensive introduction to the work of the Church overseas.

CYRIL EBOR:

(v)

CONTENTS

LIST OF MAPS

The endpapers consist of two maps of the dioceses of the Anglican Communion: one of 1845 and the other of 1945.

PART I

THE INFANCY OF THE ANGLICAN COMMUNION

Introductory : " The Greatest Fact of our Time"

1. The Expansion to England: (*a*) St. Augustine and the Roman Mission; (*b*) The Isle of Lérins; (*c*) St. Columba and the Irish Mission; (*d*) Theodore and Hadrian.

2. The Expansion from England: (*a*) The Irish Monks; (*b*) Missions to the Continent: Willibrord, Boniface; (*c*) Missions in Scandinavia.

ARCHBISHOP WILLIAM TEMPLE'S Enthronement Sermon poses the question which this book attempts to answer. " Now is arising on a scale never before seen in the world the Christian fellowship which corresponds to St. Paul's description of the Church, the fellowship in which all earthly divisions are abolished. As though in preparation for such a time as this, God has been building up a Christian fellowship which now extends into almost every nation, and binds citizens of them all together in true unity and mutual love: it is the great new fact of our era." To the question, How has all this come about? the Archbishop replies, " It is the result of the great missionary enterprise of the last hundred and fifty years." To the further question, What is the origin and history of this enterprise? this book offers only a partial answer, for it is a tale that needs many volumes for the telling: and space enough to range geographically over the whole globe, ecclesiastically over the activities of all the Churches—Roman, Lutheran, Presbyterian, Moravian, Methodist and the rest. Even an answer in terms of a single Communion, which is all that is here attempted, presents daunting difficulties of selection and compression.

Of Christian History in the Making the beginnings are unknown and the end is far off. The God and Father of our Lord Jesus Christ has chosen us in Him before the foundation of the world: not till we all attain unto the unity of the faith, unto the measure of the stature of the fulness of Christ, will the culmination be reached. Against this majestic background the fraction of Christian history in the making to which attention is here confined is dwarfed into insignificance. A hundred and fifty years is a short period in the life of the Church; moreover the Church of England, as distinct from the Anglican Communion, is the Church of a single Nation, and a Church which has no monopoly of that nation's contribution to the making of Christian history.

Yet for Anglicans there is one chapter of the great history of God's dealing with mankind which it is an obligation to study, the chapter which records the activity of the divine initiative the world over, in and through the Church which holds their allegiance and affection. Here are enshrined great memories which cannot be allowed to fade, great traditions which cannot lapse without infinite loss, great names whose glory must not be blotted out. There is nothing exclusive in thus isolating one section of Church History for special study, for these memories, traditions and great names, so far from being the private possession of a single Communion, are cherished treasures in the great common inheritance which all Christians share. Moreover, the enterprise and experience of Christian expansion has been paralleled by so many other Christian communities that what is told of one applies in large measure to all.

It is with the last century that subsequent chapters will be mainly concerned; for it was within this period that the making of Christian history proceeded apace. It would not be reasonable to exclude too rigidly all that has happened since 1900, in so far as such reference is necessary to an understanding of the legacy of the nineteenth century. But this is not the up-to-date picture of the Anglican Communion which still remains to be painted. It is with the process of its expansion that we are primarily concerned.

That process has its roots deep in the past, and we must first establish the identity of the Anglican Communion with the Church of its early progenitors and apostles, before tracing the origins of the modern missionary movement. Between the ancient and the modern missions come centuries during which English missionary activity was in abeyance. Even after this was resumed there was a period which we have called Pre-Episcopal, in the sense that Churches were growing up without the supervision of a resident Bishop. Some account must then be given of preparations at the Home Base for organized missionary enterprise. From that point we shall follow the lines of its geographical advances, country by country. Three general questions then fall due for examination. (1) The methods and motives of this expansion. (2) The degree to which expansion was accompanied by acclimatization, and the foreign origin of an imported religion outgrown. (3) The provision made for consolidating what became a world-wide Society and for counteracting the centrifugal tendencies inseparable from expansion.

But to launch without further introduction into the story of the nineteenth century would convey the impression that up to that date Christianity had been the tribal religion of a narrowly insular Church, and God a tribal deity. It is not enough to offer an explanation of why and by what stages the process of expansion began to accelerate when it did without probing into the previous question, why did it not begin before? From 597 to 1797 is a period of twelve hundred years: were the Christians of these centuries wholly oblivious of the universality of their religion? They were in possession of the Gospels which recorded a divine commission based not merely upon a verbal mandate, but upon the very nature and character of their Lord as the Light of the World, and of the God and Father whose express image He bore. They were in possession of the Book of the Acts: could they have been blind to its character as the greatest of missionary textbooks? Were they utterly out of tune with the gallant and venturous spirit of the early Church?

It must be admitted that there are stretches of Christian history the study of which is no cordial for drooping spirits. All too often *Corruptio optimi pessima* is the inevitable lament. Christianity has been adulterated and diluted. The

Church has at times been corrupt, cruel, combative, controversial, and has conformed to the values and standards of the world. Yet it has exhibited survival value. " Church history," writes Professor Foakes-Jackson, " is a record of the pursuit of an ideal which has never been realized, and of a hope which has never been fulfilled. . . . The Church has been guilty of serious crimes and inexcusable mistakes, and one cannot but be amazed that Christianity has survived in spite of all. Yet even the crimes and errors have not been able to destroy the power of the Spirit of Christ within it." [1]

The truth is that the waters of the evangelical river flowed for many a mile like a Derbyshire stream underground, emerging at last mysteriously from nowhere: or like the Nile, choked and concealed for long stretches of its course by floating sudd. The stream that in the nineteenth century emerged to invigorate the world, appearing at first as a mere trickle, gradually gathering force and flow, was the same stream which had flowed visibly and effectively in the early days of the English Church.

Those who are called to be makers of Christian history in the twentieth century forfeit a powerful incentive if they are unmindful of their ancestry. The Church in England has been classified as a " sending " Church, and the Churches of India, China, Africa, as ' receiving " Churches—but it is salutary to recall two aspects of the distant past—for how long England's was a " receiving " Church, and how early in its career it became a " sending " Church.

THE EXPANSION TO ENGLAND

Happily the belief in the universality of the Christian Gospel was strongly operative in the Church of thirteen centuries ago. It would have been a bad look-out for us if that had not been so, if no missionaries from overseas had thought our forefathers worth converting.

" Let no-one say," declaimed William Pitt in a slave-trade debate, " that Africa labours under a natural incapacity for civilization. Britons were once sold for

[1] *A History of Church History*, pp. 11, 13.

slaves in Rome . . . with equal justice might some Roman Senator have pointed the finger of scorn at the ' British barbarians,' and said, ' There is a people that will never rise to civilization, there is a people never destined to be free.' If we shudder to think of the misery which would still have overwhelmed us had Great Britain continued to the present time to be the mart for slaves for the more civilized nations of the world, God forbid that we should any longer subject Africa to the same dreadful scourge." If we shudder to think of the darkness from which England was delivered by the intervention of Gregory we may be thankful that we were once a " receiving " Church. In 864 certain Englishmen came to Rome and set up in the chapel dedicated to St. Gregory in St. Peter's a silver tablet expressing gratitude for their conversion to one whom Alfred their King had called " the best of Romans, the wisest of men."

ST. AUGUSTINE AND THE ROMAN MISSION

Our debt to Gregory is intensified by the circumstances in which he despatched his mission to our shores. The Roman Church had not been up to then a missionary Church; it had not officially reached out to become the Church of the Northern barbarians. It had indeed plenty to occupy it nearer at hand, Lombards encircling Rome, quarrels with the Franks, pestilence in the city. It is not surprising that when Gregory, as a monk, had himself set forth to make his own way to Britain and had travelled three days towards the North, Pope and people had dragged him back. Gregory himself compared the Church to " an old and violently-shattered ship, admitting the waters on all sides, its timbers rotten, shaken by daily storms and fast becoming a mere wreck." It was then that he detached a none too enthusiastic band of monks from his own monastery on the Coelian Hill, despatching them, as they complained, " to a barbarous, fierce and unbeliev-ing nation to whose very language they were strangers." The party dallied at Lérins; Augustine returned to Rome to report their apprehensions, but Gregory spurred them on to the adventure, and adventure of course it was.

Within a few years of St. Augustine's landing at Ebbsfleet, not only had Ethelbert of Kent himself become a convert, but practically the whole of his subjects had followed his example; his kingdom had become an organized part of the Western Church, with see cities at Canterbury and Rochester; and a mission had been established at London in the neighbouring kingdom of the East Saxons.

LÉRINS

The mention of Lérins recalls another debt to an overseas influence, which radiated from that romantic island of the French Riviera. St. Ambrose called it " the brightest jewel in that woven necklace on the neck of ocean." " Here were gathered the pioneers of monasticism, emulating the holy men of the Egyptian desert. . . . In its sunshine and among its pine-trees and flowers, seeds of oriental asceticism and oriental lore were transplanted to the congenial soil of the Celtic spirit." [1]   Here Martin of Tours won the monastic inspiration which he carried to Gaul; hence Ninian carried it to Galloway in the fourth century, where his Casa Candida was called the Lérins of the North, headquarters for a mission which, according to Bede, Ninian preached " to the Southern Picts who dwell upon this side of the mountains," that is of the Grampians. Hence St. Patrick carried inspiration to Ireland, and Kentigern to Strathclyde.   Here again in the seventh century, Benedict Biscop studied monastic principles, before founding Wearmouth and Jarrow.   Here it was that St. Augustine's mission halted and began to think of returning home, hearing no doubt stories about the savagery of the Saxons, stories which may have originated with those holy men from Britain such as Patrick, who, coming to Lérins in the fifth century had doubtless scattered rumours which grew with the lapse of time.[2]

ST. COLUMBA AND THE IRISH MISSION

But Augustine's mission does not exhaust our debt to " sending Churches."   The sixth century had witnessed a

[1] Hodgkin: *History of the Anglo-Saxons*, p. 7.
[2] Ibid., p. 263.

vast development of a new type of monasticism in Ireland, which blended ecclesiastical and tribal organization and effected a paradoxical fusion between extreme asceticism and enlightened culture. The year 563 saw Columba and his companions setting up their wood and wattle dwellings on Iona, having turned their backs on their beloved Ireland. " Iona," says Bishop Lightfoot, " became now the light of Christendom, for many generations the centre of the great evangelical movements of the time." [1]   Three or four weeks after the landing of St. Augustine in Kent, St. Columba passed away; a man of " heroic temper, furious energy, impetuous, masterful, with the hot blood of Irish Kings in his veins, yet homely and tender." " To do him justice you had to hear him bless the heifer of a poor peasant as well as curse a niggardly rich man." On his last day, so runs Adamnan's story, the old white pack-horse that carried the milk from the cowshed to the monastery came to the aged saint and shed tears in his bosom. When the attendant tried to drive this mourner away, Columba told him to forbear, because God had let the poor animal know that he would lose his master, though He had concealed it from human beings. A deep feeling for nature and wild things was characteristic of the Irish monks. We are told that as Columbanus used to go through the forest, the squirrels and birds would come to be caressed by him and would frisk about and gambol in great delight like puppies fawning on their master. St. Columba's true character is revealed on his death-bed of bare rock. " These, my little children, are my last words: I charge you to keep unfeigned love one with another. If you do after the pattern of the fathers, God the Champion of the good will help you."

Columba had founded an epoch " The most attractive " to quote Bishop Lightfoot again " and in a spiritual aspect the most splendid in the annals of our Church. Iona succeeded where Rome had failed." For from Iona sprang Lindisfarne. " From the cloisters of Lindisfarne," writes Montalembert, " and from the heart of those districts in which the popularity of ascetic pontiffs such as Aidan and martyr Kings such as Oswald and Oswin took day by day

[1] *Leaders of the Northern Church.*

a deeper root, Northumbrian Christianity reached in succession all the people of the Heptarchy. Am I not right in claiming for Aidan the first place in the evangeliza- tion of our race? Augustine was the Apostle of Kent, but Aidan was the Apostle of England." Lightfoot's claim is not universally conceded by historians, but the emphasis which he desired to redress still needs redressing.[1]

THEODORE AND HADRIAN

When the third-generation stage was reached in the English Church, there was yet another infusion of foreign blood. The Pope in 668 had nominated to the vacant Archbishopric of Canterbury, Hadrian, " an Abbot of African origin, excellently skilled both in the Greek and Latin tongues "; but Hadrian suggested that the Greek Theodore would be the better man for the post and offered to accompany him to Canterbury in a subordinate position. " The Church," writes Mr. Hodgkin, " canonizes its Saints; it is left for History to crown statesmen; and historians have long acclaimed Theodore as the first recognizable statesman to appear in the story of England. If any one man was the founder of the English Church, it was Theodore." [2]   He wrought a miracle in uniting, organizing, educating the Church till it " rose with massive grandeur, consolidated, learned, influential, above the petty kingdoms in which the political energies of the nation were still confined." All this we owe to a Greek of Asia Minor and an African. Theodore was sixty-six when he shaved his beard and grew his hair to conform to the tonsure required of an Archbishop of Canterbury, and he reigned for twenty-two years. "This was the first Arch- bishop," wrote Bede, " whom all the English Church obeyed. For to say all in few words, the English Churches received more advantage during the time of his pontificate than ever they had done before."

It is not only the fact that Christianity was no indigenous religion but was introduced to England by foreign mission- aries, that it is salutary to recall. It is of some significance for our subsequent history, when once more the missionary

[1] Cf. Bright: *Waymarks in Church History*, pp. 295 seq.
[2] Op. cit., p. 310.

stream emerged from its long tunnel, that there was the double current in our ecclesiastical heredity—the Celtic and the Continental. The duality still counts for something in our make-up, and in what we have to contribute to Christian history in the making. The Synod of Whitby (664) had something more serious to face than a dispute about the date of Easter, seriously inconvenient as no doubt it was for Oswy to be celebrating the feast while his Queen was still observing the fast. There met the two types of Christianity, the Irish and the Mediterranean. Christianity in Ireland had never adapted itself to the provincial and diocesan system; the Church had no centralized government. Bishops there were, but Abbots were much more important. Bishops were tolerated for their uses and special functions, as in the not very distant past they have been tolerated by some missionary societies. In some respects, monks though they were, the Celtic missionaries were not unlike some nineteenth-century missionaries, and their monasteries akin to missionary societies. Continental Christianity brought a new tradition of order, a new conception of Bishops as pioneer-founders and fathers, round whom the flock would gather, and a new monastic discipline on the Benedictine model. Bishops must no longer " foot it in the Scotic manner "—it is said that Theodore lifted Chad on to a horse with his own hands. There must be no more migratory monks, and clergy must not wander from diocese to diocese. Missions must be "diocesanised." "After the Celtic expansion, the Latin organisation." Continuous life, as Bishop Gore used to say, depends upon continuous principles. Celtic Church-building had been haphazard, non-architectural, and the new orientation promised stability and breadth of outlook. Roman organization did for England what the Irish Church had never done for Ireland, affording a unifying influence in contrast with the local particularities, which disconnected and independent monasteries inevitably aggravated.

It was in Church Synods that the representatives of the English Kingdoms first learnt to take peaceful counsel together; a common obedience to the Primate taught them in due time the reasonableness of a common obedience to a single King. " It was more profitable," is Professor

Oman's verdict, " for the infant Church of England to be in touch with the bulk of Western Christendom than with the Scots alone, if it was to be an active and useful limb of the great Christian community. The Celtic Church produced many great saints and many devoted missionaries, but it was always lacking in order and organization. Fervour and ascetic self-sacrifice are essential virtues for those who have to build up a Church, but for those who have to administer a Church already solidly constituted, tact, practical wisdom, and a broad charity of spirit are also necessary. . . . As an organization for the spiritual government of a mixed community the Celtic system left much to be desired." [1]

The confluence of these two streams issued in the main flow of what so soon became a native Anglo-Saxon religion and culture. There have been times when the two have shown a tendency to flow apart or in parallel channels, or when one has absorbed the other: the stream has flowed strongest when the two tributaries have blended their waters in one.

THE EXPANSION FROM ENGLAND

There is no more convincing evidence of the effectiveness of the early missionaries who, coming from two directions, converted England, than the precocious zeal with which the Church they founded passed from " receiving " to " sending " status. The two stages indeed overlapped. Wilfrid had seen something of Northumbrian missions on the Continent before he returned to convert Sussex and teach the barbarous people of that coast the art of catching fish in nets, while the Isle of Wight still stood out as a stronghold of heathendom. Blemishes there were in our own third-generation Christianity, the memory of which should check any tendency to censorious criticism of other countries' third-generation Christianity; set-backs and reactions there were as well as advance; the Anglo-Saxon Church was not built in a day. From a distance, the conversion of England appears to have been a swift and sweeping victory of the Cross of Christ. But it was many

[1] Professor Oman: *England before the Norman Conquest*, pp. 291, 292.

years before the Church could pass the test of adolescence implied in the inquiry, Would it survive if all missionaries were withdrawn? It is all the more remarkable that in the matter of missionary enterprise, British Christianity was so distinguished.

THE IRISH MONKS

Much was due to the Celtic strain and the example of the Irish missionaries, whose monastic colonies were the starting-point of a great expansion of Christianity. Twelve years before the death of Columba and the landing of Augustine, Columbanus had begun his thirty years of missionary activity extending from the Vosges to the Apennines. His monasteries had become centres of conversion and civilization, homes of art and agriculture as well as religion. The same movement which produced the illuminations of the Book of Kells (in which one who examined its elaborate interlacing designs under a microscope, 150 interlacements in a space of $\frac{3}{4} \times \frac{1}{2}$ inch, could not detect a single false line), exercised at the same time a profound influence on the peasants of Europe. " It was an essentially rural movement, avoiding the towns and seeking the wildest regions of forest and mountains: the monks were themselves countrymen with a Franciscan feeling for nature. Their settlements were forced by necessity to take up the peasants' task, to clear the forest and to till the ground. They stood so near to the peasant culture that they were able to infuse it with the spirit of the new religion." [1]

In his reference to the missionary enterprise of the nineteenth century and its sequel, Archbishop Temple noted that neither the missionaries nor those who sent them out were aiming at the creation of a world-wide fellowship: their aim was to preach the Gospel to as many individuals as could be reached, so that those who were won to discipleship should be put in the way of eternal salvation. " Almost incidentally the great world fellowship has arisen." Almost incidentally Ireland became the leader of Western culture from the close of the sixth century: almost incidentally was this expansion of Christianity initiated.

[1] Christopher Dawson: *The Making of Europe.*

For it is an interesting paradox, relevant to a study of missionary motive, that the Irish monks were not primarily concerned with missionary work in the sense of converting pagans to Christianity; they were pursuing an ideal of extreme asceticism, which took the form of renouncing not only family life and possessions, but even fatherland and the comforting companionship of the monastic community.

The case recorded in the Anglo-Saxon Chronicle of the three monks " who stole away from Ireland in a boat without any oars because they would live in a state of pilgrimage for the love of God, they recked not where," is typical. Even so, says Jonas, his biographer, "Columbanus began to feel the longing for *peregrinatio*, mindful of the command of the Lord to Abraham, Get thee out of thy country and from thy kindred and go into a land which I shall show you "; or to quote Strabo, the biographer of St. Gall, " St. Columbanus desiring to attain that perfection spoken of in the Gospel, namely to leave all that he had and take up his cross and follow the Lord stripped of all possessions, succeeded in persuading those of his brethren whose souls were inflamed with a like fervour, to make good their zeal by action, by renouncing the sweets of kindred and home." Inevitably, the monasteries he founded became centres of light. " People began eagerly to stream in from all directions to dedicate themselves to the practice of religion so that the great number of monks could hardly be accommodated in one community, and from them streamed the apostles of Europe."

Such was the richness of the tradition transmitted to the English Church by Aidan and his successor. The Lindisfarne Gospels are the outward and visible sign of its transmission in the realm of art. The austerities of St. Cuthbert, his fastings and immersions in the sea up to the neck, combined with complete disregard of self, a patience which was inexhaustible, a love which overflowed like that of St. Columba and St. Francis to his fellow-men and to his animal friends, transmit the ascetic tradition: while the Northumbrian missionaries in Frisia are in the authentic succession.

ANGLO-SAXON MISSIONS

WILLIBRORD

We may trace the double descent in the person of Willibrord, one of the earliest of English missionaries on the Continent; by birth a Northumbrian, he had his roots in the Celtic Church; but he was born only seven years before the Synod of Whitby and soon fell under the spell of Wilfrid, another Northumbrian, the aggressive champion of the Roman allegiance, spending twelve years of study at his monastery at Ripon. Iona also had a share in his up-bringing, though his studies there were under the guidance of another Northumbrian, Egbert, who was later responsible for converting the Iona community to the Roman rule in regard to Easter and the tonsure. But from Wilfrid and Egbert he imbibed more than the lesson of ecclesiastical order. It was Wilfrid who in 677 had spent a winter in Frisia, preaching daily to the heathen and, according to his biographer, baptizing almost all the chiefs as well as many thousands of the Frisian people; it was Egbert who after many years of learned retirement *in Ireland* formed the design of attempting the conversion of the Frisians and Saxons. He was prevented—supernaturally as Bede believed—from undertaking the work himself, but collected a band of twelve monks, the most distinguished of them and the only priest in the company being Willibrord, who had just completed twelve years of study in Ireland.[1] The first association of the English with Echternach, a bridge-head so crucial in the campaign of 1945, was through Willibrord, who founded there and at Utrecht his most important monasteries.

BONIFACE

It was to the assistance of Willibrord that Boniface of Crediton went to Frisia in 716. Frustrated on his first visit by a rising of the Frisians against Charles Martel and the Franks, led by their King Rathbod, who " would rather be with his ancestors in Hell than with a handful of beggars in Heaven," Boniface returned to England, but in 718 turned his back on a Wessex Abbacy and began his

[1] F. M. Stenton: *Anglo-Saxon England*, p. 166.

thirty-seven years of unbroken service overseas. Men and women flocked to the mission-field. " It would be difficult to exaggerate the praises of these valiant and devoted women who faced the dangers of a distant journey, only to bury themselves in wild and savage regions, exposed to hardships from which even strong men had shrunk." [1]

We must be content to dismiss in a few words the details of a career which included the founding of four sees in Bavaria and four in Saxony, and the founding of Fulda and many another monastery. To his connection with Pippin and the Frankish Court, reference will be made later. "The work of a missionary among barbarous peoples, living in dense and distant forests," writes Mr. H. A. L. Fisher, "may leave but little trace on the written memorials of his time. But the salient facts in the career of Boniface are eloquent of ardour and persistence, of capacity and success. . . . That he was assisted by other valiant workers does not detract from his achievement. In the task of binding Germany to Rome he was a pioneer, and his the decision and dynamic influence." [2]

" The Papacy found its most devoted allies and servants in the Anglo-Saxon monks and missionaries," writes Mr. Christopher Dawson. " The foundations of the new age were laid by the greatest of them all, St. Boniface of Crediton, the Apostle of Germany, a man who had a deeper influence on the history of Europe than any Englishman who has ever lived." [3]   This verdict is echoed by Mr. Hodgkin: " No Englishman has ever played so great a part in Central Europe as the first Devonian of Saxon descent to appear in history, displaying a spirit of adventure and determination which is not excelled by Gilbert or Drake or Raleigh." [4]

In Boniface are represented all the elements which had been contributed by outside influence to the formation of the English Church. " Like Augustine he obtained advice on details as well as general directions from the Papacy. Like Aidan and the Scots he perambulated heathen villages,

---

[1] E. Bishop in *Transactions of the Devonshire Association for the Advancement of Science, Literature and Art* (quoted—Hodgkin).
[2] *History of Europe*, I, p. 152.
[3] *The Making of Europe*, p. 210.
[4] *History of the Anglo-Saxons*, p. 327.

baptizing thousands of converts. Like Theodore he established new sees and formed a disciplined army out of scattered clergy." [1] To which Mr. Dawson adds that Boniface passed on the traditional culture of both Anglo-Saxon and Irish monasteries, being himself scholar and poet and extending his reforming activities to the education as well as the discipline of his clergy. His great foundation at Fulda was the centre of a revival of literary culture from which all the greatest scholars of the Carolingian period drew their inspiration.

The letters written and received by Boniface reveal a lovable man, a ruler but a friend of men, reliant on God for guidance and grace yet prizing deeply the affectionate sympathy of men and women. His was the courage of a lion, the physical courage to fell the sacred Thunderer's Oak with his own axe, unintimidated by a mob of cursing pagans; the moral courage to rebuke the scandalous conduct of a King of Mercia, to tell the Pope that his palls were too expensive, and that pagan rites were being performed in Rome under his very nose.

Boniface the missionary we have selected as representative of the second instalment of that rich legacy which the early British Church bequeathed for the inspiration of later generations. He stands for the first assertion of the status of the missionary enterprise in world affairs, of the place and potency of the spiritual in the making of history. He stands out also as the first of a long line of missionary martyrs. An old man, in his eightieth year, he had abandoned his Archbishopric of Mainz to devote himself to the wild folk of Northern Frisia. On Whitsun-Eve he was in camp awaiting the newly-baptized who were to foregather for Confirmation. When the day came there appeared in the early morning a large band of pagans who rushed upon the little band of Christians brandishing their weapons. The Christians flew for theirs. He forbad them. " Cease, my children, from conflict. Lay down the purpose of battle. We are bidden not evil for evil, but good for evil to return. Be strong therefore in the Lord. Brothers, be of one mind. Fear not those who kill the body, but cannot kill the soul. Rejoice in the Lord and

---

[1] Hodgkin: p. 328.

fix in Him the anchor of your hope." So they were all put to the sword. It is thus that Christian history is made.[1]

MISSIONS IN SCANDINAVIA

The Scandinavian Missions of the Anglo-Saxons bequeathed yet another rich legacy. Denmark, Norway and Sweden in turn numbered missionaries from England among the makers of their Christian history. " Monasticism in Denmark is said to date from the closing years of the eleventh century with the coming of twelve monks from Evesham at the request of the Danish king. The strength of the English influence in forming the Christianity of Denmark is seen in part too in the language of the Danish ritual, in the numbers of churches named after Anglo-Saxon saints, and in monasteries founded by English monks. . . .

" The Church in Norway was the offspring of the English Church. In terminology and institutions the English lineage was clearly discernible. English missionaries laboured in Norway and some of the Norwegian monasteries were founded by Englishmen. . . . Olaf Haraldson (died 1030) when he set himself to make his newly-won kingdom Christian not only in name, but in fact, had with him many priests and bishops from England whom he had instruct his people and conduct missions; throughout the eleventh century monks came in who, like the seculars, were largely from England. . . .

" The Christianity of Norway was largely the child of that of England. . . . When the conversion of Sweden took place, England seems to have had a larger part in the process than did the Germans or even the Danes and Norwegians. Much of the ecclesiastical terminology and architecture showed English influence. Eskil and David were esteemed as saints, and several English saints such as St. Alban, St. Botulf, St. Dunstan, were venerated."

These citations from Professor Latourette's *History of the Expansion of Christianity*, sketch in the outlines of a story worthy of a much fuller treatment than can here be accorded.

[1] For Boniface, *see* Bishop Browne: *Boniface of Crediton and his Companions.*

It is seen in its significance when set against the background of Anglo-Scandinavian relations in the ninth century. Alcuin's letters from the court of Charlemagne to his Northumbrian friends convey a vivid impression of the violence of the Viking onslaught, in language which our own generation is specially qualified to understand.

" Never before has such a horror appeared in Britain as we have now suffered at the hands of pagans. And it was not supposed that such an attack from the sea was possible. Behold the church of the holy Cuthbert is deluged with the blood of the friends of God: the place more venerable than any other in Britain is given as a prey to pagan races. Who does not fear? Who does not mourn? "

In the same year (793) he writes to the Bishop and Monks of Lindisfarne: "When I was with you your friendly love was wont to give me much joy. And now that I am absent the calamity of your afflictions greatly saddens me every day. The pagans have contaminated the Sanctuaries of God, have laid waste the house of our hope, have trampled upon the bodies of saints in the Temple of God like dung in the street. What can I say but groan forth along with you before the altar of Christ, Spare, O Lord, Spare Thy people, lest the pagans say, Where is the God of the Christians? " [1]

But there was worse to come. It was to be little short of a hundred years before Alfred at Edington stemmed the tide of disaster. " In saving Wessex, Alfred saved England, and in saving England saved Europe from becoming a heathen Scandinavian power. . . . Had Alfred given up the struggle, England would have been lost to Christianity."[2] Whether the Danes desired deliberately to establish the religion of Odin and Thor on the ruins of Christianity and to found a great pagan empire with its centre in England may be open to doubt, but the fact remains that they had nearly succeeded in doing so. Of all the rich conventual establishments that studded the Kingdom of Northumbria, not one escaped destruction, and to the moral effect of being an occupied country on what was still a very young Church, Alfred himself bears witness.

[1] Bishop Harold Browne: *Life of Alcuin*.
[2] Charles Plummer: *Life of Alfred*.

He laments that " There are few left on this side Humber who can understand their mass-book in English or translate a letter from Latin into English. I wean that there are not many beyond the Humber. I cannot think of a single one South of the Thames." Asser bewails that the desire for the monastic life had utterly died out.

Alfred's peace-terms included a condition that strikes oddly on a modern ear. Guthrum (according to Asser) promised " to accept Christianity and receive baptism at the hands of King Alfred. And King Alfred stood god-father to him and raised him from the holy font of baptism. After the baptism he remained with the King for twelve days and the King with all his men gave them many excellent gifts." Mr. Hodgkin quotes a story of a North-man who at a baptismal ceremony complained that he had "gone through this washing" twenty times and that the alb then given him was not up to standard nor fit for a warrior. Were there scarcely smothered guffaws ? he asks. " Is it possible that the old warrior Guthrum in his alb and his fillet looked back at his chiefs with something like a wink. . . . At least the combined effect of defeat and of the contact with a Christian of heroic type was lasting: Alfred understood his Northmen and put a double spell upon them, both the heroic and the Christian, and it worked.' [1]

It says much for the survival value of Anglo-Saxon Christianity, for Alfred's faith and for the efficacy of his reforms, that the stricken church did absorb its former assailants and win them to the faith. When Canute made England the centre of his Empire and governed according to the traditions of his Saxon predecessors, he rivalled them in his devotion to the Church. " His pilgrimage to Rome in 1026 when he assisted at the coronation of the Emperor Conrad, is one of the most significant events of the period, for it marks the incorporation of the Northern people into the Society of Christendom and their acceptance of the principle of spiritual unity." [2] It is further evidence of the genuineness of Danish conversion that the mission-aries to Scandinavia would seem to have come largely

[1] Hodgkin: op. cit., p. 571.
[2] Dawson: op. cit., p. 245.

from the Danish part of England. " The English priests or missionaries with Scandinavian names—as for instance Eskil, Grimkild and Sigurd—who went over to Scandinavia in the tenth century, for the purpose of converting the heathen, were, as their names show, of Danish origin, and undoubtedly natives of the Danish part of England. Sprung from Scandinavian families, which, though settled in a foreign land, could scarcely have so soon forgotten their mother tongue or the customs which they had inherited, they could enter with greater safety than other priests on their dangerous travels in the heathen North: where also, from their familiarity with the Scandinavian language, they were best suited to prepare the entrance of Christianity."[1]

The title, " Apostle of the North," may be claimed for the English Sigfrid, without detracting from the glory of Anskar (died 865), whose heroic reconnaissances in Sweden, instigated by Lewis the Pious, and imperilled by pirates and popular uprisings, shines out against the background of Viking violence. Anskar's little Christian group soon ceased to be, and the conversion of Sweden had to begin all over again, when soon after A.D. 1000 Sigfrid appeared at the court of the heathen King Olov. He had settled at the modern Växjö with his three English nephews, Cluniac monks and martyrs, and won many hearers. Twelve wise and aged men were chosen to represent the twelve chief tribes of the land, who were to decide about the truth of his teaching and on behalf of the commonalty to determine whether it should be accepted. Sigfrid instructed them in the cardinal truths of Christianity, laying special emphasis on God's love for the world and the joy in heaven over the repentance of sinners. The whole twelve were convinced of the truth of Christianity and agreed to return for baptism in twelve days' time. The story reached the ears of Olov, who summoned Sigfrid to court, yielded to his persuasions and was by him baptized.

By the time of Sigfrid's death (c. 1068) at a great age, the great heathen temple at Upsala was still standing, but considerable progress had been made and the ultimate issue was nearing a decision. Among his successors two

---

[1] Opperman: *English Missionaries in Sweden and Finland*, p. 57, n. quoting Worsaee.

English bishops, Eskil and David, obtained canonization, the former suffering martyrdom during a period of reaction provoked by an attempt on the part of a zealous King Inge to abolish the sacrifices at Upsala, to destroy its temple and compel the baptism of his subjects. Such outbursts were rare in the Church of Sweden in contrast with the Church in Norway, which had been taught to lay undue emphasis on the Gospel precept, " Compel them to come in that my house may be full." When the time came for monastic settlement it was the Cistercian Order, that owed so much to the Englishman Stephen Harding, which came to Sweden, and there were Englishmen among the monks. When the time came to unite the Church of Sweden more intimately with the Papacy in fulfilment of Hildebrandine strategy, it was an Englishman, Nicholas Brakespeare, who undertook the legatine mission, and it was he who as Pope Adrian nominated another Englishman to be the first Archbishop of Upsala.

It was this Bishop Henry who earned the title of the Apostle of Finland. A Bull of Boniface VIII refers to him as St. Henry the Martyr, for he was murdered in Finland after six months of journeyings through the country " working wisely and faithfully to build up and strengthen the Finnish Church." It was an English Dominican, Bishop Thomas (consecrated c. 1220), who established the Church of Finland on a firm basis. Bishop Thomas brings up the rear of a noble procession of English and Irish missionaries, who bequeathed a great heritage to their Anglican posterity; it was centuries before the procession was re-formed and advance resumed. Something must be said about the interval during which missionary activity was in abeyance in England.

PART II

THE CENTURIES OF ABEYANCE

1. The Pre-Reformation Church: (*a*) The Papacy; (*b*) The Crusaders.

2. The Post-Reformation Church: (*a*) Erasmus; (*b*) Luther and Calvin; (*c*) Roman Expansion.

THE stream of missionary enterprise now plunges underground, not to reappear for centuries: there is for the time being no distinctively English effort to extend the kingdom of Christ among non-Christians. Pre-Reformation and post-Reformation epochs have different explanations to offer of the fact that the English Church thus lost its missionary identity, and show different mitigations of what might have led to disastrous isolation.

THE PRE-REFORMATION CHURCH

THE INFLUENCE OF THE PAPACY

The identity of the English Church up to Tudor times was of course merged in a larger whole. The cessation of its missions did not, therefore, involve a lapse into insularity, or tribal religion: the œcumenical tradition was maintained, and entered into the warp and woof of the nation's religious mentality.

In his Ford Lectures of 1905,[1] A. L. Smith, late Master of Balliol, surprised many of his pupils by the vigour of his protest against any belittlement of the debt owed to the Papacy. He warned his hearers not to misread their history by reading it through their own prejudices, nor by a kind of historical fatalism to assume that what they know did happen was the only thing that could have happened, not to treat the whole of mediæval Church history as an introduction to the Reformation, nor to allow the influence

[1] *Church and State in the Middle Ages.*

of insular patriotism to lead them to forget that to be an island and to be insular need not be equally good things. We were reminded that the mediæval church had to work upon an extraordinarily complicated and barbarous mass of social custom and must not be held responsible for abuses that were forced upon it by mediæval society.

The Lectures gave a balanced picture of the good and evil of the connection of England with Rome. They recorded two powerful if contrasted impressions: on the one hand, an impression of abuses, so long unconcealed yet so long endured, which ate into the very heart of the system; of the narrow selfishness and wholly political character of the Papacy's most cherished aim, the aim of a petty territorial princedom in Italy; of its increasing concentration upon this one aim till phrases such as " the Church," " the Faith " and " the cause of God " came to mean this petty aim and this alone; and finally of the growing bitterness and even outspoken invectives which it aroused in all countries and all classes. Giraldus Cambrensis at the end of the twelfth century laments the prevailing simony: he quotes Alexander III's saying, " When God deprived bishops of sons, the devil gave them nephews "; he tells of a man stricken with paralysis of the tongue because when denied audience with the Pope he had murmured, " One can only get at Simon Peter through Simon Magus." The passionate impulse of the Middle Ages to realize its ideals and to embody them in a material form ended in a vast system of indulgences and an undisguised tariff of sins.

On the other hand, to confuse the last state with the first, to deny that what came to be so bad was ever good in intent and idea, this is not historical. The student of the records received a second impression. He must be profoundly stirred to admiration of the machinery and organization of the Papacy; its enormous superiority not merely as a religious centre, but as the centre of law and government; its all-pervading activity and almost infinite potentialities; and finally, the absolute and literal acceptance of it by the highest minds as the veritable oracle and tribunal of God. . . . The Papacy taking it all in all was the greatest potentiality for good that existed at the time or perhaps that has ever existed. . . . The ideal of the golden age of the canonists was to make a working reality of the Kingdom of God upon earth; to express the law of that kingdom in a coherent, all-embracing code, and to enforce that code upon the still half-heathen Kingdom of the world. An ideal truly, and predestined to fail; but a noble ideal. We do well to reflect on " the beauty, the majesty, the potentialities of that which the word ' Christendom ' embodied: it was a conception of the reign of God upon earth to which men did homage in their hearts, however much their conduct fell short of this ideal."

" If a man consider the original of this great ecclesiastical dominion, he will early perceive that the Papacy is no other than the ghost of the deceased Roman Empire, sitting crowned upon the grave thereof." A. L. Smith quotes this saying of Hobbes' as hitting the very central fact about the Empire of the Gregories and the Innocents, that it was a translation into spiritual terms of the Empire of the Cæsars. As that Empire of the Cæsars had been a great unifying force in the world, drawing even distant Britain into the circle of the civilized world, so was its ghost a unifying force, safeguarding the English Church from isolation through the influence of a central oracle, a universal law, and an œcumenical organization.

We may cite as characteristic English witness for this Papal section of the abeyance period the great Grossteste, Bishop of Lincoln. In his eyes not only all Christians, but the whole human race are bound to be subject to the Holy See, and no one can be saved who does not fulfil this. " This most holy See is the Throne of God, and the Sun of the world in His sight, without which sun the world would perish: those who preside over this most holy See are pre-eminent among mortals in being clothed with the person of Christ." But this does not deter him from adding in the same sermon from which these words are quoted, delivered at the Council of Lyons in 1250 in the presence of Innocent IV and his Cardinals, an audacious denunciation of the prevailing coveteousness, " Of all this evil what is the prime and signal cause ? The cause, fountain-head and origin of it is in this court: not only because it does not clear away these abominations as it alone can do,

and as is its bounden duty, but because itself by dispensa-
tions, provisions and collations, appoints these bad pastors.
The greater the sinner's position, the greater the sin. The
whole world cries out against the unbridled shamelessness
of the familiars of this court. If the Holy See do not
speedily correct itself, destruction will come upon it
suddenly."

THE UNIVERSITIES

Throughout this period, then, the English Church was
saved from insularity, and maintained an intercourse with
the Continent. Students interchanged visits. Arnold Nash
recalls that the doors of the mediæval university were
open to all and sundry. Boundaries of nationality and
language disappeared as students and teachers alike sought
to pursue that truth which transcended any local expression
of it. He quotes a letter from Foulques de Deuil to Abélard
describing how students of every land flocked to his lectures. " Neither distance nor the height of the mountains,
nor the depth of the valleys, nor the roads beset with perils
and infested with robbers, prevented them from hastening
to you. The host of young Englishmen feared neither the
passage of the sea nor its terrible storms; despising all
perils, as soon as they heard your name uttered they
hastened to you. Bretons, Angevins, Poitevins, Gascons,
Spaniards, Normans, Flemish, Germans, Swabians, inces-
santly proclaimed and praised the power of your name." [1]

THE CRUSADERS

Foreign friars penetrated English villages. English
pilgrims wandered far and wide. " There are said to have
been one hundred and seventeen separate expeditions to
the Holy Land during the eleventh century before the
beginning of the Crusades, and some of these expeditions
had included large numbers, even thousands, of pilgrims."[2]
What place should be allotted to the Crusades in a study of
the expansion of English Christianity ? Many would deny
them any right to a place at all: they owe them a grudge

[1] Arnold S. Nash: *The University and the Modern World.*
[2] D. C. Munro: *The Kingdom of the Crusaders*, p. 31.

for having permanently embittered the relation between Christianity and Islam, and for introducing ideas of Christian advance by methods wholly incongruous. Certainly if the Crusades were to be regarded as a chapter of missionary history the story of their disasters and decadence could only yield a purely negative moral. But the preachers of Crusades, Urban II, Peter the Hermit, and later Bernard of Clairvaux, who thrilled the Princes and peasants of Europe into a passion of ascetic ecstasy did not include the conversion of Mohammedans among the motives to which they appealed. Urban " dwelt upon the sufferings of their fellow-Christians in the East, and the pollution of the sacred places by the heathen: he urged his hearers to go to the relief of their brethren and to free the Holy City from the infidel; to acquire merit by fighting righteous wars instead of imperilling their souls by fighting at home; to march under the leadership of Christ with the assurance that if they died they would gain an eternal reward, if they lived they would possess the Holy Land flowing with milk and honey."[1]

" The habit of penitentiary pilgrimage for the sake of remission of sins was ancient in the West. Jerusalem—at once the most sacred and the most distant of holy places, and therefore conferring a double grace—had long been the goal of such pilgrimages. The goal was now menaced; the menace must be removed. The Crusades accordingly came as a great armed pilgrimage for the sake of clearing the routes and liberating the goal of future pilgrimages." Professor Barker thus disposes of the idea that the Crusades need be deplored as a blot upon a missionary movement to which they never belonged.

A former pupil may be allowed to quote further from Professor Barker's chapter in *The Legacy of Islam*,[2] to emphasize another point, the enlarging effect of the Crusades upon the outlook of the Island Church: " Not only did Europe find in the Crusades a new form of internal union and a new influence on its own inner life: it also gained in their course a new and vastly extended view of the world. This widening of view, with the growth of collaboration and of

[1] D. C. Munro: op. cit., p. 33.
[2] *The Legacy of Islam:* " The Crusades."

geographical knowledge by which it was accompanied is the last, as in its sweep it is the greatest, of the results of the Crusades. . . . They saved Western Christianity from any self-centred localization; they gave it breadth, and a vision. ' The people that hath no vision perisheth '; and to the peoples of the Middle Ages the vision of the Crusades, seldom seen steadily, perhaps never seen whole—was none the less a saving ideal.'' The recumbent effigies in our village Churches of cross-legged Knights, popularly assumed to be crusaders, kept alive romantic memories of new peoples, new countries, strange adventures and perils by which scarcely a village had been unaffected. " Who ever heard such a mixture of language in one army ? " asks Fulcher of Charles, who took the cross in 1095. There were Franks, Flemish, Frisians, Gauls, Allobroges, Lotha-ringians, Alemains, Bavarians, Normans, Angles, Scots, Aquitanians, Decians, Apulians, Iberians, Bretons, Greeks and Armenians." [1]

THE POST-REFORMATION CHURCH

ERASMUS

It is a far cry from Fulcher to Erasmus and their attitudes to the Turks are as distant from one another morally as temporally. In his *Enchiridion* Erasmus writes: " The most effectual way of conquering the Turks would be if they were to see the spirit and teaching of Christ expressed in our lives; if they perceived that we were not aiming at Empire over them, thirsting for their gold, coveting their possessions, or desiring anything whatever save their salvation and the glory of Christ." In the year before his death (1536) he wrote the treatise *On the Art of Preaching*, which he had promised to his friend the Bishop of Rochester. He recalls the illustrious examples of Basil, Chrysostom, Augustine and Gregory the Great, who sent forth mission-aries to far distant regions:—

> We daily hear men deploring the decay of the Christian religion
> who say that the gospel message which once extended over the
> whole earth is now confined to the narrow limits of this land.
> Let those then, to whom this is an unfeigned cause of grief,

[1] Quoted by D. C. Munro, op. cit.

beseech Christ earnestly and continuously to send labourers into His harvest, or, more correctly, sowers to scatter His seed. Everlasting God ! how much ground there is in the world where the seed of the Gospel has never yet been sown, or where there is a greater crop of tares than of wheat. Countries into which the Gospel was first introduced from Judaea with great success, are they not now wholly in the hands of Mohammedans ? Palestine herself whence first there shone the gospel light is ruled by heathens. In Africa what have we ? There are surely in these vast tracts barbarous and simple tribes who could easily be attracted to Christ if we sent men among them to sow the good seed. . . . Kings keep in their employment men whose duty it is to teach elephants to leap, lions to sport and lynxes and leopards to hunt; but has the King of the Church ever found men ready to call their fellows to the service of His dear Son ? I know there is no beast so difficult to tame as the stubborn Jew; but nevertheless even he can be brought into subjection by kindness and love. . . . Travellers bring home from distant lands gold and gems, but it is worthier to carry hence the wisdom of Christ, more precious than gold, and the pearl of the Gospel which would put to shame all earthly riches. . . . Shall princes have no difficulty in finding men who for the purpose of human diplomacy are well acquainted with various tongues, and shall we not show the same zeal in so noble an enterprise ? Since men can die but once, what can be more glorious and blessed than to die for the Gospel ? Crowds of men go every year to see the ruins of Jerusalem, but what a great achievement it is to build a spiritual Jerusalem. . . . Bestir yourselves then, ye heroic and illustrious leaders of the army of Christ. . . . Overturn, quench, destroy not men, but ignorance, godlessness and other sins. It is a hard work I call you to, but it is the noblest and highest of all. Would that God had accounted me worthy to die in such a holy work.

LUTHER AND CALVIN

Among the voices, Lutheran and Calvinist, which reached English ears from across the Channel in the early post-Reformation years, there is no echo of Erasmus' challenge to the Church. He alone showed concern for Africa, Ethiopia or the Jewish world: with the Reformers the universality of the Christian Gospel went into eclipse. It must be said in their defence that they had much to pre-occupy them. Their immediate objective was to bring back the Church to its origins. As in the early days of the Oxford Movement, the foreground was a jungle of controversy, and the immediate task was to consolidate newly-won positions. Luther's " outlook for Christendom was bounded by the conflict between the evangelistic Zion and the papal Babylon, of which he was the champion. Zwingli and Calvin, from their different standpoints, suffered from the like narrowing of the world-scope of the Gospel." [1] It might have been expected that the recovery of the Bible in the vernacular would have counteracted narrowness and inspired catholicity of outlook, but the interpretation of either the Old or the New Testament did not always tend that way. As in later days it was his understanding of the Old Testament which led the Boer to see the native people of South Africa as Hittites and Amalekites, who must be driven out of the promised land into which he himself desired to enter, or as sons of Ham appointed by Jehovah to be his servants, with the corollary " no equality between black and white, either in Church or State," so Puritan New Englanders stigmatized the dispossessed Red Indians as " Canaanites " and justified from Scripture their ruthless suppression.

The New Testament was similarly wrested to the purposes of an exclusive theology. Professor Warneck of Halle, the least willing of critics, laments that " we miss in the Reformers not only missionary action, but even the idea of missions in the sense in which we understand them to-day. And this not only because the newly-discovered heathen world across the sea lay almost beyond the range of their vision, but because fundamental theological views hindered them from giving their activity and even their thoughts, a missionary direction. This fact surprises us in the case of so great witnesses for God; it pains us." [2]

Luther's view was that the dominical injunction to preach the Gospel to all the world had in fact been fulfilled by the Apostles. In the parable of the Good Shepherd, Luther regards the " other sheep " as already brought in. " Many say that that has not yet been brought to pass. I say, nay, the saying has long ago been fulfilled." The systematic work of missions is in his judgment the prerogative of the Apostles. After them " no one has any longer such a universal apostolic command, but each bishop or pastor has his appointed diocese or parish. As for those who have

[1] Findlay and Holdsworth: *History of the Wesleyan Methodist Society.*
[2] Warneck: *History of Protestant Missions.*

rejected or failed to respond to the good news, their blood be on their own heads. They have fallen under the dominion of the Devil. . . . If men in one place will not hear or suffer Jesus He goes elsewhere." This static view was reinforced by the belief that the end of the world was at hand so that no time remained for the further development and extension of the Kingdom of God on the earth.

For Calvin, too, the apostolate was an extra-ordinary office (*munus extraordinarium*), which as such has not been perpetuated in the Christian Church. The words with which the Baptist pioneer, William Carey, was later rebuffed, " Sit down, young man, if God wants to convert the heathen, He will do so without your help or mine," were only the echo of his master's voice. " We are taught that the Kingdom of Christ is neither to be advanced nor maintained by the industry of men, but this is the work of God alone; for believers are taught to rest solely on his blessing." The period indeed dictates a warning that is never out of date, that a theology which cuts the nerve of evangelistic impulse and inhibits the exercise of the missionary instinct, is suspect and demands the closest scrutiny.

ROMAN EXPANSION

All this time Roman missions were over-running vast regions of Asia and America. " The Roman Church had inherited from the Middle Ages the missionary obligation and tradition, and in this respect she vindicated her apostolic lineage. The passionate loyalty of the Religious Orders, their soldierly spirit and the utter selflessness attained by their discipline, provided a host of Catholic Missionaries, ready to go to any clime, to endure any hardships and to lay down life without a murmur at the Church's bidding." We shall have occasion to criticize some of the missionary methods of the Jesuits, but that does not detract from their heroism nor does the greatness of their opportunity discount the zeal of Portugal and Spain in seizing it. By a curious adaptation of Luther's later principle, *Cujus regio ejus religio*, and a transposition of the pronouns to read,

" Whosoever is the true religion his shall be the sovereignty," Alexander VI, the Borgia Pope (in 1493) partitioned
" all the lands and islands already discovered or hereafter
to be discovered in the West, towards the Indies or the
Ocean Seas," between Spain and Portugal. Thus were the
dice loaded against the extension of Protestant Missions.
The stream of English missionary enterprise continued to
run underground.

PART III

A PRE-EPISCOPAL PERIOD

1. National Expansion.

2. Ecclesiastical Expansion: (*a*) Westward, across the Atlantic: the S.P.C.K.; the S.P.G.; the Indians. (*b*) Eastward, across the Indian Ocean: the East India Company Chaplains.

IT is sometimes considered derogatory to religious history to admit its entanglement in the web of secular history: still more to attribute any considerable share in its development to the influence of external factors. That the Elizabethan's appetite for pepper to spice his winter rations, or his liking for tobacco, had something to do with the extension of the Gospel, may be thought incongruous. Such was not the attitude of the Old Testament prophets and psalmists towards secular history; they saw the hand of God in the rise and fall of nations. As the individual rightly reckons his circumstances among the indications of his personal vocation, so the circumstances and secular context of the Church reflect the purposes of God for those who see in history more than " only one emergency following upon another as war follows upon war " or in " the development of human destinies more than the play of the contingent and the unforeseen." [1]

NATIONAL EXPANSION

If the power of Portugal and Spain loaded the dice against non-Roman missionary enterprises, their decadence and downfall reversed the odds. This was crudely true of Ceylon where the substitution of the Dutch for the Portuguese meant the substitution of Reformed for Roman Christianity, though without any fundamental alteration in the methods of propagation. The indirect results were more far-reaching. The dispersal of English subjects meant more than an enlargement of the English

---

[1] Preface to H. A. L. Fisher's *History of Europe*.

horizon; they carried their religion with them, and after an interval of centuries, English Christianity found itself no longer land-locked, but afloat on all the oceans and carried to unknown regions in the West and in the East. In both directions it was found that an expansion which began with ministrations to English exiles could not end there: once more there was to be close and compulsory contact with non-Christian peoples, with Red Indians in the West, Hindus and Mohammedans in the East.

The expansion of overseas enterprise in Elizabeth's reign took a great step forward with the rise of trading Companies of a new type, such as the East India Company founded by Elizabeth's Charter of 1600. " To each of these a geographical sphere of operations was assigned by Royal Charter, and no ' interloper ' from England might trade therein. . . . Only very slightly dependent on the State, these great Elizabethan Companies worked under conditions which fostered the spirit of private enterprise, self-government and self-reliance. . . . They were in many respects similar in their privileges and functions to the ' Chartered Company ' that helped to develop and disturb the interior of Africa late in Victoria's reign . . . an age, perhaps, too late for such political and military powers to be wisely entrusted to a private group of the Queen's subjects." [1]   The Master of Trinity, in his *English Social History*, adds a quotation from Peter Munday, who noted, a generation after the death of Elizabeth, as " one of the seven things wherein England may be said to excel, traffic and discoveries, viz.: so many incorporate companies of merchants for foreign trade, who employ their study and means for the increase thereof, by adventuring their good and sundry fleets and ships into most parts of the known world."

ECCLESIASTICAL EXPANSION

EXPANSION WESTWARD

" The successful founding of Colonies in Virginia, New England and West Indian Islands like Barbados were the greatest events of the reign of James I and the early years

[1] G. M. Trevelyan : *English Social History*, p. 200.

of King Charles. The English race began once more to move outside its island borders; this time in the right direction. The attempt made during the Hundred Years' War to reduce France to an English province had been the first instinctive gesture of an awakening national consciousness and a new-felt power to expand. After it had failed the English had for a century and a half been confined to England, strengthening themselves there in wealth, intelligence and naval power; now they began once more to expand, by very different methods and under very different leadership. This time the ' good yeoman whose limbs were made in England ' went forth again . . . not with the long-bow to sack and conquer an ancient civilization, but with axe and plough to found a new civilization in the wilderness." [1]

What steps did the Church of England take to keep pace with emigration ? It was *ex hypothesi* concerned not with those settlers who crossed the Atlantic for religious reasons, to escape from " prelates' rage," from Acts of Supremacy and Uniformity, from Tests and Conventicle Acts and the rest, whether Puritan or Papist: but with settlers who had emigrated mainly from social and economic motives. A complete answer would involve tracing the whole story of the Episcopal Churches in the United States of America, in Canada, Newfoundland, and the West Indies, which stand witness to the fact that however casual and inept the experiment, shoots of the old stem were successfully transplanted.

It was on June 21st, 1607, that the Holy Communion was first celebrated by Anglicans on American soil, at Jamestown—" a pen of poles with a sail for a roof, and for a pulpit a bar lashed between two convenient trees." The Virginian settlers who landed at Chesapeake Bay suffered many vicissitudes—drought, malaria, and in 1662 massacre at the hands of Indians. But the Colony grew, fervent in its loyalty to Crown and Church. Its representative Assembly, the first in America, enacted an Established Church; when the Commonwealth disestablished the Church in England the Virginians remained unmoved and with the Restoration pursued the even tenor

[1] Op. cit., p. 208.

of a way that had never been interrupted. The Church
in the Northern Colonies had the harder lot of a minority
movement and had to fight for every inch of toleration and
recognition.

With the eighteenth century missionaries began to arrive,
and it was none too soon. " Numbers of the English
settlers were in such a wilderness and so destitute of
spiritual guides and all the means of grace that they were
making near approach to that heathenism which is to be
found among negroes and Indians." [1] The great obstacles
to the free Indians embracing the Christian religion was the
" scandalous and immoral life of the white men among them
calling themselves Christians. Many of the slaves' masters
were extremely inhuman, esteeming them no other than
beasts." [1]

But missionaries did arrive in spite of the dangers of
the voyage. " It was estimated that something like one-
fourth of the men who sailed to England seeking ordination
in the eighteenth century were lost at sea by reason of
shipwreck, capture by pirates, or illness contracted on the
voyage." [2] When they did arrive they won general regard.
Colonel Heathcote writes in 1705, " I must do all the gentlemen that justice as to declare that a better clergy were
never in any place, there being not one amongst them
that has the least stain or blemish as to his life and conversation "; and Governor Hunter of New York, in 1711,
" We are happy in these provinces in a good sett of Mission-
arys, who generally labour hard in their functions and are
men of good lives and ability."

That the Church was capable of coping with this wholly
new situation may be placed to the credit of the " Religious
Societies " which had sprung up to counteract the moral
decay of the Restoration period; London and Westminster
had their first Societies in 1678, and soon had forty-two.
Their members were zealously attached to the Church of
England and the Prayer-book, but there were also Societies
for the Reformation of Manners, composed of Nonconformists as well as Churchmen, which aimed at " putting the
law into operation against Profaneness and Debauchery."

[1] Quoted in *Two Hundred Years of the S.P.G.*
[2] Lyddeker: *The Life of Charles Inglis.*

THE S.P.C.K.

The Religious Societies set out to impress on all and sundry " those divine arguments whereby themselves had been aroused out of a state of carnal insensitiveness." They were the precursors of the Society for Promoting Christian Knowledge of which the first meeting was held on March 8th, 1698. Alarmed by " that inundation of Profaneness and Immorality which we find of late broke in upon us," full of consternation at the prospect of those judgements which overtake " an Apostatis'd People," Clergy and Lay Gentlemen coalesced in this new Society to consult upon the best means and methods of promoting Religion and Learning in any part of His Majesty's Plantations abroad, and to provide Catechetical Libraries and free Schools in the parishes at home. It was amid the strains of rejoicing on account of the Peace of Ryswick on the 2nd December, 1697, and in the choir—then first opened for Divine Service—of the new Cathedral Church of St. Paul (thirty-one years after the Fire of London and thirteen years before the completion of the whole building) that " the zeal of severall persons of the best character in and about ye Cities of London and Westminster," reached and registered their resolution.

Within three years the Society found it expedient to distribute its burden; and the work of maintaining a supply of Clergy for the Colonies devolved upon another new Society, the Society for the Propagation of the Gospel. The S.P.C.K. concentrated upon the provision of schools, the publication of Bibles, Prayer Books and religious literature and the resuscitation of personal religion. It soon covered the country with a network of organizations. Its work was not all smooth sailing: the correspondence of its local representatives reveals a choppy sea. Some Bishops approved but others were " utterly averse." John Wesley's father could report that his Bishop (of Lincoln) was very well pleased with the methods of the Society and the union of clergy under Rural Deans which he intended to introduce into his own diocese; but he himself " had been labouring ten years to carry on the bussiness of Reformation with very little success, but hopes he shall not despond." He complains that he stands alone in this great work;

among seven thousand souls there is hardly one that will heartily assist him. A Kent clergyman can find but two Churchmen within ten miles round him whom he can confide in as favourers of the Society's designs. Clergy exposed it as a reviving of Presbyterian classes encouraging Fanaticism. And indeed such public " persecutings " as were levelled at the heads of the erring by the Archdeacon of Durham were well calculated to alarm. Individuals and families are denounced by name " for being reconciled to the Church of Rome "; City Constables " for being negligent and remiss in visiting publick houses in time of Divine Service and suffering Tipling and drinking on the Lord's Day, and " two Widdows for harbouring and keeping Irish and Scotch vagabons Rogges and beggers." The same Archdeacon reports that at Durham " he begins a monthly Sacrament where they used to have it but twice in the Year."

A Sherborne correspondent complains "that every Sect retains Discipline, whilst the Established and best Church is left precarious to an astonishm* and Concubinage is openly maintained in ye Diocess of Wilts." In Yorkshire " The lives of the Clergy in Cleveland are so groosly irregular, that it would render their meetings contemptible." At Spithead " The Service of God is wholly laid aside in some ships, by the Contrivance of the Seamen. That a Captain ha's commanded him in the middle of his Sermon to leave off in the King's name; and that he ha's desired him in God's Name to sit down and hear him." But Sir Cloudesley Shovell "mightily approve's of the Societies design." Another Chaplain writes: " As to the Reformation of the Seamen, he Recommends the Gift of a little Tobacco to be join'd to give advice and Instruction; which being done with a due air of Concern, he says will have wonderful Effects. And therefore wishes that the Society would send a considerable Quantity of course Tobacco to be disposed of by each Chaplain of a Ship accordingly."

The S.P.G.

These letters help to sketch in the background against which the Church's expansion must be assessed, and the magnitude of the task which Dr. Bray, humanly speaking, the founder of both the S.P.C.K. and the S.P.G., so undauntedly attacked. At the moment of the American Revolution the S.P.G. had seventy-seven chaplains in the field; during the eighty years of its service to the United States it had sent out three hundred and fifty-three missionaries. That they did not labour in vain is shown by the fact that the Episcopal Church survived the War of Independence, the cleavage which that war created in the ranks of the Clergy themselves (the future Bishop White became a Chaplain of Congress, the future Bishop Seabury Chaplain of a British regiment), and the inevitable taint of having been so closely identified with the Loyalist cause.

The chances of survival were further imperilled by the glaring weakness of an Episcopal Church which had no Bishop. Until the consecration of Bishop Seabury by the Bishops of the Episcopal Church in Scotland on November 14th, 1784, the Church in America was wholly dependent for episcopal supervision upon the Bishop of London. The Bishop of London conscientiously deputed Commissaries " to assume the reins of the Church, to exercise discipline, to reform manners, to settle disputes, to preserve order, to build up the Church." But Commissaries could not ordain; Commissaries could not confirm. The Church both rivalled and reflected the ineptitude of the regime of the three Georges in its unimaginative dealings with America. " The Bodies and Souls of men are ruined and undone and the Bounty of the Society lost," writes Talbot (who shares with Keith the rank of giant in the early American Church), " for lack of an Overseer of the poor Church in America without which the Gospel can't be planted nor any good work propagated in the world." " It seems the strangest thing in the world and 'tis thought History cannot parallel it that any place has received the word of God so many years, so many hundred Churches built, so many Proselytes made, and still remain altogether in the wilderness as sheep without a shepherd." Every effort was made on the spot to remove the misunderstandings and apprehensions of those who equated Bishops with " Prelacy " and their introduction as an " ecclesiastical

Stamp Act." Every effort was made in London by the
Society to remove the apprehension of timid authorities,
civil and ecclesiastical, but in vain.

THE INDIANS

The Charter of Incorporation granted to the S.P.G. by
William III, on June 16th, 1701, authorized the Support
and Maintenance of Ministers to instruct "our Loveing
Subjects"

> " Whereas Wee are credibly informed that in many of our
> Plantacions, Colonies and Factories beyond the seas belonging
> to our Kingdome of England, the Provision for Ministers is
> very mean . . . and whereas Wee think it Our Duty as much as
> in us lyes to promote the glory of God by the Instruction of Our
> People in the Christian Religion. . . . And whereas Wee have
> been well assured, That if Wee would be gratiously pleased to
> erect and settle a Corporation for the receiving, managing and
> disposing of the Charity of Our Loveing subjects, divers Persons
> would be induced to extend their Charity to the Uses and Pur-
> poses aforesaid, namely the ' Support and Maintenance of an
> Orthodox Clergy in Forreigne Parts.' . . . Know yee there-
> fore. . . ."

The word "Forreigne" was not to be taken as extending
the Society's lawful sphere beyond countries inhabited by
" our Loveing Subjects "—it was not till 1882 that Queen
Victoria, by a Supplementary Charter, sanctioned by
implication an extended range—but the restriction was
not held to confine activities to British-born subjects. From
the first the S.P.G. included in its designs " the breeding-up
of persons to understand the great variety of languages in
order to be able to converse with the natives and preach
the Gospel to them "—a branch of its work that it was
decided as early as 1710 " ought to be prosecuted preferably
to all others." While, therefore, its work began with the
Colonial Settlers it could not end there. In one of the
earliest reports it was recorded that " even the Indians
themselves have promised obedience to the Faith."
Attention was, therefore, directed to the Mohawks. There
was a natural desire to emulate the achievements of John
Eliot, the pioneer of Indian Missions, who had translated
the Bible into an Indian tongue in the 1660's. He had

become a legend, as to a later generation became David Brainerd, American-born but commissioned by the Society in Scotland for Propagating Christian Knowledge. He died in 1747 at the age of twenty-nine, and the tribes to whom he ministered are extinct; but to him William Carey, Samuel Marsden and Henry Martyn traced their descent as missionaries, and his influence deeply affected religious thinkers far into the nineteenth century.

The question of priorities was found difficult: it was indeed a moot point whether attention should be spared from white colonials. The first missionary to the Indians decided in the negative. To begin Christianizing the Indians before the Whites was preposterous, " for 'tis from the behaviour of the Christians here that they have had and still have their notions of Christianity, which God knows has been and generally is such that I can't but think has made the Indian hate Christianity." " They waste away and have done ever since our first arrival amongst them, as they themselves say, like snow before the sun, so that probably forty years hence there will scarce be an Indian seen in our America." Another missionary wrote that it was impossible to impart any Christian impression because the " Indians are wholly given up to drink and sottishness, rum and strong liquor being the only deities they are solicitous to worship."

In 1710 the visit of four Iroquois chiefs or sachems to London, where they begged Queen Anne to send instructors for the thorough conversion of their nations, attracted notice. The sachems were brought before the Society and promised that they should have two missionaries and a chapel. Thus was begun a daunting and dangerous work, complicated by French rivalry and hostility from Canada, for the Indian tribes served as makeweight between the competing nations. The influence of Dutch and English traders was detrimental to Indian morale. The Rev. John Ogilvie, one of the series of faithful friends of the Mohawk, deplored that the leading men of the country did not countenance the conversion and education of the Indian; but there was one brilliant exception, the Government Superintendent of the Indians, Sir William Johnson, who took the deepest personal interest in his charges, and collaborated with the Rev. Charles Inglis in working out a scheme for Indian conversion, himself building a school and church.

The Indians' was suspected to be a lost cause; their mentality was recognized to be too remote from the European to be easily comprehensible. There was no technique as yet developed for the presentation of the Gospel to the wild man. All the more, therefore, is it to the credit of the early eighteenth-century Church of America that it made so fine an attempt to help the Indian.

In a second sphere, pioneer work was undertaken far in advance of current humanitarian standards. The slave-trade was bringing hundreds of mysterious blacks, classed by some with orang-outangs as a different species of the same genus. Most owners were convinced that a policy of amelioration, which aimed not merely at protecting them from excessive cruelty, but at educating and civilizing them, was doubly bound to lead to trouble. On the one hand, the slaves would acquire new ideas, a new sense of their rights and of their power to attain them, a process which would culminate in a general and irresistible rebellion: on the other hand, their rise in the scale of civilization would make it increasingly difficult and finally impossible to justify the institution of slavery itself. As it was, in their primitive state, they could be and commonly were, regarded as virtually disqualified by nature for the enjoyment of human rights.

Yet it was as early as 1703 that the S.P.G. appointed a teacher for the negroes of New York. Elias Neau's seventeen years of unobtrusive work in this capacity not only gathered numbers of negroes into the Church, but established their claim to human privileges; not that the privilege of freedom was confirmed by baptism, the right of owners to their slaves after they had been baptized was confirmed by an Act of Assembly. There was a long way to go before public opinion would condemn the institution of slavery, longer still before emancipation. But it is to the credit of the Society that it dogmatically directed its missionaries to baptize slaves after due instruction.

EXPANSION EASTWARD

" Meanwhile," to return to Trevelyan's *English Social History*, " on the other side of the globe, the ships of another London trading company were beginning another chapter of England's destiny. The East India Company, founded by Elizabeth's Charter of 1600, held thereby a monopoly among her subjects of trading with the ' East Indies,' the power of legislation and justice among its own servants overseas, and by implication the power of making peace and war beyond the Cape of Good Hope."

This is not the place to describe the stages by which a few trading-stations developed into a territorial sway over wide dominions, and a trading company into a financial interest with wide political and social influence: nor to discuss the ethics of the monopoly of trade in the East, any infringement of which, even by Charles I, was bitterly resented. It is with the East India Company as a factor in the eastward expansion of Anglican Christianity that we are immediately concerned. Beyond the fact that neither in the East nor in the West was there any Bishop—both belonged to the pre-episcopal era—there was little in common between the two expansions. The East India Company had to do not with Colonial settlements, but with mercantile and military cantonments. From the first they showed no indifference to the spiritual needs of their employees, whether on board their ships, or on land in their Factory-Forts. " First above all men living under the sun we that be travellers by sea be much bound unto Almighty God, who see His wonders in the deep. . . . Therefore it behoves you principally to have respect that prayers be read morning and evening both ashore and aboard, and that none be wanting unless sickness be occasion, that you may jointly pray to the Almighty for a blessing upon you and your proceedings." These instructions of 1615 became Standing Orders, " and for the better performance thereof we have delivered to each of the pursers a Bible, wherein is contained the book of Common Prayer."

The roll of Chaplains reaches back to 1607; care was increasingly exercised in the selection of suitable men and their instructions were explicit. It was not the Company's fault that the Vice-Chancellors of Oxford and Cambridge had no recommendations to make in response to the Company's application (1637) for the names of ministers who would advance and spread the Gospel in India. " During your voyage (1663) we recommend unto your careful performance the daily exercise of prayer both morning and evening aboard the ship, and in especial the due observance of the keeping holy the Sabboth Day in prayer and preaching and other good duties, and as far as in you lieth to suppress all swearing, drunkenness and other un-Christian behaviour by reproofs and admonitions as you shall see occasion, that the blessing of the Almighty may accompany you in your voyage."

Nor was the Company unmindful of their obligations to those dependent on them, particularly towards the children of mixed marriages. It troubled them that " your over-much familiarity with the Portugal and French Padres becomes a snare to our factors and servants, and that the children of Englishmen, soldiers and civilians, are educated and brought up in the Popish Religion, which we cannot allow of." The Agent and Council on the spot replied that persuasion was better than persecution. Portuguese mothers, whether of pure or mixed blood, claimed to do with their children as they pleased, and some of them were not married at all. The Directors then (1667) authorized a gratuity of two pagodas to each boy of such marriages when he could say the Catechism by heart in the chapel on the Lord's Day. Six years later the Fort St. George Council ruled that " the children of seamen who intermarry with native women and settle with their Commanders' permission in Madras are to be brought up in the Protestant religion." In 1687 the Director wrote: " The marriage of our soldiers to the native women is a matter of such consequence to posterity that we shall be content to encourage it with some expense, and have been thinking for the future to appoint a Pagoda to be paid to the mother of any child that shall hereafter be born of any such future marriage upon the day the child is Christened, if you think this small encouragement will encrease the number of such marriages."

But it had already occurred to the Directors that the provision of schools was likely to effect more than bribes: a plan was afoot, and the first schoolmaster arrived in 1678. By 1718 the Governor could write to the S.P.C.K., who were bringing characteristic pressure to bear on the home authorities, "We have made a beginning this year in as handsome a manner as we could to erect and establish a Charity School," and the second half of the century saw educational progress in advance of the age, fostered by strong local Committees composed of military officers, civil servants and independent merchants.

Like the growing Church across the Atlantic, the Church across the Indian Ocean was under the Bishop of London's ample jurisdiction. When the Company's first Church, St. Mary's, Madras, was completed in 1680, built largely by local subscription, under the impetus of a vigorous Governor, it was by Latin Commission from the Bishop of London that it was dedicated. The link was no mere formality. In 1697 the Company resolved "that for the future when any Chaplains shall be tendered to the Company's service they shall be directed to attend upon my Lord Bishop of London for his approbation." When the new Charter of 1698 was granted the Archbishop of Canterbury and the Bishop of London were asked and consented to sanction a special prayer for use on board the Company's ships.

The dignitaries of the Home Church were also interested in the question whether anything was being done to propagate the Gospel among non-Christians. The question had first been raised by Richard Baxter as recorded in the Company's Minute-book for 1660. "A letter read from Mr. Richard Baxter, an eminent divine, wherein he requested the Company's commission that some number of the book named *Grotius de veritate religionis Christianae*, which are translated in the Arabicke tongue at the charge of Mr. Robert Boyle, might be prudently dispersed in such places where that language is understood, to the end Christianity may be established among infideli. The Court was very ready to promote so pious a work, so that they may be first satisfied that those books have the allowance of authority."

The philosopher Robert Boyle had re-opened the question in 1677, by commending to the Company a plan for sending scholars to Oxford to be trained in the knowledge of Arabic and Malayan. The Bishop of Oxford, Dr. Fell, wrote in warm support to Archbishop Sancroft and was ready to do the training himself. Bishop Bennett of Salisbury urged the matter on the attention of Sir Joseph Child, the autocratic Governor of the Company. Bishop Fell died, the Charter expired, and they were the wrong languages, so the Company's willingness to subsidize the scheme came to nothing.

Among the manuscripts preserved in the Lambeth Palace Library is a report submitted to the Archbishop by Dr. Prideaux, Dean of Norwich,[1] dated 1695, complaining that the Company is remiss in not propagating the Gospel among the people. " The Dutch do maintain about 30 Ministers for the converting of these poor infidels in their dominions, by whose labours they have converted many hundred thousand to the Christian Faith. They have lately erected a college or University in Ceylon, and have in that place 80,000 converted who are Communicants."

The familiar facts that Henry Martyn had to be smuggled into India as a Chaplain, that William Carey had to find sanctuary in Danish Serampore, that there was a prolonged struggle before freedom of missionaries could win the guarantee of the 1813 Charter, have perhaps thrown an unduly dark shadow on the Company's previous record. Many were the Danish missionaries to whom the Company had given free transport and supplementary salaries for services rendered to European congregations. In earlier days the London merchants who formed the Company had shown no lack of interest in the evangelization of India. The Court Minutes for August 19th, 1614 record " Captain Best having brought home a young youth, an Indian, whoe was taught by Mr. Copland to wright and reade and is very apt to learne: the Company therefore resolved to have him kept to schoole to bee taught and enstructed in religion that hereafter being well grounded he might upon occasions bee sent unto his countrye where God may be soe pleased to make him an instrument in converting some

[1] Penny: *The Church in Madras*.

of his nation, And resolved to have 20 markes per annum allowed for that purpose."

Two years later, the boy, with the Archbishop's approval, was duly christened at St. Dionis Backchurch, Fenchurch Street; the occasion being recognized to be of such unique importance that the Lord Mayor and Aldermen, members of the Privy Council, of the East India Company and of the sister Company of Virginia attended in state and there was an immense crowd in the street. History does not relate the sequel.

In relation to slaves the Company had shown a sense of Christian obligation far in advance of their time. Slaves in Surat " were to be taught and after three years as Christians set free." Slaves in St. Helena were to be " carefully instructed in the knowledge of Jesus Christ; after Baptism they were to serve seven years and no longer and then to be free planters."

The naive ardour of the seventeenth century cooled in the rationalistic climate of the eighteenth: the deceitfulness of riches and the nervousness of newly-gotten power inhibited zeal; costly and formidable conflicts with European and Indian foes distracted the attention and strained the resources of the Company. The refusal of the Directors to undertake mission work officially with the help of the public revenue at least conferred a negative benefit, by averting the worst blunders of Portuguese and Dutch official patronage of Christianity. Their opponents, as we shall see, had great difficulty in getting a clause inserted in the 1813 Charter compelling the Company to permit missionaries to go to India, but it is only fair to remember " that this same Company had not only been permitting missionaries to go to India for eighty years past, but had also paid their passage money and carried their baggage and books and printing-press and stores and remittances in silver, freight-free."[1]

* * * * * *

The pre-espiscopal period of the Church in India as in America prepared the way for the coming of the Bishops, and it closed in a blaze of glory. A constellation of Chaplains

[1] Penny: op. cit., p. 499.

appeared on the Calcutta horizon, who in spirit were as much missionaries as chaplains—David Brown, Henry Martyn, Claudius Buchanan, the future Bishop Corrie and others. They were disciples of Charles Simeon who began his fifty-four years at Holy Trinity Church, Cambridge, in 1782 : Henry Martyn had been his curate. They belonged essentially to the new century and the new dispensation, and are therefore reserved for later treatment. This chapter, however, must not close without underlining India's debt to their master. " As to Simeon," wrote Lord Macaulay in 1844, " if you knew what his authority and influence were, and how they extended from Cambridge to the most remote corners of England, you would allow that his real sway in the Church was far greater than that of any primate."[1] The two characteristics of his faith, his passion for individual salvation and his sense of Church order and corporate loyalty, led him to extend his authority far beyond England. " It was not for nothing that it was said in the religious periodicals of the day, Mr. Simeon is more of a Churchman than a Gospel-man."[1] Probably Cambridge never saw quite such a funeral as Simeon's " though less than forty years earlier it had been a University crime to speak to Simeon and he had been hissed in the Senate House on going up to vote: what was an unusual mark of respect in the University, in almost every College the Lectures were suspended." " Thus " wrote the Dean of Jesus, " is buried a true servant of God; one who (like us all) had his failings but who has been enabled to do more good for the Church of Christ in England than any person living "; to which we might add, though he never left these shores, " for the Church of Christ in India, if only as having inspired two such Indian missionaries as Henry Martyn in England and Alexander Duff in Scotland."

[1] Quoted in Charles Smyth: *Simeon and Church Order*.

PART IV

THE HOME BASE: FORMATIVE YEARS

1. Missionary Planning: (*a*) Varieties of organization; (*b*) Anglican organization.

2. Missionary Planners: (*a*) Charles Grant and his circle; (*b*) Joshua Watson and his circle.

THE Taverns of the City of London witnessed some unwonted spectacles round about the turn of the century. It was the " Castle and Falcon," Aldersgate Street, in 1795, which provided the birthplace of the London Missionary Society, and four years later, on April 12th, 1799, the original meeting-place of the sixteen clergy and nine laymen who founded " The Society for Missions to Africa and the East," better known as the Church Missionary Society. The " London Tavern " in Bishopsgate launched the British and Foreign Bible Society on March 7th, 1804, and in the same year the " New London Tavern " in Cheapside was the scene of the first valedictory meeting of the C.M.S. We have already noticed the genesis of the S.P.C.K. and the S.P.G. It was in the more decorous back parlour of a minister's house at Kettering that the Baptist Misssionary Society had been born in 1792. It was in the Leeds Old Chapel on October 6th, 1813, that the resolutions were passed which inaugurated the Methodist Missionary Society.

Bryant's *Years of Victory* has recently been published to help us to recover the atmosphere of the years in which these events, so inconspicuous yet in the end so contributory to the " great new fact of our time," were taking place. Those who have lived through two wars have some qualifications for entering into the spirit of the epoch of the Napoleonic wars and their aftermath. Those who have themselves experienced the repercussions of the Russian Revolution on thought have qualifications for understanding the mentality of those to whom the French Revolution was as recent an upheaval.

But to appreciate the significance of " the great missionary enterprise of the last hundred and fifty years," some knowledge of its origins is essential; of the plans and the planners of the Missionary Societies; of the policies framed by the founders, and of the personalities of the founders themselves.

MISSIONARY PLANNING

VARIETIES OF ORGANIZATION

It is at once obvious that there was no uniformity of policy in spite of unanimity of aim: no common model was adopted. (i) There were varieties in the relation of the new Societies to the Churches : some overstepped existing boundaries: some built on denominational allegiance. (ii) There were varieties in the relation of the Missionary Society to the Church which it represented; some were organs of the Church, integral to the life of the Church; some were distinct entities, autonomous corporations, within the Church.

(i) The London Missionary Society avowedly owed inspiration to the foundation of the Baptist Missionary Society. " Almost three years ago " it was recalled in a speech at the inaugural meeting, " Mr. Carey of Leicester published an ' Enquiry into the Obligations of Christians to use means for the Conversion of the Heathen . . .' We beg leave to recommend the perusal of this well-meant pamphlet to our readers and to remind them that it derives no small addition of value from this consideration that the author ' has given to his precepts the force of example ' ; becoming a missionary himself on the shore of the Ganges." But the London Missionary Society departed from the Baptist Missionary Society model in inviting the co-operation of all Christians irrespective of denomination. The London Society for Promoting Christianity among the Jews, founded in 1808 under the patronage of Queen Victoria's father, was also on non-denominational lines.

Similarly the Religious Tract Society (1799), and the Bible Society (1804), adopted a comprehensive basis. Hostility was excited in orthodox circles—the formation of an Auxiliary Branch of the Bible Society at Cambridge drew the thunder of the Lady Margaret Professor of Divinity. On the other hand John Owen, the Bishop of London's Chaplain, in spite of anti-Quaker prejudices, was so deeply moved by the Bible Society's first meeting that he wrote " a description of a multitude of Christians whose doctrinal and ritual differences had for ages kept them asunder and who had been taught to regard each other with a sort of pious estrangement or rather of consecrated hostility. The scene was new; nothing analogous to it had been exhibited before the public since Christians had begun to organize against each other the strife of separation. It was the dawn of a new era in Christendom."

The London Missionary Society soon became in practice the organ of the Congregational Church, and the Church Missions to the Jews early, but without any " consecrated hostility," went its Anglican way; but the British and Foreign Bible Society has weathered all storms and multiplied exceedingly.

(ii) There are three Churches which have organized their missionary enterprise as an integral part of the activities of the Church, reserving to the central governing body of the Church the responsible direction of its work throughout the world: the Methodist Church, the Church of Scotland and the Church of Rome. The Anglican Church in the United States, Canada, Australia and New Zealand has adopted a similar policy.

" Strictly speaking," writes the historian of the Methodists, " we Methodists should no more speak of the ' Foreign Missionary Society ' than we do of the ' Home Missionary Society ' or the ' Sunday School Society.' Foreign Missions are no adjunct or outlying appendage to the Church: they form equally with Home Missions or with the spiritual care of our children, a part of its structure—an interest incumbent on every Methodist in so far as he is a loyal subject of the Kingdom of Christ. . . . Our system springs from the primary conception of Missions as the charge of

E

the entire Church of Christ." From the outset the Methodist Conference has stationed the Missionaries and appointed the executive by which their operations are directed, and the funds for their maintenance are raised. All the advantages, we are told, are not on the side of this plan. Missionary work may become one department amongst many in a crowded agenda. " Where the Church officially directs the missionary campaign, the fighting force is liable to be hampered by half-hearted or ill-instructed followers, who impose a deadweight upon its march—by men who vote on missionary questions without close attention, and who serve out of duty, and because ' one must do something for Foreign Missions'."[1]

The missionary work of the Church of Scotland has been under the direction of an overseas Committee and a Presbytery with which its missionaries are as closely related as are Ministers at home with a Presbytery in Scotland.

The missionary organization of the Church of Rome reaches back to the institution of the Propaganda Fide in 1662, by the Bull " Inscrutabili." This is a congregation of Cardinals appointed by the Pope to govern the missions and everything that concerns the propagation and the preservation of the Faith in infidel and heretic countries; all missionaries are subject to it. Its original jurisdiction extended to the whole world outside distinctively Catholic countries. Pius X recently restricted it to regions which because of the absence of a constituted Hierarchy still remained as Missions, and to other regions like India and Japan where, notwithstanding the possession of a Hierarchy, Catholicism was still in the formative period.

This " Sacred Congregation " of Propaganda comprises nineteen Cardinals and thirty-five Consultors under the presidency of a Cardinal Prefect. There are ordinary weekly convocations, and solemn monthly assemblies where all-important questions are examined, reports read and decisions submitted to the Holy Father for final approbation.

[1] Findlay and Holdsworth: *History of the Wesleyan Methodist Missionary Society*, Vol. I.

The Congregation controls the whole development of Missions, Prefectures, Vicariates, Dioceses, throughout its jurisdiction. It decides where a Mission should first be sent; when, as it develops, it should be promoted to the status of a Prefecture Apostolic under a selected Priest, who as its Superior communicates directly with Propaganda and receives from it his instructions ; when, because the work has developed or because dioceses call for division, a Prefecture should be transformed into a Vicariate Apostolic, under a Titular Bishop with delegated authority from the Holy Father; when the development of the native ministry justifies a regular hierarchy and the appointment of a diocesan Bishop still under the jurisdiction of Propaganda. To countries dependent upon Propaganda this Sacred Congregation may send Delegates to represent the Holy See among the Bishops, priests and people, to handle the more important questions that arise, and to strengthen the bonds that unite them with Rome.

The Congregation has its own College of Propaganda in Rome, founded by Urban VIII in 1627 to " provide ecclesiastical education for young foreigners destined to evangelise their own countries." But it is not dependent for recruits on its own Colleges. It is the Religious Orders that place at the disposition of Propaganda the greater number of missionaries. There are forty-three Orders and Congregations that have missions entrusted to their care.

Two hundred years after the founding of Propaganda Fide, in 1822, was founded the Society for the Propagation of the Faith, whose duty it is to supply the sinews of war. It exists to help by prayer and alms. Its members are formed in groups of ten, each under a Promoter who passes their offerings to the priest of the parish, who passes them on monthly to the Diocesan Director, who forwards his receipts to the National Director, who remits to the Central Council at Lyons. " All the Popes from Pius VII to Pius X have granted a great store of indulgences to the members of the Society " but " those who specify their offerings for particular missions and missionaries cannot consider themselves members of the Society or enjoy its benefits." Copies of the official organ, the *Annals*, are distributed to all Promoters.[1]

ANGLICAN ORGANIZATION

The Church of England did not adopt the principles illustrated by the London Missionary Society, the Methodist Missionary Society, or the Church of Rome. While ready to co-operate in the work of the Bible Society, it displayed no enthusiasm for non-denominational enterprise. It had no Pope and could not therefore be expected to emulate the centralized simplicity of the Roman system. Its central life was indeed at so low an ebb that if it had relied, like the Methodists, on the Church as a corporate body for the initiation of its Missions they would never have been initiated at all. Ancient wounds in the body corporate had not been healed. The new Evangelicalism had not been assimilated; the Oxford Movement had not been heard of. The Convocations had not met since 1718. The Church therefore adopted a characteristically English compromise: it adapted and cloistered the machinery of expansion most ready to hand, namely the Chartered Company. It would be unwise to press too hard the analogy between the nation's casually haphazard management of its Colonial expansion and the Church's unsystematized expansion of its missions. But there is a factor common to both, which may be derived from the national character common to both—the spirit of private enterprise and self-reliance. Missionary and mercantile initiative both forged ahead of the powers that be: too impatient and restless in their respective spheres to wait till the authorities of State and Church had overcome their hesitations and safety-first mentalities.

There is no evidence that the Missionary Societies consciously modelled themselves upon Chartered Companies, though as we have seen, the S.P.G. was literally a Chartered Company, with both temporal and spiritual authority at its back. It is clear that when the founders of the Church Missionary Society became convinced that another Society was needed to cover fields excluded from

[1] Paolo Marina: *The Conversion of the Pagan World*, trans. by Rev. J. McGlinchy.

evangelism by the S.P.G. Charter, and to represent views excluded from favour by the S.P.C.K. (though they subscribed to both) they were equally anxious to secure something like a Charter from the Archbishop of Canterbury. They waited patiently for an answer to their letter of July 1st, 1799, till July 24th, 1800, when William Wilberforce was able to report that Archbishop Moore had overcome his caution and " spoken in very obliging terms, expressing himself concerning your Society in as favourable a way as could be well expected; though his Grace regretted that he could not with propriety at once express his full concurrence and approbation of an endeavour in behalf of an object he had deeply at heart."

It must be remembered that the missionary stream had long run underground. It took time to gather impetus, or to convince observers that its waters were unadulterated by " enthusiasm," by which our forefathers understood something as alarmingly aggressive as the Group Movement has sometimes appeared to their descendants. An English Bishop could still feel indignant enough to charge his clergy not to receive " those itinerant preachers who, neglecting their own parishes, go about through the country to draw all the money they can for the support of Societies self-constituted and unauthorized by either Church or State."

Why two Societies ? The question was asked in 1817 by Dr. Christopher Wordsworth who earnestly desired the consent of the first promoters of the C.M.S. to modifications of their system; and in 1818 by Richard Heber, still Rector of Hodnet. " The advantages of a union would, I humbly conceive, be great. It might go far towards healing the breach which unhappily exists in our establishment." He drew up a scheme of union under which the S.P.G. was to admit all members of the C.M.S.; officers were to be multiplied and distributed between the two Societies ; joint District Societies, county, diocesan or archidiaconal, were to be instituted. Perhaps, though it was the C.M.S. that Heber had joined " as apparently most active and employing with more wisdom than the elder corporation the means provided,"[1] the scheme smelt of absorption rather than union. At any rate it fell flat.

[1] George Smith: *Life of Bishop Heber.*

But that the relations between the Societies were friendly is pleasantly illustrated by the action of Josiah Pratt, Secretary of the C.M.S. in 1818, after his Society had been fiercely attacked at a meeting by the Archdeacon of Bath; the incident created such a sensation that the Archdeacon had " unwittingly served that great cause which lies nearest to our hearts." He gave the S.P.G. credit for doing so much that some of our rulers in the Church have felt it needful to do more than it had ever entered into their minds to contemplate. And now, by virtue of a King's Letter, to be issued in due time, all the Clergy will be enjoined to plead the cause of Christian Missions." Pratt at once set about compiling " an Abstract of the Designs and Proceedings of the S.P.G. with extracts from its Annual Sermons," and published it anonymously as " By a member of the Society," which of course he was.

MISSIONARY PLANNERS

The S.P.G. and C.M.S. have always been democratically governed and a host of men and women, unknown and unremembered, have had a hand in their planning, devoting years of inconspicuous and voluntary service to the management of their affairs. To only a few will it be possible to pay tribute of gratitude by according them their rightful place in the making of Christian history. It will be convenient to group them round two laymen, Charles Grant and Joshua Watson.

CHARLES GRANT'S CIRCLE

The first enjoys the greater fame, both on his own account and as the father of two sons, Charles Lord Glenelg, a future Colonial Secretary, and Sir Robert, Governor of Bombay and author of the hymn " *O Worship the King.*" Charles Grant's father was wounded at Culloden a few months after his birth, 1746, and ruined by his Jacobite loyalty. It was in 1767 that Grant first sailed for India, at a bad period in the administration of the Company : fifty years later he recalls in a letter to Lord Hastings that " the Native Government was then still subsisting in all its forms: the Europeans, the new masters of the country, though dreaded, had many things in their manner so revolting to Eastern notions as to make them objects of odium and contempt. In fact, the continuance of European ascendency was uncertain."

It was on his second visit, beginning in 1773, that Grant became a Writer in the service of the East India Company, now a family man but accumulating gambling debts, extravagantly ostentatious, though scrupulously honest in business and disapproving of Warren Hastings. The death from small-pox of his two daughters within nine days, his own illness and his brother's death, plunged him in despair from which he emerged a convinced believer. During his seven remaining years of exalted rank in Calcutta, troubled by the surrounding darkness, he put forth all possible exertions on behalf of Christian missions, helping to build St. John's Church, afterwards the Cathedral, rescuing at the cost of Rs. 10,000 the Danish mission which was involved in financial disaster, proposing a Mission to Bengal and Bihar, pleading with Dr. Cole, founder of the Methodist Missionary Society, to extend its activities to India, welcoming such pious Chaplains as the Rev. David Brown and inditing elaborate " Proposals " for a Mission to lay before the Archbishop of Canterbury and other authorities in England. His letter to Wilberforce in 1787 was a factor in bringing the C.M.S. into existence. " All objections to the extension of Christianity arise rather from Indisposition to the thing itself than any persuasion of its Impracticability."

But it is Grant's life after he had returned to England for good in 1790 that serves as an introduction to so many notable characters. As a Director of the East India Company from 1792, and later its Chairman, he was in the thick of the political and religious controversies which preceded the granting of the Company's new Charter in 1813. Socially he was in the centre of great luminaries, for he took his place as a star in the constellation " Clapham," which radiated beams of idealism across the world. One ray search-lit the darkness of Slavery; another shone upon the infant mission fields of India and Africa; another illumined Parliament. The metaphor does scant justice to the stark industry with which the championship of great causes was pertinaciously pressed home.

It was a group of laymen, but John Venn, Rector till 1813, one of the founders of the C.M.S., was the friend and confidant of all. They had another common friend in John Newton, till 1807 City Rector of St. Mary's Woolnoth, another founder of the C.M.S., whom Lecky describes as " one of the purest and most unselfish of Saints. He acquired by indomitable perseverance the attainments requisite for a clergyman, and continued for the space of forty-four years one of the most devoted and single-hearted of Christian ministers."[1] He is represented in " Hymns Ancient and Modern," by " Glorious things of thee are spoken," and " How sweet the name of Jesus sounds." He was a man to whom men turned at the crises of their lives, and not in vain—many of them men whose lives multiplied his influence indefinitely, such as Claudius Buchanan and William Wilberforce himself, whose biographer assures us that at the crisis of his life " No one at this period was more intimate with Wilberforce; none had greater influence over him ; none knew better what torments the young penitent had lately passed through, what vows he had made to prove himself worthy of grace."

Professor Coupland summarizes Newton's strange career: " Son of a master-mariner, he had gone to sea at the age of twelve; and after some years of service, partly on his father's ship, partly as a ' pressed man ' on a man-of-war, he had drifted into the position of an overseer at one of the depots on the Gold Coast where slaves were collected for shipment to America. Himself a slave to dissolute habits and to the brutal caprices of his master and his master's negro concubine, he was fast sinking into that irrecoverable degradation which is so often the doom of an outcast white man, when he was rescued, more or less against his will, by a friend of his father's, brought back to England, and finally given command of a slave-ship. It was during his career as a ' slaver ' that ' conversion ' came upon him."[2]

[1] W. E. H. Lecky: *History of England in the Eighteenth Century*, Vol. III, p. 134.
[2] R. Coupland: *Wilberforce*, passim.

There was an incongruity in the intimacy between the former " slaver " and the champion of the slave. Stranger still " During the time I was engaged in the slave-trade I never had the least scruple as to its lawfulness. I was, upon the whole, satisfied with it, as the appointment Providence had marked out for me." As it turned out, it was, as Sir James Stephen wrote " his province to work at the foundations of a great and necessary reform in the spirit of the Church of England. His weapon therefore was the pick-axe of the builder rather than the chisel of the sculptor. . . . To be, in all the comprehensive fulness of the words, a preacher of the Gospel—such was the purpose which without pause or faltering occupied during more than half a century the soul of John Newton."[1]

There were children as well as grown-ups to lighten the seriousness of the Clapham friends, " cheered, not checked, by the presence of their elders," and Sir James Stephen was one of them, for his father had married Wilberforce's sister. We may avail ourselves of his aid in picturing those amongst whom the " long-faced blue-eyed Scotchman," Charles Grant, was making himself at home. They could not be dismissed as armchair fanatics, for between them they could muster a wide experience of travel and administration. Grant himself, as we have seen, had been through the Indian mill and was now in daily contact with and control of the Company's Executive in Leadenhall Street. Stephen's father, who was to be his brother-in-law's standby in the House of Commons, had passed the most active part of his life in the West Indies as a barrister at St. Kitts, where he had been " so deeply stirred by the evils of slavery as he saw it at close quarters, that he had refused in the teeth of universal custom to own a single slave himself."[1]

Granville Sharp, the patriarch of the community (commemorated somewhat incongruously in the Poets' Corner of Westminster Abbey) had the weakest claim to the status of man of the world, and the weakest defence against being called an eccentric. He had spent seven years in a mercer's shop, and eighteen as a clerk in the office of Ordinance. But the " Ordinance clerk sat at his desk

[1] Sir J. Stephen: *Essays in Ecclesiastical Biography*.

with a soul as distended as that of a Paladin bestriding his war-horse; and encountered with his pen such giants, hydras and discourteous knights as infested the world in the eighteenth century." It was he who, sued for the illegal retention of a rescued man, "throughout two successive years betook himself to his solitary chamber, there, night by night, to explore the original sources of the Law of England, in the hope that he might be able to correct the authoritative dogma of Chancellors and Judges," until on June 22nd, 1752, Lord Chief Justice Mansfield of Kenwood (who sits enthroned in the western aisle of the North transept of Westminster Abbey) had vindicated his case by the Judgement "The claim of Slavery can never be supported. As soon as any slave sets foot on English ground he becomes free."

Zachary Macaulay, father of a more famous son and founder of a historian family, had left his father's manse at Cardross on the Clyde to superintend slave-labour in Jamaica: his abhorrence of the trade was based also on knowledge of the African end as ill-starred Governor of the new Settlement for liberated slaves in Sierra Leone. Stephen ascribes to him " a countenance at once so earnest and so monotonous, gestures uniformly prim and deliberate, an athletic though ungraceful figure; a demeanour in-animate if not austere, a charm which excited amongst his chosen circle a faith approaching to superstition, and a love rising to enthusiasm. That God had called him into being to wage implacable war with this gigantic evil was his immutable conviction, and for forty successive years it was the subject of his vision by day and of his dreams by night." His bust adorns the north-west chapel of Westminster Abbey over an inscription " en-graved by some eulogist less skilful than affectionate."

Clarkson, too, upon whom Wilberforce relied for the marshalling of the anti-slavery evidence, was of a stature that impressed Pitt in Whitehall and Mirabeau in Paris. Thornton was another friend of Pitt who himself planned for him the oval saloon wainscotted with books for his newly purchased residence at Clapham to become " the scene of enjoyments which amidst his proudest triumphs he might well have envied, and witness of the growth of projects more majestic than any which ever engaged the deliberation of his Cabinet." Thornton lived in two realistic worlds—the world of banking and the world of Parliament, and brought judgement as well as benevolence and hospitality into "this brotherhood of Christian politicans," this "remarkable fraternity, remarkable above all else, perhaps in its closeness, its affinity. It not only lived in one little village; it had one character, one mind, one way of life."

Again an ex-Governor General, Lord Teignmouth, who had risen from the bottom of the East India Company ladder rung by rung till by Pitt's appointment he reached the top, could not be lightly dismissed as a mere religious enthusiast who presided over the new Bible Society. Stephen as a boy had evidently found difficulty in believing that this humdrum man could ever have been so important, and bored with having to review two volumes of his biography, deals out more faint praise than to any other member of the fraternity. "He governed an empire without ambition, wrote poetry without inspiration and gave himself up to labours of love and works of mercy without enthusiasm. He was, in fact, rather a fatiguing man—of a narcotic influence in general society—with a pen which not rarely dropped truisms: the very antithesis and contradiction of the Hero whose too tardy advent Mr. Carlyle is continually invoking. Yet he was one of those whom we may well be content to honour, while we yet wait the promised deliverer."

The statue of Wilberforce in the Abbey is not one of those which were deemed worthy of sandbags—its mien is certainly more whimsical than devotional—but its loss would have been taken to heart by the public which does not pass him by without a glance of recognition, even if the inscription goes unread: "He was called to endure great obloquy, but he outlived all enmity." Charles Grant no sooner settled in England than he found himself deep in consultation with Wilberforce on public affairs, and also with the Prime Minister through Wilberforce's friendship with both. Grant was the only person to be invited to several days of seclusion with Mr. Pitt and Mr.

Dundas over Indian legislation. In so far as that legislation affected religion and missions, Grant was able to
bring Wilberforce the reinforcement of first-hand knowledge; he was at his elbow when he was preparing the
case for his famous Resolution, declaring " the religious
and moral improvement of the Indians by all just and
prudent means to be the peculiar and bounden duty of
the Legislature." He was in the Gallery of the House of
Commons when the clauses were struck out on the Third
Reading " and had one melancholy pleasure, that of seeing
Mr. Wilberforce in the face of that house stand forth as
the bold, zealous, animated and able champion of Christianity, and of the propriety and duty of communicating
its blessings to our heathen subjects." That was the defeat
of 1793. When victory came in 1813, Wilberforce was
still the prophet of the cause with Grant still beside him,
entitled now to speak himself from the floor of the House.
The new Charter embodied the provision that facilities
should be afforded to persons desirous of going to and
remaining in India for its moral and religious improvement,
and that a Bishop and three Archdeacons should superintend the Church. The story of Wilberforce's campaign
for the Abolition of Slavery from the day in 1787 when
" seated in the open air at the root of an old tree, in Hol-
wood, just above the steep descent into the valley of
Keston " he discussed the probability of success with Mr.
Pitt, to the news of the passing of the Bill a few days before
his death in 1833, is too familiar to need repetition. The
supreme moment of his life had been in 1807 when his
success in passing the Abolition of the Slave Trade had
carried the first objective. " The House was on its feet
giving Wilberforce an ovation such as it had given to no
other man." But the less spectacular moments spent in
making smooth the path for the infant Missionary Societies,
fostering the Africa Institution, caring for the Church in
New South Wales, legislating to reduce the hours of labour
for children or to prohibit sweep boys from climbing
chimneys—these were all contributions made by Wilberforce and his " brotherhood of Christian politicians " to
the making of Christian history.

JOSHUA WATSON'S CIRCLE

Joshua Watson was not so distinguished a public character as Charles Grant, and his friends were less conspicuous in public affairs. Lovers of symmetry like to label them the Clapton in contradistinction to the Clapham " sect " because his brother and his life-long friend, Handley Norris, were Hackney clergy and he lived for a time as their near neighbour; but for the most active years of his life he had a house in Park Street, Westminster, a great centre of hospitality. He qualifies for selection as a representative figure as having been closely associated with so many good causes and so many interesting people, in a circle which hardly intersected at all with that to which Grant belonged. Watson once sat with Wilberforce on an S.P.G. sub-committee, and he revelled in his biography; but these are the only references in his own biography to Clapham.

Born in 1771, twenty-five years later than Grant, he survived him by thirty-two years, and died in 1855. He carries us therefore well in advance of any date we have yet reached and introduces us to new aspects of the home-base stage of early nineteenth-century missions, just when the pre-episcopal stage of the Church in West and East was being left behind. He left school at fourteen to join his wine-merchant father in Mincing Lane. Yet we find Van Mildert, the Bampton Lecturer of 1814, submitting his draft to him for " strictest criticisms," and Christopher Wordsworth inviting his opinion on his forthcoming enquiry into the authorship of *Eikon Basilike*. The former, as Bishop of Durham, summoned him to Bishop Auckland for counsel when he was diverting the revenues of the see to the foundation of the University, the latter as Master of Trinity summoned him to Cambridge to talk over his building schemes. Over and above his reputation for culture and sagacity, his character won regard and affection. Bishop Lloyd of Oxford calls him " the best layman in England ": " I can tell you " writes the Archbishop of Canterbury (Manners-Sutton), " I could not love that man more were he my own son." William Wordsworth sought his company both in London and the Lakes.

Newman dedicated to him a volume of his " Parochial Sermons." Hugh James Rose, first Principal of King's College, London, whose parsonage at Hadleigh was the cradle of the Oxford Movement, was his intimate friend, that " really learned man " of whom Dean Church wrote that the Church revival " owed to him not only its first impulse but all that was best and most hopeful in it and when it lost him it lost its wisest and ablest guide and inspirer."[1]

Watson retired from his business in 1814 to fill countless voluntary Treasurerships and Secretaryships. Not all of these were ecclesiastical. He raised £11,500 in Westminster and administered a Parliamentary grant of £100,000 for the aid of German sufferers from the Napoleonic war. Thanks were effusive: " Let it never be doubted that German hearts are open to every feeling of gratitude and love for such generous benevolence shewn them by that happy country in which you reside." Watson also had a share in raising the Waterloo fund of nearly £500,000 for widows and orphans, and the Duke of Wellington attended his Committee. Among his specifically Church activities we are primarily concerned with those that affected the Church overseas, but his service of the Home Church reflects the spirit of the age.

It was in Watson's house that the founding of a new Society was plotted, that would make " the national religion the groundwork of national education " and when in 1811 the S.P.C.K. resolved that religious education must be deputed to a separate " National Society," Joshua Watson became its Treasurer and for thirty years threw himself into the development of schools, and the adoption of the new snowball methods of multiplying teachers by setting the taught to teach the less advanced, recently introduced " from the practice of the Hindoos " by Dr. Bell, one of the East India Company's Chaplains at Madras. The man and the system are portrayed in sculpture in the South Choir aisle of Westminster Abbey. Churches as well as Schools were needed, and Watson again raised funds and was a member of the Government's Church-building Commission. Into all plans for putting the

---

[1] R. W. Church: *The Oxford Movement*, p. 85.

Church's house in order, and for the construction of a
Board of Ecclesiastical Commissioners, he threw himself
with zest. When the time came for the laity to follow the
example of 7,000 clergy by addressing the Primate " with
an expression of unshaken adherence to the doctrine and
discipline of the Church, and firm attachment to her pure
faith and worship and her apostolic form of government "
it was Watson who formulated the Declaration to which
the signatures of 230,000 heads of families were appended.

These pre-Reform Bill years were full of anxiety verging
on panic for Churchmen, " who were no mere fanatics
or alarmists, but sober and sagacious observers, not
affected by mere cries but seeing below the surface of
things their certain and powerful tendencies."[1]   Men
feared the dismemberment of the English Church and
the disintegration of its doctrinal basis: " an agrarian and
civic insurrection was brewing against the Bishops and
clergy and all who desired to adhere to the existing institutions of the country."   The Prime Minister had roughly
bidden the Bishops " set their house in order " and the mob
had taken him at his word and burnt down the Bishop
of Bristol's palace.   Watson's address " rallied the courage
of Churchmen and showed that they were stronger and
more resolute than their enemies thought."[1]

Such times might well seem unpropitious for advance
overseas; their pre-occupations might have excused missionary inactivity.   But that was not Joshua Watson's
view, for his friends included three men who had lately
been consecrated Bishops of distant sees: Middleton, the
first Bishop of Calcutta; Inglis, his father's successor as
second Bishop of Nova Scotia; Broughton, first Bishop
in Australia.   With Middleton while he lived, and with
the others for a life-time, he was in constant correspondence.
Bishop Hobart of New York was another friend, and
Watson warmly defended him when public opinion
resented the unrepentant republicanism and frank criticism
which he had rather aggressively avowed on his return to
America from a visit to England.   Later in his life, friendship with Bishop Selwyn, first Bishop of New Zealand,
further extended Watson's horizon.

[1] Ibid., pp. 89, 96.

This intercourse with distant Bishops, which is taken as a matter of course to-day, was then a novelty, unknown if not unthinkable to those who for generations had been pleading in vain that the Branches of an episcopal Church should themselves be episcopal. But Watson was as deep in home organization as in overseas correspondence. As Treasurer of the S.P.C.K. he persuaded that Society of the wisdom of transferring to the S.P.G. their responsibility for the South Indian missions of Danish origin (see Part V); and as member and constant counsellor of the S.P.G. persuaded that Society to accept the transfer. His friendship with Bishop Middleton led him to agitate for the issue of the King's letter, or rather Regent's letter, the proceeds of which refloated the S.P.G. and launched Bishop's College, Calcutta. Royal Letters may sound a dubious method of missionary finance, but " it was not then considered right or lawful to collect alms for public designs such as Church building, without this form of public authority "; it was a form which Christopher Wordsworth preferred to the alternative Parliamentary grants as avoiding the unseemliness of Parliamentary conflict, but more " because I am persuaded that the raising of the money by an appeal through the clergy . . . would lay them under an obligation to understand what it is for and to shew that the object is a good one: the getting of the gold is but a small part of the business."

The Prince Regent's Royal Letter enabled the S.P.G. to send £50,000 to Bishop Middleton, and marked a rebirth of the Society. " It was at this period rather an ecclesiastical board for administering the funds which the Government supplied to the clergy in the North American Colonies, than a Missionary Society for the Church at large: its annual income from voluntary sources did not amount to a thousand pounds." Watson may have been over-sanguine in belittling the obstacles to the conversion of India, and mistaken in regarding Ceylon as " the master-key of Hindoostan "; but his advocacy of the cause is far-sighted as well as vigorous, as when in his 1817 memorandum to the Archbishop of Canterbury he urges that it was impossible to carry on the work of the ministry either in the East or West Indies with any good success unless there might be bishops and seminaries settled in them, that so ministers might be bred and ordained on the spot. . . . Christianity cannot take root effectually till there are native priests and ministers."

*   *   *   *   *   *

Our review of these two circles associated with the names of Grant and Watson registers a debt to the home-base pioneers, and those who rallied round them, and indicates directions for future study. Clapham is our junction for India, West Africa and the West Indies: lines run from Clapton to four new and unwieldy dioceses in India, Australia, Canada and New Zealand. But before starting on these journeys, there is another debt to be registered— the obligations of the Anglican Communion to foreign allies and auxiliaries.

PART V

GERMANS AND DANES: ALLIES AND AUXILIARIES

1. The Recruiting Problem.

2. German Allies: (*a*) Ziegenbalg; (*b*) Schwartz.

3. German Auxiliaries: (*a*) Gobat; (*b*) Krapf; (*c*) Isenberg; (*d*) Pfander.

THE RECRUITING PROBLEM

MISSIONARY Societies were now in being—and the missionary's right of entrance to India had been sponsored by Parliament—but would there be missionaries for the Societies to thrust through the newly-opened door ? Again it was proved that the stream that had been flowing underground for centuries emerged not in full spate but as a trickle. It took time before the missionary calling lived down the disrepute attaching to the unaccustomed.

In 1693 an impecunious young graduate of Queen's College, Oxford consulted his parents about an invitation to go over into Maryland which he was not very unwilling to accept. His father replied, " I advise you to steer your course any way where it may be for God's glory and the good of souls, *but seawards*. I earnestly desire you to banish out of your heart what thoughts, intents and purposes you have to pass over the sea. This Kingdom is large enough and places many in it. Let those go who are not so well provided as you are." To which his mother adds the postcript, " Son, I hope you have done nothing you need depart the land for."[1]

The correspondence suggests factors which to some extent explain the difficulty of securing missionary recruits, even at a time when the London Missionary Society was sending boat loads to the South Seas, and Methodists were

[1] Quoted in Prof. Syke's *History of the Church in the Eighteenth Century*.

spreading in many directions. It was from Maryland that the invitation came. Overseas service was equated with ministrations to fellow-countrymen in westward or eastward exile; the prestige of the Establishment could be invoked to cover such undertakings, but not to countenance work among non-Christians.

"This kingdom is large enough and places many in it" is a plea constantly echoed. "Is not the maze of evil here greater a thousand times" asks Dr. Arnold in 1840, "in its injurious effects on the world at large than all the idolatry in India? Look at the state of your own county (Durham) and does not that cry out as loud as India?" He adds a touch curiously reminiscent of Luther, "Remember the Apostles did indeed, or rather some of them did, spread the Gospel over many provinces of the Roman Empire: but it was necessary that it should have a wide diffusion once; not that this diffusion should go on universally and always, although the old Churches might be grievously wanting the aid of those who were plunging into heathen and barbarian countries to make nominal converts" (note the question-begging epithet). "If all our men" (note the question-begging *all*), wrote Archbishop Benson (still Bishop of Truro) in 1878, "are to go off to the frontier, then we shall all be doing for the Church what Trajan did for the Roman Empire. Augustine had prophesied that the extension of the frontier would bring downfall at home: the work for us is to prevent decay spreading any further at the core."

Neither Arnold nor Benson would claim that an exclusively insular outlook reflected the whole counsel of God. The former admits that "if a man tells me that he feels bound to go out as a missionary to India, I feel I ought not to grudge to India what God seems to wish for her." The latter admits "that we must send out our legions of missionaries." If there had not been men and women, and those not the least alive to the need for the regeneration of the English Church, nor the least sensitive to the social emergencies of the time, who could withstand such discouragements, and stake all on their faith in the universality of God's purpose, the "great new fact of our era" would never have materialized.

It certainly cannot be said that the missionary enterprise of the nineteenth century achieved what it did because
the Church carefully selected its strongest men and women,
as for tasks of exceptional difficulty: it did nothing of the
kind; and for many years first the S.P.C.K. and then the
C.M.S. depended largely on German allies and auxiliaries.

GERMAN ALLIES

When Dr. Lutkens, his Chaplain, asked permission of
King Frederick IV of Denmark to go out and start a
mission in that corner of South India which Denmark in
1621 had purchased from the Rajah of Tanjore, the
answer was " I cannot send that hoary head to encounter
the dangers of the voyage and the devouring heat of
India "; but the King countenanced a search for volunteers. Denmark drew blank, but August Francke, founder
of the Pietist University at Halle, was kindling missionary
fervour in German youth, and it was at Halle that the first
recruits were found—the first of a long line of Halle men:
for out of the forty-nine who joined the Mission between
1706 and the end of the century, only three were Danes,
and all but thirteen were Halle students. Danish is in fact
something of a misnomer, for the missionaries were German
and talked German, while their support was largely
English. The S.P.C.K. had been in close touch with
Continental Lutherans—their correspondence had an
œcumenical flavour. Queen Anne's husband was a nephew
of Frederick IV and brought his Lutheran Chaplain to
London, as did the first Hanoverian monarchs. Hence
the Society's connection with the Mission, which was not
merely formal or financial but managerial, if not magisterial.
" You have, good Sir," wrote the Society to one of its
German emissaries, " as few failings as any missionary in
India, and as warm a zeal to promote the glory of God.
Do what you can to sacrifice your chiefest failing to this
Zeal, and to mortify the least degree of pride that can
tempt you to assume a Superiority or Rule over your
fellow-labourers, altho' your merit may make you worthy
of it and would probably command it of them, if you did
not assume it."

BARTOLOMEW ZIEGENBALG

Ziegenbalg, the pioneer, arrived in India in 1766 at the age of twenty-three, after so delicate a youth that it is surprising that he could survive twelve years of exposure to climate and trials. His arrival in Tranquebar was not encouraging. He and his companion were advised to make all haste home again. No one would give them shelter. Two ships bringing funds foundered at sea. The Governors withheld the pittance allowed them by King Frederick, and for four months Ziegenbalg was kept under lock and key without trial, till a letter arrived from the King peremptorily enjoining the Governor to befriend the missionaries. No Tamil grammar or dictionary was to be found and the new arrival had to depend for language study on a teacher who knew no English; they took their places in class with the children spelling out their words in the sand. Ziegenbalg would have books read over to him again and again till he almost knew them by heart and had mastered every tone and inflexion. The lives of Europeans did not commend their religion: " Christian religion, devil religion; Christian much drunk, much rogue, much naughty, very much naughty."

Amid derision from his countrymen, though a few offered contributions, Ziegenbalg set to work on a Church. How would he ever finish it, or ever fill it if he did " unless they can persuade enough slaves and outcastes to change their religion, in the hope of bettering their condition in life? " But within thirteen months of landing, the Church was dedicated and already baptisms were taking place, not without stringent preparation of the candidate and his subsequent discipline: the administration of the Holy Communion was always preceded by eight days of preparation. Ziegenbalg's sermon at the dedication of a second Church ten years later reveals a strong sense of the Church " of which Christ as Prophet, High Priest and King is alone rudiment and foundation." Fearless and plain-spoken, his disputations and even his denunciation of idolatry excited little resentment. There was authority in his emaciated form, and his complete mastery of Tamil commanded a hearing. His Tamil New Testament was complete within five years as well as a dictionary, and a press had been sent out by the S.P.C.K. so that books could be printed in Tamil on the spot.

Ziegenbalg paid one visit to Europe. Frederick IV was busy in camp besieging Charles XII of Sweden. One evening there was a profound movement among the Danish troops. A stranger of note had an audience with the King, who had shown him singular favour and for hours they had been closeted together. Then they saw that he was " only a clergyman, but a man of commanding presence, of a wonderful dignity and fire, resolute and calm with a keen eye, a winning courtesy and lovableness of manner: when he opened his lips and preached to them there were some at least who ceased to wonder at his welcome from the King."[1] In London he addressed the S.P.C.K. in Tamil which was translated into Latin: he was welcomed by George I who later wrote to him in Latin, " Your letters were most welcome to us; not only because the work undertaken by you, of converting the heathen to the Christian faith doth, by the Grace of God, prosper, but also because in this one Kingdom such a laudable zeal for the promotion of the Gospel prevails. . . . You will always find us ready to succour you in whatever may tend to promote your work and to excite your zeal."

A letter in eighteenth century idiom from Archbishop Wake arrived a few days after Ziegenbalg's death in 1778, and may serve for epitaph: " Let others indulge in a ministry, if not idle, certainly less laborious, among Christians at home. Let them enjoy in the bosom of the Church titles and honours, obtained without labour and without danger. Your praise it will be to have laboured in the vineyard which yourselves have planted; to have declared the Name of Christ where it was not known before, and through much peril and difficulty to have converted to the faith those among whom ye afterwards fulfilled your ministry. Your province therefore brethren, your office, I place before all dignitaries in the Church. Let others be pontiffs, patriarchs or popes; let them glitter in purple, in scarlet or in gold. Ye have acquired a better name than they, and a more sacred fame."

---

[1] Quoted in *Schwartz of Tanjore*.

CHRISTIAN FREDERICK SCHWARTZ

Schwartz is our best introduction to the Danish Missions in the second half of the eighteenth century. He reached India in 1750, befriended on his way through England by the S.P.C.K. and the "Revd. Mr. Ziegenbalg, the venerable Chaplain of His Majesty," and there he served without break till his death in 1798. He found Christianity still handicapped by the example of Christians. An honest and venerable enquirer is astonished to be told that sincere Christians existed. "Sir, you astonish me, for from what we daily observe and experience we cannot but think the Europeans with few exceptions to be self-interested, incontinent, proud, full of illiberal contempt against us Hindus and even against their own religion"; and a dancing girl cried bitterly when told that no wicked or unholy person could possibly enter the Kingdom of Heaven, for "Alas, sir, in that case hardly any European will ever enter it."

Schwartz set about his preparation for life in India as thoroughly as if he had known there was half a century's service ahead of him: Tamil, Hindustani, Portuguese and English were mastered. "Deeming it necessary in order to converse with advantage with the people to be well acquainted with their system of theology, he spent five years in reading their many mythological books only, and reaped this benefit, that he can at any time command the attention of the Malabars by allusion to their favourite books and histories which he never fails to make subservient to the truth."

The mission had extended from Tranquebar to the neighbouring coast towns of Cuddalore and Negapatam, and a hundred miles northward to Madras, country much overrun by war in the 1750's; wars between English and French, Clive and Dupleix, and between rival Maharajahs; "the fortunes of the mission appeared to be the shuttlecock of the contending parties in the game of war." Schwartz was responsible for an extension inland, making Trinchinopoly his headquarters. Here he acted chaplain to British troops, but made himself very accessible to the Brahmins who were attracted by his personality and discussed religion without reserve. " For the first time they had come in touch with a man who had a profound knowledge of their own position and a friendly sympathy in meeting their difficulties "; he never rebuffed them as beyond hope. It was a Brahmin who bestowed a fine title on Schwartz: " You are a universal priest."

An important official of the East India Company recorded his surprise at discovering Schwartz at Trinchinopoly, to be so different from his expectations: " His garb which was pretty well worn, seemed foreign and old-fashioned, but in every other respect his appearance was the reverse of all that could be called forbidding or morose: a short well-made man, erect in his carriage and address. A European in England may live much better on £24 per annum than on Schwartz's income of £48. He lived in a room in an old Gentoo building, just large enough to hold his bed and himself and in which few men could stand upright. A dish of vegetables dressed after the manner of the natives was what he could always cheerfully sit down to, and a piece of Chintz dyed black and other materials of the same homely sort, sufficed him for an annual supply of clothing. Thus easily provided as to temporalities, his only care was to " do the work of an evangelist."

So homely and other-worldly a figure might have seemed out of place in palaces and ill-fitted to cope with social and political crises. Yet it was Schwartz who saved the situation when famine followed in the wake of Hyder Ali: it was his foresight which had purchased twelve thousand bushels of rice and his practical wisdom which persuaded the people " who had lost all confidence in the word of a European, to bring in their animals and stores, making himself personally responsible that they should be duly paid. . . . The Lord also enabled me to consider the poor, so that I had it in my power to feed a large number for the space of seventeen months."

It was Schwartz in his black chintz who established such a personal influence over the Rajah of Tanjore that he implored him to take over the guardianship of his heir: " This is not my son but yours, into your hands I deliver him," and that in spite of much plain speaking. " More than once have I entreated him to have mercy on his subjects, for which plain declaration I lost in some degree his good opinion." Schwartz had added Mahratta to his languages to facilitate this intercourse. When the Government was compelled to take over the administration of Tanjore they urged Schwartz to take a seat on the Committee with the compliment " Happy indeed would it be for this country, for the Company and for the Rajah himself if he possessed the whole authority, and were invested with power to execute all the measures that his wisdom and benevolence would suggest."

This was not the first or only occasion on which Government resorted to Schwartz. In 1779, Sir Thomas Rumbold, Governor of Madras, asked him to undertake a very important mission to Hyder Ali at Seringapatam. " As the intention of the journey is good and Christian, namely to prevent the effusion of human blood, and to preserve this country in peace, this commission militates not against but highly becomes your sacred office, and therefore we hope you will accept it." Accept it he did for these reasons, and on the condition that he received no reward. It was a dangerous and tricky mission and had very limited success, but that the fierce tyrant was not unimpressed by his unusual visitor is shown by a subsequent order in the thick of war " to permit the venerable padre to pass unmolested and to show him respect and kindness, for he is a holy man and means no harm to my Government." Schwartz was once more asked to accompany a commission to Mysore after Tippoo had succeeded his father, but declined because he disapproved the official policy of appeasement. Colonel Fullerton, the English Commander, in his report to Government bore witness that " the knowledge and the integrity of this irreproachable missionary have retrieved the character of the Europeans from imputations of general depravity."

" The similarity of this situation to that of the first preachers of the Gospel produced in him a similar resemblance to the simple sanctity of the Apostolic character." This is part of the inscription recorded on the Flaxman monument erected by the Rajah of Tanjore who had been " delivered into Schwartz's hands " as a boy. The East

India Company was not to be outdone. An eminent sculptor was commissioned to represent in marble the scene of Schwartz's death, and a Director composed an inscription a page and a half long testifying the regard of the powers that be for one " whose life was one continued effort to imitate the example of his Blessed Master." Employed as a Protestant missionary from the Government of Denmark, and in the same character by the Society in England for the Promotion of Christian Knowledge, he, during a period of fifty years " went about doing good," maintaining, in respect to himself, the most entire abstraction from temporal views, but embracing every opportunity of promoting both the temporal and eternal welfare of others."

The Danish Mission of the S.P.C.K. was manned by a succession of missionaries, and extended to Tinnevelly and Palamcottah in South India, and to Calcutta in the North. When war and rationalism over-ran Germany, the supply of University recruits ran dry, and the first Bishops in India found the Mission in parlous state. It was subject to the limitations of an experimental epoch and a patriarchal outlook, and its attitude to caste will come up for later reference, but it bequeathed a grand tradition, and laid the foundation of an Indian Ministry. As early as 1728, the Mission wrote to their authorities in Denmark that the best solution of their pastoral difficulties would be to ordain a minister for these people from among themselves, if one could be found with suitable qualities. Had they the power so to act ? Five years later Aaron, the son of Hindu parents, kindled by what he learnt at a charity-school in Cuddalore to seek out the missionaries at Tranquebar, was promoted from catechist to ordained minister. His twelve years' ministry produced a good effect on his countrymen " because they see one of their own nation devoting himself to teaching a congregation in the things connected with God and eternity, without seeking his own advantage. From the increased consideration in which he is held, the way to Christianity has been made easier to many, for they have thus overcome the disgrace connected with it."

But few Indians rose beyond the rank of catechist and Schwartz was not over-sanguine on the subject of a native ministry: he devoted time every day to training catechists and felt more confidence in placing them under German than Indian guidance: but in 1790 he approved the ordination of Sathanaden who had accompanied him to the court of Hyder Ali and done pioneer work in Palamcottah : this beginning of a twenty-five years' ministry was marked by the publication of a sermon of Sattianaden's by the S.P.C.K., "in order to evince the capacity of the natives for the work of the ministry, and as an evidence that the efforts of the missionaries had not been in vain, but that the light of the Gospel was spreading throughout those regions of darkness and idolatry."

GERMAN AUXILIARIES

The habit of engaging German and Swiss mercenaries to fight the country's battles overseas was familiar to our forefathers, and it was to some such expedient that the Church Missionary Society was reduced in its early days. Mercenary is the last adjective that could be applied to the spirit of these German auxiliaries, but they were engaged to do something for their employers which their employers ought to have done through the instrumentality of their own fellow-countrymen. Dr. Warneck's *History* is humiliating reading on this point: " In its beginnings the Society had to struggle with extraordinary difficulties. Apart from the general disfavour under which it had to suffer, missionaries were wanting. Out of this misfortune they were helped by having missionaries provided from two German mission seminaries, Berlin and later Basle, to the number, as time went on, of 120 in all. Only in 1815 did two Bishops join the Society, and in 1840 the two had only become nine."[1]

In contrast with the missionaries of the S.P.C.K. period, these Germans did not hail from Halle, and most of them came to England for training and episcopal ordination. They and their wives and innumerable children added many names to the roll of martyrs for the faith, for the casualties at first were very heavy, though Dr. Stock's

[1] *History of Protestant Missions*, p. 91.

record of the years 1824–1840 shows twenty-eight missionaries averaging twenty-eight years of service.

These were the men and women who founded the first C.M.S. mission in West Africa, among the Susoo tribes a hundred miles north of Sierra Leone on the Rio Pongas. " It was a very humble enterprise and far from satisfactory according to our modern standard: little more than two or three schools in which German missionaries, while still trying to pick up Susoo, were teaching English, also very imperfectly understood, to a few African boys who were clothed and fed at the expense of the Mission."[1] Thousands of slaves taken from slave-ships were being landed at Freetown by British cruisers and the Government turned to the Mission to come and befriend them in Sierra Leone itself. The mission was sore let and hindered by the hostilities of chiefs (Susoo had to be abandoned), by dissension and by death. Of twelve persons who landed in 1823, six died in that year and four more within eighteen months. But the Home Committee triumphed over sorrow and firmly resolved " we will not abandon West Africa." The survivors rose to a new sense of purpose and unity, and the news of disasters kindled new zeal among the students of Basle. The Society girded itself to provide ministers and schoolmasters for the multitude of liberated slaves whom the Government was settling into the peninsula of Sierra Leone, now divided into parishes.

Further afield the Society was exploring Abyssinia, its interest excited by the possession of Bible manuscripts in Ethiopic and Amharic. It was a short-lived and hard-living expedition. Gobat reached Abyssinia in 1830, Krapf and Isenberg were evicted in 1843. The Red Sea voyage in a boat laden with Negro and Abyssinian pilgrims is described by Gobat : " Each passenger had his place measured, about five and a half feet long by two feet broad, and in this disagreeable position he had to abide twenty-one days, exposed to the burning sun." The anathemas of Coptic priests must also have been disagreeable. " They committed our souls to Satan, our bodies to the hyenas, our property to the thieves, and excommunicated every one who would come near us."

[1] Eugene Stock: *History of C.M.S.*, Vol. I, p. 157.

Try as he might, Isenberg could not convince them that " we come with a message of love from a sister Church, which desires to communicate to you the best treasure of the Church of God, His Holy Word. She does not demand that you should change your customs." He urged (as in later years B.C.M.S. missionaries insisted) that he did not intend establishing an English Church in Abyssinia— on the contrary he would not administer the sacrament to any Abyssinian and only requested that the missionaries might observe their own form of service in their own hours. But it was of no avail. Nevertheless Isenberg succeeded in translating the New Testament and collected much valuable philological material. Nor was his knowledge of Ethiopian languages and customs wasted: years later in Western India he took charge of a colony of rescued slaves of many African nationalities and among them Abyssinians, some of whom afterwards carried their Christianity to Africa, nine of them in the company of Livingstone. He had at one time under his roof five Abyssinians from Adowa.

The dispersal of the three Abyssinian missionaries illustrates a threefold development of the Church's activities. Isenberg we have seen in Western India. Gobat became the second Bishop in Jerusalem, for which he had special qualifications " as being allied in nearly equal measure by birth, education and career to three great and distinct nationalities: by speech a Frenchman, in sympathies a German, and an Englishman by virtue of your connection with Church and mission." Krapf was the first missionary to land on East African shores, a solitary figure standing by the grave of wife and child, and writing: " Tell our friends that there is now on the East African coast a lonely missionary grave. This is a sign that you have commenced the struggle with this part of the world: and as the victories of the Church are gained by stepping over the graves of her members, you may be the more convinced that the hour is at hand when you are summoned to the conversion of Africa from its Eastern shore."

Yet one more German auxiliary must be mentioned, Karl Gottlieb Pfander, who after twelve years' wandering in Turkey, Persia, Armenia, and Georgia, entered C.M.S. service in India equipped as no other of his generation to interpret Christianity to Moslems: a master of the languages, the thought, the scholarship, the idiom of Islam. We shall meet him again in Part IX

Many another German auxiliary merits tribute of gratitude; those mentioned here represent five main fields of activity, where, as we follow their beckoning, we shall find growth owing its origin to their beginnings: West Africa, East Africa, Palestine, India, and the world of Islam.

PART VI

THE COMING OF THE BISHOPS
SEVEN SEES

1. The See of Nova Scotia: The See of Newfoundland.

2. The See of Calcutta—Sidney Smith, Claudius Buchanan, Bishop Middleton, Bishop Heber.

3. The See of Barbados: The See of Jamaica.

4. The Sees of Australia and New Zealand—Samuel Marsden, Bishop Broughton, Bishop Selwyn.

5. The Home Base and the Coming of the Bishops.

OUR study of the circles which centred round Charles Grant and Joshua Watson dictated the directions in which to explore the expansion of the Church under episcopal auspices: the former pointed to India, to West Africa and the West Indies: the latter introduced us to Watson's four episcopal friends in Nova Scotia, Calcutta, Australia and New Zealand. Sierra Leone must be postponed for later reference, as no Bishop came to West Africa till 1852. The dioceses of Jamaica and Barbados were twins and must be considered together. The Mother diocese of Nova Scotia cannot be separated from the daughter diocese of Newfoundland. There are then seven Sees, all of them destined to be fruitful and multiply; and we must make the acquaintance of the men who presided over their origins, and what were the conditions with which they found themselves confronted.

THE SEES OF NOVA SCOTIA
AND NEWFOUNDLAND

Nova Scotia takes precedence as being the senior Colonial diocese, its first Bishop Inglis having been consecrated in 1787, only three years after Bishop Seabury, the first and up to that date the only overseas Bishop. Joshua Watson's

friend was the son of the first Bishop Inglis and the third
to hold the See. As long ago as 1758, the Nova Scotia
Legislature had "established" the Church according to
the liturgy and laws of the Church of England. The
Governor was "directed to induct the minister into any
parish that should make presentation of him, and to
suspend and silence any other persons assuming the
functions of ministers." At the same time Dissenters and
Roman Catholics had liberty of worship and freedom
from tithes or taxes for the support of the established
Church. In each township 400 acres of land were set
apart for the parson, 200 for the schoolmaster. Church
and State were so completely identified that on Bishop
Inglis' death in 1816, the House of Assembly at once
recommended to the Crown the appointment of their
Chaplain, who was duly consecrated, and reigned for
eight years while under medical treatment in England.

When the second Bishop Inglis succeeded him in 1825,
his diocese had shrunk. It still covered Nova Scotia,
New Brunswick, Newfoundland and Bermuda, but Upper
and Lower Canada had become the daughter diocese of
Quebec which was in turn to become mother and grand-
mother of other dioceses. It had been his father's duty
to organize a Church for the multitude of fugitive "Loyal-
ists," between thirty-five and forty thousand of them,
including many of the foremost colonists of New York and
Massachusetts, who found refuge in Nova Scotia from the
violence and confiscation to which their pro-British
sentiments exposed them in the aftermath of the American
Revolution: he himself was one of them, losing his New
York Rectory, together with the majority of the S.P.G.
clergy who felt bound by oath of allegiance to George
the Third.

The son's task was to consolidate. He subdivided his
scattered diocese into four Archdeaconries and visited them
all; in fifteen years one hundred and nineteen chapels and
churches were consecrated; clergy multiplied in spite of
the reduction of State subsidy, and education developed
in spite of the withdrawal of grants and confiscation of
school lands dictated by the prevailing preference for what
was then called a "liberal" or secular education. King's

College, Windsor, produced a line of notable alumni, though the fact that its statutes were modelled on those of the University of Oxford restricted its influence. It was only in 1830 that a new charter waived subscription to the Thirty Nine Articles as a condition of graduation. Bishop Inglis throughout his twenty-five years kept up a close liaison with the Mother Country and conducted vigorous campaigns in England on behalf of the S.P.G. "He did not adopt a course which has been taken up by some younger colonial bishops, and which the circumstances might have justified, of soliciting funds for his own province, but pleaded the general cause, trusting to a sense of justice in those who administered the funds of the Society that his own clergy would not be neglected." "He was led to adopt a measure of doubtful promise, the advocacy of his cause at public meetings and on public platforms," the novelty of which Joshua Watson was inclined to regret, doubting its permanent efficacy.

New dioceses, Newfoundland 1839, New Brunswick (Fredericton) 1845, Bermuda (1917) reduced Nova Scotia to its present limits. It is of the first of these that some notice must be taken, for it illustrates the reach and variety of the Church's expanding range. Newfoundland and Calcutta present climatic extremes, but even within the diocese which embraced Labrador and the Bermudas (in which the Bishop had to pay visits of several months every alternate year) there were contrasts of temperature, population and problems. Like his contemporary Bishop of New Zealand, Bishop Feild conducted his visitation by water : in a " Church Ship," the *Hawk*, a vessel of fifty tons, carrying eight passengers and fitting a congregation of sixty-three into its cabin.

Here began a wholly new chapter in Anglican history: here was the unwonted spectacle of a Bishop depending for victuals on Newfoundland fare of tea, biscuit and eggs, varied with the flesh and heart of bottle-nosed whale; battling with Arctic gales; his palace uncarpeted and servantless; his study a " literary chaos " of pamphlets and letters; his tithes dependent on the supply of blubber and the price of seals; his new Cathedral " lacking all the usual properties," though with all the seats free, daily

Offices and weekly Communions. Strict Churchman as
he was, to the point of declining presidency of the Bible
Society, he was too pre-occupied to feel it mattered vitally
whether Dr. Lushington in London ruled credence-tables
legal or illegal. Bishop Blomfield might well contrast his
own lot at Fulham and London House with " the necessities
and difficulties which embarrass and impede the bishop
of such a diocese as Newfoundland, in the discharge of
his pastoral duties." Here was a new call to ascetic
service: " I offer bread and fish and £100 a year." Here
was His Excellency the Governor with three A.D.C.'s
and a hundred applications for the post. Were there no
clergy of any spirit in England ? " Was I perhaps too
stern ? " he asks himself, after the failure of his first campaign, in bidding candidates " having food and raiment
therewith to be content." Stern he certainly was with
himself (though blithe and humorous). Stern he was with
his diocese at the cost of disfavour, egging it on to self-
support. It must learn to finance itself out of a central
fund contributed directly by heads of families, not from
pew-rents or assessments: every mission must send twenty-
five per cent. of its receipts to this fund as a condition of
obtaining assistance. All S.P.G. grants for clergy stipends,
his own included, were at his request reduced by fifty
per cent., the economies to go to new missions, nine of
which were started around the coast, in addition to new
churches.

Stern too were the demands made on the clergy, but
the Bishop sustained them by his understanding and
example. On the coast of Labrador, a Mr. Gifford " was
to be put ashore to commence work alone and unfriended."
It was no common trial to be left alone, among utter
strangers, in a fisherman's cottage, with no probability of
retreat or escape, no prospect of seeing a friend or even
receiving a letter for nearly a year: what a contrast to my
first curacy! He was rowed off by two hands with his
bundle and so set on shore and stood there alone watching;
while the good Church ship got under way. Perhaps I
have dwelt too long upon such an event, the landing of a
clergyman in his mission, or, as the sailors roughly phrased

it, ' shoving the gentleman on shore '; but the place, the prospect, the purpose, if duly weighed, so surely show signs of Christian daring and devotion not to be mistaken, not to be despised."

THE SEE OF CALCUTTA

SIDNEY SMITH

Sidney Smith's articles in the *Edinburgh Review* of 1808 on Methodism and on Indian Missions outrage decency and their invectives are often unquotable, but they afford evidence of the formidable forces against which the champions of an Indian Bishopric had to contend. While protesting himself a sincere friend to the conversion of the Hindus as being a great duty and if it could be effected a great blessing, for was it not an obligation on Christian people to disseminate their religion among the pagans subjected to their Empire? the time was not yet. The desire of putting an end to missions might be premature and indecorous, but for circumstances which made India an exception to the rule. In the Vellore mutiny two years before, 164 Light Dragoons had been killed and 600 mutineering Sepoys shot. The Commander-in-Chief had reported that fears of forcible conversion by the Government had had little to do with it. It would be surprising that people should be brought to believe " that those who apparently conduct themselves with so much apathy in respect to what concerns the adoration of the Supreme Being should have formed any serious scheme for converting whole nations to the Christian faith. None but the weakest and most superstitious could have been deluded by so improbable a tale."

But Sidney Smith was convinced that " if missionaries are not watched the throat of every Englishman will be cut. . . . No man not an Anabaptist will contend that it is our duty to preach the Natives into an insurrection; to lay before them the scheme of the Gospel so fully and emphatically that they rise in the dead of night and shoot their instructors through the head." The loss of our settlements would mean the loss of " that slow, solid and

temperate introduction of Christianity which the superiority of the European character may ultimately effect in
the Eastern world."

Hindus moreover were a comparatively civilized and
moral people. " Christianity would improve them (whom
would it not improve?), but if Christianity cannot be
extended to all there are many other nations who want it
more." Hinduism at any rate provided " some restraint
on the intemperance of human passions: it was better
that a Brahmin should be respected than that nobody
should be; better that the Hindu should believe that a
deity with a hundred arms and legs will reward and
punish him hereafter than that he is not to be punished
at all." It was alarming to find that the men who wielded
the instruments of government could not be trusted for
an instant; they were insane and ungovernable on this
subject and would " deliberately, piously and conscientiously expose our Eastern Empire to destruction for the
sake of converting half-a-dozen Brahmins, who, after
stuffing themselves with rum and rice and borrowing money
from the missionaries, would run away, covering the
Gospel and its professors with every species of impious
ridicule and abuse."

In any case failure was inevitable: caste was impregnable
and the converts were exposed to intolerable misery.
Failure was rendered doubly certain by the contemptible
character of the agents employed: " shoals of jumpers
exhibiting their nimble piety before the learned Brahmins
of Benares ": " little detachments of maniacs "; " didactic
artisans "; " delirious mechanics." " The wise and
rational part of the Christian Ministry find enough to do
at home. But if a tinker is a devout man he is infallibly
set off for the East, benefiting us much more by his
absence than the Hindus by his advice." The gossip
at Mr. Farington's table in May 1813 was that while no
danger need be apprehended from missionaries, " if a
regular Church establishment should be formed with all
the show attendant upon it, an insurrection of the natives
would be the consequence, and the English would be
driven out of the country."[1]

[1] *Farington Diaries :* Vol. vii, p. 254, May 4, 1813.

Claudius Buchanan

Had the principles of the *Edinburgh Review* prevailed in the time of the Apostles the Church would have been strangled at birth: had they prevailed in the nineteenth century there would be no Indian Church to-day. It was the Rev. Claudius Buchanan, D.D. who took up the cudgels and won the day. Never did champion arise from a more unexpected quarter or serve a more incongruous apprenticeship. Buchanan left school at Inveraray in 1780, at the age of fourteen, and entered at once on a succession of tutorships to the children of a series of Highland lairds, the Campbells of Dunstafnage, Knockmelly in Islay, and Carradale in Kintyre: but this did not preclude the completion of a Glasgow University course by the time he was twenty. A frustrated romance induced him to trump up a story that he had been engaged to conduct an English gentleman's son on a continental tour. The deception was kept up for several years: he replied as from Florence to his mother's letter announcing his father's death. He tramped his way to Newcastle dependent on his violin for half-crowns and free dinners, and thence took ship for London where he sank to the lowest extreme of wretchedness and want, till a clerkship to an attorney opened the way to three years' service in a respectable City Solicitor's office. He afterwards deplored his dissipated and irreligious London life, wasting his money on theatres and his time in debating Societies. An introduction to Newton (p. 56) altered his course, and an introduction to Henry Thornton of Clapham led to his joining Queens' College, Cambridge, at his expense: (he did not omit to refund the £400). It was not easy for an ordinand of twenty-five to settle down to Mathematics and Philosophy, but here he remained till his ordination by Bishop Porteous at Fulham in September 1795, having learnt to shudder at his own temerity in thinking himself prepared for the Church without the discipline of winning freedom from " unnecessary prejudices and prepossessions," and the drudgery of " converting every species of mental food into spiritual nourishment, whether it be Homer or Milton or Gibbon or Hume."

Buchanan entered on his Indian Chaplaincy in 1797, commissioned by Charles Grant (p. 55). It was some years before he got nearer the capital than Barrackpoor, sixteen miles from Calcutta, where he had no Church and little society, and his letters show that he grew depressed. " The climate tries the mind like a furnace: deterioration seems inherent in Indian existence . . . no Englishman turned of twenty who is only acquainted with the labials and dentals of his mother-tongue can ever acquire an easy and natural use of the nasals and gutturals of the Bengal language . . . a rapid spread of the Gospel is not to be expected; its dawn has appeared; after many centuries have revolved there may be a general light . . . instead of thirty missionaries I wish they would transport three hundred; they can do little harm and may do some good." A Miss Whish, not yet nineteen, dispelled the clouds, with "a very proper education for my wife. . . . I did not expect that I should ever have found in this country a young woman whom I could so much approve." William Carey and his Bengali Bible excited interest which bore fruit in later joint plans for fifteen vernacular versions: " this like Wickliff's translation may prove the father of many versions."

The Marquis Wellesley, the Duke of Wellington's elder brother, was now turning his attention from military exploits which had led to the despair of his parsimonious Directors to educational plans that were to cause them no less embarrassment. It was Buchanan to whom he entrusted the constitution of Fort William College, founded primarily " to fix and establish sound and correct principles of religion and government and a knowledge of eastern literature in junior civil servants from England, but with a yet more ambitious aim: " to enlighten the oriental world; to give science, religion and pure morals to Asia." Chaplain David Brown became Provost, Buchanan Vice-Provost.

We cannot follow the fortunes of the College, nor accompany Buchanan on his travels, in the course of which he did homage at the shrines of Ziegenbalg and Schwartz, investigated the situation of the Syrian Church, and poked his nose into the mysteries of the Inquisition, still operating in Goa. It is his campaign for an Indian Bishopric, or as he would have preferred, Archbishopric, which is our immediate concern. It opened in 1803 with a barrage of Prizes, intended to " soften " the front. The Vice-Chancellors of Oxford and Cambridge, the Principals of the four Scottish Universities, and the Headmasters of Eton, Westminster, Winchester and Charterhouse, were approached, with offers amounting to £1,650 from his private purse: £100 to each University for an Essay on " The best means of extending the blessings of civilization and true religion among the sixty million inhabitants of Hindustan subject to British authority." For the best English poem on the revival of letters in the East, £60 each; for the best Latin ode on " Collegium Bengalense " £25, and the best Greek ode on " Let there be Light " £25. Each of the schools was offered £50 for Latin and £50 for Greek poems. In 1805 Oxford and Cambridge each accepted £500 for a prize essay on the probable design of Providence in subjecting so large a portion of Asia to British dominion, the duty, means and consequence of translating the Scriptures, and the historic progress of the Gospel since its first promulgation, illustrated by maps." But it was heavy artillery that Buchanan brought to bear, first at long range in his " Memoirs for an Ecclesiastical Establishment in India " which he discharged from Calcutta in 1805, and later after his return to England at shorter range in his elaborate " Sketch " of an Ecclesiastical Establishment in India, published on the eve of the debate on the Company's new charter of 1813.

Some of Buchanan's arguments read oddly to-day, and reflect transient conditions: Napoleonic conditions, for example: " Nothing would more alarm the portentous invader of nations than our taking a ' religious possession ' of Hindostan. Five hundred reputable clergy of the English Church, established in our Gentoo cities, would more perplex his views of conquest than an army of 50,000 British soldiers." None the less it is doubtful whether the reforms would have materialized without his persistent exposure of the paralysing timidity of Lord Minto's administration, which had indeed reported him to the directors as a dangerous firebrand for having

" assumed a latitude of censure disrespectful in its nature
and unwarranted by facts."

BISHOP MIDDLETON

Buchanan in his " Sketch " had stipulated that when a
man " receives consecration as a Bishop for India, it ought
to be with the spirit of a man who is willing to live and
die among the people committed to his charge." A contemporary critic comments in the margin: " Where shall
we meet with such a man among the respectable Part of
the Clergy, or what Man would pledge himself to live
and die in India ? " Happily such a man was discovered
in Thomas Fanshaw Middleton, and nobody could accuse
him of not belonging to the respectable part of the Clergy.
He was an Archdeacon, and Vicar of St. Pancras, where
50,000 people still had only a village church holding 200,
and his plan for its replacement was so ambitious as to
provoke the unkind comment that it had little else in view
but the aggrandisement of the Vicar. He had written a
book on the Doctrine of the Greek Article. He was in
fact the living embodiment of the Established Church:
the worst that the opposition could say against him was
that he was a diligent attendant at S.P.C.K. committees
which had passed strong resolutions in support of Mr.
Wilberforce's policy.

The Bishop's consecration in Lambeth Palace Chapel,
at the age of forty-five (May 8th, 1814) was a hole-and-
corner affair. " It was regarded with so much jealousy
and by some with such positive aversion and alarm, that
it was thought prudent to abstain from any proceeding
which might have the effect of more particularly calling
to it the attention of the public, or provoking unnecessary
discussion as to its probable results; and for these reasons
the admirable sermon of Dr. Rennell was suppressed."
None the less, one of Mr. Farington's guests reported
" that the Prince Regent addresses the Bishop as ' my
Lord ' which was not expected as the Bishops in England
have that title as Barons in Parliament."[1]

The arrival of Bishop and Mrs. Middleton in Calcutta
was also a hole-and-corner affair. Lord Teignmouth,

---

[1] *Farington Diaries:* Vol. vii. June 2, 1814.

when asked by the House of Commons Committee whether the appearance of a Bishop would not increase the danger of native misunderstanding, had replied, " I should think it would be viewed with perfect indifference," as indeed it was. We have the Bishop's own account: " My public reception was certainly so arranged as not to *alarm* the natives: I believe it might *surprise* them, as they would naturally suppose, considering the high reverence which they pay to the heads of their own religion, that the arrival of a Bishop would make some little stir. My private reception, however, was kind and respectful." No public mark of welcome was forthcoming ; no residence had been provided.

Thus began seven and a half years of unfurloughed and courageous service. The position was full of embarrassments for a mind " naturally anxious and not permitted ever to be at ease," a body ill-adapted to the climate, and a temperament prone to assume " high notions of his office, leading to an assumption of a formal and rather haughty manner," which concealed from all but his intimates his " keen perception of pleasantry and humour "; he was in consequence thought pompous, repulsive and too acutely alive to any supposed want of respect on the part of others." But the same obituary letter applauds his judgement, sobriety, good sense and moderation, and ascribes " the beneficial change which has certainly taken place in our society, of late years, mainly to the Bishop."

The fact was that the Bishop had no precedents to guide him, while everything he did or left undone established precedents for better or worse. His status was ambiguous and he wished it clarified for his successors. His Staff was exiguous, an Archdeacon in each of the three Presidencies; for his diocese included Australia as well as Ceylon and Penang. His Chaplains were few, for the establishment had not kept pace with the extension of territory. " We ought to have from twenty-five to thirty, but after January next I question whether *twelve* will remain. . . . A large proportion of the Christian subjects of this government are virtually excommunicated, for they have not the use of the sacraments. . . . Is it not strange to read in the newspapers, ' On such a day was married, by the brigade-

major . . . ' where everything but the Church establishment
is kept up in the highest efficiency." The Chaplains
moreover served two masters : the Company paid them
and expected to dictate their appointments, and these
went by seniority. " It would be but a bad rule that the
senior clergyman in Middlesex, being of unimpeached
moral character, should succeed on a vacancy at St. James'
or St. George's, Hanover Square. . . . The Bishop has the
power of censuring and correcting offences, but scarcely
any of stimulating and encouraging exertion, for he had
no power of promotion. The Churches themselves were
mean : I cannot think these barn-like edifices are very
honourable to those who possess the revenue of the country.
What must the worshippers in mosques and pagodas think
of men who, possessing all the resources of the country
and pretending to a better faith, worship their Maker in
buildings not distinguishable from barracks ? "

Missionaries were beginning to arrive. Here was an
additional embarrassment to the Bishop. They held no
episcopal licence, and it was doubtful whether the Bishop
could conscientiously license them under the terms of
his Letters Patent, which only authorized him to govern
an established Church of Christians, not to propagate
Christianity among non-Christians. His perplexity was
great. " If they are not to be recognized by the Bishop
there would be two Churches of England in the country:
with the shortage of Chaplains in a few years there will be a
Bishop in India with hardly any clergy, and a numerous
clergy not acknowledging episcopal jurisdiction. If I
license them to preach in English, that were to acknowledge
them as performing the duties of parochial clergy, and
that the Company need not send chaplains to India: if I
should forbid them to preach in English while so many
European congregations are without any pastor, it would
excite horror and hatred both of my person and my office."

The Letters Patent offered an even more serious obstacle
to the fulfilment of episcopal functions. In Ceylon the
Bishop had felt prohibited from ordaining a most worthy
Tamil, Christian David, " though he was, poor man,
sadly disappointed and hurt, to my great concern." He
writes : " A difficulty was started about my power of

ordaining persons born in this country. It turned upon the question whether they are the ' King's loving subjects ' in the sense of the Letters-Patent." Without the removal of this difficulty it had been better never to have sent a bishop to India. They who would enter into the service of the Church cannot—though they may enter into the service of the sectaries. The Church is now made to appear to *reject* the well-disposed: for a bishop who *cannot* ordain at his discretion is something new and quite inexplicable." That the difficulty was genuine is shown by the fact that it took an Act of Parliament to remedy it.

It will be seen from these laments that the Bishop was not indifferent to the progress of the Gospel. " The case is not desperate: it is full of blessed hope: the tide is turning: India is not the scene of British glory; we have been successful in war and skilful in finance; but these things will make a sad figure in the page of the Christian historian; we have done nothing for Christianity and have acted as if we were ashamed of it: and with some I believe this is really the case. This feeling I am labouring to subvert." His laborious visitations of his diocese bring out this side of his character. He is profoundly moved by his visit to Tanjore, the scene of Schwartz's " almost apostolic labours, the place to which his name has given a sacredness which belongs perhaps to few spots besides on the habitable globe, with the exception of those which were trodden by the feet of the first Evangelists "; and he finds in Schwartz's pupil and successor, Kohloff, " another Schwartz." " I have inspected the state of the mission minutely and have conversed with the sons of converts: they are in knowledge and manners as much superior to their pagan neighbours as a well-educated Englishman to a peasant." No Letters Patent could deter him from taking the impoverished mission under his wing. He urges on the S.P.C.K. the necessity of more missionaries and deplores their difficulty in procuring them.

Wherever the Bishop went, whether Madras, Bombay, Colombo or Penang, he threw his energy into founding branches of the S.P.C.K. and organizing the supply of literature for soldiers, seamen and Anglo-Indians, for he was convinced that " the Gospel had much more to fear from the practical atheism of nominal Christians than from the bigotry of ignorant idolators," and that " if every Englishman really wished to disseminate Christianity, recommending it both by his example and influence, or even not checking it, it would find its way."

His second and over-mastering enthusiasm found vent in the foundation of Bishop's College, Calcutta, which a timely vote from the S.P.G. encouraged him to plan, and contributions from the King's letter collection (see p. 64) the S.P.C.K. and the C.M.S. enabled him to complete. Here were native and other Christian youth to be trained as preachers, catechists and schoolmasters; Mussulmans and Hindus were to study useful knowledge and the English language; the Scriptures and the Liturgy were to be translated, and newly-arrived missionaries were to be received. Lord Hastings granted an ideal site of twenty acres on the Ganges. The Bishop is aglow. " At this moment I would not exchange my duties for those of any individual in my profession. My mind in truth cannot contemplate anything greater or more worthy of a bishop of the Church of England, than the foundation and organization of such an institution. Can you forgive the feelings of a founder if I tell you that the other day, as I listened to the woodman's axe employed in clearing the ground, I actually began to muse upon what might hereafter be the studies and glories of this place ! I know that such enthusiasm is very irrational and ought to be checked, but really without some little indulgence in this way, I should never get through my difficulties."

On this human and self-revealing note we say farewell to one who is entitled to rank among the makers of Christian history and well merits the monumental effigy familiar to all visitors to St. Paul's Cathedral.

BISHOP HEBER

It was ten years from the date of Bishop Middleton's death that Bishop Wilson arrived as the fifth Bishop of Calcutta in 1832. Three Bishops—Heber, James, Turner— had reigned and died between April 1826 and August 1831, and it had fallen to the lot of Archdeacon Corrie to preside over the diocese for sixty-five months of inter-regnum. So slow was the pace of news that Bishop James' consecration in June 1827 was not known in Calcutta till towards the close of the year: hence the long delays in filling the vacant see. The tragedy of Bishop Heber's death and his fame as a hymn-writer[1] and journal-writer won him such a secure place in the history of the Church in India that it is surprising to find his " contemporaries " wondering whether he was quite the man to succeed. " His early career as a poet, traveller (in Russia) and accomplished gentleman, rather than zealous parish priest or studious divine, had led him towards the homes of the nobility and gentry, to enliven and refine by his wit and talents the mirth of their assemblies, with compliancies sometimes scarcely consistent with the clerical office. . . . His Bampton lectures were ' distinguished by his graceful appearance in St. Mary's and his graceful delivery of eloquent sentences, rather than by anything remarkable in the argument of his discourses, except some crude speculations on the angelic nature now deservedly for-gotten.' "[2] Joshua Watson had his misgivings. There was some disappointment that the Bishop scamped his references to Bishop's College in his reports.

Nobody could accuse the Bishop of undue attendance in the palaces of the nobility and gentry of Calcutta. After five months he left wife and child and started on his first visitation which last sixteen months; and after three months he started on his second which ended with his death. These journeys had their moments of tragedy, danger, drama and romance, but were mostly monotonous and unspectacular: their records vividly depict the India of the day viewed from a Ganges pinnace, a Himalayan pony, a Rajput elephant, or from the courts of the Emperor of Delhi, the King of Oudh or the Gaekwar of Baroda. The last insisted on providing so splendid an escort that " I could not help thinking that since the days of Thomas à Becket or Cardinal Wolsey, an English Bishop had seldom been so formidably attended."

[1] There are eleven of Heber's hymns in the *English Hymnal*, including " Holy, Holy, Holy ! Lord God Almighty ! " " Brightest and best of the sons of the morning," " The Son of God goes forth to war " and " From Greenland's icy mountains."

[2] Churton: *Memoir of Joshua Watson.*

In Gujerat occurred the famous interview with the Hindu reformer Swami Narain, who sent his salaams and desired a meeting, thus raising the Bishop's hopes that this preacher of monotheism and denouncer of caste " might be an appointed instrument to prepare the way for the Gospel. He came having near two hundred horsemen mostly well-armed with matchlocks and swords, and several of them with coats of mail and spears, besides a large rabble on foot with bows and arrows. When I considered that I had myself more than fifty horse and fifty musquets and bayonets, I could not help smiling at the idea of two religious teachers meeting at the head of little armies and filling the city with the rattling of quivers, the clash of shields and the tramp of the war-horse. But in moral grandeur what a difference between his troop and mine. Mine neither knew me nor cared for me. His were his own disciples and enthusiastic admirers, who would cheerfully fight to the last drop of blood rather than suffer a fringe of his garment to be handled roughly." Homesick for his Cheshire parish, he adds " in Hodnet there were once perhaps a few honest countrymen who felt something like this for me."

The Bishop could always be trusted to dramatize a situation, but it was the less dramatic visits to regimental cantonments or village Christians which kindled his keenest interest. " The Archdeacon (Corrie, whose travels with the Bishop led him to ' praise God that such an one had been placed at the head of affairs ') had never told me of the native Christians at Buxar; yet they are most of them the children of his own quiet and unwearied exertions in the cause of God. Curreem Musseeh, ' mercy of Messiah ' came up to ask me to see his scholars assembled, and I found his little schoolhouse full of women and children on the ground which was spread with mats, with their books in their laps. This served too as a Church where they met three times a week in the evening for prayer, and a few of their husbands, European soldiers who understood Hindustanee: they are sometimes but very rarely visited by a Missionary. I was extremely pleased and surprised at all I witnessed." At Benares fourteen Indians were confirmed and a visit paid to the C.M.S. School endowed

" by a rich Bengalee Baboo, Jay Narayen, who, without becoming a Christian has settled in a sort of general admiration of the Gospel and a wish to improve the stock of knowledge and morality among his countrymen. Here were 140 boys, mostly wearing the Brahmanical string but very fond of the New Testament. I wish a majority of English schoolboys might appear equally well-informed."

Both by temperament and by amendment of laws Heber was freed from the inhibitions which had embarrassed his predecessor. Boldly he proclaimed himself " Chief Missionary." Readily and in Calcutta he ordained the disappointed Christian David. Diligently he investigated the affairs of the C.M.S. and found " great reason to be satisfied with the manner in which they were conducted." Relentlessly he impressed upon the highest officials the duty of initiating Committees not only of the S.P.C.K., but of the S.P.G. " assuring them that nothing was involved which would ' give offence to their unconverted fellow-subjects or be at variance with a wise respect for their feelings.' " Like his predecessor he was impressed by the aged Kohloff (" I have seen many crowned heads, but not one whose deportment was more princely "), and deeply moved by the associations of Tanjore and Trinchinopoly, and it was after a confirmation in Schwartz's church that he died. " We have lost our second Schwartz " lamented Kohloff; " if St. Paul had visited the mission he could not have done more."

No explanation has ever been forthcoming of the Bishop's *faux pas* in regard to Ceylon. Bishop Middleton had found his first visit to Ceylon among the most gratifying experiences of his life. Not only did every prospect please, but man was far from being vile. " The character of the people appeared to be open, smiling and confiding, without a suspicion of any sinister or unfriendly motives. Their very countenance showed that they were without jealousy or misgiving." Bengal was a " melancholy contrast," for in Ceylon, " the inhabitants, instead of gazing on the party with a stare of vacant apathy, gave the stranger a cheerful and smiling welcome."

Heber's welcome was no less exuberant. His journey from Galle to Baddegama to Kotte and up the newly-engineered road to Kandy was a triumphal progress through pandal after pandal. In Kandy he confirmed and celebrated the Sacrament in the Audience Hall of the Kings. " Here a few years ago no European or Christian could have appeared except as a slave: now in this very place an English Governor and an English congregation, besides many converted natives of the Island, were sitting peacefully to hear an English Bishop preach."

Perhaps it was his dislike of Roman Catholic and nominal Christians that alienated Bishop Heber. There were many of both as a legacy of Portuguese and Dutch occupations. He was, however, impressed by the rows of Confirmation candidates, by the Kotte and Kandy schools, and not least by the four C.M.S. missionaries who had arrived in Ceylon seven years before: " they are really patterns of what missionaries should be, and the younger generation afford excellent hopes of repaying richly and even in our own time the labours of these good men who have given up parents and friends and country in their service." It was to be another twenty years before Ceylon achieved a Bishop of its own.

THE SEES OF BARBADOS AND JAMAICA

Claudius Buchanan in his *Brief Review of the state of the Colonies in respect to Religious Instruction*, published in 1813, reports that " not the Church of England but other denominations of Christians are forming the religion of the natives. In the West Indies the Church of England has six missionaries, viz.: those belonging to the S.P.G.; whereas those belonging to other denominations are ninety-two in number, viz.: The United Brethren, sixty-four, the Wesleyan Methodists twenty-five, the Missionary Society three. It will be seen hereafter that the parochial clergy in the West Indies do not, in general, take an active part in the instruction of the Negroes." " The number of converts belonging to the Moravians who have laboured in this good work, with success continually augmenting, ever since the year 1732, is by the last returns nearly

25,000: those belonging to the Methodists who followed their example about the year 1785, amounted to 13,042."

Buchanan culls from the cross-examination of witnesses by a House of Commons Committee evidence of the high regard in which the character and work of these missionaries were held by some of them, and quotes the testimony of Dr. Porteous, Bishop of London: " One thing we know from fact and from the experience and example of the Moravians, that the Negroes are capable of being made *real Christians*." He denounces two anti-Methodist edicts promulgated by the legislative body of Jamaica in 1802 and 1807 respectively, under the first of which " preaching or teaching in a meeting of Negroes or People of Colour by a person not duly qualified exposed a Methodist for the first offence to one month's imprisonment, and hard labour in the common workhouse, and for a second offence to imprisonment and hard labour for six months, or such further punishment ' not extending to life as the Court should see fit to inflict.' A black man for a similar crime could be sentenced to a public flogging, not exceeding thirty-nine lashes." The second edict prescribes punishment for all " false enthusiasts " who unless duly authorized should " presume to preach or teach or offer up public prayer, or sing Psalms in any assembly of Negroes." "Opposition to the instruction of the Slaves still continues, notwithstanding the repeated interference of his Majesty's Governments. As we apprehend public dishonours have been put upon Christianity and as the interests of more than 360,000 hapless Africans are concerned in the event, it appears to be a case which ought to be submitted, in its full dimensions, to the Imperial Parliament. . . . Our native subjects in the West Indies stand in a closer relation to us than those in the East and claim a prior regard. Our native subjects in Hindustan remain on their native soil; these our African subjects are in different circumstances. We have dragged them by force from their native country and appropriated their bodily services to our use. Justice therefore requires that we faithfully acquit ourselves of every moral obligation toward them." It says much for Buchanan's largeness of heart that, wedded to India as he was, he could thus write: " and it is pleasant to find a

H

contemporary Anglican thus appreciative of the Methodist missionaries." He could not, of course, foresee how greatly their difficulties were to be accentuated during the next twelve years, as the relations between Great Britain and its colonists became embittered, as the slave population grew more and more restless, and as the " abolitionist taint " incurred more violent punishment, of which Methodists bore the brunt. Few stories are less flattering to British self-esteem than that which is told in the second volume of Dr. Findlay's *History of the Wesleyan Methodist Missionary Society.*

It need not be assumed that no Rectors of the Established Church succeeded in transcending the prejudices of the race and class from which they sprang, or that all succumbed to the temptation to conform to the views of their congregations. How difficult was their position and how remiss some of them were is shown in the reflexions of Christopher Codrington, a Fellow of All Souls, and an officer in the army of William III in Flanders, who administered estates in Barbados acquired by his grandfather in 1644.

> " I have alwaies thought it very barbarous that so little care should be taken of the bodys and so much less of the souls of our poor slaves. Their condition has cost me many a mortifying reflection and yet I know not how I shall be able to amend it in any one respect, but feeding my slaves well. I shall certainly be opposed by all the Planters in generall if I should go about to secure their limbs and lives by a law (though I shall certainly recommend something of that kind), but much more if I should promote the baptising of all our slaves : 'tis certain the christening of our negroes without the instructing of them would be useless to themselves and pernicious to their masters, and 'tis evident the few and very ill-qualified clergymen who goe to the Islands are not only insufficient for such work, but can doe noe service to the whole Heathens they find there. Indeed a work of this nature is only fit for a regular clergy who are under vows of poverty and obedience. If the Archbishop and Bishop of London can find such a number of apostolical men who are able to take much pains for little reward my protection and countenance shall not be wanting. As an inconsiderate zeal shall not put me upon an attempt that will not answer its end, soe noe consideration shall hinder me from promoting boldly and impartially a design that shall be pleasing to God and truly beneficial to my fellow-creatures."

Codrington died in 1710, bequeathing a Library to his college and two plantations to the S.P.G., with the expressed desire " that they be continued entire and three hundred negroes at least always kept thereon, and a convenient number of Professors and scholars maintained there, all of them to be under vows of poverty and chastity and obedience and obliged to study and practise Physick and Chirurgery as well as Divinity, that by the apparent usefulness of the former to all mankind they may both endear themselves to the people and have the better opportunities of doing good to men's souls." The Trust was to involve the S.P.G. in considerable embarrassment, so difficult is it for the Church to detach itself from its economic environment; emancipation was not immediately practicable; it could only be prepared for by enhancing the amenities and the moral and religious education of their heritage of slaves.

Bishop Coleridge and Bishop Lipscomb

The first Bishops of Barbados and Jamaica arrived in their dioceses with ten years to run, in which to prepare for the revolution which the climax of the anti-slavery campaigns of Wilberforce and Sir Thomas Fowell Buxton would precipitate. The controversy which had been hot enough to divide Johnson and Boswell at the time of Lord Mansfield's ruling in 1777 reached boiling-point as Emancipation grew nearer; but Boswell's presentation of the issue cannot be bettered as an indication of the forces engaged. Dr. Johnson dictated to him an " argument ": " The constitutions of Jamaica are merely positive and apparently injurious to the rights of mankind, because whoever is exposed to sale is condemned to slavery without appeal, by whatever fraud or violence he might have been originally brought into the merchant's power. The laws of Jamaica afford a Negro no redress. His colour is considered as sufficient testimony against him. It is to be lamented that moral right should ever give way to political convenience. No man is by nature the property of another." Boswell cannot let this pass " without my most solemn protest against Dr. Johnson's general doctrine with respect to the Slave Trade."

" For I will resolutely say that his unfavourable notion of it was owing to prejudice and imperfect or false information. The wild and dangerous attempt which has for some time been persisted in to obtain an Act to abolish so very important and necessary a branch of commercial interest must have been crushed at once had not the insignificance of the zealots who vainly took the lead in it made the vast body of Planters, Merchants and others whose immense properties are involved in that trade, reasonably enough suppose that there could be no danger. The encouragement which the attempt has received excites my wonder and indignation. . . . To abolish a status which in all ages God has sanctioned and man has continued would not only be robbery to an innumerable class of our fellow subjects; but it would be extreme cruelty to the African Savages, a portion of whom it saves from massacre or intolerable bondage in their own country, and introduces into a much happier state of life."

The new Bishops, who arrived in the West Indies at this historic moment, held jurisdiction over many islands separated by many miles of Caribbean Sea. Barbados included all that is now covered by the dioceses of Antigua, the Windward Islands, Trinidad and Guiana: Jamaica included the later dioceses of the Nassau and British Honduras. Bishop Coleridge seems to have been the more fortunate in his reception: not only was it a ceremonial arrival with salutes and guards of honour but:

" Wherever a human foot could stand was one appalling mass of black faces. As the barge passed slowly along, the emotions of the multitude knew no bounds: they danced, they jumped, and rolled on the ground; they sang and screamed and shouted and roared; they broke out into a thousand wild exclamations of joy, uttered with such vehemence that, new as it was to me, it made me tremble."

Jamaica was not so sure that it was pleased to see Bishop Lipscomb. The abolition agitation was at its height: the majority of the Assembly had threatened to transfer their allegiance to the United States or even to assert independence. Outbreaks among the slaves were constant, for they were persuaded that emancipation had been agreed on in England and was being withheld in Jamaica. Crops to the value of £666,000 were destroyed on a single occasion. Even the clergy were quick to resent discipline.

At last the Day of Emancipation dawned. An Antiguan Methodist reports:

> " Our most sanguine hopes have been more than realised. I have not heard of a single disturbance of the public peace. We held watch-night services in all our Chapels on Thursday evening, July 31st: a very large and solemnised congregation. About two minutes before midnight I desired all the Negroes and friends of freedom to kneel down—the first to receive their liberty at the hands of God, and the latter to take from Him the consummation they had so devoutedly wished. We felt the ' speechless awe which dares not move, and all the silent heaven of love.' The clock struck twelve, and I exclaimed: ' The first of August has arrived. You are all free.' At this the voice of weeping was heard, mingled with subdued cries of ' Glory be to God ' and the like. We sang, ' Praise God from Whom all blessings flow.''

Bishop Coleridge was no less moved. " Eight hundred thousand human beings lay down at night as slaves, and rose in the morning as free as ourselves. There was no gathering that affected the public peace. There *was* a gathering but it was a gathering of young and old in the House of the common Father of all. It was my peculiar happiness on that ever memorable day to address a congregation of nearly 40,000 persons, of whom more than 3,000 were just emancipated. Such was the order, such the deep attention and perfect silence that you might have heard a pin drop. . . . To prepare the minds of a mass of persons, so peculiarly situated, for a change such as this, was a work requiring the exercise of great patience."

The Church in Great Britain put forth every exertion to rise to all that so great an occasion demanded. The King's Letter machinery was set in motion (see p. 64), Parliamentary Grants were invoked, and the S.P.G. found itself administering a Negro Education Fund of £172,000, a sum almost the equivalent of its own expenditure in the West Indies over the years 1835–1850. By 1838 the C.M.S. had thirteen ordained missionaries in the field, twenty-three English schoolmasters and seventy schools.

It was not altogether unnatural that where so much had been done it was not realized how much more there was to do. In the State's sphere local legislatures were incompetent to supervise the sociological adaptations involved: the Imperial Parliament assumed an economic

stability in the West Indian plantation-system sufficient
to withstand the unrestricted competition of slave-grown
sugar from Cuba and Brazil, and in deference to consumers
cancelled all preferences on Colonial sugar.   There was a
somewhat analogous ineptitude on the part of the Home
Churches: insufficient allowance was made for many
decades of brutalizing degradation, and the entail of
slavery.   The C.M.S., hard-pressed financially and pre-
occupied with other commitments, were gone within ten
years.   State subsidies dwindled.   By the '60's the S.P.G.
was beginning to look askance at appeals from Jamaica,
sternly stating that the present number of clergy and
schoolmasters in the diocese was sufficient for the spiritual
education and wants of the people, if clergy and schoolmasters " devoted themselves zealously to their duties."[1]

In the '70's the Methodists felt that the time had come
for their Church in the West Indies to stand on its own
feet and relieve the parental purse; and a West Indian
" Conference " was set up charged with the onus of self-
support and self-rule: but after nineteen years of separation it was found necessary for the London Committee to
resume responsibility: it is a story with a moral.

But this is to wander beyond the compass of a chapter
which has the limited objective of telling the circumstances
in which Anglican Bishops assumed new responsibilities
and called upon their Home Church to shoulder new
burdens.

THE SEES OF AUSTRALIA AND NEW ZEALAND

A smouldering controversy upon the relative claims of
fellow-countrymen and of the heathen world on the resources of the Church has periodically burst into flame.
Mr. John Walter of *The Times*, for example, once told an
S.P.G. meeting that the heathen deserved more sympathy
than the fishermen and colonists of Newfoundland, and by
a coincidence a *Times* leading article appeared a few days
later on the same thesis.   Bishop Feild of Newfoundland
was indignant.   " Are the Colonies no longer to merit
extraneous aid ?   Are they to maintain their own clergy

[1] J. B. Ellis: *The Diocese of Jamaica.*

out of current local resources ? Do you ? What about endowments and tithes ? Are your new districts expected to rely on local contributions for the support of their clergy ? Is any stigma attached to a clergyman who applies for assistance to the Pastoral Aid or Additional Curates Societies ? "

This book must by-pass this controversy, and the major space it allots to the expansion of the Church among races and nations other than our own implies no verdict. The fact is that once the foundations were laid in Canada, Australia, and New Zealand, the rising superstructure can be pictured without any great strain on the imagination, for its architecture follows familar models; this is all too true of Oriental or African Churches also in their early days, but it becomes less so as they become more self-expressive. It will therefore be permissible, in order to avoid unwieldiness and overwhelming detail, to jump from the opening phases of these Colonies of the Mother Church to their arrival at what may be called Dominion status. It does, however, involve some strain on the imagination to picture the infant Churches of Australia and New Zealand as they looked to Londoners of the 1830's and '40's.

Samuel Marsden

Their stories are too intertwined for separate treatment. The great figure of Samuel Marsden, for example, was in at the birth of both. He reached Sydney as a Government Chaplain less than five years after the first batch of Botany Bay convicts, and seven missionary voyages between 1814 and 1838 established his claim to be called " The Apostle of New Zealand." A practical Yorkshireman, he discerned a future for Australian farming, and was the first to persuade wool-experts in Leeds that the specimens he brought home would " produce a cloth which was at least equal and in the opinion of the manufacturers superior to that of the best French looms." George III gave him " five Merino ewes with young " to take back with him. But this was not the primary purpose of Marsden's visit to England in 1809. He wished to stir public opinion on the subject of the convicts, their temporal and spiritual needs, the lodging of their women and the care of their orphans: a stern magistrate himself, he incurred libel actions and the wrath of Governors in the combative assertion of his conscience.

Marsden regarded his success in inducing the C.M.S. to sanction a New Zealand mission as the crowning achievement of his stay. He had been deeply stirred by what he had heard from fugitive L.M.S. missionaries, of their adventures in Tahiti. As early as 1795 an official visit to the convict settlement on Norfolk Island had opened his eyes to the existence of Maoris. Captain King, R.N., told him of two kidnapped chiefs who had displayed " keenness of intellect and manliness of character." " I waited upon the Committee several times, and it was ultimately resolved to send three missionaries. No clergyman offered his services. The character of the New Zealanders was considered more barbarous than that of any other savage nation, so that few would venture out to a country where they could anticipate nothing less than to be killed and eaten."

When Selwyn became Bishop, Sidney Smith was still jesting about " Tête l'Evêque " being the most recherché dish on the menu, and " cold clergyman " on the sideboard.[1] Marsden at length found two mechanics who agreed to accompany him, and hoped that like Caleb and Joshua of old they might open the way for others. They were Hall, a Hull shipwright, and King, a Cotswold shoemaker. On the return voyage Marsden found to his astonishment among his fellow-passengers a young Maori Chief, Ruatara, who had worked his passage to England " having long entertained an ardent desire to see King George." This was a providential opportunity of learning New Zealand lore, and " adding some new word to my vocabulary every day." Several years went by, long enough for lucrative employment in Sydney to cool the ardour of Hall and King, before the arrival of Kendal, a London schoolmaster aged 36, with five children, gave the signal for the first expedition to start. Marsden could return after two months, having established missionaries in the Bay of

[1] R. G. Wilberforce : *Life of Bishop S. Wilberforce.*

Islands, and feeling that all was propitious, except the death of Ruatara, on whom great hopes were set. He reported that the New Zealanders were all cannibals; when he expressed his horror at their eating one another, they said it had always been their custom, but whether " they ate human flesh as a meal or from choice or in cold blood, or only from mental gratification and in retaliation for some great injury" remained a moot-point.

Whether a mission so amateurishly begun, so beset with dangers, so discredited by white pirates and by internal friction and frailty, would survive, might well appear doubtful; that it did must be largely credited to the vigilance and adventurous voyages of Samuel Marsden, who on his last visit at the age of 73 could report peace and security in what had been one of the most warlike districts, a great number of the inhabitants baptized and living like Christians, and the missionaries a very pious, prudent and laborious body.

WILLIAM GRANT BROUGHTON

Like Claudius Buchanan, Broughton (born in Bridge Street, Westminster in 1788) served an apprenticeship in a City office before a legacy enabled him to go to Cambridge, and he was thirty before he was ordained. It was the Duke of Wellington who put him in the way of appointment first to the Chaplaincy of the Tower, and in 1828 to the Archdeaconry of New South Wales. The Duke was very considerate to the local curate and now took pains to discover whether a pension was attached to the post, without which it would be unfair to wife and children to embark on so " distant and perhaps dangerous " an expedition. The Archdeaconry covered a population of 36,000, of whom more than 17,000 were convicts. " When I first landed, Melbourne was uninhabited and South Australia in a similar state. The ecclesiastical organization had altered little since 1802, when the Governor had directed that " in all spiritual, judicial and parochial proceedings, the district of Sydney was to be comprised within a parish to be henceforth named St. Phillip, in honour of the first Governor, and the Paramatta district within a parish to be named St. John's, in honour of the late Governor, Captain John Hunter." The Archdeaconry included Van Diemen's Land, where the Archdeacon authorized free use of the rubric which sanctions the admission to Communion of those " desirous " of Confirmation. " After the Nicene Creed I should feel satisfaction in delivering an address to the candidates, and in receiving their promises according to the form directed by the Order of Confirmation, omitting only the imposition of hands and the Collect having reference to it."

However, these awkwardnesses were removed when Broughton returned from his first visit to England in 1836 as Bishop of all Australia. Lord Glenelg (Charles Grant's son) was the Colonial Secretary who submitted his name to the King, and from whom he extracted the assurance that there was no intention to impose any condition upon acceptance of the Bishopric, or to fetter the free exercise of his judgement. Broughton strongly disapproved of the Governor, Sir Richard Bourke, and his educational policy, and was determined not to put himself in a position in which in the existing relations between Church and State in the Colony, his concurrence and co-operation might be assumed.

How entangled these relations were is shown by the inclusion of clergymen's salaries in the Colonial estimate, just as the salaries of Chaplains to the Forces to-day are included in the Service estimates; and when Bishop Broughton had to supervise a transition to the voluntary system, the strain was comparable to what would be felt if the War Office threw back upon the Church the payment of Chaplains. The Bishop foresaw that his successors would be faced with " a very furious assault from Papal and anti-Christian powers. My anxiety is, whilst it is day, to provide some kind of defence and shelter for them, that they may not come to such a contest quite naked and defenceless." He had no cause to complain that the S.P.C.K. and S.P.G. were backward in facilitating the transition.

Next to securing that the Church should not be regarded as a mere department of colonial administration, it was the safeguarding of the religious foundation of all education which roused the Bishop to combat. The British Government, after depositing 100,000 convicts on Australian shores (13,700 in the last three years) had thrown the entire charge of providing for their religious and educational needs upon the Colony, leaving the Bishop at the mercy of the strong secularist bias of local educational policy. In this context he could rely on Methodist allies, who had welcomed him on his consecration with an address, than which none " had accorded him more sincere gratification." " Firmly and conscientiously attached as a body to the United Church of England and Ireland as by law established, and taught by the example of our reverend founder, we cannot but rejoice in every measure which promises to extend the usefulness and to increase the prosperity of that venerable hierarchy." So strong were the Bishop's convictions that he declined his allotted seat in the Senate of the new University with its secular constitution.

But the main problem was to keep pace with the population. He writes in 1843: "Five years ago Melbourne contained but three houses deserving the name, and its population consisted of a few hundred souls: it is now a large metropolis with suburbs covering a large extent of ground, and a population approaching to 8,000. . . . I have lately been in one county, Durham, in the whole extent of which there is one Church and one clergyman. In the adjoining county of Brisbane there is one Church and no clergyman. In three counties there is neither minister nor any ordinance of religion. These five contain a fourth part of New South Wales and from a sixteenth to an eighteenth of the whole population." To meet these differences Broughton began to look to the products of King's School, Paramatta, already in pre-Arnold days a flourishing " Public School," and to the Theological College which he was able to build, thanks to a local benefaction of £20,000.

Bishop Broughton was not unmindful of the original inhabitants of either country. At the request of the C.M.S. he decided to visit New Zealand, though it was not within the terms of his commission, "for Letters Patent do not confer spiritual powers; they only define the range within which a Bishop is authorised to exercise them, and beyond the limits of British sovereignty (as New Zealand still was) he has an inherent right, in virtue of the powers conferred on him at his consecration, to officiate episcopally wherever the good of the Church demands." On Christmas Day, 1838, the Bishop confirmed forty Maoris, together with missionaries' children, and on the Feast of the Epiphany held the first ordination on New Zealand soil, ordaining a missionary, Octavius Hadfield, afterwards Selwyn's intimate friend, Bishop of Wellington, and first Primate of New Zealand.

Of his own aborigines the Bishop never despaired, repeating in 1850 what he had said as a young Archdeacon. Of course obstacles were to be anticipated, as in every advance of Christianity from its origin to the present day. " The erratic habits and inconsiderate disposition of Australian natives were no more adverse to Christianity than those properties which its earliest preacher had encountered. Shall we look on and see them perish without so much as an effort for their preservation ? I answer unhesitatingly, No. Persevere as you regard the honour of God and as you value the souls of these your helpless and unhappy fellow-creatures."

THE SEE OF NEW ZEALAND

By 1843, when Bishop George Augustus Selwyn arrived in New Zealand aged thirty-three, the Maori Mission had lived down its unpromising infancy. There were twelve missionaries by 1830 and twelve more arrived in the next twelve years. Charles Darwin had taken off his hat to them. " It is admirable to behold what they have affected. I firmly believe they are good men working for the sake of a good cause. I much expect that those who have abused or sneered at the missionaries have generally been such as were not very anxious to find the natives moral and intelligent beings."[1]

Henry Williams, an ex-Naval Officer and his brother William of the medical profession, both now ordained, had begun their forty years of united work in 1822, pledged

[1] *Life and Letters of Charles Darwin,* i, p. 264 ; *Letter from H.M.S. Beagle,* Jan. 1836.

to carry no arms for " as you are about to enter the territories of a savage and powerful people, to commit yourselves to their hospitality, it would be vain to think of protecting yourselves by force against their violence. It is impossible to shut your eyes to the fact that, as far as human means are concerned, you must be considered as in their power, and at their mercy." It was unarmed that Henry Williams intervened between two contending camps of warriors eager for battle, persuading them to remain quiet over Sunday and attend his Service, and making peace between them on the Monday morning. By 1840, 30,000 Maoris took part in public worship.

" The missionaries " writes Professor Hancock, " in their pursuit of souls attacked the wilderness: their evangelising journeys opened the interior of the North Island to European knowledge. . . . The missionaries themselves were no laggards, but their ardent converts raced in front of them to spread the Christian gospel. The story is told of a missionary who, far from his home station, encountered an unknown tribe. He gathered the tribe for a first reading of the Anglican Service. The gathering, to his astonishment, devoutly interjected the proper Anglican responses."[1]

But the Mission wanted two things. It wanted ecclesiastical authority. " The appointment of a bishop had long been desired " wrote Bishop W. Williams after he had himself become Bishop of Waiapu. " The Christian Church had grown to an extent which made a presiding authority expedient, to which all could look with confidence, together with the exercise of those ecclesiastical functions which are essential to its complete efficiency." It also wanted the authority of government. " If an effective government can be established," Samuel Marsden had written as long ago as 1824, " a colony may be established and benefit the natives." " European civilization showed in its first coming to New Zealand its most reckless and ruthless face. . . . In free competition between its good and evil elements, the evil elements were winning . . . the introduction of fire-arms had inaugurated a series of

[1] W. K. Hancock: *Survey of British Commonwealth Affairs*, II; *Problems of Economic Policy*, Part i.

ghastly tribal wars. . . . The missionaries desperately
wanted some authority which would impose order upon
the Maori and upon the very mixed European community
which during the eighteen-thirties was growing by migra-
tion from New South Wales."[1]   In this they were at
loggerheads with their headquarters in England.   While
Salisbury Square, the C.M.S. Headquarters in the heart
of the City, was taking a realistic view of the land-grabbing
designs of the New Zealand Company and showing un-
compromising hostility to colonizing projects that could
bode no good to the Maori, the missionaries on the spot,
taking a realistic view of the menace of anarchy, were doing
all they could to induce the Maoris in their best interests
to accept annexation and sign the Treaty of Waitangi
(1841). Captain Hobson, the first Governor, warmly
acknowledged their "zealous and effective assistance."

The two desires, for temporal as well as spiritual authority
were not unrelated, for annexation removed the necessity
for what would then have been regarded as an awkward
precedent, the consecration of a Bishop for a sphere outside
the Queen's dominions. Legal obstacles were now cleared,
and Mr. Gladstone's friend and contemporary was duly
appointed, a dazzling Etonian and Fellow of St. John's,
Cambridge. The C.M.S. were not consulted, though they
had offered half the episcopal salary; but Henry Venn,
the Secretary, wrote to congratulate the missionaries on
the appointment of one whose talents and Christian
devotedness merited their welcoming him " with the confidence becoming the paternal relation in which he now
stands towards them."   " The Society," said the preacher
of the Annual Sermon " had not tarried till haply there
might be a Bishop set over the wild Western Isle of New
Zealand, but had at once introduced amidst the ferocious
cannibals of that seemingly inaccessible land, the messengers
of grace and peace and love. Now they had the blessed
privilege of welcoming to a garden, which they had been
the honoured means of winning from the waste, this master
husbandman in the vineyard of God."

Bishop Selwyn at his second Synod described what the
Oxford Movement had meant to him. He had followed

[1] Hancock: op cit.

those who seemed likely to " develop in all its fullness the actual system of the Anglican Church, neither adding aught or taking aught away; purifying corruption, calling forth its latent energies, encouraging its priesthood to a more holy and self-denying life; exhorting it to fast and watch and pray more frequently and more earnestly, to be more abundant in alms-giving—in a word, to do in our own system and ritual what the apostles did in their days and what our own Church still prescribes. . . . When a change came upon the spirit of their teaching and it seemed as if our own Church were not good enough to retain their allegiance, when we seemed on the verge of a frightful schism; then indeed I shrank back."

Here was a situation fraught with possibilities of friction: here was a Wilfrid set down amongst the monks of Lindis-farne. It was obvious that the Bishop spoke an idiom unfamiliar to the Maori, who " could not understand his fast-days and saints'-days ": that the Bishop could not help feeling how much better things might have been if there had been a master-husbandman in the vineyard from the beginning: (" If I could get some good Arch-deacon from England the case would be altered "). That the missionaries watched him searching " my massive folios of Fathers and commentators. . . . . attempting to adduce a plan of operations suitable to the peculiar case of New Zealand from the records of the first three centuries of the Church," founding a College within a year of his arrival " on the best precedents of antiquity ":—they might have been excused if they wondered whether this young man might not have been well-advised to seek his authorities nearer at hand. It was encouraging that the Bishop could preach in Maori on the day of his arrival, and that he preferred to make the mission compound his headquarters, in the midst of the Maoris, rather than Auckland in the midst of European settlers.

But difficulties there were bound to be, only to be resolved as mutual admiration and affection grew. " William Williams " writes the Bishop, " is an episcopally-minded man, and it would give me great pleasure to divide my diocese with him; yea, let him take all, as I cannot pretend to equal his piety or maturity of wisdom." " The Bishop,"

writes Williams, " has laboured hard and set us in a noble
example: he does the work of the best two missionaries I
have ever known."

As war-clouds thickened, irritation over episcopal edicts
could not be allowed to weaken support of the Bishop,
exposed as he was to the suspicion of the natives as pro-
British and to the animosity of the colonists as pro-native.
The main Maori war of the '60's falls outside the span of this
chapter, but the convulsions of the '40's were disturbing
enough. Deterioration had already set in, and the relations
between the races were entering upon a discreditable
history which only subsequent recovery and reconciliation
makes tolerable reading. The Bishop did not hesitate to
incur the wrath of Lord Grey, the Colonial Secretary (and
the description of himself in the House of Commons as
" a turbulent priest ") by arraigning a policy which
threatened to reduce to a scrap of paper the Waitangi
Treaty, on which the honour of the Church was staked.
" Why," asked Bishop Selwyn, " should not the two races
form as it were two colonies ? " which would safeguard
the parallel development within a single territory of two
different communities. " Many experienced and intelligent observers believed that the British Government ought
to preserve the institutions of the Maori people and build
upon them, instead of allowing the colonists to destroy
them," and the Bishop was one of them. "Some of the
phrases which occurred in the discussions," Professor
Hancock continues, " anticipate the later terminology of
' indirect rule '."

In his educational plans the Bishop was also well ahead
of his time. Though himself a classic, and his primary
aim the supply of men for the Ministry, the curriculum of
St. John's College, which he soon moved to Auckland, included from the start industrial classes for manual training
in farming, gardening and forestry, and he spared no
pains to learn how coarse cloth was made by the peasants
of Scotland and Wales, that weaving might be learnt by
the girls in his boarding-school. Impetuous though he had
been in planting the College, Bishop Selwyn was prepared
to wait long for its fruits: his standards for ordination
were as exalted intellectually as spiritually: it was eleven

years before he would ordain a Maori deacon, twenty-four before he bestowed priest's orders on a Maori, but by the time he became Bishop of Lichfield in 1867, he and the Bishop of Waiapu between them had a staff of twenty-three clergy.

In his view of ecclesiastical organization the Bishop was also ahead of his time. " I believe the monarchical idea of the Episcopate to be as foreign to the true mind of the Church as it is adverse to the Gospel doctrine." These words are from his charge to his second Synod in 1847; he had held his first as early as 1844, scandalizing critics in England who saw in it " priestly assumptions, if not an infringement of the royal supremacy."

But Bishop Selwyn's contribution to the development of Church government must be reserved for a future chapter, as must also the founding of a Melanesian diocese which has so justly secured him a place in the first rank of makers of Christian history.

THE HOME BASE AND THE COMING OF THE BISHOPS

Three symptoms of a revived and an official interest in the overseas Church can be recognized in the history of the 1840's.

(1) The consecrations of Middleton, Heber, Broughton, Selwyn, Coleridge, had taken place in semi-private in the seclusion of Lambeth Palace Chapel; it was a concession for Mrs. Heber to be allowed to bring two friends. Edward Coleridge (an Eton master, later Rector of Mapledurham, whose practical friendship with Selwyn and Broughton entitles him to rank among the builders of the Church in Australia and New Zealand) had protested vigorously after Selwyn's consecration:—

" I could not help feeling that we ought to have been thousands rather than ten, gathered together as with one consent in St. Paul's or Westminster Abbey, to witness the sending out by the Church of the first Bishop of the appointment, and not as we were, a few persons in an upper chamber—as if we were afraid or ashamed of that great deed which we came to sanction by our presence and our prayers. It is an actual fact that my own cousin, the present Bishop of Barbados, was admitted to that

I

sacred office in the presence of only two persons besides the necessary attendants. Such cannot last much longer. The feeling of the Church will become so strong and the cry of indignation so loud that it will pierce even the walls of Addington, and so rouse the Archbishop from his slumbers."

It was therefore considered epoch-making when three new Australian diocesans, and Bishop Gray for Capteown were consecrated in Westminster Abbey on St. Peter's Day, 1847. The wooden screens then dividing the transepts from the choir were removed for the occasion, but even so accommodation was strained to its limits. The Eucharist was choral, there were 760 communicants, the alms amounted to £550, and the Bishop of London preached on the Church's obligations towards her "remoter branches."

(2) Bishop Blomfield is also associated with the second symptom, the initiation of a " Colonial Bishoprics' Fund " in 1841, a corporation which still operates, though the overseas episcopate has long outgrown both the fitness of its title and the extent of its resources. At a time when the overseas episcopate is dependent to the tune of £14,000 on the current revenue of Missionary Societies, and demands additonal provision for each new diocese, it is stimulating to recall the enthusiasm of Archbishop Howley's inaugural meeting, and the magnitude of its financial fruits. £230,000 raised in thirty years enabled thirty new dioceses to be wholly or partly endowed. Mr. Gladstone was one of the speakers and for long Treasurer of the Fund. Archdeacon (afterward Cardinal) Manning was another: he poured scorn on those within and without the Church who bemoaned her diversities, struggles and divisions, which were marks of the exuberance of her life. " There has been no time when the Church of England stood stronger than now, in the apostolic doctrine and discipline."

(3) Thirdly the Church was beginning to take seriously the recruitment and training of reinforcements for the overseas dioceses. The Church Missionary College at Islington, which had been opened in 1825, was now turning out a distinguished succession of students of British birth: and Mr. Beresford-Hope delighted Bishop Broughton's heart by purchasing the ruins of St. Augustine's monastery

at Canterbury and established (in 1848) the College which Edward Coleridge had designed " for the education of young men for the service of the Church in the distant dependencies of the British Empire."

PART VII

AFRICA: BEFORE AND AFTER LIVINGSTONE

Introduction : David Livingstone

1. Pre-Livingstone Days: (*a*) Expansion from the West, Sierra Leone, Abeokuta, The Niger; (*b*) Expansion from the South, The See of Cape Town.

2. Post-Livingstone Days: Expansion from the East, The See of Zanzibar, The See of Eastern Equatorial Africa.

IF the unmanageable scale of Africa makes it difficult to fit a picture of its infant Church into a small frame, perspective presents an even more insoluble problem. To recover the outlook of the pioneers stretches the most elastic imagination. Yet justice demands that their achievements be magnified and their mistakes minimized by making due allowance for the fact that they were initiating Christian history, in a pre-gold, pre-diamonds, pre-railways, pre-quinine, pre-anthropology, pre-survey, and *ex hypothesi* pre-Christian Africa. Slave-raiding for many a long year remained the dominant issue. A map of 1842 labels great tracts of Africa as " unknown parts," the home of " tribes of which very little is known." Not only were internal communications restricted to the pace of oxen, if not of human porterage, but England and Africa were far apart: the first missionaries to West Africa in 1806 only reached Sierra Leone in September after leaving Liverpool in February. Livingstone first reached the Cape in 1841 after a fourteen-weeks' passage. First contacts between European and African occurred under unpropitious auspices. " The fact that the institution of slavery was closely identified with difference of colour must have helped to bring into prominence the idea of White superiority."[1] The southward penetration of Bantu

[1] Lord Cromer: *Ancient and Modern Imperialism.*

warriors gave equal prominence to the idea of white security. These basic ideas have a long and sinister history.

If it was strange to find Claudius Buchanan, a boy who left Inveraray Grammar School at fourteen, attaining to such influence in the early history of the Anglican Church in India, it is stranger to find a boy who at the age of ten went to work in a Blantyre cotton-mill, not only attaining universal fame, but affecting the destiny of a Church other than his own, in the depths of Africa. "Whereas all other great missionaries have been identified more or less with one place or one people, it might almost be said of Livingstone that his field was not a country but a continent."[1] David Livingstone's grave in Westminster Abbey, at the very centre of the nave, is symbolic of the place his rugged, dogged character had won in the nation's affection and the world's esteem. Livingstone's return to England in 1856 after his first fifteen years in Africa marks more than a " great divide " in his own career: it is comparable to the watershed which he had just discovered whence waters flowed by way of the Congo into the Atlantic, and by way of the Zambesi into the Indian Ocean. The history of the continent henceforward is different from its past. Its secrets now begin to be disclosed, its rivers, lakes and mountains mapped, its fortunes linked for better or for worse with the outside world. For the outside world Africa was now on the map, and in their different ways the diverse elements that composed that world, statesmen, explorers, merchants, humanitarians, missionaries, were compelled to take notice of the great new fact of their generation.

It was from bridgeheads on the Western, the Southern and the Eastern coasts that the Anglican expeditionary forces took off for their advance into the interior. The Sahara, till the opening up of the Upper Nile, proved an impregnable obstacle to advance from the North; the White Fathers pressing on from the French bridgehead of Algiers made gallant attempts to cross it, but after two parties had perished, their founder, the great Cardinal Lavigerie, withdrew the more exposed desert posts: their

[1] Professor Coupland's Introduction to David Chamberlin's *Some Letters from Livingstone.*

later entry into the French Sudan was from the west, by way of Senegal and Timbuktu, and into Uganda and the Belgian Congo from the East by way of Zanzibar. Advance from the East belongs to the later period ; it is the Churches of West Africa and South Africa which have pre-Livingstone origins.

PRE-LIVINGSTONE DAYS
EXPANSION FROM THE WEST

Precedence must be given to the Western bridgehead though no Bishop was appointed till 1852. The C.M.S. had been forty years in the country and it was for no lack of importunity on their part that the delay was so long. It was indeed almost exactly a century since the Church had first set foot in West Africa in the person of Thomas Thompson, an S.P.G. missionary in North America, who at his own request was transferred to " the Coast of Guiney, that I might go to make a Trial with the natives, and see what Hopes there would be of introducing among them the Christian Religion." After five years on the Gold Coast, at the end of which " the Rage of the Distemper " drove him home, he could record his conviction that " the Blacks of the Coast of Guinea may be brought over to the Christian faith, being more removed from Barbarity and Savagery than others and fitter to be dealt with in the way of Christian Instruction; neither are they uncon- scious of the Folly and Vanity of their own Way of Religion; their Adherence to it is in some sort involuntary: it rather sticks to them than they to it." Thompson's solitary adventure bore fruit in Philip Quaque, whose father, an influential Chief, allowed him to go to England with two other Negro boys at the invitation of the S.P.G. There he was ordained in 1765—the first of his or any non- European race to receive Anglican orders—the beginning of a half-century's ministry among both his own people and the Europeans of Cape Coast. A memorial was erected to him at Cape Coast Castle by the African Com- pany " in token of their approbation of his long and faithful service," and was still standing when Samuel Crowther happened upon it in 1841.

SIERRA LEONE

The heavy mortality which shadowed the early days of the Sierra Leone Mission lasted on. Five consecutive years saw the death of four Governors of the Colony, all but one of them by disease: a fifth, Major Octavius Temple, father and grandfather of Archbishops of Canterbury, died in 1834. Of thirteen missionary arrivals in January 1840, five were dead by July and five evacuated. Yet the Church multiplied. By 1842 there were 7,000 at worship, and 1,500 communicants, and a Parliamentary Committee could testify to " the invaluable exertions of the C.M.S., to whom and to the Wesleyans the highest praise is due: by their efforts nearly one-fifth of the populations are at school and the effects are visible in considerable intellectual, moral and religious improvement." The three first women missionaries came out to start schools for girls between 1846 and 1848.

The serious casualties dictated and accelerated a policy of self-support in men, money and ministry; for the African Church could not depend on the precarious lives of European missionaries. From very early days the weekly offertory, still a suspected Tractarian innovation in England, was the accepted symbol of self-respect. The African Church took over responsibility for all village schools in 1854, to the tune of £800 a year; and it was in line with this policy that an annual charge of double that amount was, six years later, transferred from the shoulders of the Society. The principle was at the same time enshrined in a new constitution which transferred all responsibility for African clergy and congregations from the C.M.S. to the Bishop and Church Council on the spot. Except for major educational institutions, Sierra Leone was henceforth regarded " as outside the Society's official range.

The first three Bishops of Sierra Leone averaged a working life of only two years, but between them they ordained twelve Africans and saw an African ministry well launched. It was with this ultimate aim that a College had been started in 1827 at Fourah Bay, later to be affiliated, like Codrington College, to Durham University. For

twenty years it was ruled by a coloured clergyman of the
Episcopal Church of the United States. Most of the clergy
and many of the leading laity owed their education to it.
Samuel Crowther's name was the first on its roll among
the original six students, and he taught as a member of
its staff.

SAMUEL CROWTHER : ABEOKUTA

The mention of Crowther's name is a signal for a journey
farther afield; but before starting eastward it must be
recalled that the Diocese of Sierra Leone extended also
northward. Its offshoot, the Diocese of Gambia and the
Rio Pongas, is too youthful to be included without anachronism in this context, but the West India Mission in the
Pongas goes back to the 1850's and must be noticed as the
first Mission of a " Younger " to a still younger Church.
Men were trained at Codrington College for a mission to
Africa, among them a young African, John Dupont, who
after the death of Mr. Leacock, the leader of the expedition, kept its flag flying. The start was propitious, for, on
arrival at Fallangia, Mr. Leacock was met by the Chief
who, taking him by the hand, said "Welcome dear Sir,
thou servant of the Most High." He seemed greatly
agitated, and a few moments after rose from his chair
and recited the Te Deum with great solemnity and accuracy.
The explanation was that he had been to England as a
boy and received Christian teaching ; on his return he had
at first relapsed into pagan practices, but had long been
praying that God would send a missionary to his Pongas
country before he died.

Sierra Leone had for forty years been the place of
settlement for thousands of slaves rescued by sloops of
Her Majesty's Navy on the ocean. It was reckoned that a
hundred tribes and languages were represented among
them ; many of them, when return to their own countries
became possible, carried back at least a smattering of
Christian knowledge: some of them became the foundation members of local Churches. " Our God had turned
the curse into a blessing."

Samuel Crowther was one of these rescued slaves: he left a fragment of autobiography which reveals what it was like to have your town suddenly sacked, to be snatched from your family at the age of fourteen or fifteen, to be passed from purchaser to purchaser, to be embarked for the notorious Western passage, and finally to be taken aboard a man-of-war and deposited once more on African shores. After his ordination in England, Crowther made his way in the company of two missionaries to the country of his birth, which had now become stabilized under the name of Abeokuta. This was a twelve-hundred mile voyage eastward from Sierra Leone, and fifty miles inland from Lagos. After twenty-five years, to their mutual astonishment and joy, mother and son were reunited, each with a tale of captivity to tell. Crowther's mission among the Yorubas prospered. " This Mission is three years old to-day. What hath God wrought in this short interval of conflict between light and darkness. We have five hundred constant attendants on the means of grace, eighty communicants and two hundred candidates for baptism. Others have cast their gods away and are not far from enlisting under the banner of Christ."

But the Yoruba mission was not to be allowed for long to occupy the main attention of its founder, nor was it to escape grim tests of its sincerity. War broke out between Abeokuta and the neighbouring state of Ibadan—the capitals were only forty miles apart—the bloodthirsty King of Dahomey took the opportunity to attack Abeokuta, and the slave-trading King of Lagos to attack the neighbouring port of Bagadry where a Christian Church had been planted. Lord Palmerston, determined to strike a final blow at the traffic in slaves, in 1861 dethroned the King of Lagos and annexed the port. The Lagos government came to be regarded by the Abeokutans as having taken sides with Ibadan. This inevitably reacted upon the missionaries, who were for thirteen years banished from Abeokuta. Churches were wrecked and Christian assemblies banned, but three African clergy remained at their posts, and under their guidance the Church grew: no small testimony to the soundness of the foundations laid.

SAMUEL CROWTHER: THE NIGER

Samuel Crowther's name and destiny were to be for ever associated primarily with the Niger. The Niger had been a captivating but perplexing geographical mystery. Where did it rise ? Where did it end ? In the west or in the east ? Many lives were lost in attempts to find a solution of these riddles. At last Mungo Park, doctor son of a Scottish farmer, had seen " with infinite pleasure the great object of my mission, the long-sought-for, majestic Niger, glittering to the morning sun and flowing slowly to the *eastward*. I hastened to the brink and having drank of the water, lifted up my fervent thanks in prayer to the great Ruler of all things, for having thus far crowned my endeavour with success." Clapperton, another Lowland Scot, had taken up the quest, but it was reserved for his Cornish servant, Lander, after burying his master with many tears, to make the final expedition with his younger brother. On November 15th, 1830, they sailed out of the Delta in triumph. Lander is honoured by a memorial column set up in the heart of Truro.

Within ten years an elaborate expedition was afoot to explore the Niger in the reverse direction. It sailed with what Claudius Buchanan would have stigmatized as " carnal éclat." Prince Albert, still a bridgeroom, had presided over the inaugural meeting of a new Society for the Civilization of Africa, on June 1st, 1840, supported by five and twenty peers and bishops and a host of M.P.'s. Sir Thomas Buxton, after carrying to a dazzling climax Wilberforce's campaign for the Abolition of Slavery, was once more on the war-path. The evil must be scotched at its source. " The deliverance of Africa is to be effected by calling out her own resources. . . . It is the Bible and the Plough that must regenerate Africa." *The Times* and the *Edinburgh Review* might scoff and Dickens deride the scheme in *Bleak House,* but Prince Albert, Palmerston, Sir Robert Peel, and Buxton were unflinching in their support. The noble Buxton still broods broken-hearted in the Abbey aisle over the ill-fated venture : forty-two out of the hundred and fifty who left England had died in two months.

But it is with Samuel Crowther that we are concerned. The C.M.S. had been invited to send two representatives on the 1841 expedition, and Crowther was one of them. He was also a member of the second expedition of 1854, and is given the credit for securing its immunity from a second disaster by his diagnosis of the cause of the first: the green firewood to which he traced poisonous vapours was no longer carried on board but in canoes, and the party thrived. It was the experience gained and the resource displayed on these expeditions which suggested Crowther as the obvious nominee when Henry Venn, the Secretary of the C.M.S., insisted that if the Niger Mission was to materialize, it must be under the supervision of an African Bishop. That so novel a proposal surmounted all obstacles was no doubt due partly to Venn's pertinacity and influence with Prime Ministers ; his brother-in-law Sir James Stephen was Chief Secretary in the Colonial Office, and Lord Glenelg, Grant's son, Colonial Secretary ; partly to the impression Crowther himself had made on Queen Victoria and the Prince Consort when they had given him audience eighteen years before. Her Majesty had been so simply dressed that " in blissful ignorance before whom I stood I conversed freely and answered every question put to me about the way slaves are entrapped, how I was caught and sold, to which they listened with breathless attention ; and it was only when the lamp blew out and the Prince said ' will your Majesty kindly bring a candle from the mantelpiece ? ' that I became aware before whom I had been all the time. I trembled from head to foot."

Oxford conferred a D.D. Degree, Crowther's Yoruba dictionary and translation of the Bible being submitted as evidence of scholarship, and the consecration took place in Canterbury Cathedral. It was a momentous event and the beginning of a very notable espiscopate. If there were some weaknesses which the vigilance of an experienced white Bishop might have counteracted, there was far more that an African Bishop could do that a European could not. It was not only the matter of being acclimatized to the physical climate of the Niger : there was a moral and psychological climate as mysterious to the European as it was familiar to Bishop Crowther. He could enter by instinct into the minds of his clergy. " Christianity does not undertake to destroy national assimilation: guard against the common prejudices which are apt to prevail in your minds against native images in general, because they have their origin from a heathen state. If judicious use be made of native ideas the minds of the heathen will be better reached than by attempting to introduce new ones quite foreign to their way of thinking." The Captain of H.M.S. *Lynx* with four of his officers and his coxswain were the only white men present at an ordination. " It was an impressive sight. There was the Bishop, once a slave, but rescued by British cruisers, dressed in the usual robes of the English Bench and surrounded by his clergy, seated within the rails of as primitive a Communion Table as ever was seen; in front the candidate for Holy Orders. All, Christians, Mohammedans and Pagans (who had come from curiosity) could see the simple earnestness of Bishop and Clergy."

Bishop Crowther could also enter by instinct into the minds of Chiefs. Captain East records that " having to arrange a dispute between the King and the merchants about trading matters, the King expected me to send for the Bishop, " for " he said, " I know he is a man of truth and will know what is right." It was a delicate matter to commend to autocratic chiefs the toleration of Christian innovations and the suppression of traditional barbarities. It could be a dangerous business. A traveller on the Niger was an easy prey to a hostile archer. A British consul was killed by a poisoned arrow in the act of rescuing the Bishop from an angry Chief who had imprisoned him and demanded £1,000 in ransom. Bishop Crowther lived on into extreme old age, and it was inevitable that he should have to deal with some "second-generation" problems; but when he died in 1891 it was felt that only one text was fitting for his monument, " Well done, thou good and faithful servant."

EXPANSION FROM THE SOUTH

Bishop Robert Gray had been one of the four Bishops consecrated in Westminster Abbey on St. Peter's Day,

1847 (see p. 114). It was not long before he realized that the Church of England had arrived late in the day. Some of the most romantic pages of South African history had already been written, great events had come and gone, and the seeds of dissension between Briton and Boer, Briton and Bantu, Bantu and Boer, had already been sown. The first issue had come to a head in the Great Trek—at its zenith at the time of Queen Victoria's accession—when seven thousand Dutch farmers in-spanned for the unknown North, resenting the liberalism of the Cape which had triumphed in the emancipation of Hottentots and Slaves. Anna Steenkamp, sister of a famous Voortrekker leader, gave as the main reason for the great Trek, " the shameful and unjust proceedings with reference to the freedom of the slaves, and yet it is not their freedom that drove us to such lengths as their being placed on an equal footing with Christians, contrary to the laws of God and the natural distinction of race and religion; so that it was intolerable for any decent Christian to bow down beneath such a yoke; wherefore we rather withdrew in order to preserve our doctrine in purity."[1]

The second issue, Briton and Bantu, had been exacerbated by bloodshed on a constantly shifting frontier; interludes of peace and war lasted till the peace of 1853, and the Governorship of Bishop Gray's friend, Sir George Grey, under whose " humane and enlightened rule " the Cape took its first serious steps towards civilizing the natives. Henceforth they were to be " inhabitants of one country " along with their European conquerors. Sir George was not only a notable pioneer of native education, but the originator and founder, before the days of medical missions, of the first great hospital for Natives. Hostilities between Briton and Boer were paralleled by outbursts of sharp-shooting between Downing Street and Exeter Hall, ammunition for the latter being supplied by the L.M.S. missionary Dr. John Philip who had stoutly championed the Hottentot, the Coloured People and the Griquas and now incurred the reputation of a fanatical " Negrophile." Of the Bantu he writes: " The Caffres are not the savages one reads about in books: they are intelligent and not

[1] McCrome: *Race Attitude in South Africa.*

afraid of conversing with strangers; they are well acquainted
with their own history; they have humour and are clever
at giving characteristic nicknames. True they go almost
naked, but they have their points of delicacy."[1]

Philip riddles the evidence on which "they have been
declared to be a nation of thieves, robbed of their cattle,
their only means of support, and from time to time of their
country." Philip enjoyed the confidence of the Governor,
Sir Benjamin D'Urban, and even conducted fact-finding
expeditions at his request, but when his warnings (that the
Kaffirs would resist if the existing Frontier system and the
harassing conduct of the Frontier authorities continued)
were disregarded, when the Governors procrastinated,
talked of irreclaimable savages, and on reaching the
frontier came down heavily on the side of those whose chief
faith was in "powder and ball," fresh supplies of powder
and ball were hurriedly despatched to Sir Thomas Fowell
Buxton to be discharged from the platform of Exeter Hall.
Philip became the prototype of the meddlesome missionary,
but "the obloquy which attaches to his name is the lot of
men who attain great ends."[1] He won the regard of
David Livingstone who admits that "I came to the Cape
full of prejudice against him, but after living a month in his
house and carefully scrutinizing his character, that prejudice was entirely dissolved and affection and the greatest
respect took its place. I have heard a great deal said
against him but now I am fully satisfied it is all, or at least
the greatest portion of it, sheer downright calumny. . . .
The Boers hate him cordially. Many of them would think
it doing God service to shoot him. They have an inveterate
hatred to the coloured population and to him as their
friend and advocate; you can't understand it, it is like
caste in India. Can you believe it?"

This brings us to the third issue, between Bantu and
Boer. Livingstone's letters shed a lurid light on their
relations. He was in Bechuanaland when the spear-head
of the Great Trek was forcibly penetrating native lands
and meeting forcible resistance. Livingstone's mission in
Kuruman was attacked in 1852. "Had I been able to
travel as quickly as my desire dictated, I would have been

[1] W. M. Macmillan: *Cape Colour Questions.*

at Kolobeng at the very time of the attack. The Com-
mandant repeatedly expressed sorrow at not having caught
me and also his determination to cut off my head: they
say ' that horrid Doctor must have taught them to fight '.
It is necessary to distinguish between the Colonial farmers
of Dutch extraction who are usually called Boers, and those
in the Interior of the same name whose independence has
lately been acknowledged by the Government. The latter
are the dregs of the Colonial population, and if we do not
bear in mind the general belief they entertain that black
people are soulless, it is difficult to believe the records of
their barbarity and callousness in shedding the blood of
the coloured people. Cannot say that I take joyfully the
spoiling of my goods. If they had made any use of my
books and medicines I could have forgiven them, but
tearing, smashing and burning them was beyond measure
galling." Celestial atlas and sextant were among the losses.

The See of Capetown

Such was the political background of Bishop Gray's
episcopate. He started off in his coach and eight-in-hand
on his first visitation in August 1848 (after " a very friendly
conversation in a call upon Dr. Philips the Independent
Bishop, and another with Dr. Adamson, the head of a new
sect called the Apostolical Union and another with Mr.
Faure of the Dutch Communion: these three all in one
day will show my catholic spirit, I hope.") He did not
expect to return to Capetown till December. These
prolonged tours by routes that were sometimes impossible
for a rough cart, let alone a coach and eight, across dangerous mountain passes and swollen rivers, exposed the Bishop
to exertions and discomforts ill-suited to one beset with
chronic opthalmic trouble; they were carried through
against a background of political and no less thorny
ecclesiastical problems.

The Church of England was late in the field. " Since
I left Capteown I have met with *one* English Church;
but I travelled nine hundred miles before I came to it. . . .
The Church population is far larger than I imagined,
but they have been and still are in various places aiding

the erection of dissenting chapels, for want of any effort
upon the part of the Church. . . . Everywhere I found
men of education and intelligence who, for lack of means
of grace, had availed themselves of the ministrations of
the Dutch Wesleyan Independents. . . . We have suffered
great spiritual destitution from the long neglect shown by
the Mother Church, for half a century there is no one of
our Colonies that we have for so long a time and so entirely
neglected. . . . People do not seem to be aware that up
to this time the Church can scarcely be said to have had
a footing in South Africa." There was no corresponding
neglect on the part of non-Anglican Churches. Livingstone was writing home that " the Colonial market is
literally glutted with missionaries. I do not believe that
equal advantages are enjoyed by any town or village in
the United Kingdom as those which are pressed on the
people of Algoa Bay, Uitenhagen, Graaf Reinet and
Colesberg: our missionaries should be moving to the
regions beyond."[1]

All this was very distressing to a Bishop who had been
" much pleased " with the *Tracts for the Times* as they
appeared, in spite of passages to which he could not assent,
who loved John Keble and leant on the advice of Dr.
Pusey. Mr. Hawkins, the Secretary of the S.P.G., in a
letter urging him to accept the bishopric, based his case
on the plea that " What are called extreme opinions on
this side or on that exclude so many," and the Bishop did
not come under that ban, but he held " Church principles "
passionately and felt a vocation to inoculate the Christianity
of South Africa with a strong injection of episcopal serum.
" We have to engraft a new system, a new phase of religion
upon a previously existing one. Everywhere we appear to
those who have been before us as intruders. . . . I feel at
every step I take principles are involved and precedents
established."

Perhaps a playful letter of David Livingstone's to the
head of the L.M.S. Mission in South Africa, in which he
addresses him as the Right Reverend and Venerable
William Capetown, and signs himself David Zambesi,
with a cross " his mark," may be taken to indicate that the

---

[1] D. Chamberlin: *Some Letters from Livingstone*, p. 109.

Bishop's personality was beginning to count for something. He did not escape a measure of persecution and " much abuse from the Press: we never attack others but almost every paper that is published attacks us: their determination is to write us down. Then there are tirades against priestcraft and so forth." On the other hand, " To-morrow I have some leading Dutch ministers to meet some of ours, to let it be understood that we help one another in any way we can without compromise of principles. . . . I get on very well with the Dutch clergy, and hope to get three leading men to dine and spend the day with me. . . . I must send you a line, if it be only to comfort you with the information that I have lately taken to preach in the Methodist Chapels ! I have preached three times and am in high favour with that respectable Society in consequence. The Archdeacon has been preaching in a Moravian chapel, so you see we are in a fair way of getting rid of our bigotry! I could not well avoid addressing the poor heathen at the Mission when sharing the hospitality of the Missionary, even if I wished to do so, which was not the case."

It was the Moravian Mission, already a hundred years old, that had a special appeal for Bishop Gray. On his first visit to Genadendal (a settlement founded by three musicians, singer, flutist and violinist in 1789) he wrote " would to God the Church in this Colony could point to a work of equal importance with this as the result of her own labours in the cause of Christ among the heathen." And when the time came for him to start a mission for Kaffirs—a project which had figured in his very first sermon—it was the Moravian model which suggested itself. " The Moravians are the Archdeacon's model missionaries." " Both myself and the Archdeacon are more interested in the Moravian Missions than in any others. He thinks those on the frontier almost pefect, and he has been much with them and loves them heartily. I like what I have seen, but think the system at Genadendal in some respects faulty. It is however a sweet place and they are gentle people and receive me with much affection. But there are too many substantial meals ! There is no excess but there is fulness. But I am again becoming censorious."

K

" My Mission scheme is briefly this: Government propose to make ten locations of the natives, 10,000 souls in each. In each I propose to found a Mission Institution, somewhat on the plan of the Moravians. There is to be a community; they are to live in common. There must be a Priest, Schoolmaster, mechanic, agriculturist. An Industrial system is to be taught in combination with mental and moral training. The plan embraces the reception of male and female pupils, and a hospital." In commending the scheme to the Governor's approval, which he won, and applying for grants in aid out of the Hut tax, the Bishop concludes " I have only to add that the working out of the plan, if I engage in it, must be left altogether to myself. If I am to be in any way responsible for its success, I must have the entire control of it." Similarly he writes home " If you like to sound the Church Missionary Society as to funds, I have no objection; but nothing would induce me to submit to any dictation or interference on their part. The whole Mission shall in every respect be managed by the Church here, or there shall be none. If they mean to bargain for power I will have nothing to do with them. I see every day I live, more and more clearly, that the whole Church work must be done by the Church and not by any other agency."

Autocratic as this may sound, we shall see in a later chapter dealing with constitutional machinery, that nobody played a more conspicuous part than Bishop Gray in the development of synodical government. Unhappily his reforms led to the first but not the last litigation to harass the minds, divert the energies and deplete the resources of South African Bishops. The Bishop was not left in peace to consolidate the great work he had begun, both among the Colonists and the Natives. The young Church caught the backwash of two storms which were breaking over the Church in England. One tidal bore after another created alarm bordering upon panic, threatening as it seemed, to drown all familiar landmarks beneath overwhelming floods and to sap the very foundation of both Church and Bible. There was the rising tide of Erastianism and the rising tide of Infidelity.

Bishop Gray by this time had become a Metropolitan: he had planted dioceses in St. Helena, Grahamstown, Natal and Bloemfontein; but he could not shelter his Province from these shocks. Indeed the South African Church became itself doubly a storm-centre. In battle with the Erastians, Bishop Gray contended with all who would enmesh the Church in the toils of the State, whether the local Government or the Imperial Government. In battle with the Heretic, Bishop Gray found himself compelled to issue the fiat of excommunication not against distant prelates but against one of his own Suffragans. Mr. Keble might assure him that all would be well with the Church if we could " mend the Bishop-makers "; but that was little consolation to Bishop Gray, for he had been his own Bishop-maker, and had himself selected Dr. Colenso for the new diocese of Natal, " a noble-hearted man," and his voyage out with him in the same boat had only confirmed his hopes of him. Father Osmund Victor in his *Salient of South Africa* boldly avers that " in losing Bishop Colenso the Church lost the greatest missionary it has ever produced "; but it is not altogether surprising that his contemporaries, shocked first by the theology of his *Commentary on the Epistle to the Romans* and by his criticism of the Pentateuch, and secondly by his adhesion to his See after he had been excommunicated and his successor consecrated, in sole reliance on the letter of the law, saw in him the embodiment of each of the two evil spirits which menaced religion: the spirit of Infidelity and the spirit of Erastianism.

The later years of Bishop Gray's episcopate—he died at his post in 1872, aged 63—were thus overclouded with three tragic phenomena new to our narrative—heresy, schism and litigation. There was, however, a fourth element of novelty which afforded some relief and compensation to the harassed Bishop. On a visit to England he had made a thorough study of the Religious Communities which had sprung up during his absence, and consulted with their founders and superiors. On his return he was able to bring with him eight " very sterling women, very sensible and very nice, with a diversity of gifts " to be the nucleus of a Sisterhood of St. George. The Bishop drew up their

Rule of Life and bestowed on them a motto " Adoremus et Laboremus " which may also serve as epitaph for his own life.

II. POST-LIVINGSTONE DAYS
EXPANSION FROM THE EAST

THE SEE OF ZANIZBAR

The first edition of *Livingstone's Missionary Travels,* an issue of twelve thousand at a guinea, was sold out before publication. He had returned to England in 1853 to find the public avid for his story, and even the shadow of the Indian Mutiny did not eclipse his glory. It was an epic tale to tell: Linyanti to the west coast and back again, 3,000 miles; Linyanti to the east coast, 1,300 miles: thirty months of travel. " It will be gratifying for you to hear that I have been able to follow up without swerving my original plan of opening a way to the sea on either the East or West coast from a healthy locality in the Interior of the Continent . . . . I am not so elated in having performed what has not to my knowledge been done before in traversing the continent, because the end of the geographical feat is but the beginning of the missionary enterprise." Healthy was an exaggeration, for it was here that the Helmores, L.M.S. missionaries, perished; nor were the new routes yet a working alternative to the long line of communication between the Highlands and the Cape; but that did not dim the grandeur of the achievement.

As has been said, the visit to England marked a great divide both in Livingstone's personal career and in Africa's relations with Europe. It was the end of a fifteen years' apprenticeship: he had landed at Algoa Bay on May 19th, 1841, and reached the mouth of the Zambesi on May 20th, 1856. He had formulated and began to apply certain resolutions of far-reaching significance for the future of the African Church. We can give them in his own words. *First* there was the resolution to stand or fall by the hypothesis that extension took precedence of concentration. " If we call the actual amount of conversion the direct result of Missions, and the wide diffusion of better principles the indirect, I have no hesitation in asserting that the latter are of infinite more importance than the former. I do not undervalue the importance of the conversion and salvation of the most abject creature that breathes, it is of overwhelming worth to him personally, but viewing our work of wide sowing of the good seed relatively to the harvest which will be reaped when our heads are low, there can, I think, be no comparison . . . . The more concentration the less success . . . . Those who regard this as a mere journey of exploration ought perhaps to remember that we bring to view a large section of the human family." " The indications of Providence ? I don't think we ought to wait for them. Our duty is to go forward and look for the indications."

Secondly there was the resolution to pay the price of loneliness. " To orphanise my children will be like tearing out my bowels, but it is the only way . . . . Have I seen the end of my wife and children ? . . . I think much of my poor children . . . . If I allowed my mind to dwell constantly on the miserable degradation, wickedness and sad prospects of the people here, I might become melancholy and soon die. But we have a fair world and all the wonderful works of our Father in it, and I believe we ought to allow our minds to dwell on the beautiful more than on the evil. I am never low-spirited. It might be different if I had a crusty companion. I have experience of it and my thoughts never turn with any longing except for my family . . . . Such a rush of thoughts and trembling sensations when I opened letters from my family you may imagine if you can, taking it into consideration that I have been without information for nearly three years."

Thirdly there was the resolution to exterminate the ubiquitous slave-dealer. "Shame upon us if we are to be outdone by the slave-traders." " One had sixty slaves and will take away from the villages 100 or 150 more." "The Arabs were all intent on the slave-trade. It must be profitable."

Fourthly, Livingstone was resolved that an illicit was to vanish before the advance of a licit commerce. " Commerce breaks up the sullen isolations of heathenism. It is so far good though Christianity alone reaches the very centre of the wants of Africa and of the world. Here is a most desirable central point for the spread of civilisation and Christianity . . . . If the movement now begun is not checked by some untoward event, the slave-trade will certainly come to a natural termination in this quarter."

Lastly there was the conviction, and the resolve to stand by it, that God, to Whom he had offered his service, had accepted it. " Then my life is charmed till my work is done. We are immortal till our work is done . . . . I am doing something for God . . . . It is God, not the devil that rules our destiny." He had received a message from the Directors that they held themselves restricted in their power of aiding plans " connected only remotely with the spread of the Gospel." It was a stinging phrase, and arrived at the worst psychological moment, at the end of 4,300 miles of pilgrimage. " Indeed so clearly did I perceive that I was performing good service to the cause of Christ that I wrote to my brother that I would perish rather than fail. The wonderful mercies I have received constrain me to follow out the work in spite of the veto."

Such was the man who stood before Cambridge University in the Senate House on December 4th, 1857, apologizing for uncorrectness of language because for seventeen years he had spoken African dialects: even as a young candidate before the Board of Selection he had been criticized for " his heaviness of manner, united as it is with a rusticity not likely to be removed." But the words rang out; fifty years later, an eyewitness described it as a sudden shout: " Do you carry on the work which I have begun. I leave it with you." Bishop Gray was in Cambridge next year and watered the seed sown. All Saints' Day, 1859, saw its efflorescence in a great meeting at Oxford addressed by Mr. Gladstone, William Wilberforce's son, now Bishop of Oxford, and Sir George Grey, Selwyn's Governor in New Zealand and Gray's in Capetown. So was launched what, with the adhesion of Dublin and Durham, came to be known as the Universities' Mission to Central Africa.

Never did ship, so propitiously launched, come so near and so soon to total wreck. Charles Frederick Mackenzie, Archdeacon to Bishop Colenso of Natal, had been

selected as chief navigator, and was consecrated at Capetown by Bishop Gray, who, so remote were contemporary
from modern ideas, was disappointed that the new Mission
was not to be within the Province. Livingstone himself
chaperoned the Bishop on a trial trip up the Rovuma;
he accompanied the *Pioneer* up the Shiré River, and
himself selected the site for settlement at Magomero in
July 1861. Together they met and liberated a convoy of
slaves, and the gentle Bishop was left to wrestle with a
moral dilemma, to let the slaves continue in bondage or
to use force. But by January 1862 the Bishop had paid
the price of inexperience and his companion Burrup
survived only long enough to bury him, struck down by
the same malaria. Within a year, Scudamore was dead,
and Dr. Dickinson, the beloved physician. It was not
surprising that Bishop Tozer braved criticism by strategic
withdrawal to Zanzibar. Here the work bifurcated in two
equally urgent directions, among the hosts of freed slaves
confided to the Mission's care on the Island, and among
the free men of the mainland, where what came to be a
second headquarters of the Bishop was established at
Magila, among the mountains and oranges of the Usambara
country. Both kinds of experience were invaluable preparation for missionaries who were going to carry the work
into country where normal tribal and village life subsisted,
though slave-raiders roamed to and fro on their nefarious
quest. Bishop Steere in a single journey met nine caravans
representing from 1,500 to 2,000 slaves.

Two great Cathedrals symbolize respectively these two
aspects. Zanzibar Cathedral was built, Bishop Steere
himself the architect and master-builder, on the actual
site of the old slave-market; the altar stands where the
whipping-post stood. Its campanile, the long line of its
solid concrete roof, and the arcading of its semi-circular
apse, dominate the old city: hospital, and hospital clergy-
house and school nestle among the Flamboyants and
Petraeas at its base. Likoma, a younger but even more
majestic Cathedral, enshrines the memory of Chauncy
Maples, William Johnson, Charles Janson, Arthur Douglas,
among many whose lives were hid in the foundations of
the Nyasa diocese.

It is with Bishop Steere (Tozer's successor), linguist, scholar, architect and builder-up of the spiritual temple not made with hands, as of the coral-stone basilica, that the second mainland expansion is associated. It was he who led the expedition from Lindi, 300 miles south of Zanzibar, advancing by himself to the upper waters of the Rovuma, and founded the settlement, which, in spite of subsequent sack, survived to give its name Masasi to the youngest of the dioceses of Central Africa. It is with Bishop Smythies (Steere's successor) that the further extension to Lake Nyasa, the launching of the *Charles Janson* upon its stormy waters, and the settlement upon its beautiful island of Likoma, are associated. It was to serve " the tribes dwelling in the neighbourhood of the Lake Nyasa and River Shiré " that Bishop Mackenzie had been consecrated. The abandonment of that arena had been a heart-breaking disappointment to Livingstone. Now at last two Missions were at work on Lake Nyasa, the U.M.C.A. on the West Bank, the Livingstonian Mission of the Free Church of Scotland on the East, with Blantyre for capital; the Scottish hospital and Doctor Laws eager from the start to save the life and cultivate the friendship of the saintly Johnson, whose physique and semi-blindness held out little prospect of his being able to withstand the hardships and perils of a pioneering life for fifty-two years.

The last great extension westward, associated with Bishop Hine and the diocese of Northern Rhodesia, was an outcome of the U.M.C.A. Jubilee in 1907, and falls therefore outside our period; as also does the later development of Theological and Training Colleges, Schools and Hospitals, and the Community of the Sacred Passion. It remains only to note in passing, some points of contrast between a Mission started in the middle of the nineteenth century and those of an earlier foundation. The support of persons eminent in Church and State, and of crowds, was, as we have seen, forthcoming to a degree that would have been unthinkable fifty years earlier. That the principles upon which the Mission was to be founded should be debated in Convocation, would have been unthinkable ten years before, for the Canterbury Convocation had only just been revived. In both the Houses it was agreed that there were cases where it might be "expedient to send out presbyters in the first instances as evangelists," others where it may be desirable to send forth a Bishop at once as the head of a Mission, that Central Africa belonged to the latter category, and that it was hoped "that the Bishop of Capetown and his Comprovincials may be able to see fit to admit the head of this mission into the Episcopal order."

The Bishops of these dioceses were held to be bound by the decrees of the mother-Church, in force at the time of their consecration, though not to new decrees or canons. This "special need of combined councils to maintain in unity the Church as it extends" suggested a regular gradation of duly-constituted Synods, Diocesan, Provincial, National, culminating in a General Council.

The episode marks an epoch in the attitude of the "official" Church towards expansion overseas. The Mission, however, was not overawed by the dignity of its antecedents into undue subservience to precedent or prejudice. It was founded at a time when many were kicking against the pricks of ecclesiastical coercion, restless for freedom of expression according to new or revived patterns. It was natural enough that when like-minded men found themselves members of a celibate brotherhood, living hard lives, confronting over-whelming odds, remote from the frowns of conscientious objectors, they should experience a sense of liberation and express themselves in forms of worship and articles of association congenial to their convictions.

To listen to Bishop Smythies in Synod must have relaxed many men's tensions: " I wish to allow the largest liberty in all methods which may be adopted by individual priests for the sake of deepening devotion and reverence, especially in the direction of ancient custom and Catholic precedent. Holding that the Church of England is a part of the Catholic Church, I will not hamper the liberty of any priest who interprets her rules in the most Catholic sense. " Quod semper, quod ubique, quod ab omnibus." Here, therefore, a new and deeply-interesting factor appears in the expanison of the Anglican Communion which must be approached with reverence and understanding. Several generations of African Christians have been reborn and bred according to this one tradition; they know no other; this is the guise in which Christ came to them. It holds accordingly their love and loyalty and evokes the response of their hearts. No one could doubt that who, however bewildered by an unfamiliar liturgy in an unknown tongue, has shared in the worship of Zanzibar Cathedral or the Choral Eucharist at Kiwanda School, sung corporately in rich harmonies by the boys themselves as they gather soundlessly, because bare-footed, round the altar, to partake of the Holy Sacrament in which all difference is transcended.

Yet another distinctive characteristic of the U.M.C.A. is that it disclaims the style and title " Missionary Society." As Bishop Steere wrote in 1881, " Our Universities' Mission is not a Society to encourage and support a Mission to Central Africa—it is an actual Mission living and working in the country itself. . . . Our Missionaries are not dictated to by any home committee. The Church has been a missionary body from its foundation, and its Episcopate are by the very nature of their office the chiefs of its Missions." In other words, the executive is on the spot: dependent upon home organization for maintaining knowledge and interest in Great Britain; for the replenishment of its resources in men and women and money, and for the counsel of such leaders as Edward Talbot, Gore and Scott-Holland; but independent in the sphere of local government, administration and " use." Here again is material to be examined when we consider the constitutional expansion of the Church.

THE SEE OF EASTERN EQUATORIAL AFRICA (1884)

UGANDA (1897), MOMBASA (1897), CENTRAL TANGANYIKA (1927), THE UPPER NILE (1926)

In *East Africa and its Invaders*, the first volume of his classic trilogy, Professor Coupland devotes a chapter to " The Missionary Invasion ":—

> " The figures of these early-Victorian missionaries stand at the very front of the stage on which this book is set. They were

true 'invaders' of East Africa. Before they came, American and German business-men had skimmed the coast for trade, but Krapf and Rebmann invaded the mainland itself. Since the Portuguese were swept southwards in the seventeenth century they were the first Europeans to make their homes on the coast for many years. And they were the first Europeans of all time to penetrate to Kilimanjaro and the outskirts of the Kenya Highlands. Nor was the objective of their 'invasion' limited in space or time. They contemplated a steady advance right through the continent. 'A missionary,' Krapf once noted in his journal, 'often shares in common the desires and aspirations of a great conqueror'; and indeed Krapf's 'chain of missions' was akin in principle to Seyyid Said's chain of trading-posts, and Cecil Rhodes' 'Cape to Cairo' railway. Nor were these missionaries to come and go like raiders. Their chain was meant to grip the people of Africa as a railway grips its soil. . . . The founding of the Rabai mission marks the first appearance of a dominant and permanent factor in the process of invasion.

We left Krapf at the end of our chapter on German Auxiliaries (p. 78) sorrowing in solitude over the grave of wife and children, but assuring the Home Committee that " the victories of the Church are gained by stepping over the graves of her members," or as he put it on other occasions " God bids us build a cemetery before we build a Church; though many may fall in the fight, yet the survivors will pass over the slain in the trenches and take this great African fortress for the Lord." This was in 1844.

The Sultan of Zanzibar had been surprisingly gracious and armed him with a passport: " This comes from Seyyid Said. Greeting to all our subjects, friends and governors. This letter is written on behalf of Dr. Krapf, the German, a good man, who wishes to convert the world to God. Behave well to him and be everywhere serviceable to him."[1] Hamerton, the British Consul also, though trained in the traditions of the East India Company, received him with his famous cordiality and exuberant hospitality. " Hamerton," wrote Speke, " literally studied the mode of making people happy." Krapf certainly needed all the encouragement he could get. His journeys and his colleague Rebmann's, won them fame as the discoverers of snow peaks on the equator, but they landed him in

[1] Krapf's *Travels*, p. 127.

desperate adventures.   Their settlement at Rabai on the mainland opposite Mombasa was an oasis, but exposed to the incursions of disease and violence.

Krapf was not destined to forge more than the first links in the chain of his vision—he was invalided home after twelve years' service leaving Rebmann to hold the fort for twenty years longer—but he had a Swahili Bible ready for his successors.   He had moreover convinced the authorities at home when in their cautious fear " lest they be led away by grand schemes foolishly to risk the lives of missionaries and the expenditure of sacred funds," they proceeded " rigidly and faithfully to try the question whether these extensive aims were the dreams of enthusiasts or the sober calculations of wise men."   How little data had they on which to base so massive a decision ; but Henry Venn, the Secretary of the C.M.S., boldly charged their missionaries not to settle down in one place but " to branch out far and wide, witnessing to the truth of God in successive tribes and countries."

That was in 1851.   Nearly a quarter of a century was to pass before the chain began to unroll to any spectacular length.   Missionaries lost their lead in the race for the interior.   They were outstripped by the explorers Burton and Speke, Baker and Grant, though Speke was generous in acknowledgement of their help:—

> " The missionaries are the prime and first promoters of this discovery (of the Victoria Nyanza).   They have for years been doing their utmost with simple sincerity, to Christianise this Negro land.   They heard of a large lake or inland sea. . . . Not being able to gain information of any land separations to the said water, they very naturally, and I may add fortunately, put upon the map that monster slug of an inland sea which so much attracted the attention of the geographical world and caused our being sent to Africa."[1]

This was an allusion to Krapf's map of 1843, and his speculations on the sources of Nile and Congo.   The " monster slug " was discovered to be triple.   Three great Lakes punctuated the " enormous African rift system, extending nearly 2,000 miles from South of the Zambesi to the Sudan and Abyssinia."[2]   We have already visited

---

[1] Speke: *Nile Sources*, Vol. I.
[2] Julian Huxley: *Africa View*.

the Southern Lake, Nyasa, and must now turn our attention
to the Northern Lake, Victoria Nyanza.

It was in 1875 that H. M. Stanley, already famous for
his discovery of Livingstone, wrote from the capital of
Mutesa, King of Uganda, challenging Christendom to
send a mission to Lake Victoria. Airborne travellers can
now eat their breakfast on the Lake and their lunch at
Mombasa, but the first missionary party took six months to
cover the ground. They reached the southern end of the
Lake on January 29th, 1877, and the capital of Uganda
on June 30th.

Almost at any moment in the course of the next two
decades, plausible reasons could have been and were
adduced for abandoning the Uganda "Arnhem." Smith,
the Aberdonian Doctor, died in May. Mutesa's cordial
reception was of the nature of a false dawn. Within a few
months Sherwood Smith, the leader of the expedition, son
of a midshipman on the ship which rescued young Samuel
Crowther, and O'Neill, a diocesan architect from Cork,
had been killed in a fracas between Arabs and a local Chief.
How could Wilson be left month after month alone in
Mengo ? Worse still, how could Alexander Mackay be
left there alone for year after year ? Of the rescue-party
of three, who with General Gordon's active help had
succeeded in reaching Uganda by the Nile route, two had
soon to be invalided home. James Hannington with two
companions was sent out as reinforcement in 1882, but he
had no sooner reached the Lake than he was sent straight
back to England a sick man and told that he could never
hope to return. Before any lasting impression could be
made on the mind of Mutesa, Roman priests arrived and
bewildered him by denunciation of the Protestants as
deceivers. " Every white man has a different religion.
How can I know what is right ? "

True, Mackay's charm and grace were not unfruitful:
five well-tested converts were baptized in 1882, and a sixth
who had been smuggled to the coast out of reach of per-
secutors was received into the Church by the Fathers of
the U.M.C.A., to return later to a conspicuous share in
the making of Christian history in his own country. By
October 1883 there were twenty-one to be admitted to

the Holy Communion.   But in 1884 " Mutesa was succeeded by his eighteen-year-old son, Mwanga, who with
more vices but far less courage and political acumen than
his father, soon found the presence of Mackay and his two
colleagues irksome.   Christian notions of conduct were
already becoming known, and Mackay, with his long
residence and acquaintance with Mwanga as a youth,
did not fear to expostulate with him.   Mwanga showed
his spite as early as January 1885, when he found a pretext
for burning to death three lads from Mackay's personal
following, who are accordingly commemorated as the first
Christian martyrs."[1]

Worse was to follow.   In the next year, persecution
broke out which moved *The Times* to recall in a leading
article the saying that the blood of the martyrs is the seed
of the Church.   " On the success of the Uganda experiment, with its alternation of favourable and adverse circumstances, depends the happiness of the interior of the
vast continent for generations. . . . There would have been
no shame had the Mission voluntarily broken itself up in
the face of the young King's insolent enmity.   Its per-
sistency is not only magnanimous; it is the one way of
testing the ability of Christian truth and humanity to hold
its ground, without the accessories of gun-boats and rifles
against both heathendom and Islam."   Some thirty-two
Protestants were burned to death and thirteen Roman
Catholics, while others to a total of 200 perished for
suspected complicity in dangerous thinking.

The inviolability of Europeans had been disproved for
Mwanga, and any inhibitions he may have had had been
relaxed, first by the death of Gordon, and less remotely
by the death of Hannington.   Great expectations centred
round the coming of Hannington: he had made a marvel-
lous recovery and no physical unfitness any longer discounted the spiritual fitness of his noble character for
leadership of the Uganda venture.   Hopes revived with
his consecration, and at Frere Town, the Mission's base
on the coast, guns fired and horns blew.   He braved a new
route, pioneered by James Thomson, one of the gentlest
and most attractive of nineteenth-century explorers, making

[1] Thomas and Scott: *Uganda.*

a northern arc through Masrai country to the northern end of the Lake instead of the usual southern arc sweeping round to the southern end. But this was an approach jealously guarded for fear of an enemy finding entrance by Uganda's back door. The Bishop had separated from his party when he was seized: after eight days of captivity in a verminous hut, while the Chief waited for his instructions, he was put to death; the journal's record has survived. Sadly his party returned to Rabai, bearing a banner with the strange device " Ichabod " (I Samuel, 4. 21).

In the capital, Mackay's position was becoming more and more precarious; it might have become impossible much earlier if his skill with forge and lathe had not made him indispensable to the King. The sinister darkness of Mwanga's still-standing court, its thatch-roof supported by a forest of poles, its approach through one guard-house after another, strikes dread in the most casual visitor: but Mackay was habitually in this den, serenely confronting the lion's angry roar. When he was banished, though Mwanga accepted a gallant substitute, it might well have seemed that the Mission was doomed. All the more so when Hannington's successor, Bishop Parker, died within a few months of arrival on the Lake. The next year a Mohammedan rising dispersed into exile Christian chiefs and converts both Protestant and Catholic, while missionaries, both Protestant and Catholic, with difficulty escaped together on the Mission steamer.

A year later (1890) Mackay himself died. He had served for an unbroken spell of fourteen years, never losing his nerve, never abandoning his reading, never slackening in his work of translation, never wanting in tenderness nor truculent in argument, never too pre-occupied with his visions to turn his hand to printing-press or boat-building. Indeed, his visions of Africa for the African and its regeneration by the African, found expression in engineering terms. The new Forth Bridge and the Canti-lever principle suggested by analogy his strategy for the African Church; for strategist he was, as aware as the sternest critic of the weakness of a long line of communications thinly held, and of the necessity of a stronger base of

operations on the coast.   H. M. Stanley had recorded his
impressions of a visit to Usambiro:—

> " God knows, if ever man had reason to be doleful and lonely
> and sad, Mackay had, when, after murdering his Bishop and
> burning his pupils and strangling his converts and clubbing to
> death his dark friends, Mwanga turned his eye of death on him.
> And yet the little man met it with calm blue eyes that never
> winked.   To see one man of this kind, working day after day
> bravely and without a syllable of complaint or moan among the
> wilderness, and to hear him lead his little flock to show forth
> God's loving-kindness in the morning and His faithfulness every
> night, is worth going a long journey, for the moral courage and
> contentment that one derives from it."

Ten days after the news of Mackay's death had reached
England, Bishop Tucker was consecrated; hopes revived
and this time were vindicated, for his episcopate lasted
eighteen years; though three of his party of seven died,
Hooper began a great work at Jilore near Mombasa, and
Pilkington in the seven years before his untimely death,
completed the translation of the New Testament.

But there was still fuel for the pessimists' fire.   Were
political conditions stable enough to justify further commitments ?   Mwanga was favouring the French and had
made a treaty with the Germans.   The Imperial British
East Africa Company, founded by those who put welfare
before dividends, had been empowered by Royal Charter
to adminster the country, but it was coming to the end of
its resources.   Unless the British Government could be
induced to subsidize the railway to the Lake which the
Company had begun as the most effective check to the
Slave Trade, it must resign its Charter and evacuate
Uganda, and where would the Mission be then ?   *The
Times* answered the question on September 28th, 1892:—

> " The probable and almost inevitable result would be an im-
> mediate massacre of the Native converts and European mission-
> aries; a state of anarchy . . . the resurrection of the Slave Trade
> in its worst form; the entire collapse of the policy which whether
> as regards the Slave Trade or the development of the African
> continent, the Government has so courageously and hitherto so
> successfully followed.   Indeed the consequences of withdrawal
> might well assume the proportions of a national disaster."

This was the justification for the most flagrant and the
most felicitous incursion of the Church into politics.

Bishop Tucker's passionate denunciation of torn-up treaties was responsible for raising £16,000 towards the £40,000 required to secure postponement of the decision. He maintained that it was not a case of the missionaries compromising the Government but of the Government compromising the missionaries. When the three months' grace expired, orders were actually sent to Captain Lugard, the Company's Agent in Uganda, to withdraw; " an astounding communication," he wrote, " a thunderbolt indeed, a collapse terrible in its results, a cruel wrong." But by this time public opinion was aflame. Government capitulated; the new Foreign Secretary, Lord Rosebery, made it a condition of accepting office in Mr. Gladstone's Ministry that Uganda should not be deserted:—

> " Continuity of moral policy is a moral force by which in my opinion this country has to be judged. It is the salt which savours our history; it is a spirit which has exalted it and it is by that when we have passed away that in my belief we shall come to be judged. As Greece is best remembered by her literature, Rome by her laws, so this country, when this country stands before history, will stand not by her fleets or her armies or her commerce but by her herioc self-denying exertions which she has put forward to put down this iniquitous traffic."

In June 1894 the establishment of a British Protectorate in Uganda was proclaimed and the Company's Charter annulled. Colonial affairs were seen to have assumed too great an importance and to be fraught with too many international complications to be left any longer to a Chartered Company, however enlightened; they must be placed under a Minister responsible to Parliament. Tenniel's cartoon in *Punch* shows John Bull opening his front-door to find a black foundling baby in a basket on the step, under the caption, " What, another! Well, I suppose I must take it in! " But the pessimist could still point to the hostilities, not so much between Protestant and Catholic as between pro-English and pro-French parties, which it took all Lugard's strength and wisdom to allay, and to the dangerous instability of the country as a field for missions as long as it depended for its security on Sudanese mercenaries. It was at the end of the second decade that Pilkington met his death as the result of a Sudanese insurrection.

The young Church which had passed through so many vicissitudes was none the less strong enough to extend into neighbouring Kingdoms outside Uganda proper: 20,000 worshippers gathered in its Churches on Sundays, and in Bishop Tucker it had a leader well-qualified for the work of consolidation. As in Ireland a Church that has grown up cheek by jowl with a strong Roman Catholic rival develops a strong Protestant tradition; such is the tradition in which Uganda Anglicans have been reborn and bred; they know no other: this is the guise in which Christ came to them: it is the tradition which evokes their love and loyalty: its strength is in its Biblical foundation. No one can doubt that who has watched a congregation finding the place of the text as soon as announced, even though it be from one of the less easily identified books. There is, too, a numinous quality in the worship of a village con- gregation or a Choral Eucharist at King's College, Budo, or Nyakasura School.

Sixty years after the entry of the Gospel into Uganda the event was commemorated in the domed Cathedral on Namirembe Hill. A procession of ninety African clergy and eighty African choirmen and boys wound its way to the west door past the garden of roses where lie Hanning- ton, Mackay, Pilkington and many other makers of Church history, African and European. In this setting the words of the Te Deum, " The noble army of martyrs praise Thee," the words of the hymn, " For all the Saints, who Thee before the world confessed, the Saints who nobly fought of old, the fellowship divine where all are one in Thee for all are Thine," acquired a deep significance. An immense congregation joined in the hymn " Daily, daily, sing the praises," which Uganda's first martyrs had sung at the stake. The service closed with the Hallelujah Chorus, conducted by the African organist. Something of the blood and sweat and toil and tears which were the cost of the ascent to this summit it has been the purpose of this section to relate.

PART VIII

THE FAR EAST

1. The Church in Burma; Adoniram Judson; The Karens; John Ebenezer Marks.

2. The Church in the Straits and Borneo; Sir Stamford Raffles; Rajah Brooks; Bishop McDougall.

3. The Church in China: (*a*) China a closed door; (*b*) China between the Treaties; (*c*) China between the Treaties and the Revolution.

4. The Church in Korea ; Bishop Corfe ; Bishop Turner ; Bishop Trollope.

5. The Church in Japan; Anglo-American partnership; The Nippon Sei Ko Kwai; Bishop Edward Bickersteth.

THE Churches in Burma, Borneo, Malaya, China and Korea, which were overtaken by the Japanese avalanche in 1942, were among the youngest and the most hardly won of the nineteenth-century extensions of the Anglican Communion. The Church in Japan itself was no farther distant from the date of its foundation than the birth of Bede from the coming of St. Augustine. Time will reveal the full story of how these Churches have stood the test, and weathered the rigours of what in respect of their youth may be likened in severity to a late Spring frost. This chapter sets out to sketch the background against which the story, when it can be told, can be seen in its full significance. The task is the easier in that names which a few years ago would have meant little or nothing have lately become household words, and the scenes of early missionary activity have become familiar as the arena of naval and military activities in which our kith and kin have been engaged.

THE CHURCH IN BURMA

ADONIRAM JUDSON

Mandalay, for example, so long a mere symbol of romance, so recently a symbol of heroism, has been associated with some of the finest episodes in the history of Christian expansion since long before it superseded Ava as the new King's capital in 1857, for it was to this region that Adoniram Judson, the American Baptist, penetrated in 1821. Judson's arrival in Burma in 1812 was to all appearances curiously fortuitous. He had intended to throw in his lot with Carey at Serampore, but reached India at the only moment in the nineteenth century when an American, owing to hostilities with Canada, could be regarded as an enemy alien. The ban on missionaries was not yet lifted and Judson received short shrift from the authorities. After four months in French Mauritius he set sail for Penang, but his ship got into difficulties off the Andamans and deposited him on the coast of Burma. For ten years Judson and his wife endured a very primitive Rangoon, " a miserable dirty town containing eight or ten thousand inhabitants, almost without drainage and intersected by muddy creeks through which the tide flowed at high water." Four years of study enabled him to complete the Gospel of St. Matthew in Burmese, but it was six years before he could preach, and six years before the first convert was baptized. Buddhism presented an impregnable front and an arbitrary monarch threatened torture for heretics and forbad the distribution of books. It was Dr. Price's reputation for successful cataract operations that won the King's ear, and the prospects at Ava seemed promising enough to justify a move to the capital It was an ill-fated moment. The first Anglo-Burmese war broke out and Judson starved in a noisome gaol as a suspected spy. Judson survived a further twenty-five years in Burma; he completed the Burman Bible and a Burman dictionary, and saw an infant Church in being.

THE KARENS

The Baptist Church had taken root in Karen rather than Burman soil, and it was the story of the growing Karen Church which stimulated the Anglican Church to an active interest in Burma; there are Karens in the ranks of the Anglican ministry to-day. The Karens are the most numerous of the peoples of Burma, numbering over eleven million: they reached Burma some centuries ago from the borders of Tibet across the Gobi desert, held themselves aloof in the agricultural Highlands, fostered a folk-lore rich in picturesque and moralizing fables, and maintained a religious tradition so full of Biblical analogies that some have supposed them to be one of the lost tribes of Israel Their version of Creation, of a Garden containing a Tree of Life and a Tree of Death, of the Temptation and Fall of man, and of the moral code, have been traced to contact with Armenian Jews who made their way to China in the early Middle Ages. The Karens held by immemorial tradition that their ancestors had been in possession of a Book containing the Word of God. It had been forfeited by neglect and given to their younger brother, the white man, who was placed under obligation to restore the volume once they had atoned for their sins; the white man would one day arrive, riding in ships and boats. " God will again have mercy upon us; God will yet save us again." The first convert, Judson's water-carrier, greeted the Gospel as the fulfilment of the long-predicted return of God to his nation through the white man. " Now is fulfilled that which was spoken by the prophets " became the burden of his message to his fellow-Karens, and it awoke them to new life. The Chief Commissioner of Burma wrote in 1863 that when, ten years before, British troops had occupied Toungo, the Karens were in a savage state. " In process of time, from the constant labours of the American missionaries, many thousands of the mountain Karens were instructed in Christianity, abandoned their savage mode of life and their cruel wars, and lived as Christian men and women. I assert, from long experience among similar tribes, that such results could not be attained by the civil administration unaided by missionary teaching."[1] By 1852, two years after Judson's death, there were sixty-two missionaries and 7,750 Karen Christians belonging to the American Baptists who were also at work among the Chins, Kachins and Shans; by 1910 the Karen Church numbered over 50,000.[2]

[1] D. M. Smeaton, I.C.S.: *The Loyal Karens of Burma.*

[2] Bernard Fergusson in *Beyond the Chindwin* writes: " Nobody who has served with Karens could fail to like them. They are mostly Christians (to a degree which would put to shame most people who profess and call themselves such). They make admirable soldiers, intelligent, willing, energetic, brave."

JOHN EBENEZER MARKS

It was on a far more modest scale that the Church of England entered the field. The S.P.G. sent its first missionary in 1859. Within the next thirty-three years, twenty-seven names appear upon its roll. The records show that their average period of service was six years: Marks was still in Burma in 1892 after thirty-three years' service: Fairclough, after twenty-six years: only three others had reached double figures: it cannot therefore be said that the mission was over-staffed. John Ebenezer Marks was so dominant a figure throughout this period that the story is inevitably focussed on his biography. He was pre-eminently a schoolmaster, modelling himself upon Dr. Arnold, and proud to serve under Bishop Cotton of Calcutta, formerly Master of Marlborough and the " new master " of *Tom Brown's School Days*. It was as a lay schoolmaster that he started life at Moulmein in 1860. But he was much more than a schoolmaster, and St. John's College, which he founded in Rangoon, was much more than a self-contained educational institution. Pre-occupied as he was with the building of his school, and possessed of all the instincts for individual dealing with his pupils, his mind roamed at large over problems of educational and mission strategy. He was determined to extend the benefits of Christian education to people and places not yet reached. " I constantly pointed out how useless it was to continue the education of Burmese boys, if on arriving at manhood, they only had ignorant uninstructed girls to marry." While on furlough, he secured in Miss Cooke the first Principal of St. Mary's School, Rangoon, which she opened in 1865: " almost every race in Rangoon is represented in it."

" At a meeting called to sponsor an orphanage for children of mixed parentage whose European fathers accepted no responsibility for their Burmese ' wives,' I got no sympathy. I was assured that I was attempting to condone immorality and promote concubinage : the proposition was almost unanimously negatived "; nevertheless the orphanage was established within the St. John's College compound.

Marks initiated a chain of outpost schools up the Irra-waddy and Sittang valleys: " all the schools founded by me were conducted upon the same plan, so that boys migrating from one to the other found themselves at home in their new school as much as in the one they had left." It is reckoned that 150,000 pupils came under his influence in these S.P.G. schools in the thirty-five years of his life in Burma: they were bound together by strong ties of loyalty as " Dr. Marks' pupils "; amongst those whom he baptized, three had been ordained before he left the country. All this time the foundations were being laid for a future University of Rangoon, in co-operation with the Roman Catholic Bishop Bigandet, whose relations with Marks were so happy that in an emergency he offered to lend the services of two Brothers: " they shall teach nothing that you do not wish, merely directing the secular instruc-tion and carrying out your own plans." In 1913, when the University was established, Sir John Jardine wrote to Dr. Marks (he had been given a Lambeth D.D. by Archbishop Tait): " I write in fulness of heart to you, as I shall never forget how thoroughly you worked in this great cause, and how constantly and warmly you sup-ported our early efforts. You and I had to frame a policy, and to fight for it and spend many weary hours over it. I hope that our labours and honest hopes have been blessed, and that we have done something for the public welfare, and in the spirit of the Author of our Faith."

But Marks' strategy was not confined to Lower Burma: he was determined to carry the Mission across the for-bidden frontier to Mindon Min's new capital of Mandalay. Authorities were sternly discouraging. " We have had two expensive Burmese wars. Our relations with the King are more amicable and advantageous than we have ever had with his predecessors. He prides himself on being entitled the ' Great Chief of Righteousness and Defender of the Buddhist Faith.' He is a very devout Buddhist. The Government of India is very anxious to continue on good terms with him. He would resent our permitting the entry of an English missionary." But His Majesty had heard of St. John's College from one of his sons and commanded the presence of its Head. Up went Marks accompanied by six of his boys. Ceremonial visits followed, and less ceremonial conversations, as a result of which not only a school but a Church were built at the King's expense, Queen Victoria presenting the font. Bishop Milman came from Calcutta to consecrate the Church in 1873.

King Thibaw, who succeeded in 1878, was not one of the more satisfactory products of the royal S.P.G. school. "He killed his brothers and sisters, and he drinks gin. He had been a surly and morose boy, sitting apart and never coming to school on the same elephant with the other Princes: he was fond of cricket but used unprincely language to anyone who bowled him. When the servants of 'the Foreign Woman,' Her Most Gracious Majesty Queen Victoria, protested against his summary settlement of domestic matters, he swore a royal oath that he would never look on a white man again. Secret treatings with France and autocratic dealings with the Bombay Burma Trading Company brought about a rupture. The Burmese Kingdom fell with the suddenness of a paralytic stroke, and King Thibaw was a prisoner within a month of his rejection of the British ultimatum."[1]

There had been exciting episodes in the early days of the reign. A young missionary, James Colbeck, describes in his blithe letters home his ingenious rescues of some of Thibaw's intended victims, which came near to involving him in a repetition of Judson's fate. But now Lord Dufferin arrived in state, a railway was begun, Marks found himself preaching to British troops in the audience hall of the Palace with his back to the throne. The modern epoch had begun.

The mention of Colbeck, one of the most winsome and saintly of S.P.G. missionaries (he died in 1888 at the age of thirty-six) recalls aspects of the Church in Burma with which Dr. Marks was less intimately associated. On his arrival in 1874, he worked among the Tamils, large numbers of whom, educated and uneducated, migrate to Burma from South India, many of them from Christian homes. In Kemendine, a Rangoon suburb, Colbeck lived in a native house in a single upper room, which served as

[1] Shway Yoe: *The Burman: his Life and Notions.*

study, bedroom and dining-room, with the lower storey for Chapel. " I shall not easily forget my first visit." wrote the first Bishop of Rangoon; " when climbing up to his room by a rough ladder and afterwards attending service in his little chapel I witnessed the simplicity and earnestness of his long labours for the Lord."

Bishop Titcomb also visited the newly started Karen Mission at Toungo in 1878, and ordained the first four Karen deacons: the nucleus of the Church were seceders from the Baptist Church, who after ten years of hesitation and with the consent of the Baptists had been received into the Anglican Church to save them from lapsing into paganism. Bishop Strachan visited the Karens in 1884 at their annual conference and was impressed by the growth of the Karen Church. " There has been an increase of 2,500 in three years. There used to be constant deadly feuds between these tribes, but the recognition of a common brotherhood in Christ Jesus has altered all this. The missionaries have wisely left everything almost entirely in the hands of the natives. Besides building their own churches and schoolrooms without any extraneous help, they subscribed last year nearly Rs. 1,000." The Bishop was a doctor of medicine. " I had provided myself with a good supply of medicines and soon had a large number of patients."

The Diocese of Rangoon had been separated from Calcutta in 1877, one-fourth of the endowment (£10,000) being contributed by the diocese of Winchester. Winchester thus set a precedent for the adoption of an oversea by a home diocese. The link was further strengthened by the formation in the early '90's of a Winchester Brotherhood for service in Burma.

THE CHURCH IN THE STRAITS
AND BORNEO

Two romantic Englishmen exercised a conspicuous influence on the Eastward expansion of the Church— Stamford Raffles (born at sea off Jamaica, 1781), and James Brooke (born at Benares, 1803). Each had a minimum of schooling but a life-long passion for self-education. They shared an Elizabethan flavour, a roaming disposition, a capacity for rule, an instinct for liking and understanding Malays, and a humanitarian outlook in advance of their age. Both came to loggerheads with Governments to whom the defects of their qualities were more obvious than the qualities themselves. Both incurred the obloquy of those whose vigilance for the national honour is only exceeded by the intensity of their conviction that no good thing can come out of Britain.

Raffles won his way by unassisted merit from a stool in Leadenhall Street to a £1,500 a year post in the Government of Penang. Nothing Malayan was alien to him; the people, their history, archæology, customs, language and prospects became his absorbing interest. A fierce report on the proposed restoration of Malacca to the Dutch won the ear of Lord Minto, who commandeered his services for the invasion of Java, and established him in authority for the five years of British occupation. The Dutch East Indies had become French when Napoleon appropriated Holland. With the peace, Java was restored to the Dutch, but Raffles' original experiments in Indirect Rule were not wholly wasted. He withdrew to Sumatra as Lieutenant Governor at Bencoolen. There is now a strong self-respecting Church of a half-million Bataks in Sumatra, but that belonged to the still distant and unforeseen future of the 1860's when the German pioneers of the Rhenish Missionary Society would begin their perilous adventure. Raffles' Sumatra was primitive and precariously held, but it served as an observation-post for his watch upon the interests of British Far Eastern trade. This is not the place to tell how Raffles put his telescope to his blind eye and in daring defiance of his own Government and the Dutch won Singapore by treaty with the local Sultan and created out of " a derelict native village a city and free port commanding the shortest route between Europe and China."[1]   " But for my Malay studies," he wrote, " I should hardly have known that such a place existed; not only the English but also the Indian world was ignorant of it. . . .   Our object is not territory but trade; a great commercial emporium and fulcrum whence

[1] R. Coupland: *Raffles of Singapore*.

we may extend our influence. One free port in these seas must eventually destroy the spell of Dutch monopoly; and what Malta is to the West, that may Singapore become in the East."[1]

Raffles' interests were by no means exclusively political or commercial. The Institute which he founded in Singapore is a monument to his enthusiasm for culture. It was to be not merely a College but a centre of research for all studies connected with the Malay race. "Thus will our stations become not only the centres of commerce and its luxuries, but of refinement and the liberal arts. If commerce brings wealth to our shores it is the spirit of literature and philanthropy that teaches us how to employ it for the noblest purposes. If the time shall come when Britain's Empire shall have passed away, these monuments of her virtue will endure when her triumphs have become an empty name. Let it still be the boast of Britain to write her name in characters of light."[2] When he came home to live next to William Wilberforce at Mill Hill, and to arrange such of his vast collection of flora and fauna as had survived a disastrous fire on the voyage, he founded the Zoo. He died before Wilberforce had settled at Mill Hill, but they sit on contiguous pedestals in Westminster Abbey, guarding the grave of Purcell.

Nor was Raffles indifferent to the religious implications of European contact with Eastern peoples. He was among the first to welcome Bishop Middleton on his visitation of Penang in 1819, and to subsidize the branches of the S.P.C.K. in Penang and Bencoolen. Antipathy to Dutch monopoly did not blind him to the value of their missionary penetration of the Archipelago. "The propagation of Christianity among these islands is liable to none of those objections which have been urged against it in our Indian possessions. A great proportion of the nation are still pagans under the influence of a wild and almost incorrigible superstition. . . . The attachment of the Malays to the religion of Islam is by no means of that strength to inspire them with that contempt and hatred for other religions as is found in many of the older Moslem Kingdoms." Writing to a missionary cousin he admits

[1] H. E. Egerton: *Sir Stamford Raffles.*   [2] R. Coupland: *Raffles of Singapore.*

that " I am a good deal more inclined than you are to let people go to heaven their own way, and foresee much bitterness and contention by an inordinate desire for conversion. . . . I abhor and abominate the tenets of Mohammedanism and verily believe that it is the religion of all others most likely to enslave the minds and bodies of mankind. I am Utopian enough to think that a new system altogether founded on the principles of Christianity and modified according to the temper of the people, would be better than the naked revelation at once, which they would neither desire or relish." " Religion and laws are so united in these countries that I don't see what good can arise by giving people a new system of the one without also a new system of the other. . . . I will commute with you by recommending a vigorous conversion of Borneo, almost the largest island in the world and thickly peopled by a race scarcely emerged from barbarism."

BORNEO

Raffles may be credited with a larger influence on the expansion of the Church to Borneo than this playful recommendation. It is doubtful whether Sir James Brooke could have achieved the Rajahship of Sarawak without Raffles' Singapore within call. It is doubtful whether Christianity could have been introduced to Borneo without the Rajah's encouragement and the comparative peace and civilization which his rule ensured. The Rajah's life was written by one who confessed to an antipathy to the Bishop and his mission, based largely on anti-theological prepossessions. The fact remains that when a Borneo Church Association was formed and invited McDougall to be its first missionary, the Rajah showed himself gratified by the selection. It is likely that his motives in welcoming the Mission did not coincide with those of its supporters. Though sufficiently interested in theological debate to toss off a long reply to Tract XC in a leisure moment, his mind was " sceptical and controversial rather than unbelieving."[1] But he was anxious to civilize his people and acknowledged in Christianity " the highest form of religion, and believed the Church

---

[1] Bunyon: *Memoir of Bishop McDougall.*

of England to be the most free, as he trusted she would be the most patient and most loving, of communions." In later days, the Bishop, as the friend of both, became involved in the controversy between the Rajah and the nephew, whom he curtly disinherited, but that should not be allowed to eclipse the earlier years of intimate friendship between the two, and the Rajah's gratitude and admiration for the Bishop's medical skill and courage in moments of crisis. This is not the place to tell the story of Rajah Brooke's adventures and adversities. The carping criticism of Gladstone and Cobden, their scepticism as to his motives and their blindness to his humanitarian reforms, the appointment of a Commission to scrutinize his conduct (from the distance of Singapore) and undermine his authority, the uncertainty over the British Government's intentions, on which the stability of his regime depended, combined with local reverses and a tropical climate to elicit the defects of his qualities.

The Bishop as a soldier's son had had an abnormal upbringing, in Corfu, Cephalonia, Malta. An Admiral had made him a Midshipman at the age of nine and instilled a knowledge of navigation which stood him in good stead; he was an amateur jockey at fourteen, and a medical graduate of Malta at eighteen. Not till twenty-four, after completing his medical course at King's College and walking the hospitals, did he enter Magdalen Hall (now Hertford College) and row bow in the University boat: after which he spent a year in a South Wales iron works. He was twenty-eight when he was ordained by Bishop Blomfield, and thirty-one when he arrived at Sarawak in 1848.

The vicissitudes of Mr. and Mrs. McDougall illustrate the costly character of pioneer work. They lost five children, including, on their first leave, the boy whom they had left at home. They had to start from scratch, gradually raising Church, School, Bungalow, and making their influence felt among Dyaks, Malays, Chinese. As the only surgeon in the country the Bishop's skill was in constant demand. As the only available hostess, Mrs. McDougall had to keep open house to such naval visitors as Jane Austen's Admiral brother, and such ecclesiastical

visitors as Bishop Wilson of Calcutta who came to consecrate the new Church in '51; he expressed himself
gratified by all that he saw except the volumes of Newman,
Manning, and Bishop Wilberforce on the library shelves:
he recommended Scott's *Commentaries*, and " don't tie
yourself to any book of prayer in your family devotions:
you have a copious utterance and could easily command
words in uttering your desire to God."

Translation work went forward, lithographed, not
printed, because " the Malays associate printing with
printed tracts of a violent controversial character circulated
in the Straits by Dutch and Dissenting missionaries both
American and English, whose want of judgement and
ill-sustained proselytizing efforts have certainly made the
work more difficult for those that come after." Dispensary
and hospital—McDougall's was the first Anglican medical
mission—won the confidence of Chinese (as well as Malays)
who confided their children to the Mission school. " I
have thought it best to allow the children to continue their
native dress and all Chinese customs that are not incompatible with Christianity, as by so doing they will prove
the more helpful and influential as missionaries among
their countrymen." In 1851 the Mission advanced a
step in stability by becoming a branch of the S.P.G. and
the Society began an agitation " to add to the existing
missionary the spiritual powers belonging to a Bishop—
not to make him less a missionary than before, or much
to add to the state or expense of his living." The erection
of a missionary bishopric beyond the dominions of the
Crown still presented difficulties: these could be evaded
by the happy chance that in 1846 Britain had acquired
an uninhabited island (as it then was) off the coast of
Borneo which could conveniently lend its name, Labuan,
to the proposed see. The Rajah scented an intrusion by
the Crown on his jurisdiction, and was not disposed to be
treated as a dependency of Labuan. He proposed therefore
in the exercise of his prerogative to appoint Bishop Mc-
Dougall Bishop of Sarawak, thereby enabling the Bishop's
authority to become effectual over the clergy in Borneo as a
" consensual jurisdiction " by the agreement of all parties
concerned. Hence the cumbrous title attached to this See.

The stability thus attained was not of long duration. Borneo lay midway between India and China, and suffered the repercussions of the Mutiny in the one and the "Arrow" war in the other. Chinese goldminers from across the borders of Sarawak launched a wholly unexpected attack upon Kuching, came within an ace of wiping out the whole community, and were with difficulty routed by Malays and Dyaks. "The Dyaks have all proved themselves good men and true, and shown the greatest devotion to the Rajah, and respect and consideration for us, both as teachers of religion and white men in distress. The conduct of the Chinese in sparing us and allowing this house to be a general refuge proved the influence that the work of the Mission had acquired. It is true that on their return (when I mercifully escaped) I was marked for vengeance, because I had done what I could to bring back the Rajah, and had hauled down their flag, but that was as natural on their part as it was the plain path of duty on mine. The conduct of our Chinese Christians was exemplary." The Bishop was active in attending to the wounds of friend and foe. This was not the only interruption of the smooth tenor of the Mission's ways; there were perils from cholera, perils from plots, perils from pirates; but enough has been said to explain the origin and early vicissitudes of the Church in the diocese of Labuan and Sarawak.

THE CHURCH IN CHINA

CHINA: A CLOSED DOOR

Sir Stamford Raffles alludes more than once to the activities of a Mr. Milne. He writes to his cousin in 1815: "we had a very good man of your caste among us some time since, the Rev. Mr. Milne, who is attached to the mission in China. He is a liberal, well-informed, excellent man, and I cannot say too much in his favour. Such men must do good wherever they go and are an honour to their country and to the cause they espouse. If he had remained longer among us I verily believe it would have gone hard with some hardened sinners. As you are a Director of the Missionary Society you may have it in your power to promote Mr. Milne's views. He is an honour to your Society and a jewel that cannot be too highly prized." Eight years later he writes from Singapore: " The death of my friend Dr. Milne of Malacca has for a time thrown a damp on missionary exertions in this quarter: but I expect Mr. Morrison of China to visit this place in March, and I hope to make some satisfactory arrangement with him for future labours."

A conversation between Morrison and Raffles would have been worth listening to. What had happened was this: Robert Morrison was the son of a Dumfermline farm-labourer who had settled as a boot-tree maker at Newcastle-on-Tyne, and after leaving school had been apprenticed to his father's trade. By concentrated self-education he qualified as a candidate for the Ministry, and in the year of Trafalgar, at the age of twenty-three, was accepted by the London Missionary Society and told to specialize in Chinese, medicine, and astronomy. He sailed in January 1807, in an American ship, as the East India Company would not carry him, and reached Canton via New York in September. Having arrived, what could he do ? China was bolted and barred to "barbarian" intrusion. Only on the doorstep of Portuguese Macao or on a fringe of river frontage at Canton could British merchants do business with Chinese. The Emperor accepted George the Third's gifts as a vassal's tribute, exhorted him to keep peace among his people and see to the security of his territory without relaxation, and assured him that further envoys were superfluous. " Know only to show the sincerity of your heart and study goodwill and one can then say, without the necessity of sending representatives to my Court, that you progress towards civilised transformation."[1]

One well-wisher warned Morrison that Europeans were prohibited from learning the language under penalty of death to the native teachers; another that the East India Company " forbad any person to stay but on account of trade." Life was ruinously expensive, even when living in a go-down, adopting Chinese food and clothes, and economizing to the detriment of health. Any avowal of missionary intention would mean expulsion. Morrison

[1] W. E. Soothill: *China and the West.*

solved his own problem by accepting a post as Chinese Translator to the Company, having profited by secret tuition, and from 1809 till his death in 1834, he held this position, acting Interpreter to Lord Amherst and Lord Napier on their missions to Peking. His duties did not prevent him from completing his translation of the whole Bible in twelve years and when he left on his only furlough in 1824, he could report " the Dictionary is all printed."

This did not solve the problem for anyone else. Morrison's own position was precarious enough—the Roman Catholics had succeeded in banishing his printing-press from Macao—and the introduction of missionaries would be impossible till the gates of China were unbarred. It was against that day that Morrison founded in 1820 the Anglo-Chinese College at Malacca, " the object of which should be the cultivation of English and Chinese literature in order to spread the Gospel." Milne was his partner in the enterprise and first Principal. It was a policy to commend itself to Raffles: was he not himself founding an Anglo-Malayan College at Singapore, and dwelling with characteristic foresight upon the probability of a great Chinese immigration? " Borneo and the Eastern islands may become to China what America is already to the nations of Europe." Unhappily Milne died within two years, but the College served its purpose till the Treaty of 1842 made possible a transfer to Hong Kong. It was here that the great scholar James Legge began his career, with forty-five Chinese students, on whom his hopes were set for the future Church of China. " He will prove the most efficient labourer who shall raise up workers from among Chinese young men, men who are able to teach others also, speaking to their countrymen as brother to brother. They must be pervaded with the idea that they have a great work to do, and yet must their preparation be made so that they shall not be puffed up."[1]

Meanwhile the Protestant Episcopal Church of the United States was making parallel preparations: finding work at Canton impossible, their three missionaries settled at Batavia in 1835 to work among the Chinese in Java, while they learnt the language and mentality of their

[1] H. E. Legge: *James Legge: Missionary and Scholar.*

M

pupils. They were thus equipped to start work at Shanghai when opportunity offered, and one of them, William Boone, became the first Bishop in China in 1844. " I'd give my life if I could but oil the hinges of the door," he had exclaimed when told that entry to China was impossible.

CHINA BETWEEN THE TREATIES

The early history of the Church in China cannot be regarded with any special satisfaction by the Church of England. The Roman Missions, whatever their methods, look back on centuries of service and suffering and count more martyrs than the non-Roman. Among the non-Roman the non-Episcopal outstrip the Episcopal in the magnitude of their operations. Among the Episcopal the palm must go to the Church in America rather than to the Church of England which was slow off the mark and parsimonious in support. It had not, like its sister Church in America, looked ahead to the day of Treaty-ports. The day is perhaps not far distant when British and Chinese scholars can get together to present an objective history of the events which led up to the Treaties of 1842–44 and 1858–60, marshalling the data for a final judgement which might not prove flattering to the pride of either party (though not necessarily for the traditional reasons) but might dispose of some of the obstacles to a good understanding between the two peoples. Here we are only concerned with the wars and the Treaties in their relevance to the propagation of Christianity.

The opening of Canton, Amoy, Foochow, Ningpo and Shanghai for residence and trade, and the cession of the barren island of Hong Kong under the Treaty of Nanking (1842) extended to missionaries the opportunities which had been denied to Robert Morrison. These were further extended by the Treaties of Tientsin and Peking (1858 and 1860) which not only opened more ports, and a legation in the capital, but licensed penetration into the interior and guaranteed some measure of protection for missionaries and Chinese Christians. These were great gains but they were won at a price. The Chinese could not be expected to discriminate between diplomatic, commercial and religious motives: the distinction was particularly difficult to draw when French protection of Roman Catholic Missions appeared to be based on motives of national aggrandisement. The edict which ordained that Roman Catholic bishops and priests should hold official rank—bishops equal in rank to viceroys and governors, vicars-general and arch-priests to treasurers and judges, priests to prefects—though only passed at the end of the century, was the logical climax of French policy.

Christianity has had a long struggle to live down its identification not merely with foreigners but with foreign force and foreign opium:—

> " Although the campaigns which Great Britain launched against China in 1840, 1857 and 1860, would assuredly be condemned by British standards of conscience to-day, there is clear enough evidence that they were entered into by the responsible English statesmen less in a spirit of 'jingoism' ... than in a spirit of revolt against what was genuinely felt to be intolerable grievance.
>
> " It is undeniable that the traffic in opium imported from India to Canton was morally scandalous, and none the less so because the anti-opium laws of China were habitually disregarded by the Chinese themselves, both merchants and officials. . . . On the British side the incentive to indulge in the trade lay partly in the great profits to be gained by the interested parties in India, including the government, and partly in the value of opium sales as a means of redressing the very heavy and embarrassing adverse balance of Great Britain's trade with China."[1]

It was not to be expected that the Chinese should regard the British record as otherwise than unrelievedly black; and the missionaries, obsessed by daily evidence of the moral and physical ravages of the insidious habit of opium-smoking, and embarrassed by the memory of the wars which heralded their arrival, were disposed to agree. To make amends due for wrongs done in connection with opium was as great an incentive to serve China as was their country's share in the Slave traffic to serve Africa. Exeter Hall supported the future Lord Shaftesbury, whose protest in the House of Commons against the trade in opium *The Times* pronounced " grave, temperate and practical; far more statesmanlike in its ultimate and general views than those by which it was opposed."

[1] Royal Institute of International Affairs: *British Far Eastern Policy.*

The lash of the *Church Missionary Intelligencer* was wielded remorselessly and consistently: " our whole course upon the coast of China has been one of injustice. . . . We are the great opium producers, the great poison-vendors of the East." The dilemma was posed by the future Bishop Russell in 1860: " By the Treaty now ratified, the whole of China is opened up to the preaching of the Gospel: but while we recognize in it the Hand of God, we recognize in it at the same time the hand of man, of cruel, covetous, Godless man. By the very instrument by which China is declared to have thrown open her gate to the free and unrestricted preaching of the Gospel, it is equally declared though somewhat more covertly that she has been forced by Christian England to throw open her gate to the free and unrestricted introduction of opium." The son of Lord Elgin who for their preservation had removed the marbles of the Parthenon, committed to destruction the treasures of the Summer Palace at Peking after the torture of British prisoners, to " punish the court and spare the people."

It cannot be said that the Church of England took an energetic share in availing itself of the openings offered by the Treaty of Nanking. Dr. Legge's L.M.S. College at Malacca moved to Hong Kong; Dr. Boone's settlement at Batavia moved to Shanghai, of which he was consecrated Bishop in 1844. In the same year the C.M.S. sent a Caleb and Joshua to spy out the land. Of the two, one remained in Shanghai and with three recruits three years later started a mission there and in Ning-po. The other, George Smith, of Magdalen Hall (now Hertford College) was invalided home but by 1849 was able to return as the first Bishop of Hong Kong; with four reinforcements he was able to enter another port, Fuchow. But the Anglicans were a small minority among the non-Roman missionaries whose numbers rose from thirty in 1844 to a hundred in 1865.

If heresies are, as is sometimes assumed, a symptom of vitality, the Tai'ping Rebellion may perhaps be reckoned as evidence of the extent to which the message of the Missionaries had penetrated. It arose out of the sowing of Christian ideas as less directly did the Revolution of sixty years later, and both were indebted to Christian leaders, though as might be expected the Christianity of Hung, the Tai'ping leader of 1851 was more inchoate than Sun Yat Sen's in 1911. From 1851 to 1865 rebel forces swept over Southern China and came within an ace of laying low both the Manchu dynasty and the European regime in Shanghai. The missionaries were at first perplexed, whether to bless or curse. Even Dr. Legge, who was more alive than most to the spurious elements in the movement, wrote that " the starting up on a sudden of hundreds and thousands of men and women professing such views in stereotyped and benumbed China is a phenomenon in which I dare not but magnify the power of God." Four hundred printers were employed in the production of copies of the Scriptures and of tracts which " though containing some things of doubtful character yet clearly abjure idolatry, recognize the duty to serve the living and true God, make known Jesus Christ as the only and all-sufficient Saviour, and lead the people to rejoice in the prospect of the future life disclosed by Christianity and in the duty of possessing and reading the Sacred Scriptures." The movement was Sabbatarian, anti-opium, and well-disposed to the foreigner. Even as late as 1860 the Tai'ping chief in command of the forces threatening Shanghai proclaimed that all is being done " in a spirit of real regard and consideration for our common faith."

But degeneration set in with the intoxication of power and luxury. The " Heavenly King's " visions distorted his theology and exalted himself to Messianic status. J. S. Burdon, afterwards third Bishop of Hong Kong, who visited the rebels at Soochow with the L.M.S. missionary, Griffith John, found that polygamy was compulsory for chiefs, massacres were the order of the day, and the Sacraments had fallen into desuetude. " This strange being who combines in himself much that is both childish and blasphemous, true and false, leaves the management of the war of extermination which he began and of the kingdom to his subordinates, while he applies himself mainly to the study of the Bible and Mr. Burns' illustrated translation of *The Pilgrim's Progress*." General Gordon became the Chinese

Government's instrument for the ruthless suppression of the rebels, but Professor Soothill is not convinced that the Powers backed the right horse: "In the rebels they had nominal friends. Had they early thrown in their lot with them and organized the movement, history might have been changed; certainly the Manchu dynasty would have speedily fallen and the moral tone of the movement probably been restored and strengthened."[1]

CHINA BETWEEN THE TREATIES AND THE REVOLUTION

The "Arrow" war, the capture of Peking, the Tai'ping rebellion, General Gordon's exploits, were sensational enough to awaken Church and public to the great new fact of their generation, that China was astir. It was a moment if ever there was one for the Church to concentrate its resources on a general advance. "When the earthquake of the Rebellion was over, conspicuous among the ruins were to be seen—as I saw with my own eyes, 'the idols utterly abolished by Chinese hands.' The temples were burnt and thrown down and not a whole image was to be seen in city or country for hundreds of miles. No tongue was raised in defence of idolatry; it was admitted with a sad smile of perplexity and despair that gods which could not keep their own heads on their shoulders could not be expected to preserve their worshippers from murder and rapine." So wrote Archdeacon Moule who, with his brother the Bishop, represented the C.M.S. in Chekiang.

The American Church at this time was represented by a giant: Samuel Isaac Joseph Schereschewsky (pronounced Sherry-sheffsky). By birth a Lithuanian Jew, educated at Breslau University and there converted by a missionary of the London Society, a student in turn of the Presbyterian and the Episcopal Theological Seminaries in New York, he reached China in a momentous year, 1860, and plunged at once into a profound study of the languages. "The Gospel of Christ is to be made honourable in every respect. To preach in an incomprehensible gibberish to such a

---

[1] W. E. Soothill: *China and the West*.

people as the Chinese who more than any other are fastidious about language is anything but making it honourable." It was upon a massive accumulation of Chinese learning that Schereschewsky was to base his great translations, in close partnership with Bishop Burdon of Hong Kong. But the American mission at this critical moment fell on evil days. For three out of the four years of the Civil War the American Board of Missions could send no funds to China, and of the twelve volunteers who arrived in 1859, only two were left in 1863. Eight had been recalled, one had died of cholera, one had been murdered by the rebels in Shantung. In 1864, Bishop Boone himself died.

The English Societies were in no better case. They had as we have seen in earlier chapters growing commitments elsewhere. The Church at home was more than usually preoccupied with setting its own house in order and with controversy: heresy-hunting was in full cry: Frederick Temple in *Essays and Reviews*, Frederick Denison Maurice, Kingsley, Colenso, Seeley's *Ecce Homo*—there was no lack of quarries: questions of ritual diverted much nervous energy into channels of domestic debate. The C.M.S. had ten men in China in 1862: eleven went out in the next eleven years, but the total was still only fifteen in 1872, and no university graduates had been among the recruits. The S.P.G. sent its first missionary to China in 1863, a medical man, but his purchase of a site in Peking was regarded as too grandiose and speculative and he was recalled. It was not till 1874 that another start was made. At the first Shanghai Missionary Conference in 1877 out of 126 missionaries present only twelve belonged to the C.M.S. and one to the S.P.G.

Anglican developments centred round five sees, Shanghai (1844), Hong Kong (1849), North China (1872), Mid-China (1880), West China (1895).

(a) The American diocese of Shanghai stretched six hundred miles up the Yangtze Kiang to Hankow. Here Schereschewsky who had reluctantly left his scholars and his newly-founded St. John's College to succeed Bishop Boone, set himself to establish what had been "too sporadic" and "pitifully undermanned" a mission on a firm basis.

Gradually the intervening Yangtze centres of population were occupied and adorned with Colleges, Schools and Hospitals.

(*b*) The British diocese of Victoria has throughout its history been hampered by its name. There were Victoria's in every continent. The ambiguity could be evaded by colloquial use of the title " Bishop of Hong Kong " but identification with an island colony, as it disguises to-day the character of a diocese extending across the mainland as far West as the Burma road, disguised also the juris-diction of Bishop Smith and his successors Alford and Burdon which covered all C.M.S. stations in the three coast provinces of Chekiang, Fukien, and Kwantung. From the ports the work spread inland, fostered by a growing band of Chinese evangelists. The first Chinese clergyman was ordained on Bishop Alford's arrival in 1867; four were ordained by Bishop Burdon in Chekiang in the '70's, nine in the '80's. In Fukien the number of baptized grew from 2,400 in 1882 to 5,900 in 1894; many stood firm under torture. Trinity College, Dublin, began its association with Fukien in 1887. Reinforcements also began to arrive from the Church of England Zenana Missionary Society; though founded, as its name implies, for service among the women of India, it sent thirty women to China in the decade 1885–95.

(*c*) William Russell, the first Bishop of North China, had sailed for China in 1847 and commanded the affection and regard of the Chinese to an exceptional degree. It had been maintained that the same man could not be a Crown Bishop and a missionary Bishop and that therefore the Bishop of Hong Kong should be confined to British territory and the new Bishop of North China be given supervision of all Christians owing allegiance to the Emperor of China. The twenty-eighth parallel of latitude was ultimately adopted as the boundary between dioceses, and a racial line of demarcation avoided.

On Bishop Russell's death in 1879 it was decided to carve out of North China a new diocese of Mid-China. Charles Perry Scott who, with Greenwood, had come to represent the S.P.G. in China in 1874, was consecrated to the charge of the six Northern Provinces. As a novice Scott found himself indebted to the friendship of two non-

Anglican guides. For three years he was the guest of the aged American Presbyterian, Dr. Nevius, at Chefoo, and accompanied him on his tours. During the great famine of 1878 he was introduced to the technique of relief distribution by the great Welsh Baptist, Timothy Richard. He spent nine months in remote Shansi villages, visiting from family to family: it was estimated that from nine to thirteen millions had perished: in some districts seven-tenths of the population had died. It was a grim introduction to Chinese life, but an apprenticeship that stood him in good stead. Soon after he became Bishop, Scott made Peking his headquarters: not only was the C.M.S. compound made over to him, but Brereton, a C.M.S. missionary, with the goodwill of the Society, transferred his allegiance to the S.P.G. and remained on in Peking after the C.M.S. had withdrawn. New stations were opened but the work was hampered by lack of staff. Two S.P.G. missionaries in Tai An Fu, at the foot of the sacred mountain Tai-shan, adopted Chinese dress, but that did not safeguard them from boycott. Scott resigned his diocese into the hands of Bishop Norris in 1913, but remained in Peking till his death in 1927. His period covers over half a century of Chinese history and witnessed startling transformations. The Bishop had his share of his family's architectural gifts and left as a memorial in Peking a Cathedral of his own design, one of the first and most successful experiments in the adaptation of Eastern architecture to the purposes of Christian worship.

(d) The new diocese of Mid-China fell to Bishop George Moule, like Bishop Scott in being the representative of a missionary dynasty and in completing half a century of service. He and his brother, Archdeacon Arthur Moule, had been several years together at Ningpo before the former moved to Hangchow. Seven of their children became missionaries. Hangchow became a conspicuous centre of medical missionary work under Dr. Main, and Ningpo College of educational work under Hoare, the future Bishop of Hong Kong. The Moules did distinguished literary work, interpreting Christianity to the Chinese and the Chinese to the West. Shanghai was adopted as the see-city of the new diocese, though the

American Bishops at the Lambeth Conference pointed out to their British colleagues who " were evidently astonished to learn that our labours had preceded those of the Church of England", that according to ancient precedents an English bishop officiating to native converts in Shanghai could not regard himself otherwise than as intruding on a missionary diocese already supplied by an episcopal head "; and the impropriety of having two Anglican bishops and two Cathedrals in the same city is obvious.

(e) The diocese of West China was formed because it was obviously difficult for Bishop Moule to conduct episcopal visitations two thousand miles away. William Cassels, one of the seven notable Cambridge men whose simultaneous offers of overseas service had aroused considerable enthusiasm in the autumn of 1884, had sailed in the following year under the banner of the China Inland Mission. Twenty years earlier this Society had been launched by Hudson Taylor. Though still only thirty-three, Hudson Taylor had had six and a half years' experience of China, and (after being invalided home) four years in Whitechapel. Stung by the contrast between the vast map of China and the diminutive scale of missionary operations, he became convinced that existing methods would take centuries to cover the ground. The Chinese had a right to the Gospel whether they would hear or whether they would forbear: it must be the will of God that consecrated men and women should volunteer in numbers sufficient to bring the message within earshot of all. They might belong to any denomination—they must depend unreservedly upon the Lord for maintenance— there must be no begging for funds and no collections. All would be provided if they prayed. Men and women of the Mission adopted Chinese coiffure and clothes.

> " The main purpose was not to win converts or to build a Chinese Church but to spread a knowledge of the Christian Gospel throughout the empire as quickly as might be. . . . Once the Christian message had been proclaimed the fruits in conversion might be gathered by others. The China Inland Mission did not seek primarily to build Churches, although these were gathered. Nor, although Chinese assistants were employed, did it stress the recruiting and training of a Chinese ministry."[1]

[1] Latourette: *History of the Expansion of Christianity*, Vol. VI, p. 329.

As early as 1866 Hudson Taylor while maintaining his non-denominational principle decided to make provision within the Society for denominational convictions.

> " Those already associated with me represent all the leading denominations of our native land, Episcopal, Presbyterian, Congregational, Methodist, Baptist and Paedobaptist. It is intended that those whose views of discipline correspond shall work together. Each one is perfectly at liberty to teach his own views on these minor points to his own converts, the one great object we have in mind being to bring heathen from darkness to light, from the power of Satan to God. We all hold alike the great fundamentals of our faith, and in the presence of heathenism can learn the discussion of discipline while together, and act as before God when in separate stations."

It was an *interimsethick*, an emergency policy. Cassels was the first Church of England clergyman to join the Mission. To develop a Church of England work within the borders of an interdenominational Society was a novel departure and Bishop Moule had misgivings about it. But it was Hudson Taylor's intention that the untouched part of Szechwan to which he sent Cassels should be the rallying-point for members of the Church of England who joined the Mission and for them only, and this understanding was scrupulously respected. When, therefore, ten years later, the question of the Bishopric arose, Archbishop Benson felt no scruple about appointing Cassels, nor the C.M.S. in accepting his episcopal oversight, for both C.I.M. and C.M.S. in the diocese were equally Anglican; the arrangement was unconventional enough to draw together *Record* and *Guardian* in an unwonted unanimity of condemnation. Cassells himself felt no difficulty in reconciling the two loyalties and held firmly to the principles underlying both. Thus began an episcopate of thirty years: the Bishop died in harness in 1925. He had come to Paoning forty years before as a lonely pioneer, encountering difficulty in securing possession of a house. He had looked to a time when " these little dots of light all over China shall become great fires and then will the Gospel be carried with power all over the country. The building up, strengthening and sustaining of his converts, in the spirit of St. John xvii and St. Paul's Epistles, had been his dominant care.

By the date of the consecration of its Cathedral in 1914, Paoning had become the centre of a diocese with over one hundred stations and a strong corporate life, and the Bishop was able to baptize " fourth generation Christians " whose parents, grandparents and great-grandparents had become Christians. But progress had been costly. There had been personal perils: the Bishop was twice wrecked in the Yangtze Gorges: travel in his own diocese was not safe; his assistant Bishop Mowll and his wife were captured, and two of his clergy murdered by brigands; nevertheless in a period of eight years Bishop Cassels spent over 700 days on the road. The thirty years were punctuated with outbursts of civil war and anti-foreign violence: " not proceeding as of old from the supercilious Confucian who was unacquainted with the outside world, but from the more educated and advanced party in China." Even Chengtu, the capital, was not immune from burning and looting, and the Student Hostel for which the Bishop had worked so assiduously was seriously damaged.

The persecution and wholesale martyrdoms of the Boxer period focused the attention of the West, but as a leading article in *The Times* had said in 1891:—

> " It is often forgotten that persecution is the normal condition of the Chinese converts to Christianity. We hear of these persecutions only when they touch the foreign missionaries; of the daily and sporadic outbreaks against the Native Christians we hear nothing. The descriptions lately published of the persecutions of the little Christian communities in Szechwan and Yunnan during the past two years are heart-rending. Men, women and children are murdered by scores, their little property is destroyed, and hundreds of them are fugitives from mob violence. To support the hatred and social ostracism with which the converts are regarded, there must be genuine, energetic conviction."

Such were the qualities that went to the making of Christian history in nineteenth-century China.

THE CHURCH IN KOREA

When the Church in Korea was isolated by war from all contact with the West, it was less than fifty years old: which must exonerate our trespassing on twentieth-century ground. Bishop Corfe established a diocese in 1890, but insisted that five years' study of the language, literature and mentality of the people must precede any active evangelization.

There had been Christians in Korea in the eighteenth and even the seventeenth century in contact with Christians in China and Japan. A Chinese priest appointed by the Bishop of Peking had ministered for eight years to several thousand but he was executed and several hundred perished with him. Christianity remained a prohibited religion through the first half of the nineteenth century and persecutions continued into the '70's. It was not till the '80's that her Treaties with America and the European powers exposed Korea to outside influences. American Presbyterians and Methodists were soon on the scene in considerable force: the last available statistics show over 160,000 baptized members and a native ministry of over 1,000. The Presbyterian Mission in 1907 was swept by a wave of revivalism of a kind wholly alien and indeed uncongenial to Scottish-American missionaries. "They were not revivalists; they had not encouraged it; they did not believe in it; they disliked an emotional religion; and here they were in the face of a movement which was beyond not only their experience but that of the greatest revivalists. They tried to stop it but unavailingly."[1] Open confession of sin could not be restrained and was implemented by redress of injuries. But this picture of Korean Christianity under American auspices must be balanced by evidence of its stability. It is distinguished by its high standard of self-help and the thoroughness of its Biblical studies. Every congregation had its annual Bible class, lasting a week; during the day all business in the town stopped and the people studied together for two, three or four hours under pastors or elders. In the afternoons all scattered through the town doing personal work among their friends and inviting them to Church. There were Bible Institutes running six weeks a year for men, ten for women, with a total course of five years: these were purely for laymen to train them more intensively for local leadership. Above these came the Bible Seminary for women and the Theological Seminary for men with full three-year courses,

[1] Lord William Cecil: *Changing China*.

and a yearly enrolment of 150–200 in each.   In a single year 4,500 so studied, at their own expense.   Japanese regulations enforcing on all schools an obeisance at shrines, compelled the closure of many schools which could not conscientiously consent.

In 1887 Bishop Scott of North China and Bishop Bicker-steth of Japan appealed to the Archbishop of Canterbury for a Mission to Korea.   Two years before, two Chinese Christians had been sent by the infant Church of Fu-chow to learn the language and start such a Mission. In 1889 Archbishop Benson invited Bishop Corfe to become the first Bishop—the first Naval Chaplain to become a Bishop since Ken.   He had had some experience of the Far East under Bishop Scott at Chefoo: but he was forty-six and viewed with dismay the " shoreless ocean which seemed to be before us, as we contemplated the task of deciphering numberless hieroglyphics which had to be mastered.   It took years to cross this ocean."   The episco-pate of Bishop Corfe (1890–1904), Bishop Turner (1905–11), and Bishop Trollope (1911–30) correspond to three stages in house-building—foundations, fabric, furniture.

BISHOP CORFE

Bishop Corfe's Korea was still " The Korea of ' ante-bellum ' days," before the foundations of the great deep were broken up by the China-Japan war of 1894–5. Railways and regular posts were unknown.   Seoul was still a mediæval city, boasting of hardly a single foreign building, whose ponderous gates were locked every night as the old city bell tolled the curfew.   Missionaries and other foreigners only enjoyed a restricted right of residence in Seoul and the three recently-opened treaty ports. Travel in the interior was forbidden, on pain of deportation, without a passport which distinctly specified " trade or pleasure " as the only two grounds on which such journeys were allowed.[1]

" The Archbishop told me that he had no pay to offer, that the ground was yet untrodden by English missionaries, that he had no one to give me as a companion, and that

[1] *Memoir of Bishop Trollope.*

the country was unsettled and hostile to Christianity."
As though this was not discouraging enough, the project
was assailed by critics, some of whom regarded Korea as
a preserve of the Church of Rome in which an Anglican
mission would be an unwarranted intrusion: others like
Bishop Gore " felt that Korea might be left to the Russian
Church: we felt that the English Church had no special
mission to go there. I think in consequence we gave
Bishop Corfe scant support. I recanted long ago. Korea
has passed under the influence of Japan, not Russia, and
without doubt there is no country which would have greater
difficulty than Russia in evangelising Korea." It was all
very slap-dash. S.P.G. promised £600 a year, and Corfe
asked for five priests to come and share it with him : they
must stand shoulder to shoulder with him on the main
points of " Catholic faith and practice," and abandon all
hope of marriage. The Rev. Fr. Kelly, hearing that no one
had responded to the call, offered to go himself, but it was
decided that he would be better employed at home training
and despatching volunteers for the mission: eight men
were sent in eight years, members of a Brotherhood which
became the nucleus of the Society of the Sacred Mission
at Kelham. Corfe had the support of many personal
friends in England banded together in an Association in
which membership was by prayer, not subscription; for
he was as convinced as Hudson Taylor of " the superior
value of a list of members who pray over a list of members
who pay," and there was to be no begging. The Quarterly
Intercession Paper traces its genealogy back to this Association.

BISHOP TURNER

What had been known as Bishop Corfe's Mission became
under Bishop Turner an acknowledged responsibility of
the Church as a constituted diocese. A structure began
to arise on Corfe's foundations, both living stones, and
bricks and mortar. The revivals of 1907 had effects
beyond the Presbyterian fold: the numbers of the Anglican
Church increased. The old Korea, as described above,
was beginning to vanish; interest in the outside world was
so intense that the announcement of a lecture by a youthful

layman from England could at a moment's notice fill a
large hall to overflowing. Placed like Palestine or Belgium
between two greater nations, Egypt and Assyria, Germany
and France, Korea between China and Japan was becoming
acutely aware of its own identity and anxious about the
chances of maintaining it. It was less fortunate than
Belgium in that the powers who had guaranteed its independence did not honour their word. Bishop Turner worked
quietly and vigorously from his modest quarters in Seoul;
staff was still exiguous, but pastoral and medical work
went on, the latter focussed in Dr. Weir's S.P.G. Hospital
at Chemulpo.

BISHOP TROLLOPE

By the time Bishop Trollope succeeded, Japan's annexation was a *fait accompli*: " Racial feeling, racial difficulties,
are now something beyond expression. However inevitable may have been the annexation of Korea by
Japan, it has led and must lead to great bitterness of feeling
between the two nations." Could the Christian Church
draw together elements so dissimilar ?

Trollope had served for twelve years under Bishop
Corfe: he was a " thorough scholar and one of the few
who had made himself at home in the old Korean literature; this he read as you and I might run through light
literature in our own language. His interest in this
literature led him to collect specimens till his library of
old Korean books numbered something around ten
thousand volumes, and contained many priceless editions."
So run the *Proceedings* of the Korea Branch of the Royal
Asiatic Society.

It was therefore as no stranger that the new Bishop
returned, after nine years spent mainly in Poplar as Father
Dolling's successor. He brought very definite ideas about
the furniture most appropriate to the house of which he
had helped to lay the foundations. It must of course be a
modest house, for Church, like country, found itself between
two numerically more powerful neighbours, the French
Roman Catholics and the American Protestants. " Nothing is to be gained by trying to cover the world or Korea

with a thin layer of Anglicanism, whereas a pinch of such Catholic salt as an English Church Mission can provide may be of real service, if applied within a judiciously limited area." It must be recognizably Korean; the time was ripe for "a caveat against the wholesale adoption of unsuitable Western habits and customs." But it must be " native " without being " national." " It is quite possible to build up a ' native ' Church, racy of the soil, without attempting to organise a ' national ' Church with all its undesirable political implications: the surest way of stifling and perverting the healthy and legitimate development of a ' native ' Church lies in clamping it to the wheels of the ' national ' chariot." The appointments of the house must symbolize universal as well as local origin: they must bear the imprint of the Catholic.

The Bishop looked forward to the day when Koreans who owed their conversion respectively to the French Catholic, the American Presbyterian or Methodist, and the Anglican Mission, would cease to be dominated by French, American and English missionaries.

> " What better pledge could be given of the possibility of these divergent masses being ultimately welded into one consistent whole than the presence of a nucleus of Christians trained in the Catholic Faith, as understood by the Anglican Church ? If God could bring the unity of our great Ecclesia Anglicana out of the jarring controversies of the Celtic, Italian and British Churches, which all helped to give her life, we may trust that He can and will, in His own good time, in Korea and elsewhere, bring peace and unity out of the divergent and apparently inconsistent elements which distract our minds."

There was always the presence of the Japanese to remind the Korean of the tensions involved in catholicity. " It makes all state prayers as difficult as in the old Jacobite days." The language difficulty militated against corporate worship and conference: but the Anglican Mission prided itself on ministering to the spiritual needs of immigrants from Japan, among whom there were some who belonged to the Nippon Sei Ko Kwai, and the Bishop struggled manfully with their language. His sympathy did not prevent him from bringing to bear what influence he could against the worst injustices of the government or

from denouncing in print the " nameless horrors " of their
efforts to suppress the independence movement.

There were certain defects in the furnishing of the
diocese which the Bishop was determined to make good.
" A Bishop is bound to hold a Synod at least once a year;
it is as much a part of his duty as holding confirmations
or ordinations." A Synod therefore there must be,
" following the canonical practice of the Catholic Church,
not the secular precedents of modern parliamentary
institutions " which had in the Bishop's view exercised a
sinister influence over modern efforts to revive synodical
government, reflecting the King, Lords and Commons
of the British Constitution. Laity could have no place in
the Synod. The " *consenus plebis* " must be secured by
diocesan and deanery conferences with an electoral roll
of " Practising Communicants."

The lack of a Cathedral was another glaring defect;
" to present the liturgical worship of the Church with the
dignity which is its due, and to set a norm for the scattered
communities of Christians throughout the country, was
something that ' the Mission ' could contribute to the
future Christianity of Korea which could not be supplied
by other Missions, Protestant or Roman, for the former,
remarkable as they are for their evangelistic zeal have,
as they themselves agree, no special talent for worship in
the strict sense of the word, while the use by the latter of
a Western tongue, and that a dead one, is an effective
obstacle in the way of any great acts of corporate worship
on the part of an Oriental race." To this end, experts must
be consulted so that the Korean Liturgy might be the
perfect vehicle of such worship: experts must be consulted
so that the terms used to translate such words as Bishop,
Priest, Deacon, were free from the inadequacies which
Trollope deplored in the Japanese renderings: " Lord
of the Doctrine "; "The Offerer of Sacrifice"; " Assistant
at the Sacrifice," are the equivalents of the terms.

Lastly, "when we think of the tremendous part played
by monasticism in the building up of the Kingdom of God
all over the world, it is difficult to see how any Church can
be regarded as in any sense ' thoroughly furnished ' which
leave this side of Church life entirely out of account."

Trollope had hoped that the American Cowley Fathers would work in his diocese: two priests actually arrived but a new Superior cancelled negotiations. The Sisters of St. Peter, Kilburn, had begun work under Bishop Corfe, but it was long before there were any signs of a vocation to the " religious life " among Korean women. It was only a few years before his death that the Bishop saw his diocese " thoroughly furnished " in this respect, and dedicated a home for the Society of the Holy Cross. He did not expect the contemplative life in its strict observance to find many adherents: he " had a sympathy and respect for the Korean mind and desired to preserve its individuality: he wished to impose no narrow peculiarities of the religious life upon the Koreans, but rather that the essentials common to that life might form the basis upon which the Korean Order might develop in its own way."

Looking to the future, Bishop Trollope saw clearly that the arrangement by which an isolated diocese in the Far East was loosely attached to a distant Metropolitan, unavoidable as it was in the early stages, could not last: " The detached existence of a single autocephalous diocese permanently subordinated to a metropolitan the other side of the world is an unheard-of phenomenon." He saw equally clearly that racial and political considerations rendered the absorption of the Church in Korea into either the Chinese or Japanese Churches inconceivable. He fully expected that " at the present rate of increase, in the course of the next ten or fifteen years, Korea will be as entitled to three or four Bishops as Japan now is to six or seven. This would form as good a foundation for a separate province as it did in England north of the Trent until 1542, when Henry VIII by the creation of Chester raised the number of prelates in the Province of York to five."

Meanwhile, he felt it his duty to avoid any act or speech which might produce confusion of mind in the newly-made Christians who looked to him for guidance, or any " slackening of discipline or weak-kneed sacrifice of principle " from which his flock might suffer injury. For this reason he maintained Bishop Corfe's insistence on a homogeneous staff, " for whatever may be said of the

' glorious comprehensiveness ' of the Church of England *in England*, missionaries in a non-Christian land are plainly very seriously handicapped unless they can agree to a substantially unanimous presentment of the faith which is in them."

THE CHURCH IN JAPAN

It was in 1859 that the first three missionaries arrived in Japan from the United States, two of them Episcopalian. It was in 1940 that the foreign missionary was politely but firmly bowed out of the country. In that year it was recorded that baptized Christians numbered approximately 311,000: Anglicans, 27,000, Roman Catholic, 100,000, other Communions 184,000. But the history of the Church can hardly be said to cover the whole of these eighty years. Though the American Treaty of 1858 had guaranteed them the free exercise of their religion, and, the right to erect places of worship, public notice-boards still displayed a list of " forbidden things," and " the evil sect of Christians " was the first on the list; district headmen were still expected to sign a declaration that " we have not been negligent in searching for the sect of Christians." " So long as the sun shall warm the earth, let no Christian be so bold as to come to Japan: and let all know that the King of Spain Himself, or the Christian's God, or the Great God of all, if he violate this command, shall pay for it with his head." It was only in 1873 that this ancient edict ceased to be displayed, and it could be assumed that Christianity was no longer to be punished. Conditions were very unsettled in Japan in the '60's; the effect upon Christianity of the revolution which overthrew feudalism and re-established the Emperor's authority in his new capital, Tokyo, was very uncertain. It was not surprising that hesitation prevailed as to whether the moment had yet come for missionary activity.

Among the last to suffer under the Edict were the members of a Roman Catholic community which had survived in obscurity from the seventeenth century in the wilds of Kyushu, maintaining their faith loyally if not in its purity. Once the Government was aware of their existence they were arrested, tortured and deported in detachments to distant provinces. They profited by the clemency of 1873 to return to their homes. Ten thousand accepted admission to the Roman Communion.

Other Communions had no such nucleus from which to expand: their numbers crept up slowly. By 1882 Anglicans numbered 760, and their missionaries 36 (Americans 10, C.M.S. 11, S.P.G. 7). There were 3,700 Christians and 114 missionaries of seven North American denominations. These figures illustrate the important fact that the makers of Christian history in Japan were predominantly American. At the first missionary conference at Osaka in 1883 only 18 out of 106 delegates were not American: of the 22 Anglicans, twelve were American. Till 1884 the only Anglican Bishop in Japan was the American Bishop Williams.

" The Bishop's personal characteristics led him to place emphasis upon intensive rather than extensive development: he insisted on very thorough preparation of candidates for baptism and confirmation. While he was not a rapid builder, he laid solid foundations which have stood the test of time. His great contribution was the influence exerted by his own faith and character upon the first generation of Christians. The Japanese still revere him not only as the founder of their Church, but still more as its patron saint."[1]

The Congregational policy was on rather different lines—for example they committed responsibility to their young Japanese pastors at an earlier stage—and resulted in more rapid growth. " So far as numbers go both methods seem to have produced in the long run approximately the same results. In the statistics for 1907 the Congregationalist Church is credited with 79 ministers and 15,600 members, the Anglican with 72 and 14,350 respectively."[1]

American influence benefited Japanese Christianity in other ways. Teachers accepted posts in Government Colleges and, refusing any undertaking to abstain from Christian teaching, exercised a profound influence. " It is impossible," said Dr. W. S. Clark, who had been engaged to organize an official Agricultural College, " for a

[1] Bishop H. St. George Tucker: *The History of the Episcopal Church in Japan.*

Christian to dwell three years in the midst of a pagan people and yet keep entire silence on the subject nearest his heart."

Japanese students also were early pilgrims to the United States, among them Joseph Niisima, who returned to found the first Christian Univeristy in Japan. Though Government educational and medical policy did not make it necessary or desirable to multiply such institutions as were so impressive a characteristic of American Episcopal Missions in China and the Philippines, St. Paul's University and St. Margaret's School, St. Barnabas' Hospital at Osaka and St. Luke's in Tokyo, played a great part in imparting to the medical, nursing and teaching professions of Japan the traditions of Christian service.

All three Anglican agencies were at work in Tokyo: Kobe was the second main station of the S.P.G., Osaka of the C.M.S. The C.M.S. were also extending in Hokkaido, the island in the extreme north, and Kyushu, the island in the extreme west. Each of the three Missions started its own Divinity School; candidates for the Ministry served an apprenticeship as Catechists before ordination.

So marked a change in the prospects of the Church occurred in the '8o's that missionaries began to talk of the danger of Christianity becoming a popular religion. Converts increased in number within six years from 5,000 to 27,000. So far from being alarmed at the progress of Christianity, the leaders of Japan appeared to welcome it. The change of attitude may be illustrated from the writings of a newspaper proprietor, Mr. Fukuzawa. In 1881 he insisted that " the national religion of Japan is Buddhism. That Christianity is harmful to our national power is evident. . . . Buddhist priests are immoral and shameless; it is very unsafe to entrust this weighty cause (the opposition to Christianity) to them. Unless they are assisted by the influence of the upper classes, nothing can obstruct the intrusion of Christianity." In 1885 he was writing in a different tone: " The civilised nations of Europe and America have always held that non-Christian countries could not be treated as enlightened nations. There is no alternative for our own country but to adopt the social colour of civilised nations in order to maintain our independence on a footing of equality. As an absolutely necessary preliminary the Christian religion must be introduced. . . . We must change our professed belief and wear a religious dress uniform with others. We mean by professed belief what we profess to believe apart from the question of what may be our true doctrine. . . . We do not mean that the majority of our countrymen should become Christians. All that is required is the assumption of the title of a Christian country."

Bishop Tucker, who quotes these passages as representative of the change of view, recalls that the rejection or adoption of Christianity had become purely a question of national policy. The political leaders were primarily interested in securing a revision of the Treaties, and hoped that a sympathetic attitude towards missionaries would help in obtaining the consent of the foreign governments. " While such patronage was precarious it did have the effect of arousing a pro-Christian movement among the progressive section of the people. Crowds of eager enquirers began to pour into mission stations. Numerous invitations to open work or send instructors were received. Rapid growth under such conditions was necessarily accompanied by grave dangers."[1] It was natural that extravagant hopes were entertained of a Christian Japan in the immediate future, but perhaps it was as well for the stability and soundness of the Church that the State found it possible to attain the status desired without donning a religious uniform. The revision of treaties and tariffs, the abjuring of extra-territoriality, and victory over Russia, removed the necessity for a bolstered-up prestige.

With the uninhibited self-confidence of the adolescent, Japan in the '90's was in haste to shake off all dependence upon the advice and guidance of European elders and quick to resent criticism. In a quarter of a century she had improvised the whole apparatus of modern civilization, mastered the technique of parliamentary and municipal government, and equipped herself to challenge a great Power. Japanese outside the Churches saw nothing to

[1] Tucker: op cit.

be gained by conciliating the foreigner; those within
became impatient for independence of foreign influence.
Motives of self-defence as well as native self-assertion
accelerated the movement, for Japanese Christians were
rightly jealous of the honour of their Church, and sensitive
to whatever prejudiced their religion in the eyes of their
fellow-countrymen. Many of their leaders hankered after
" a grand national Church, such as the world has not yet
seen, free from all sectarian teaching and the crippling
influence of creeds."

It was providential that at this critical moment the
Anglican Communion was given in Edward Bickersteth a
Bishop of the stature that the times demanded. Grandson
of one of the master-builders of the C.M.S., himself founder
and for five years first Head of the Cambridge Mission to
Delhi, he understood and commanded the confidence of
all the types of Anglicanism represented in Japan. Happily
his episcopate overlapped by three years that of the aged
Bishop Williams. History does not relate the reactions of
the veteran of thirty years' service in Japan to the impetuous
vigour of the new arrival, still in his thirties. Within a
few weeks they were hard at work together formulating
a scheme for consolidating the ranks of Anglicanism, as
Presbyterians and Congregationalists had consolidated
theirs, in a single coherent whole. Within a year Bickersteth was presiding over the first Synod of what was henceforth to be known as the Nippon Sei Ko Kwai (Holy
Catholic Church of Japan) at which its Canons and
Constitution were unanimously adopted.

It is at first sight surprising that such a culmination
should have been reached so early in the life of the Japanese
Church; less than thirty years since the first missionary
had landed, only fourteen years since the Edict condemning Christians had disappeared from the notice
boards. China, though an older Church, had to wait
till 1912, seventy years from the date of the bursting open
of the doors, for the parallel inauguration of the Chung Hua
Sheng Kung Hui. The configuration of the country, the
composition of the Church, and the character of the people
combine to offer an explanation. British and American
missionaries had long been colleagues in China as in Japan,

but only in Shanghai was there any chance of their getting in one another's way. Vast distances separated their spheres and hindered communications between them. In compact Japan a closer fellowship was possible and inevitable. Separate organizations, for example the three Divinity Schools, became indefensible.

Further contrasts are evident in the composition of the Churches. The Church was in China predominantly rural, in Japan predominantly urban; in China composed mainly of peasants, in Japan of the professional classes. Restrictions on freedom of movement into the interior accounted for the early concentration on Treaty Ports. The period of infatuation with Western culture had brought students thirsting for English education within the orbit of the missionaries who alone could satisfy their desires. Among them were many of the Samurai class, dethroned by the revolution from a status of privilege and security, heirs of a great tradition of chivalry and learning, and adherents of a school of Confucianism to which the moral teaching of Christianity seemed to show some affinity. Though the reaction in favour of the "Preservation of National Excellencies" effected a winnowing, the Church retained a firm enough hold on its intelligentsia to make available the educated leadership which the Church of China had still to find.

It was not till after the Revolution of 1911 that progress began to make rapid strides in China. In Japan the pace was breathless from the time of the new Constitution in 1889, and the Church had perforce to hasten. It could not be impervious to the independent spirit of the community. It had recognized from the start that the Christianizing of the country must be entrusted to a Japanese Church, and that the missionary's task was to bring such a Church into being.

Bishop Bickersteth's Canons provide an interesting page in the story of the constitutional development of the expanding Church, but we are here concerned with the central principle embodied in them. His own account describes the Synod as a freely elected body in which Europeans and Americans were greatly outnumbered by Japanese. No distinction was made between Church and

Missions; the latter were integral to the former. No distinction was made between races within the Church. American and European missionaries were subject to the constitution and canons of the Nippon Sei Ko Kwai. While majority control was to some extent nullified as long as all the Bishops were foreigners, this stage was soon outgrown; when the foreign Bishops withdrew in 1940, Japanese successors were ready to take their place. The constitution gave the N.S.K.K. complete control of its Prayer Book and formularies except in the matter of the Creeds which were accepted as fundamental. The Prayer Book was revised in 1895 and the differences between the English and American books adjusted. The Thirty-Nine Articles were not retained, except as a temporary measure, advantage being taken of a Lambeth Conference resolution, which, while it required evidence that a newly-constituted Church held substantially the same doctrine as the Anglican Communion, did not insist on the Articles in their entirety. Bishop Bickersteth thought Article IX, *Of Original Sin,* very liable to misinterpretation by Eastern Christians; with regard to Article XIII, " is it necessary in the East to have any authoritative decision at all on the problems of election and free-will ? Article XIX might well seem offensive to Archbishop Nicolai and the 20,000 members of the Greek Orthodox Church in Tokyo. The circumstances of the sixteenth century in England offer no parallel to our own in Japan. The doctrinal confession of an Eastern Church, if its formularies be deemed requisite, should be the work of Oriental theologians, be ' racy of the soil ', spring out of a surrounding of Eastern circumstances, and carry to those who study it the obvious meaning of its own allusions and references."[1]

Bishop Bickersteth knew what he was about. " We are not met to constitute a new Church: not so is the Church of Christ propagated: a new branch of the Church has germinated, not a new tree with a separate root and stem and independent life of its own. . . . By virtue of common membership of the Body of Christ, through union in one faith, and participation of the same sacraments this Church exists, and is in communion with other Churches in other

[1] *Life of Bishop Edward Bickersteth,* p. 341.

lands." It could not have been foreseen that the Church of Japan would, within fifty years, assert a total independence of European and American missionaries and subsidies. Still less could it have been foreseen that the time was coming when that Church would find itself severed morally and physically from all contact with the outside world by the tragic barriers of war. But if Bishop Bickersteth had had the power of foreseeing the future, he might have claimed with justice that his policy was well calculated to prepare the Church for such a day of testing.

PART IX

THE THREE MONOTHEISMS

Introduction: Christianity and Other Religions

1. The Church's Approach to the Jew; Dr. Edwyn Bevan on the Christian Attitude to Judaism; Palestine Place; The travels of Way, Wolff, and Stern; The nineteenth-century achievement.

2. The Jerusalem Bishopric.

3. The Church's Approach to the Moslem: Henry Martyn; Karl Gottlieb Pfander; Thomas Valpy French; George Alfred Lefroy ; Douglas Thornton and Temple Gairdner.

IT has been possible in previous chapters to invoke the aid of maps in tracing the expansion of the Church; the impact of the Christian upon the Jewish and Mohammedan worlds conforms to no territorial pattern. Even if Jew and Moslem were less ubiquitous, a geographical approach would be inappropriate where the relations between three great religious systems are to be considered.

Christian missions to Jews and to Moslems are commonly regarded as being on a different footing to missions " to the heathen," and more difficult to justify. Their history suggests that they have been checked by certain inhibitions. Between monotheism and polytheism there is a great gulf fixed, and those who stand together on one bank feel instinctively that they have something very fundamental in common over against those who stand on the other. They share the belief in the unity of God: they share an abhorrence of idolatry: they are religions of a Book, to a limited extent of the same Book; the worship of the Jewish Synagogue shows some kinship with the worship of the parish Church: the worship of the Mohammedan Mosque is deeply impressive, while the unselfconscious performance of his devotional duties by the individual Moslem worshipper by the wayside, betokens a conscientious discipline such as the average Christian neither observes in private nor could display in public without embarrassment. Every schoolboy knows that the Jew has had a cruel deal from Christians in the past, that the Crusades were an assault in force on Islam, and that his ancestors' behaviour towards both, hardly warrants an attitude of moral superiority. Whatever their subject, students know that it has been adorned by Jewish genius. The soldier has found much to admire when fighting against or alongside the Moslem warrior.

There have also been less defensible inhibitions. Governments have quailed before the risk of exciting the fanaticism of their Mohammedan subjects. Prejudice against missions to the Jews has been tainted by prejudice against the Jewish race. Before both Moslem and Jew the Christian has been apt to show himself intimidated, if not defeatist. The conversion of either has been regarded as so improbable as not to be worth attempting: it is only a step further to argue that Moslem and Jew have a right to resent any effort to deflect them from their hereditary loyalties, or detach them from their corporate allegiance to committees of historic antiquity.

THE CHRISTIAN ATTITUDE TO JUDAISM

That this last point can be argued courteously and frankly between Jew and Christian is illustrated by consecutive articles in the *International Review of Missions* for April 1933, where Rabbi Cohen and Dr. Edwyn Bevan join issue in what may be ranked as a classic disputation. That this should be possible in a missionary magazine is itself an encouraging symptom. The Rabbi deplores that an international conference at Budapest on " The Christian approach to the Jew " had not wholly discountenanced the gaining of converts by unworthy means, had touched but lightly upon the barest fraction of the wrath and fury visited upon the Jews by the established Churches from the days of Constantine to those of Czar Nicholas, and had not denounced the bigots who deny the Jew the right to remain a Jew. The findings of the Conference had been couched in military terms—" the occupation of the field," " strategic centres," " open warfare." The branding of the Jew as an inferior spiritual and moral being was feeding

the flames of hatred and persecution. To the argument
that there is but one true religion, the Rabbi replies: " As
man's faculty of speech, so that of his faith expresses itself
in varied dialects and idioms. There is more than one
true way in which the human heart can reach out after
the Holy One. As there is no absolute language, so there
is no absolute religion." " To tear away a person from
the religion of his people, to which he is linked with all
the fibres of his being, both physical and psychical, amounts
to cutting him off from the source of life and idealism."
To a Christian's argument that " By accepting Christianity
you do not give up Judaism; you only add to it the
belief in Jesus Christ," the Rabbi replies, " In some instances, an addition transforms the original. Should the
pharmacist add a single grain to the physician's prescription
he thereby alters its character and may harm instead of
benefiting the patient. Jesus is the extra grain in the composition of Judaism which radically changes its own nature"
One of the conference speakers had said that " Not to
offer the Gospel to the Jew would be to discriminate
against the Jew and thus be guilty of doing the very thing
against which the Jews protest to-day." " No, we should
not mind it in the least. Indeed, this is what we ask for."
" The missionary character of Christianity gives it no
mandate to invade other religious communities and to
interfere with their modes of living and thinking."

Dr. Bevan could be trusted to meet the Rabbi with
reverence and insight. He repudiates, of course, unworthy methods of propaganda, but claims that it is the
Christian's duty to do everything he can to lead other
men to choose for themselves the Christian view of the
universe as the view to live by: he concedes the same
freedom to the Jew to convince Christians of the truth of
the Jewish view. He invites the Rabbi to agree with him
on three principles—(1) That certain elements in religion
ought to be universal; (2) That in regard to them a Jew
or a Christian could never admit that a religion which
lacked them was satisfactory, could never be other than
intransigent; (3) That it was a duty of charity to draw
one's neighbour's attention to what one believed to be

the missing or defective elements.   Dr. Bevan expanded
these points:—

1.   It is common to both religions that there are some
elements in religion which ought to be universal, for
example, the belief in God as one God: for both, polytheism
is definitely wrong wherever it occurs, an aberration, not
a legitimate variety.   To treat something in religion which
ought to be universal as something which need not be
universal, and thus regard a religion which lacks that
element as nevertheless just as good as religions which
have it, is as wrong as to treat something which rightly
varies according to differences of tradition and temperament as something which ought to be universal.   Jews
and Christians would have made this mistake if in the days
of ancient paganism they had agreed to recognize other
forms of religion as equivalent to their own.

2.   Pagans resented the "intolerance" of Jews and
Christians; call it rather "intransigence."   It was the
intransigent religions which survived; it was an essential
intransigence.   All religions may direct their followers to
God, but that does not mean that all lead men to salvation
equally well, that all differences are legitimate varieties.
"All religions may be pipes through which the divine
water may flow, but through some it flows comparatively
pure, through others very muddy and mixed with de-
leterious matter."   Jews and Christians ought always to
be tolerant of other religions but ought always to hold fast
to their intransigence.   It is a contradiction in terms to
affirm that an element in religion ought to be universal,
and to say that any religion which lacks it is as good a
religion as a religion which has it.   A religion which lacks
it is in that respect defective, and that defect a loss to its
adherent; his religious life must in some way suffer from
the want of it, his way to God be to that extent broken.

3.   If that be so it is a duty of charity in the follower
of the more perfect religion to do anything he can to help
his neighbours to get the missing element.   A Jew who
showed his pagan neighbours the wrongness of polytheism
was performing a duty of charity.   A Christian who regards
belief in Jesus as an element which ought to be universal
ought to refuse to regard any religion as satisfactory which

lacks that element and do all he can to draw his neighbour's attention to the claims of Jesus. It is not an element which Jew or Christian can regard as indifferent: the man who thinks the belief definitely false and the man who thinks it definitely true may both agree in this, that the belief makes an important difference, one way or the other, to religion. For the Christian belief would be nonsense if belief in Jesus were not something which ought rightly to be universal, just as the whole of Jewish belief would be nonsense if belief in the unity of God were not a belief which ought to be universal.

Dr. Bevan then drew the distinction between the ethnic type of religion and religions which make a universal claim, and adherence to which is, when genuine, an act of individual determination. When each nation or tribe had its own god, to abandon the religion of a community was disloyalty to the community as a national or racial unit. It is here that the tension between Jew and Christian becomes acute, for the Christian believes the ethnic type of religion to be the one now superseded; while for the Jew to become a Christian seems a disloyalty to his national community.

It may be true that Christianity is out to destroy all other religions, as also is Judaism when true to its highest visions: but what the Christian wants to destroy is not the truth in any other religion, but that admixture of error in another religion or that limitation which prevents the adherents to it seeing their own truth englobed in the fuller truth: even as a pious Jew would not consider that if an atheistic humanitarian added to his belief in the brotherhood of man a belief in the Fatherhood of God, his belief in the brotherhood of man would thereby be destroyed; it would gain new significance by being englobed in the larger truth.

Dr. Bevan enters fully into the pain which Christian propaganda and still more the conversion of Jews to Christianity must cause, but asks the Rabbi to recognize that Christians could not renounce their propaganda without giving up their Christian faith; that he cannot prove to Christians that they ought to give it up till he had first proved that Christianity itself was a mistake.

" The chief way, as it seems to me, in which the inevitable pain can have the bitterness taken out of it is by a real recognition on both sides that, while there is a difference of worth between different forms of religion, while one religion may be believed to contain the truth fuller and purer than any other, and all other religions may be seen in a scale of values only as they contain more or less of truth with less or more of error, the relative spiritual level of individuals by no means corresponds to that rate of values between religions. It does not follow that because one religion contains a larger range of truth than another, an individual adhering to it reacts as fully in will and emotion to that range of truth as some individual adhering to another religion may do to a smaller range of truth. This recognition that the scale of spiritual attainment between individuals does not correspond with the relative worth between the religions they profess, still leaves it right for men to try to bring others to what they believe to be the largest truth: but it might prevent that assumption of spiritual superiority in individuals which causes the worst bitterness in religious disagreements. It is really very humiliating for a Christian to say that he believes in Jesus and then look at the quality of his own life as compared with what his life ought to be if what he says he believes is true."

This lengthy preamble to the annals of the Church's approach to the Jew in the nineteenth century may be forgiven if only as placing on record the mellow wisdom and delicate Christian touch of a great teacher: it also serves to summarize the relations reached between Christian and Jew after a hundred years of controversy. But its presentation of the rationale of Christian propaganda and of the spirit in which it should be undertaken is of wider application; the missionary to Buddhist or Hindu may profit from it as much as the missionary to Moslem or Jew.

THE CHURCH'S APPROACH TO THE JEW

To recover the outlook of 1809 when the " London Society for Promoting Christianity among the Jews " was born, requires some effort of the imagination. It was in the Spring of 1833 that Macaulay supported a motion in the House of Commons " to remove all civic disabilities at present existing with respect to his Majesty's subjects professing the Jewish religion." It was in the Spring of 1933 that the Nazi revolution unleashed the pack of anti-Semitic hounds to hunt down the Jews of Germany. Much had happened between these dates to alter the geographical distribution, the economic status, the cultural prestige and even the religious outlook of Jewry. A westward dispersion had gathered impetus to escape the reach of Czarist Russia. Two million Jews had crossed the Atlantic. Rich Jews had appeared on the European and South African scene. Fourteen Jewish Nobel prize winners indicate the intellectual renaissance of their race. The emergence of Liberal Judaism was one sign of religious ferment. The emergence of secularized Judaism was another, while the publication in Jerusalem in Hebrew by a learned Hebrew, Dr. Klausner, of a profound study of *Jesus of Nazareth* was a third.

By 1933 the consequences of the revision of frontiers at the end of the first world war, which had spelt the end of the ghetto, were becoming apparent. The consequences ensuing from the Balfour Declaration of 1917, and the Zionist immigration to Palestine, were beginning to assume the aspect of an insoluble dilemma. Since 1933 the fate of the Jews in Germany, and later in the occupied countries, has seared the conscience of the world. Competent authorities estimate a death-roll of four million. It is reckoned that half the Jewish population of the world is to-day in Anglo-Saxon lands.

It may be thought as unprofitable as it is difficult to hark back to an antediluvian period. But, so far from being prehistoric, the story of the Church's approach to the Jews is entitled to an honourable place in the history of mission-ary expansion of the nineteenth century, and its omission would render that history seriously incomplete. Looking back over the century from the standpoint of 1897, the Lambeth Conference of that year found no cause for congratulation. The Bishops lamented that Christians generally are much more interested in the conversion of the Gentile. One of the greatest hindrances arises from the

" strange lack of interest " manifested by the Church in the evangelization of the Jews. " Missions to the Jews have shared but little in the rising tide of evangelistic effort which marks our age. Yet our Lord gave them precedence, and the Gospel is the power for salvation to the Jew first. . . . Zeal in this cause is still the enthusiasm of the few."

Many would have called it the fanaticism of the eccentric few, for Jewish Missions had come to be associated with ingenious but speculative interpretations of Old Testament prophecy, a morbid interest in the fate of the ten Tribes, and a dogmatic Second Adventism. It must be admitted that Jewish Missions were apt to attract theological eccentrics in spite of the efforts of the C.M.J. to dissociate itself from them, and that current apologetic had a *naïveté* and literalism as far removed from the modern understanding of Biblical inspiration as the allegorical exegesis of Origen. The blame for this lies at the door, not of the gallant adventurers who pioneered in this field, but of those who failed to reinforce and equip the enterprise with the learning, thinking, and spiritual leadership which such an enterprise demanded.

THE CHURCH MISSION TO THE JEWS

The " London Society for promoting Christianity among the Jews " which later assumed the title of " Church Missions to Jews " (C.M.J.) owed its origin to the Clapham group described in Part IV. The inclusion of London in its title distinguishes the new Society from Scottish Societies which were soon to start on their honourable career; it recalls its original adoption of the non-denominational basis of the London Missionary Society, which, however, was soon abandoned by consent in favour of an exclusively Anglican basis; it also suggests that London was the intended sphere of operations, a sphere which soon outgrew the original limits. Queen Victoria's father, the Duke of Kent, was the first Patron of the Society, and laid the foundation of the Society's first home in Cambridge Road, Bethnal Green, the Lord Mayor and Sheriffs in attendance, making a speech worthy of the great occasion.

Here for eighty years the Society possessed in Palestine Place a local habitation and a name appropriate to its designs. A spacious quadrangle, five acres in extent, provided a dignified architectural setting for a Church, a Boys' School and Girls' School, a Missionary College, a Library, residence for the Staff, and an " Operative Jewish Converts' Institution." The last was the nineteenth-century idiom for an Industrial School, where converts could spend three years in learning, for their self-support, the trades of printing and book-binding. The name and the need re-appear later in Baghdad and Warsaw, and provide a clue to the economic status of the converts. In East London, the Society was neighbour to an immigrant population whose poverty called for charitable relief, which it was difficult to administer without incurring the imputation of bribery and the risk of interested motives. The Society gradually extended its sphere to other cities where Jews congregated. Alexander, for example, the future Bishop in Jerusalem, was baptized in Plymouth. Soon it became an axiom that " the chief field for exertion was not to be looked for in England." C.M.J. missionaries were in journeyings oft, and there were few of St. Paul's perils which they did not experience. Like St. Paul, they frequently won a hearing in the Synagogue, and like him they were frequently ejected.

LEWIS WAY

The first expedition was undertaken by Lewis Way, a barrister and Fellow of Merton, who devoted himself and his fortune to refitting and refloating the Society when it was in danger of shipwreck. No sooner was the Continent re-opened to travellers, after Waterloo, than Way set forth to visit Holland, Germany and Russia. He established friendly relations with the 25,000 Jews of Amsterdam, with the Jewish students in the University of Berlin, with the Emperor Alexander I in St. Petersburg, securing from him " the warmest assurances of zealous support in all measures tending to promote Christianity among his Jewish subjects "; in token of which the Rev. B. N. Solomon, a Christian Polish Jew, was furnished with an imperial rescript bidding all authorities, ecclesiastical and secular, afford him every possible protection and assistance in the free exercise of his duty. This led to missions in Warsaw, Posen and Cracow among the 400,000 Jews of Russian Poland. The work was interrupted by the Crimean War, when Russia could not be expected to tolerate an English Mission: the enforced departure of the missionaries evoked a demonstration at the Warsaw railway station, which testified to the respect in which they were held by the crowds of Jews, converts, Protestants, Catholics and members of the Greek Church, who assembled to say farewell. It proved to be a twenty years' interval, but from 1875 to 1939, Warsaw was the centre of fruitful work. Way's exploratory tour brought a fund of information to the Society, and qualified him to draw the attention of the Allied Sovereigns round the Peace table at Aix-la-Chapelle to the state of the Jewish people; in consequence of his representations a protocol was there agreed to, promising further consideration of their condition.

JOSEPH WOLFF

Way was also instrumental in establishing a mission in Palestine, and it was in Syria that he met Joseph Wolff whose travels will take us yet further afield. Way's sketch of Wolff illuminates the character of both.

" Wolff is such an extraordinary creature, there is no calculating *a priori* concerning his motions. He appears to me to be a comet without any penhelion and capable of setting a whole system on fire. When I should have addressed him in Syria I heard of him at Malta; when I supposed he was gone to England he was riding like a ruling angel in the whirlwind of Antioch or standing unappalled among the crumbling towers of Aleppo. A man, who at Rome calls the Pope the dust of the earth, and at Jerusalem tells the Jews that the Gemara is a lie; who passes his days in disputation and his nights in digging the Talmud; to whom a floor of brick is a feather-bed and a box a bolster; who finds a friend alike in the persecutor of his former or his present faith; who can concilate a pasha or confute a partriarch, who travels without a guide, speaks without an interpreter, can live without food and pay without money: forgiving all the insults he meets with and forgetting all the flattery: who knows little of worldly conduct and yet accommodates himself to all men without giving offence to any. As a pioneer I deem him matchless, but if order is to be established or arrangements made, trouble not Wolff. He is devoid of enmity towards man and full of the love of God. All perceive as they must that whatever he is he is in earnest; they acknowledge him to be a sincere believer in Jesus of Nazareth, and that is a great point gained with them; for the mass of the ignorant and unconverted Jews deny the possibility of real conversion from Judaism."

It is left to the *Greville Memoirs* to describe the appearance of Joseph Wolff: " I had figured to myself a tall, gaunt, severe, uncouth man, but I found a short, plump cheerful person with one of the most expressive countenances I ever saw, and so agreeable as to compensate for very plain features; eyes that become suddenly illuminated when he is warmed by his subject and a voice of peculiar sweetness and power of intonation. He came prepared to hold forth with his Bible in his pocket; and accordingly after dinner we gathered round him in a circle and he held forth for a couple of hours, in fluent and sometimes eloquent language and not without an occasional dash of humour or drollery."

The early years of Joseph Wolff, the son of a Bavarian Rabbi of the tribe of Levi, held little promise of his becoming for ten years an Anglican missionary and for thirty the Vicar of Yorkshire and Somerset villages. He left home in 1806 at the age of eleven and roved from school to school. A friend introducing him to Goethe said that he wanted to become a Christian and a man like Francis Xavier. " I advise him to remain a Jew, in which case he will become a celebrated Jew." Goethe said to Wolff, " Young man, follow the bent of your own mind and don't listen to what he says." Under the spell of a Franciscan friar he was baptized at Prague, aged seventeen, by a Benedictine Abbot. He wandered to Italy where he was presented to Pope Pius VII and entered the seminary of the Collegio Romano, and later the Collegio di Propaganda itself; his views failed to pass the test of orthodoxy: he publicly attacked the doctrine of infallibility and assailed obstreperously the teaching of the professor. By 1819 Wolff was in England, and came under the influence of Lewis Way and Charles Simeon. The London Society sent him to Cambridge to study theology and Oriental languages: by 1821 he could be held in leash no longer and his missionary travels began.

Wolff left Cairo for Jerusalem with twenty camel-loads of Bibles; here, quartered in an Armenian monastery, he was able to establish contact with the four parties represented among the 700 Jewish families in the Holy City: Rabbis proved surprisingly accessible, and there was no lack of opportunity for presenting his faith and improving his knowledge of the Talmud.   He was able to bring comfort to his fellow-Jews in Damascus on the sudden imprisonment of their Chief Rabbi, in Aleppo over a devastating earthquake, in Shiraz over their squalor. He pressed on eastwards, through Ur and the ruins of Babylon and Nineveh to Baghdad and the Persian Gulf, investigating as he went every scattered colony of Jews, every congregation of Oriental Christians and such obscure sects as the Sabeans, the disciples of John the Baptist, and the Rechabites: he had an unfortunate encounter with Kurds who bound and robbed him and beat the soles of his feet.   Wolff did not omit to study Islam: at Damascus he was invited by the great Moollah of the Mohammedans to come in the night-time to argue over the merits of Christianity; in Shiraz and Isfahan he held amicable argument with both Sunni and Sufi authorities.

Wolff returned to England in 1826, married Lady Georgina Walpole, and made friends with Edward Irving whose views were little calculated to temper his own extravagances.   But by 1827 Wolff was again on the move and this time his travels took him still farther afield.   He was determined to reach Bokhara and reach it he did, undaunted by warnings of danger which proved by no means groundless.   Dressed in Persian costume he threw in his lot with a Mohammedan Hadjee (or pilgrim) returning from Mecca to Herat, Wolff exclaiming: " I also am a Hadjee, but I am more, I am a Dervish.   I am a believer in three books, first the book of Moses and the Prophets, secondly the Psalms of David, and thirdly the Gospel of Christ together with the Epistles of His Apostles." The first danger came from " the Turcomanns who are also called All-Ammann, undoubtedly the ancient Scythians, the ancestors of the Germans or Allemanni or Allemands "; the second from the tribe of Kerahe, followers of a formidable Khan: by them Wolff was stripped and beaten, tied to a horse's tail. Wolff found 2,000 Jews at Meshed, and Moosaaee (followers of Moses) at Sarakhs, by whom he was welcomed as "fore-runner of the Messiah": he heard the Psalms of David at Meri. At last he was across the frozen Oxus and at the gates of Bokhara, where a three months' stay among the Jews convinced him that they were of the tribe of Naphtali. We must not follow Wolff through his adventures on the way through Afghanistan and the Khyber Pass to the Punjab and " Simlah " where he was the petted guest of the Governor-General and Lady William Bentinck, and preached startling sermons, committing himself to a time-table of the Millennium which he afterwards regretted.

HENRY AARON STERN

It was Wolff who ascertained the existence of " Falasha " Jews in Abyssinia to the number of 200,000: but they belong to the story of another adventurous missionary, Henry Aaron Stern, born in 1820, the son of strict Jewish parents in Frankfort on Main. When he came to take up an appointment in London at the age of 19 he had no conception that he was never to return to his home. It was a visit of curiosity to Palestine Place, to see what was going on among those whom he called " apostates " that led to his study of the New Testament. " If there be a Saviour, I mentally exclaimed, it must be Jesus. No-one ever exhibited such love, put forth such supernatural energy, nor uttered such words of wisdom. I longed to be His disciple, but dreaded the grief the intelligence would inflict on my parents." Stern survived the Society's searching tests, was baptized in 1840, and four years later appointed a Missionary to Baghdad and ordained in Jerusalem.

After eight years in Persia and Mesopotamia and three in Constantinople, Stern was asked to penetrate into the interior of Arabia. Dressed as a barefoot Arab he set out from Jiddah to scale the heights of Hassan, and was well received in Jewish settlements. The report that a man had arrived who spoke Hebrew and yet was no Jew, dressed like a Mohammedan and yet despising the Koran, caused much mystification, but in Sana with a population of 18,000 Hebrews and 22,000 Muslims, he was invited to speak for an hour in the Synagogue on the Sabbath Day, and the Scriptures were eagerly bought. It was the Mohammedans, not the Jews, who drove him out: the Jews old and young flocked to bestow farewell embraces.

It was the experience of these Arabian adventures that marked out Stern as the obvious supervisor of the Society's mission in Abyssinia. A trial-trip convinced him that there was work waiting to be done among the Falashas, and established tolerable relations both with King Theodore II and the Aboona, the ecclesiastical head of the Abyssinian Church. Nobody knew when or whence Jews had settled in Abyssinia: their name, Falasha, signified exile. They prided themselves on the purity of their blood and their morality, and they scrupulously observed the feasts and ritual, chanting psalms on the Sabbath Day. There were Jewish monks who resented Mr. Stern and his teaching, but the common people heard him gladly.

It was Stern's second visit to Abyssinia which coincided with a change of front on the part of King Theodore. Stern and his colleagues, and also Cameron the British Consul, were thrown into gaol and subjected to indescribable suffering, only to be terminated after four and a half years by the rescue expedition sent out by the British Government in 1868 under Lord Napier of Magdala. It might have been supposed that the subsequent isolation of Falasha Christians would have been fatal: communications were interrupted for years at a time: but native missionaries carried on the work, helped only by consignments of books in Amharic and occasional conferences with missionaries beyond the frontier. The Mahdi and his Dervishes broke into the country from the Sudan, but there were thirty families of Christians who died rather than become Mohammedans. Several hundred Falashas were baptized into the Ethiopian Church.

BARCLAY AND GINSBURG

The exploits of Way, Wolff and Stern give some indication of the range of the Society's reach. To these for the sake of completeness must be added the names of Barclay, afterwards Bishop in Jerusalem, and Ginsburg. The travels of Barclay centring on Constantinople covered the Balkans, Salonica and Smyrna: Bucharest has always been one of the main centres of the Society's educational and evangelistic work. Ginsburg was one of two Rabbis who were baptized in Jerusalem in 1845. From his centre at Algiers, where he built a Church, he travelled through ancient Barbary, comprising Tunisia, Tripoli, Algeria and Morocco, which contained more than a quarter of a million Mugrabi or Western Jews: he made a hazardous journey through the oases of the Sahara and preached in the synagogues. North Africa is another of the Society's main fields, which, like Poland and Rumania, has been exposed to the violence of war.

THE NINETEENTH-CENTURY ACHIEVEMENT

By the end of the century the C.M.J. had built Churches in many centres and had 138 missionaries in the field: 77 of these were Christian Jews: many of them had become Christian at great cost: many served for long periods; they had to live down the imputation of apostasy, but this disadvantage was counter-balanced by their instinctive understanding of Jewish tradition and mentality. Men like Bishop Alexander who were learned in Rabbinic lore, did not need the elaborate training in Talmud and Mishna which English missionaries required but did not always receive. The Society doubtless suffered in its hold on the imagination of the Church from the fact that so many of its missionaries bore foreign names and necessarily lacked intimate links with normal parish life. It was a more serious drawback to its work that in common with other missions in their early stages it had often no corporate Church life to offer to converts to compensate them for their severance from the intense corporate life of their community. Hebrew Christian Communities grew slowly and under stress of persecution. Its missionaries were often lone scouts in a no-man's-land; it was for this reason that much of the continental work of the Society was resigned to local Churches which could provide a spiritual home and fellowship where the Anglican Church had no standing. In some places the anti-semitism of Churches offered a further hindrance.

The value of the nineteenth-century achievement in the approach to the Jew is not to be assessed solely in terms of statistics showing the numbers of converts and Jewish clergy: though these results when allowance is made for the sacrifice and suffering involved in facing boycott and persecution, are not to be scoffed at. " The Society has spent £x in one year, and has produced x converts." That such a calculation should solemnly figure in the columns of the *Saturday Review* in 1863 is a sign that very crude criteria of success were applied to the Society's work. The writer reckons that the cost of converting a Jew at Jerusalem worked out at exactly £1,111, while the Abyssinian mission which produced 30 converts only cost £1,000. "An African Jew can be done into a Christian at the low price of £33." This is the *reductio ad absurdum* of the statistical argument.

Happily those who took the initiative in pursuing the Church's mission took a broader view of their responsibilities. They worked and prayed for individual conversion, but they were willing to invest their lives and labour in far-flung adventures without being over-anxious for an immediate reward. Their work was exploratory. It was not merely geographical exploration, though in the prevailing ignorance of where the Jews were to be found, that was an elementary but necessary preliminary. Way, Wolff, and Stern and many another pioneer were collectors of indispensable information. But there were answers to be sought to deeper questions. What was the attitude of Jews towards Christianity ? It was found that what many Jews assumed to be Christianity was a travesty of the Christian faith: their picture of Christ was a gross caricature.

It was to remove these misunderstandings that the Society flooded the Jewish world with literature, with the Scriptures in many tongues, and with tracts: these, though orthodox in their generation, would not always pass muster with theologians of to-day; their interpretation of the book of Daniel might provoke a smile, but the prophecy on which they concentrated chief attention was the fifty-third chapter of Isaiah, and on that they could be spiritually convincing. What was Judaism? That was not a question which they had expected to find any difficulty in answering: but they soon discovered that Christian misunderstandings of Judaism were not less misleading than Jewish misunderstandings of Christianity: to assume that there had been no development in Judaism since Biblical times, and that modern Jews stood exactly where St. Paul stood, was an undue simplification: the Talmud at least must be taken into account. The nineteenth century missionaries had not the benefit of the profound researches in Judaism which have enriched the twentieth century. Nor had they the benefit of recent historical researches into the relations between Jew and Christian in the Middle Ages: they could not therefore be expected to make allowance for what still haunted Jewish memory of Christian atrocities: it would be an anachronism to charge them with insensibility on that score. What remains to their lasting honour is that at great cost they succeeded in bringing the Church face to face with the forgotten Jewish world, and by their explorations made possible the later researches which provide a basis for mutual knowledge and understanding and ultimate reconciliation in the totally changed context of Jewish-Christian relationships.

2.　THE JERUSALEM BISHOPRIC

Jerusalem is a Holy City to all the three Monotheisms, and is also central to the Church's approach both to Jew and Moslem: the Jerusalem Bishopric therefore finds an appropriate place in the central section of this chapter. It dates from 1841. An Act of Parliament of that year empowered the Archbishop of Canterbury to consecrate British subjects or the subjects or Citizens of any Foreign Kingdom or State to be Bishops in any Foreign Country, without Queen's Licence for their Election or Royal Mandate for their Consecration, and without requiring them if Subjects or Citizens of a Foreign Kingdom or State to take either the Oaths of Allegiance and Supremacy, or the Oath of due Obedience to the Archbishop: Bishops

so consecrated were authorized to exercise within such
Limits as might be prescribed Spiritual Jurisdiction over
the Ministries of British Congregations of the United
Church of England and Ireland, and over such other
Protestant Congregations as might be desirous of placing
themselves under their authority.

The Act provided a valuable constitutional precedent,
and relieved the Church of a serious handicap to its
expansion. It made no reference to Jerusalem but came
to be known colloquially as the " Jerusalem Bishopric Act "
because it owed its origin to the desire to facilitate a
response to certain proposals of King Frederick William
IV of Prussia for the formation of that See. The Powers
had driven the Egyptian dictator Mehemet Ali out of
Palestine and guaranteed the integrity of the Turkish
Empire. It seemed to the King of Prussia an opportune
moment for the Protestant community to secure from the
Turkish Government such guarantees as already safeguarded the interests of other Christian communities in the
Holy Land. The chances of success would be improved if
the British would co-operate. He was willing to pay a price
for their consent, even to the extent of agreeing that the
proposed Bishopric should be a Bishopric of the Church
of England: candidates for Holy Orders would be ordained
by the Anglican Bishop, who would administer the rite
of Confirmation to young persons of the German or of
other congregations within his jurisdiction. German
congregations in Palestine (none of which had as yet come
into being[1]) were to be free to worship in their own tongue
and to use an approved German liturgy. As the King was
providing half the necessary endowment he asked for the
right of nominating alternate Bishops to be consecrated,
with Queen Victoria's approval, by the Archbishop of
Canterbury. There is evidence that the King desired to
introduce episcopacy into Prussia as a bond of union
between Lutheran and Calvinistic elements: a letter from
one of his Chaplains disclosed that this desire was based
on a very loose interpretation of the principles of episcopacy,
and was regarded with abhorrence by his subjects as a
step towards the Church of Rome, but it is tempting to

[1] The King of Prussia's letter to his Minister of Ecclesiastical Affairs, June 28, 1842.

speculate upon what might have been the result if a satisfactory basis of union could have been discovered.

The Jerusalem Bishopric was from the start beset with misfortune. In the first place it became a focus of controversy. The scheme was welcomed by supporters of the Church Missions to Jews, who voted £3,000 towards its endowment. It was known that the King of Prussia was deeply interested in Jewish Missions; he himself had stated that the C.M.J. was the senior of the missions in Palestine, and it was the fact that they were building a Church in Jerusalem that established the right of the English Church to be the dominant partner. On the other hand the scheme was bitterly assailed. Even the gentle and judicious Dean Church, writing fifty years later, condemned it as " only active for mischief . . . never was an ambitious scheme so marked by impotence and failure from its first steps to its last." He could not forgive it for being one of the blows which broke Newman. Readers of the *Apologia* will recall Newman's protests " when I was on my death-bed as regards my membership with the Anglican Church." His first protest fastened on the words of the Act " and such other Protestant congregations ": this was " fraternising with Protestant bodies without any renunciation of their errors and heresies." Later it was the intrusion into the Orthodox Patriarchate which shook his faith in Anglicanism. " The Jerusalem Bishopric was the ultimate condemnation of the old theory of the *Via Media*; if its establishment did nothing else, at least it demolished the sacredness of diocesan rights. If England could be in Palestine, Rome might be in England."

The next misfortune was the early death of the first Bishop after an episcopate of four years. The selection of so learned a Hebrew Christian as Michael Solomon Alexander had been hailed as peculiarly propitious. He was a Polish Jew who had been baptized at Plymouth in 1825 at the age of twenty-six: he had been on the staff of Palestine Place, and Professor of Hebrew and Rabbinical Literature in King's College, London.

It was the King of Prussia's turn to nominate a successor, and he chose Samuel Gobat, a German-speaking Swiss, whose career and sufferings as a missionary in Abyssinia had won him fame (see p. 76). He was Bishop from 1846 to 1879, when he died at the age of 80. He became the target of much criticism, and the four Archbishops of England and Ireland found it necessary to publish a defence against the charge that he was introducing schism into the Eastern Churches. His position was not easy. For the Germans he was too Anglican, for the Anglicans he was too German. He was genuinely anxious to maintain good relations with the Patriarchs and to honour the undertaking to eschew proselytism, but " in Jerusalem itself there are many Latins, Greeks and Armenians who are more or less earnestly seeking the truth; but they are nearly all poor and their dependence on the monasteries is a terrible hindrance. Two families belonging to the Latins were suddenly turned out of their homes, forcibly ejected, because they would not deliver up their Bibles to be burnt." " A year ago I daily received petitions and deputations from all parts of the country, entreating me to take them under my guidance, and to give them teachers. Of course I could not do so, but I exhorted them to persevere in reading the Word of God and to remain in their Churches, seeking at the same time to purify them. Many have followed my advice, but now a new difficulty has arisen. The priests excommunicate those who will not promise not to read the Bible and refuse to kiss a picture and kneel before it, or invoke the Saints. I have never wished to make converts from the old Churches. What am I to do ? "

Gobat was succeeded by Barclay, an Irish missionary who had served the C.M.J. in Constantinople and Jerusalem. There were expectations that he would counteract any disadvantages that the Bishopric had suffered from the old age of a Bishop whose foreign extraction and broken English had inevitably tended to discount the interest of the Church in England in its affairs. But again misfortune dogged the see, and Bishop Barclay died within two years. The Bishopric lapsed for nearly seven years, the Germans having lost interest and withdrawn from an expenditure which accrued mainly to the benefit of the dominant partner. Many hoped that the scheme would lapse. Dr. Liddon reported to Archbishop Benson that the Bishopric was identified with an open system of proselytism, that the

Greek Orthodox Patriarch was opposed, and that it would be better to empty the Endowment Fund into the coffers of the Patriarch to enable him to improve his printing-press and provide editions of the Greek Fathers. The *Guardian* published an article on " The Dead See." Two days later the Archbishop's plan for reconstituting the Bishopric was announced. He could quote the definite judgement of the Greek Patriarch of Jerusalem: "We are moved by fervent desire to see nearer intercourse between the two Churches, that so every spiritual assault may be the more easily and effectively baffled and rendered fruitless. We consider it necessary that a Bishop of the Church of England should be placed in this Holy City. We shall receive him with much affection."

Weighty protests reached the Archbishop, but the decision stood. Letters were despatched to the Orthodox Patriarchs commending the new Bishop Blyth and assuring them that he was instructed not to call himself Bishop *of*, but Bishop *in* Jerusalem, not to use any insignia denoting territorial jurisdiction or authority, not to sign himself, like Gobat, " Angl. Hierosol :"

The Archbishop defined the purpose of the Bishopric as fourfold.—

1. The oversight of English congregations in Syria, Egypt, Asia Minor, Cyprus and the shores of the Red Sea.

2. The supervision of missionaries to the Jews.

3. The supervision of missionaries to the Moslem. In Bishop Gobat's time the C.M.S. had developed Arab work and planted schools and hospitals.

4. The improvement of relations with the Orthodox Church.

It was to support the new Bishop and his successors in pursuing these four ends that the Jerusalem and the East Mission came into existence in 1887. Egypt became a separate diocese in 1920, but the development of Chaplaincy work in Basra and the Persian Gulf counterbalanced the reduction in the Society's area. The Bishopric unites the institutional, pastoral, and evangelistic work of the three Societies, the C.M.J., the C.M.S. and the J. and E. M.

Its Collegiate Church of St. George the Martyr, colloquially known as the Cathedral, is not only a centre of worship, but a centre of study and research. Its canonries are allotted to scholars who concentrate respectively on Jewish and Moslem research, and on the cultivation of reconciliation and understanding between the Communions represented in the Holy City.

THE ARCHBISHOP'S ASSYRIAN MISSION

It was this last responsibility which was Archbishop Benson's special legacy. The spirit in which he reconstituted the Jerusalem Bishopric is reflected in the mission which he sent to the Assyrian Church. " To make English proselytes or to draw any children against the wishes of their parents is not after the spirit or usage of this foundation, although the liberty of enquiry and of conviction which exists in England is not intended to be diminished here." The Nestorian Church had appealed more than once to the Church of England for aid in preserving its existence as a national Assyrian Church. Archbishop Tait had sent embassies of enquiry; Archbishop Benson sent Mr. Athelstan Riley and received despatches from Bishop French. Mr. Riley reported a priest reading Syrian service-books which he did not properly understand, while many of his congregation could not comprehend a word. Assyrian Christians on the borders of Turkey and Persia suffered from grinding taxation and were reduced to squalor and poverty. Yet apostasy was unknown. " This Church of ours," wrote the Archbishop, " has long owned the vocation, though she has been feeble and intermittent in her efforts, to maintain the energies of the more failing Churches of the East and quietly to aid their own yearnings after more light and restored discipline." In 1886 Archbishop Benson sent out Browne and Maclean as the first missioners to organize a regular system of schools in Kurdestan. " A great function of Church towards Church is begun in you." Their instructions were not to Anglicanize, not to draw men away from their allegiance, not to propagate anything contrary to orthodox doctrines as defined by General Councils, but to " infuse

P

fresh life into that which was faint, courage into those who
were afraid, knowledge into those who had but inaccurate
rudiments, faith where everything on earth fought against
faith." The Patriarch was assured that the sole desire was
to "strengthen and illuminate your ancient Church"
by educating those who would hereafter become its
spiritual guides and instructors. The Mission was a
further sign of the vitality and expanding outlook of the
nineteenth-century Church, and remained active for
thirty years. Its duties and responsibilities passed lately,
at the desire of Archbishop Lang, to the Jerusalem and
the East Mission.

3. THE CHURCH'S APPROACH TO THE MOSLEM

Missions to Jews had at least the advantage of a clearly
limited objective and enlisted recruits for a specific purpose.
There were no corresponding Moslem Missions in the
nineteenth century. Moslems in India and Africa were
an element in the population which no missionary could
overlook; presentation of the Gospel to Moslems was
part of the occupation of a missionary, but it was a part-
time occupation and it had to compete with spheres which
presented less formidable obstacles and demanded less
specialized knowledge.

HENRY MARTYN

Even Henry Martyn, whose name has rightly been
identified with the School of Islamic Studies, was not a
Moslem missionary. Strictly speaking he was not a missionary at all, for it was as one of Charles Grant's Chaplains
of the East India Company that he landed at Calcutta in
1806 after a nine months' voyage. He was then twenty-
five and had brought honour to the Truro Grammar
School as Senior Wrangler and Fellow of St. John's College,
Cambridge. He was identified with the group which (as
we have seen in Part IV) was represented by Simeon and
Wilberforce in England, and by Buchanan, Brown and
Corrie in the chaplaincies of Bengal. His voyage was not

uneventful, for the regiment to whom he ministered on board went straight into action on arrival at the Cape for a final tussle with the Dutch, closely followed by Martyn, who tended the wounded. A month on shore gave opportunity for friendship with his hero, Dr. Vanderkemp, the eccentric but intrepid Dutch missionary of the London Missionary Society. Martyn's message was strong meat for the troops in Dinapore and Cawnpore; they had said on the ship, " Mr. Martyn sends us to hell every Sunday." " Major Davidson told me that I set the duties of religion in so terrific a light that people were revolted. I felt the force of this remark and determined to make more use of the love of God in the Gospel." But there was something about him which won the attention of His Majesty's Light Dragoons, won the confidence of sick soldiers, and filled his bungalow with enquirers of the rank and file.

It was because he underrated the difficulty of converting the Hindu that Henry Martyn concentrated upon Mohammedans. " How shall it ever be possible to convince a Hindu or Brahmin of anything " he asks, after two years in Bengal. "If ever I see a Hindu a real believer in Jesus I shall see something more nearly approaching the resurrection of a dead body than anything I have yet seen." What happened was that he was asked to abandon his Sanskrit studies because the need of the moment was the translation of the New Testament into Hindustani, and the revision of translations into Persian and Arabic. Hindustani, the tongue of sixty million Moslems, was as yet unstandardized. The possibilities of Arabic fired his imagination. " So now, *favente Deo*, we will begin to preach to Arabia, Syria, Persia, India, Tartary, China, half of Africa, all the south coast of the Mediterranean and Turkey, and one tongue shall suffice for them all." Martyn immersed himself in the society of learned Mohammedans and threw himself into his work with the diffidence and meticulous fidelity of the scholar, helped and hindered by the temperamental Sabat, an undisciplined Arab convert who ultimately disappointed Martyn's " conviction of the power of God to make him another St. Paul." The Hindustani New Testament was completed within the short four years of Martyn's ministry in India, but the

Persian and Arabic demanded further polish and it was this which consoled him for a departure enforced by rapidly deteriorating lungs. " Arabia shall hide me till I come forth with an approved New Testament in Arabic."

Martyn's voyage was enlivened by the company of Mountstuart Elphinstone, lately ambassador at Kabul, whose picture of him balances the melancholy impression of morbid introspection and disappointed love conveyed by journals that were never intended for the public eye. "We have in Mr. Martyn an excellent scholar and one of the mildest, cheerfullest and pleasantest men I ever saw. He is extremely religious but talks on all subjects, sacred and profane, and makes others laugh as heartily as he could if he were an infidel." The picture of Martyn standing by the grave of St. Francis Xavier at Goa appeals to the imagination.

The *Benares*, on which Martyn acted Chaplain to the European crew, was hunting down Arab pirates in the Persian gulf, but " having received notice of our approach they are all got out of the way, so that I am no longer liable to be shot in a battle or decapitated after it." After all it was not Arabia but Persia that proved to be Martyn's destination—he was only allowed a few hot nights on the " burning, barren rocks " of Muscat. Fitted out with Astrachan cap, baggy blue trousers, red boots and flowing cloak, he made for Shiraz, tried beyond endurance by the thermometer at 126 : " death was inevitable." Of the two versions, the Arabic and Persian, which Martyn submitted to the fastidious scrutiny of Mohammedan scholars, it was the former which passed the test. Sabat's Arabic was good, very good, but his Persian needed thorough revision. Martyn settles down to a six months' " captivity "; " the men of Shiraz propose to translate the New Testament with me. Can I refuse to stay? I am often tempted to get away from this prison, but placing myself twenty years on in time I say, why could I not stay long enough at Shiraz to get a New Testament done there, if it took three or six years? What work of equal importance can ever come to me ? "

Martyn was in Shiraz from June 1811 to May 1812: by February the New Testament was complete. He was a mystery to the people and an offence to the orthodox, but he met with hospitality and courtesy: even a public disputation with the " Preceptor of all the Mullahs " was conducted with mutual chivalry. One of the royalties was heard to growl that the proper reply to Martyn was the sword, but he remained unmoved. " If Christ have work for me to do I cannot die." On his way northward to Tabriz he became involved in angrier scenes. The Shah's Vizier challenged the stranger to recite the Moslem creed: " Say God is God and Mohammed is the Prophet of God." " I said ' God is God,' but added ' Jesus is the Son of God.' They all rose up as if they would have torn me in pieces, and shouting ' What will you say when your tongue is burnt out for this blasphemy ' ? "

Martyn was indeed within sight of the end, but it was not to be martyrdom at the hand of man. He hoped to reach Constantinople and had applied for leave to return to England from there: " a measure you will disapprove " he writes to Simeon, " but you would not were you to see the pitiable condition to which I am reduced." He crossed the Araxes and passed Mount Ararat, but extremes of climate, forced marches, and night after night " the smell of the stables so strong that I was quite unwell," combined to hasten the course of his disease. " I sat in the orchard and thought with sweet comfort and peace of my God, in solitude my Company, my Friend and Comforter." This was the last entry in the journal and ten days later Henry Martyn died at Tokat on October 16th, 1812, where Armenian clergy gave him Christian burial.

KARL GOTTLIEB PFANDER

It was in Armenia that a young German, Karl Pfander, the son of a Wurtemberg baker, took up the torch that had fallen from the hand of Henry Martyn. He had his headquarters at the Basel mission at Shusha from 1825 till 1837 (when the Russians annexed Georgia and suppressed the mission) and travelled perilously in Persia. He later attached himself to the C.M.S. in Agra and Peshawar and was ordained. At Agra the gap between Pfander and Martyn was bridged by the saintly Abdul Masih, Henry

Martyn's only convert, who had been ordained by Bishop Heber. At Agra also, Pfander is linked with Thomas Valpy French to whom he may be said to have passed on Martyn's torch. Pfander's books had attracted attention among Moslems: his *Mizan-al-Haqq*, or *Balance of Truth*, had been translated into several languages and remained for long the classic presentation of the Christian-Moslem argument. Learned Mohammedans challenged him to a public discussion. " I could not do otherwise than accept the proposal, although I was well aware that generally very little good is done. . . . The discussion was carried on for two successive days, lasting two hours each day, and was attended by most of the learned Mohammedans of the city. . . . I feel confident that however much they may boast against us, God in His own way will bring good out of this stir." Faith was rewarded, for two of the protagonists on the Moslem side became stalwart Christians: Safdar Ali, a Government Inspector of Schools, agonized over his religious difficulties for ten years, and was baptized in 1864; another, Moulvie Imad-ud-din, after twelve years of renunciation as a fakir, restudied the Scriptures in order to reclaim his apostate friend Safdar Ali, but finally resolved to follow in his steps. In 1872 he was ordained priest. After writing many controversial books he decided to devote the rest of his days to showing the Moslems " the mercies of God and excellencies of the holy teaching of the Gospels." " Let us pray for those who curse us, let us lead them in the deepest humility, and with tenderest sympathy and love." He was the first Indian to receive the D.D. degree from an Archbishop of Canterbury.

Pfander, though he also preached to Hindus was as nearly a specialist missionary in the Islamic sphere as the Church possessed in the nineteenth century. He dedicated great gifts as scholar and linguist to profound research. Sir Herbert Edwardes of Peshawar, no mean judge of character, wrote of him: " Who can ever forget that burly Saxon figure and genial open face, beaming with intellect, simplicity and benevolence. He had great natural gifts for a missionary, a large heart, a powerful mind, high courage and indomitable good humour. His mastery of the Mohammedan controversy was, in India at least, unequalled. He had thoroughly explored it and acquired the happy power of treating it from Asiatic points of view, in Oriental form of thought and expression. His arguments were all cast in native mould and had nothing of the European about them. Pfander was the very man for a controversy. He not only was the essence of good nature but *looked* it." Sir William Muir described Pfander as the most distinguished Christian opponent of Islam that had yet appeared, and French concurred in this judgement. " Dr. Pfander," wrote French, " though not equal to the beloved Henry Martyn in acuteness and subtlety, was a master of practical straightforward Christian controversy and far out-topped all the missionaries of his day as the Christian champion against Islam. It was no small privilege I had in being the disciple of Pfander in my youth, a worthy successor to the heroic Martyn."

BISHOP FRENCH

French was in the Sixth at Rugby under Arnold and Tait; he won University prizes at Oxford and a Fellowship at University College: he had a passion for languages and when he reached India spared no pains to test his book learning in colloquial talk with the villagers, making a special study of the more popular songs. To a novice who consulted him about the study of vernaculars he wrote: " You must of course commence with Urdu or Hindustani; you had better give some six to eight hours a day to that, and also two or three hours to Persian, and all your spare time to Arabic so as to be able to read the Quran." He himself to the end of his life aspired to that level of industry.

When he took part with Pfander in the public discussion at Agra in 1854 he had already been in India three years; he and Stuart, afterwards Bishop in Australia and a C.M.S. missionary in Persia, were sent to inaugurate what became the renowned St. John's College, Agra. With wife and children he was beleaguered six months in the Fort during the Mutiny. His second spell was spent on the Frontier, establishing contact with the Pathans, and studying Pushtu. Illness soon drove him home under sentence of final banishment from India: but neither health nor eight children could hold him back. A very definite plan obsessed his mind of a College for training Native Evangelists, Pastors and Teachers for North-West India and the Punjab, and he could not rest till he had persuaded the C.M.S. to despatch him to Lahore to translate his vision into actuality.

" We must not compromise the future character of the native Church," he wrote, " by attempting to trammel it with too rigid adherence to our institutions, holding it thus swathed as it were and bound tight in our leading strings. Its growth if it is to be healthy must be spontaneous and unwarped. In the early Churches it was an object from the very first to form rallying points for the diffusion of the Gospel. A small body of Christian teachers always devoted themselves to the firmer building up in the truth of the choicest and ablest converts with a view to their becoming in turn teachers and preachers. It was never left to be a desultory and discretionary spare-time occupation." In the proposed College, Christianity would be domesticated on the Indian soil and could reckon on a home and hearth of its own.

For seven years French nursed his Divinity School, setting an exacting standard for the students who, contrary to current missionary expectations, increased in numbers. It was by no means an exclusively academic curriculum. " As regards our training Colleges, we must not forget that over against the Colleges of Christian learning in the early ages there was a multitude of hermits living isolated lives in the desert, as like to Hindu Gurus and Sunyasses as can be conceived, who had an extraordinary influence in leavening the masses outside the cities. We must be very careful about damaging the work of men of this class to whom all great religious movements in India have been owing: helping them from our institution with good vernacular theology, without stunting their growth and repressing their strong individualities. We must not forget to stimulate our students by word and example to choose rather the Indian Guru's life than the hot-bed artificial life of the foreign missionary."

" We have all been struck in studying this year the history of St. Aidan and his fellow-workers with the much greater resemblance which the work of those old evangelists bore to purely native models than most of what our modern missionaries exhibit. Hindu sect-leaders, Mohammedan moollahs, Anglo-Saxon missionaries, were alike in laying stress on giving a few instruments the finest polish possible, imbuing a few disciples with all that we ourselves have been taught of truth, ' lighting the scholars lamp at the master's light '."

All this was characteristic of the man and reflected his insatiable desire to come to grips with the people, and especially with those most opposed. " I find no plan so successful for gathering a good and attentive audience as making straight for the mosque and inquiring for the moollah. Instead of hanging about the village and having one's object suspected, this was a definite and straightforward object, and besides often meeting in this way on equal terms with the moollah, the khans and other villagers would congregate in the mosque."

French's ten years as first Bishop of Lahore (1877–87) necessarily involved him in many activities, such as building a Cathedral and building up a Synod, that were not strictly relevant to his Moslem interests, but his diocese included eleven and a half million Mohammedans in the Punjab and the Frontier Province. It was characteristic that he followed close on the heels of Lord Roberts to Kandahar, and seized the opportunity of exploring beyond the Khyber Pass. To give up his See would be to release him for what had always been his primary concern, the approach to a deeper knowledge and understanding of the Moslem world.

While Bishop of Lahore he had been asked by the Bishop of London and the C.M.S. to visit missions that were still in embryo in Persia. " A call to follow in the steps of Henry Martyn had irresistible attraction." That part of the Moslem world which lay between the Persian Gulf and the Caspian he had already traversed: he had followed Henry Martyn to Shiraz and experienced something of what he had suffered: " If we would win these Moslem lands for Christ we must die for them." was his formula for encouraging missionaries, and he was ready to practise what he preached. Released from office, he had three

years left of life: only six months of this period was spent
in England. On his way home he travelled slowly through
Mesopotamia, " by foot as Abraham travelled," preaching
and talking in Arabic, and writing long despatches to
Archbishop Benson on the condition of the Assyrian
Church. He spent some months in Syria, encouraging
American missionaries and the British Syrian Schools.
On Christmas Day he preached in Bethlehem in Arabic,
and two days later an address to Moslems in the heart of
Hebron, curtailed by Turkish soldiers, was " an opportunity
worth the year's hard fagging at Arabic I have had, and
I hope the next three months may go far to remove defects
in pronunciation and the use of inappropriate words."

French had kept in close touch with the Uganda mission
and in reading the life of Alexander Mackay was deeply
moved by his appeal for a mission at Muscat " the key
to Central Africa." The Arabs used to say to Mackay:
" All you come and try to convert the Uganda people and
other idol worshippers; you never tried to convert us at
Muscat." French was sixty-five and aged beyond his years
by tropical disease, but could he not at least explore the
ground and perhaps prepare the way for a C.M.S. or
U.M.C.A. mission ? The spirit of Henry Martyn beckoned.
He spent a month at Tunis on the way, where he found
" Plymouthists and Baptists who seem to tolerate, if not value,
the interest taken in them and their work by an Anglican
Bishop, and there seems much one can learn from their
devoted self-sacrifice. It seems needless at least to exaggerate differences in such wild outlying regions. . . . I
am giving six hours a day to Arabic and like studies. . . .
I may yet return here, where the great Panislamic movement to fight a last desperate battle with the Gospel of
Christ and the Kingdom of God is likely to have very
momentous issues." At Kairowan, French found himself
in touch with the Mohammedan brotherhoods, the Senous-
siya, Qadirigas, Madaniya, and found that readings from
his " favourite author " Ald-ul-Kadir, " whose deep
spiritual fervour and mystic devotion and intense thirst
of the soul for nearness to God exceeded anything in
average Moslem works," attracted audiences at the gates
of the stately Mosques.

French reached Muscat in February 1891; accompanied by Maitland of the Cambridge Mission to Delhi. They arrived not in the least knowing how or where they could put up. Mosquitos, sand-flies, dust-storms and the sun were formidable antagonists. French plunged into bazaar preachings in Arabic, or pleadings, as he characteristically called them. "I am pushing on very hard into Arabic." "Two days ago a large party of Arabs made almost a dead set at me to induce me to turn Mohammedan. It was a new experience and useful as enabling me better to understand the feeling an Arab or Hindu would have in being so approached with a view to changing a faith dear to him as life itself, as with the Moslem usually it is." "To be courteously, almost cordially welcomed by Arab desert-rangers, if it be once out of five visits paid, is cheering beyond description." "Some may have been set thinking and the fruit yet appear: to me it has been a ' going forth weeping', bearing precious seed, apparently over a very ungenial barren drought-stricken soil."

In his last letter to his son-in-law, the Rev. E. A. Knox, afterwards Bishop of Manchester, he writes: "I have seldom experienced such trying bafflings and baulkings of purpose, but I don't think I shall ever be sorry that I made an attempt, how feeble and unsuccessful soever to reach the poor Arabs." A few days later, on May 13th, 1891, the Bishop died. His grave is on the shore at the foot of precipitous and barren rocks, and on its cross the inscription runs: "He endured as seeing Him Who is invisible."

It was the Cambridge Mission to Delhi which inherited the torch. It had been in Bishop French's episcopate and diocese, and as an outcome of his talks at Cambridge with Bishop Westcott and Edward Bickersteth its first Head (see p. 184) that the Brotherhood had been started. French wrote rather whimsically: "To join a brotherhood for seven years and (if need be) to marry afterwards seems the more excellent way, though my example has not been sufficiently in favour of it." The mantle descended upon George Alfred Lefroy, afterwards himself Bishop of Lahore and Metropolitan of India. From his arrival at Delhi in 1880 till he became Bishop in 1899, Lefroy's main energies went into the task of presenting Christ to the Moslem. Discussions in the Bazaar or in the Bickersteth Hall were exacting, " terribly trying on judgement and temper in an atmosphere of 105 or so "; but night after night for year after year Lefroy was to be found accessible, patient and understanding.

THE TWENTIETH-CENTURY SEQUEL

The work of these four pioneers and of the many missionaries associated with them illustrate the efforts which the nineteenth century made to explore what had been an unknown and forgotten field. The Lambeth Conference of 1897 summarized the lessons they had taught. " It is essential that there should be on the part of missionaries a thorough and patient study of Mohammedans, and knowledge of Arabic—absolute fairness in dealing with the doctrines of Islam and the character of Mohammed—care not to lose sight of points of contrast whilst discussing points of difference. Those who undertake this work should receive a special training for it and be set apart exclusively for it."

With the turn of the century a new chapter opened in the Church's approach to the Moslem. Two of the countries explored by Bishop French, Persia and Palestine, have seen the birth of churches composed of ex-Mohammedan congregations and clergy. The diocese of Persia, founded in 1912, with its C.M.S. Missions and educational institutions, has been exposed to many vicissitudes, corresponding to the phases through which the country has passed. In Palestine both the C.M.S. and the Jerusalem and the East Mission have undertaken medical and educational work, and a canonry in the Cathedral is allotted to an expert in Moslem studies. But the twentieth-century history of the Church's approach to the Moslem would have to cover a wider range of country and problems than come within the present scope.

Islam, which had been assumed to be an extinct volcano, was discovered still to possess powers of eruption. These explosive forces altered in some respects the outline and contours of the mountains: what had seemed unchangeable, the position of the Khalifat, the traditional attitude towards womanhood, towards western knowledge, towards Mohammedan faith and law, was seen to be once more fluid. At the same time molten lava issued from the old volcano to inundate new regions. The Lambeth Conference of 1908 was alive to "the aggressive propaganda of Islam which is challenging the Christian Church to a struggle for the possession of Equatorial Africa. The door is still open for the Christian Church, but if she fails to press through it in a few years it will be shut." The U.M.C.A. felt it necessary to safeguard the young African Church by forearming Christians with knowledge of the faith and practice of Islam and instilling in them a sense of responsibility for witnessing to Moslems in their midst. At the same time efforts had to be redoubled in Moslem lands, such as the Sudan and the Emirates of Northern Nigeria, from which Christian missions had been excluded.

Thornton and Gairdner stood for a new strategy in the Church's approach to the Moslem world, with Cairo as the centre of the Mohammedan world and the clue to Moslem evangelization. In the cloisters of its El Azhar University Mosque, the oldest of the mediæval universities, mediæval still in aspect and curriculum, were to be found students from all quarters of the Moslem world. From Cairo Arabic literature circulated throughout the Moslem world. Thornton and Gairdner laid themselves out to be accessible to students, to master both classical and colloquial Arabic, to get inside the Mohammedan mentality, and to provide literature that would interpret Christianity in terms that would be understood. *Orient and Occident* shares with the Oxford Mission to Calcutta's *Epiphany* the honour of being one of the first experiments in missionary journalism, if the name can be applied to a magazine of such serious literary and theological character. Douglas Thornton died in 1907 at the age of thirty-four. Temple Gairdner served on till 1929; an example of what has been all too commonly the price paid for shortage of man-power, a razor of tempered steel being squandered in sharpening pencils.

The approach to the Moslem must always involve tension and intransigence in Dr. Bevan's sense of the word;

it cannot altogether escape an intellectualist and controversial tone. But Gairdner brought to it, over and above
exceptional powers of mind and spirit, trained in the
discipline of Islamic studies, a distinctively personal and
affectionate touch. He would have approved his colleague,
Dr. Cash's, warning: " Controversy is a futile line of
approach both from Christian to Moslem and Moslem to
Christian: both Moslem and Christian as long as they use
this method are in a vicious circle from which there is no
escape. . . . The supreme qualification for the missionary
is love, the love that thinks no evil, the love that seeks the
good of others without any ulterior motive. . . . One who
carries the message of Christianity to Islam must ever
centre his own life as well as his message in Christ."[1]

[1] Wilson Cash: *Christendom and Islam.*

PART X

THE PROCESS OF EXPANSION

Introduction: *Some Statistics*

I. EXPANSION IN BRITISH COLONIES

1. A Process of Adaptation: (*a*) Fluctuations of Colonial Policy; (*b*) Social and Economic Conditions; (*c*) Change of Status.

2. Keeping pace with Emigration.

II. EXPANSION IN NON-CHRISTIAN ENVIRONMENTS

1. The Influence of Power: The Church and Temporal Powers; Olaf Tryggvason; Charlemagne; The King of Portugal ; Queen Victoria; The Emperor of China.

2. The Power of Influence: (*a*) Individual Conversion; (*b*) Mass Conversion, Mediæval and Modern; (*c*) Missionary Mediums, Literary, Medical, Educational.

ATTENTION has hitherto been concentrated upon the experimental stages in the expansion of the Anglican Communion: the questions to which some reply has been attempted have been, how came it that the Church of England colonized ? If, like the banyan-tree, the ancient stem put forth branches which in turn drew sustenance from the soil, through pendent streamers that established their own roots, how did this come about ? Who were the pioneers to whom the process owed its origins ? Two further questions now suggest themselves : (1) By what instruments was the process of expansion developed ? (2) What evidence is there that the Church thus transplanted is genuinely rooted and not an exotic growth ?

Both questions demand answers in terms of quality, but since they assume the fact of expansion, some quantitative presentation of this fact is a necessary preliminary to their discussion. The outstanding fact of this generation is the contrast between the Church of to-day viewed territorially or numerically and the infants " mewling and puking in the nurse's arms " whose precarious hold on life we have been observing: we are now in a position to appreciate this contrast.

Territorially the expansion may be measured by the increase in the number of Anglican dioceses: 75 in 1800; 320 in 1939. In 1800 only twelve of the 75 were outside the British Isles; ten in the United States and two in the rest of the world: in 1939 there were 105 in the United States, 146 in the rest of the world. At the first Lambeth Conference in 1868, of 79 Bishops present 19 came from the United States, 24 from Colonial and Missionary Dioceses. There were 308 Bishops at the Lambeth Conference of 1930, and the analysis of their places of origin is worth studying as evidence of territorial expansion:—

The British Isles	...	113	Tropical Africa	14
U.S.A.	61	Argentine, Bermuda,	
India, Burma, Ceylon ...	12	Korea (2), Egypt,	
Canada	24	Falkland Islands,	
Australia	24	Gibraltar, Jerusalem,	
South Africa	15	Labuan and Sarawak,	14
New Zealand	6	Madagascar, Mauritius,	
West Indies	9	Newfoundland, Persia,	
China	9	Singapore ...	
Japan	7		

Numerically there is evidence of expansion in the statistics available showing the approximate number of baptized Anglicans in 1938, and the number of the Native Clergy:—

	Baptized	Native Ministry
Australia, Aborigines... ...	5,500	12
British Malaya	22,500	11
Burma	23,000	45
Ceylon	40,000	91
China	65,000	283
Egypt	658	2
India	695,000	580
Japan	27,000	225
Korea	8,500	19
Melanesia	43,500	61
N.Z. Maoris		
Palestine	4,000	9
Persia	600	3
Polynesia	4,500	...
South Africa	526,000	177
Tropical Africa	729,000	480
West Indies	526,000	?

These figures illustrate the growth of the Church in countries where Christianity had to start from scratch, and take little account of the expansion of the Church among peoples of British descent and Christian antecedents. The two lines of this dual process of expansion run parallel and extend simultaneously, but demand separate treatment.

I. EXPANSION IN BRITISH COLONIES

A PROCESS OF ADAPTATION

The long and chequered history of the advance from Colonial to Dominion status, from representative to responsible institutions of government, is not strictly relevant to Church history except in so far as it illuminates the context in which the Church expanded. The Church could not but be affected and its energies quickened or retarded by the fluctuations in public interest in the Colonies and the vacillations of British Colonial policy. Where that policy was suspected of riding roughshod over Native interests, the Church could not evade issues which overstepped the boundary between the political and the moral. As Colonial independence developed, the Church found itself compelled to adapt itself to conditions of Bush, Veldt and Prairie as far removed morally as physically from the sheltered life of an Established Church in the English countryside of the nineteenth century.

ADAPTATION: (a) TO THE FLUCTUATIONS OF COLONIAL POLICY

" Under the pressure of great distress and financial embarrassment," wrote Lord Grey in 1848, " there is a growing disposition in the House of Commons and amongst the public to grumble at the heavy cost of the Colonies "; and again in 1849, " There begins to prevail in the House of Commons and I am very sorry to say in the highest quarters, an opinion (which I believe to be utterly erroneous) that we have no interest in preserving our Colonies and ought therefore to make no sacrifice for that purpose. Peel, Graham and Gladstone, if they do not avow this

Q

opinion as openly as Cobden and his friends, yet betray very clearly that they entertain it, nor do I find some members of the Cabinet free from it."[1]

The British took many years to recover their nerve, which had been severely shaken when the first British Empire met its doom in the American Declaration of Independence. Separatism and probable secession were the morals drawn from that experience and an eventual parting company on good terms was all that could be hoped for, or indeed desired. Up to the late '60's, the issue was discussed in the cold and calculating accents of commerce. Direct monetary gain was the only criterion. The Manchester School regarded the colonial connection " as artificial and associated with mercantilism." Free-trade and *laissez-faire* biassed their adherents against it. From the point of view of profit and loss the Colonies seemed to have lost their *raison d'être*, and glory was only " an imagined advantage."[2] There were voices attuned to other notes—Carlyle who believed in the civilizing mission of the Anglo-Saxons; Ruskin who saw imperial Britain as "a source of light, a centre of peace; mistress of learning and of the Arts, faithful guardian of time-tried principles under temptation from loud experiments and licentious desires, and amidst the cruel and clamorous jealousies of the nations, worshipped in her strange valour of good-will towards men ";[1] Disraeli who acclaimed England as " the metropolis of a great maritime Empire extending to the boundaries of the farthest Ocean."[2] But these were minority voices.

The Church, therefore, so far from being carried on a rising tide of imperial ardour, had to battle against prevailing tendencies that discouraged if they did not discountenance overseas adventure.

ADAPTATION: (*b*) TO SOCIAL AND ECONOMIC CONDITIONS

We have already seen in relation to the Slave-trade and Opium-traffic, to the Maori, to Hottentot and Bantu, the Church ranged on the side and in the van of the

[1] *Cambridge History of the British Empire*, pp. 383, 384.
[2] Quoted by E. A. Walker: *The British Empire, its Structure and Spirit*.

humanitarian movement. " The missionaries opposed the grant of local legislative powers to mixed Colonies where the white inhabitants might be tempted to oppress their coloured fellow-subjects, and often advocated the annexation of tribal areas in which they themselves had failed to buttress up an effective native government, lest uncontrolled European immigration, that most deadly solvent of tribal policies, should induce chaos." It was a delicate course to steer.[1]

Henry Venn, the great Secretary of the C.M.S., felt it necessary in 1854 to draw the attention of missionaries to the Society's rule: " Every Missionary is strictly charged to abstain from interfering in the political affairs of the country or place in which he may be situated." He admitted that " political affairs " is a wide term. " There are worldly politicians who would desire to include in their exclusive province, national education, the State support of idolatry, the social institution (as it is called) of slavery, the treatment of the aborigines, the private religious action of Government officers. As soon as a minister of religion touches these questions an outcry is apt to be raised, as if he were meddling with politics. But such subjects are not simply ' political affairs '; they are of a mixed character The great principles of justice, humanity and Christian duty lie at the root of these questions, which are the special province of ministers of religion."

There follow words of sage advice. The Committee affectionately but earnestly warns each missionary, especially every young missionary, not to take up supposed grievances too hastily, to err on the side of abstinence from doubtful cases, to stand clear of party strife, recourse to public censure of ruling powers or the lash of newspaper invective, to shun entanglement in political discussions, to avoid all appearance of political intrigue. Use your influence to preserve or restore peace in conformity with the spirit of a minister of the Gospel.[2]

Henry Venn's approbation of the prominent part played by missionaries in helping Captain Hobson to make the Treaty of Waitangi with the Maoris and in lifting up their

[1] *The British Empire: its Structure and Spirit.*
[2] *Memoir of Henry Venn*, Appendix E.

voices against what they believed to be its violation illustrates the razor-edge path which the missionary treads.
A South African historian in defending against his detrac-
tors the "notorious Negrophile," Dr. John Philip (see p. 125)
insists that the obloquy attached to his name is the lot of all
men who attain great ends. " Christian missionaries set
in the midst of any backward people, like the Churchmen
of the Middle Ages, must be the responsible representatives
of civilization and culture in the widest sense. Theirs is a
truly political though not a partisan function, that cannot
be fulfilled by eschewing politics. To disregard questions
affecting the social welfare and economic security of their
people is to doom their work as teachers of religion to
sterility. Efforts to fulfil a ' purely ' religious function may
be completely overwhelmed by social and economic facts
that are thought to be outside the proper sphere of missionaries."[1]

ADAPTATION: (c) TO CHANGE OF STATUS

The transplanting of the Church in Canadian, Australian
and South African soil had legal and constitutional consequences which are reserved for examination in a later
study. Here we are concerned with adjustments, recognized in the end as salutary though resented at the time,
affecting the social status and finances of the Church. It
was at first assumed that the Church of England carried
with it overseas the privileges enjoyed at home. In fact
the subsidizing of sees in Nova Scotia, Quebec, Calcutta,
Jamaica, Barbados, out of Government revenue, the setting
aside of a fixed proportion of public lands for the support
of the Church and its schools in Australia, the instructions
to the Governors of British Guiana to provide schools for
instruction in religion according to the Doctrine of the
United Church of England and Ireland, the Parliamentary
Grants to the S.P.G. which reached a total of £22,664 in
1825, these were all calculated to encourage the expectation
that the Church overseas was to be more rather than less
favoured than the Church at home. But by the 1830's,
even such staunch Churchmen as the Colonial Secretary,
Lord Glenelg, Charles Grant's son, and his Permanent

---

[1] W. M. Macmillan: *Bantu, Boer and Briton*.

Under-Secretary James Stephen, Henry Venn's brother-in-law, realized that the time had come to bow to the growing insistence in the Colonies upon complete religious equality. Glenelg in 1835 admitted the futility of choosing " any one Church as the exclusive object of Public Endowment." Stephen admitted that " the state of the world is very unfavourable to the maintenance of exclusive ecclesiastical pretensions, and it is evident that the exclusive privileges of the English Church in Canada cannot be supported—except at the expense of great unpopularity." He even doubted whether the real interest of the Church of England would be promoted by maintaining any such exclusive principle.[1]

By 1834 the Parliamentary grant to the S.P.G. had dropped to £4,000. The cut did not apply so austerely to the West Indies, where the Church of England was still regarded as Established, but funds were voted by Parliament for the education of negroes by Wesleyans as well as Anglicans. As the Imperial Government gradually divested itself of responsibility for purely local affairs, the cessation of State aid became general. Freedom in religious matters became the test of England's good faith in renouncing all right to interfere with self-governing colonies.

> " It had seemed to England a worthy system of colonisation to found a Christian Church simultaneously with a civil polity. But established Churches could not be acclimatised in the new Colonial societies. It was soon apparent that what the Colonists wanted was to substitute the voluntary principle for Church establishment."[2]

It was the Home Government itself, influenced by the desire to secure religious equality and following the example of the disestablishment of the Church of Ireland, that urged on the West Indian Colonies the disestablishment and disendowment (or concurrent endowment) of their Churches The Governor of Jamaica had estimated that out of a population of 500,000 the Nonconformists had charge of 200,000, the Established Church of 100,000, while no religious provision was made for 200,000. Religious feuds were so pronounced that the Governor of the Windward

---

[1] *The Cambridge History of the British Empire*, p. 294.
[2] *Ibid.*, p. 685.

Islands declared that Jamaica exhibited the lamentable spectacle of a people of whom it might be said " see how the Christians *hate* one another." £38,000 out of a gross revenue of £314,000 were appropriated to the support of the Established Church. Lord Granville, the Secretary of State, wrote " that the moral and religious culture of the subject race, and not the ascendancy of any one community ought to be the object of your Government." An Act of Disestablishment was passed by the Jamaica legislature in 1870, without protest from the local Church. The other West Indian Colonies followed suit, although in Trinidad there was concurrent endowment of the Church of England and the Roman Catholic Church, in British Guiana there was triple endowment of the Anglican, the Dutch Reformed and the Presbyterian Churches, and in Barbados the Bishop and Clergy are still paid direct from the Island Treasurer and qualify for Government pensions. The Church in Ceylon was disestablished in 1886.

It may therefore be claimed that the expansion of the Anglican Communion in the Dominions and Colonies has not, except in the earliest stages, been favoured with advantages denied to other Communions. It has indeed laboured under a handicap. It was required to bring into action muscles that had grown atrophied by disuse. Whereas the rank and file of the Free Churches, if the name may still be used where all are free, had been accustomed to maintain their own Ministry and Chapels, in their Home Church Anglicans had been wont to take for granted their inherited Church buildings and endowments.

2. THE PACE OF EMIGRATION

With all its multiplying responsibilities for missions in India, Africa, the Far East, the South Seas, the Caribbean Sea, Central and South America, the Church found itself summoned to keep pace with the British Dispersion. Hosts of emigrants were leaving these shores, a large proportion of them children of the Church and entitled to expect the ministrations of the Church in whatever part of the world their lot might be cast. The Lambeth Conference of 1888 reported that since the Battle of Waterloo, 11,740,573 emigrants had left the United Kingdom, nearly two and a half million British subjects in the last ten years. In 1887, 281,487 had gone from the British Isles, 201,526 to the U.S.A., 32,025 to Canada, 34,183 to Australasia, 13,753 to other destinations. In 1852 the discovery of rich deposits of gold at Ballarat and Bendigo had driven up the Australian annual increment of population from 6,000 to 100,000.

But 1888 stood only at the beginning of a quarter of a century of accelerating emigration. Gold and diamonds drew men to South Africa. In 1882 scientific processes of refrigeration had first been adapted to the holds of ocean-going ships. New Zealands' exports of meat rose from £120,000 to £3,000,000; butter and cheese from £50,000 to £1,500,000 in twenty years. At the beginning of the '90's, Canadian wheat began to flow to the United Kingdom; by 1900 it had become a torrent. There were less than 2,000 new homesteads in the Prairie Provinces in 1897, over 5,000 in 1900, over 24,000 in 1903. Trans-continental railways were planned to link the Atlantic with the Pacific, the Cape to Cairo, Sydney via Melbourne and Adelaide to Perth in the far West, via Brisbane to North Queensland. Trans-continental the Church had to become: diocese begot diocese.

Bishop George Jehosophat Mountain's single see of Lower Canada gave birth to dioceses in Upper Canada; Toronto, 1839; Montreal, 1850; and beyond Upper Canada in Manitoba to Rupertsland, from which sprang the nine daughters of the Province to which it gave its name, and the six grand-daughters of the Province of British Columbia. The Church of Canada to-day comprises four Provinces and twenty-seven Dioceses. Bishop Gray's solitary South African see stretching from Cape Town to the Zambesi has become a Province of fourteen dioceses, extending beyond the civil boundary of the Union to the self-governing Colony of Southern Rhodesia, the Portuguese territory of Lebombo, the mandated territory of Damaraland and St. Helena in mid-Atlantic. Bishop Broughton, as we have seen, had only to wait from 1836 to 1842 before he was furnished with an episcopal colleague in Tasmania, and only five years longer before he could change his title of Bishop of Australia to Bishop of Sydney, when Newcastle, Melbourne and Adelaide became separate sees. The Church of Australia and Tasmania to-day includes four Provinces and twenty-five Dioceses. Bishop Selwyn in the 1850's divided his diocese of New Zealand into four, Christ Church, Wellington, Nelson, Waiapu, and founded the missionary diocese of Melanesia in 1861. There are now nine dioceses in the Province of New Zealand.

Further afield, one of the smallest but not least historic of the Crown Colonies, the Falkland Islands, at the southern-most tip of South America, gave its name to a diocese founded in 1869, which, till a new diocese of Argentina and Eastern South America in 1910 relieved it of responsibility East of the Andes, was charged with the oversight of scattered British congregations over the whole continent, exclusive of British Guiana. The whole story of the British Dispersion is not yet covered, for there were countless settlers in India, Ceylon, the Straits Settlements, the ports of China, and later in the diocese of Mombasa, to whom the Church owed its ministrations. There were sailors as well as settlers. The Missions to Seamen traces its origin back to 1835, and planted Churches and Institutes in over a hundred ports in all continents.

The older Societies were among the foremost instruments in this process of expansion. The Colonial Bishoprics' Fund, till with the growth of autonomous provinces it resigned its original function of establishing and endowing new dioceses into their hands and became itself little more than a trust-holding body, had for its first fifty years been the primary agent of the Church in the enlargement of the episcopate throughout the world: it had raised close on £1,000,000 for the cause.

The S.P.C.K. and the S.P.G. contributed largely to these funds, and were the main channels of supply between the new dioceses and the old, faithfully goading the home Church into acknowledging that it could not fairly impose upon the young Churches of the Empire the burden of assimilating unassisted the hosts of British emigrants.

The C.M.S. though not constituted to minister to fellow-countrymen, played nevertheless a conspicuous part in the expansion of the Church of Canada, through its pioneer missions in the territories of the Hudson Bay Company, within the Arctic Circle, along the Red River and Mackenzie River, among Red Indians and Eskimos. Bishop Anderson's fifteen years as first Bishop of Rupertsland with its jurisdiction from Labrador to the Rockies laid the foundations for the great forty years' episcopate of William Carpenter Bompas, first Bishop in turn of Athabasca, Mackenzie River, and Yukon.

Younger Societies came into existence as auxiliaries to the Church of Canada. The Colonial and Continental Church Society, founded originally in 1823 as "The Society for Educating the Poor of Newfoundland", adopted its present name in 1861, and adopted Saskatchewan as its major field in Canada, and Emmanuel College for the training of ordination candidates, many of whom it recruited in England, as its major contribution to the Ministry of the Church of Canada. The Archbishops' Western Canada Fund brought reinforcements of English clergy and laymen. The new dioceses across the Rockies have been aided by the British Columbia and Yukon Church Aid Society. The Fellowship of the Maple Leaf has sent over 500 British teachers to the rural schools in the West, and established Hostels for teachers in training.

In the Bush Brotherhoods of Australia the Church has evolved a substitute for the traditional parochial system which proved unadaptable to small communities widely scattered in sheep and cattle stations. A Bush Brothers' membership in a group of priests, bound together by a simple rule of life and meeting at regular intervals at headquarters, counteracts the strain of spiritual isolation. It is in the form of recruits for these Brotherhoods that the Australian Church has in recent years most welcomed assistance from the Church in England.

It would be a mistake to suppose that the making of Christian history in the Dominions and Colonies compares unfavourably with the story of expansion in the non-Christian world, as lacking the elements of exacting and costly adventure or as merely reproducing the familiar apparatus of Church life. In Bishop Feilds' early exploits in Newfoundland we had a glimpse of the conditions which fall to the lot of pioneers, calling for dogged persistence in the face of hardship and resolute determination to press on into the unknown. It is true that the settlers' church establishes gradually and with adaptations, institutions modelled on inherited customs: there is too large a common element in what all Churches need for the building up of their corporate life to make probable any wide diversity in the methods employed. There is the inevitable similarity in the provision made for the erection of places of worship, for the education of the young, the care of the sick, the training of teachers, the theological preparation of the Ministry. There is the universal acceptance of a Church's missionary obligations. The Church of Canada made itself responsible for dioceses in China and Japan; Australia for the dioceses of Central Tanganyika, and New Guinea; New Zealand for Melanesia and a mission in Sind; South Africa for extension into Damaraland; while all these Churches held within their own borders populations originally non-Christian, Indians, Eskimos, Oriental immigrants, aborigines, Maoris and Bantus.

Yet the Churches overseas are no replicas of the Mother Church; they tell an absorbing tale of the process of adaptation: adaptation to immense distances and climatic extremes; adaptation to the status of a "Free" Church; adaptation to Bush, Veldt and Prairie; adaptation to the fluidity of expanding frontiers.

II. EXPANSION IN NON-CHRISTIAN ENVIRONMENTS

3. THE INFLUENCE OF POWER

The extension of Christianity in the ancient days was conditioned by circumstances. The security of the Roman Empire, the system of communications, the disposition of monarchs, the mysterious emergence of migrant peoples, the play of politics, all had their influence in opening or closing doors to the Gospel. The makers of modern history have similarly, though unwittingly, played a part in the making of Christian history—Pitt, Fox and Burke, successive Governor-Generals of India, Speke and Burton and other African explorers, Commander Perry, Cecil Rhodes, Sun Yat Sen.

It may be well, therefore, before enumerating the more spiritual instruments of the Church's nineteenth century expansion, to ask how much was owed to reliance upon temporal power. Here a distinction must be drawn between taking advantage on the one hand of new opportunities, of access or new conditions of security afforded by Governments, and taking advantage on the other hand of favours extended, and force exerted or held in reserve by Governments in deliberate support of religious propagation. It is in respect of the latter that the nineteenth-century missionary may confidently challenge comparison with his predecessors.

OLAF TRYGGVASON

On an earlier page we noted that the Church in Norway laid undue emphasis on the Gospel precept " Compel them to come in that my house may be full." The development of the Church and the consolidation of the Kingdom under one rule were part of the same process. When Olaf Tryggvason became King the Saga tells us that he bade all men take up Christianity, and those who spake against it he dealt with hard: some he slew, some he maimed, and some he drove away from the land: none dared oppose the King and wherever he went the folk were baptized.

CHARLEMAGNE

Charlemagne's conversion of Saxony was as bloody. Ambition and religion went hand in hand; successes in arms were successes for Christianity. The bribes and menaces by which he urged the conquered to the font, his wholesale massacres and ruthless deportations provoked remonstrance from Alcuin. In 794 Charlemagne transported 7,000 Saxons, in 797 every third household, in 798 sixteen hundred of the chief men, in 799 a great multitude. His legislation for the Saxons was written in letters of blood. " If any man depise the Lenten Fast let him die the death. If any man shall hide himself and refuse Baptism let him die the death." We may be glad that it was a Yorkshireman who had the courage to protest. " If the easy yoke and light burden of Christ had been preached to this most hard race," so Alcuin told the King, " with as great insistence as the legal penalties for the very smallest details, it may be that they would not have abhorred the Sacrament of Baptism. . . . Let the Teachers of the Faith preach not prey: Sint Predicatores non Praedatores. . . . The perfectly converted soul is to be fed with the milk of apostolic piety until it grows and becomes strong enough to receive solid food." Alcuin echoed Aidan's rebuke of the austere Scot who returned to Iona from a mission to Northumbria discouraged because he could do no good to a nation of uncivilized men of a stubborn and barbarous disposition. " I am of opinion, brother, that you were more severe to your unlearned hearers than you ought to have been, and did not at first, conformably to the apostolic rule, give them the milk of more easy doctrine, till being by degrees nourished with the word of God, they should be capable of greater perfection, and be able to practise God's sublime precepts."[1]

The only plea in Charlemagne's favour, wrote his biographer, Professor H. W. C. Davis, was his success. " To the conquest of Saxony, Germany owed her brightest seats of learning, and her most splendid dynasty." The Saxons soon forgave and were grateful to their terrible preceptor. It is certainly startling to read in the Annals of a Saxon poet less than a century later:—

> " He swept away the black deceitful night
> And taught our race to know the only light.
> The strife was lone, the peril great and sore
> And heavy toil and sleepless watch he bore.
> The host of all his realm did he combine
> To drag this people from the devil's shrine.
> For who can turn fierce heathen from their bent
> By soft persuasion and sage argument ? "

With all deference to an honoured tutor, Charlemagne's success with the Saxons must be discounted by their subsequent conduct, and the quality of their Christianity. It is true that when they came to power they extended Christianity eastwards, but by the same methods as they had themselves been taught, imposing Baptism as symbol

[1] Bede: III, p. 5.

of acknowledgement of their overlordship and as a step towards assimilation. The spread of Christianity was a phase of Teutonic expansion and checked by recurring reactions which were anti-Christian because anti-German. The conversion of Bohemia and the Czechs was delayed until the close of the ninth and not completed till late in the tenth century, because Christianity was identified with German dominion and culture. Poland in turn suffered similar reactions and in turn pursued a Charlemagne policy against the Pomeranians, carrying its inhabitants captive and requiring them to renounce paganism and embrace Christianity.

THE KING OF PORTUGAL

Identification of the sword of the Spirit with the sword of State was not a mediæval monopoly. It is startling to find so great a missionary as St. Francis Xavier writing in 1545 to the King of Portugal:—

"I have discovered a unique but as I assuredly believe a sure means by which the number of Christians in this land may without doubt be greatly increased. It consists in your Majesty declaring clearly and decidedly that you entrust the propagation of our most holy faith to the Viceroy and all the Deputy governors in India, rather than to clergy and priests. Let your Majesty demand reports from the Viceroy and Governors concerning the numbers and quality of those heathen who have been converted . . . At the appointment of every high official your Majesty's royal word should be most solemnly pledged to the effect that if in that particular town or province the number of native Christians were not considerably increased its ruler would meet with the severest punishment. Yea, I demand that your Majesty shall swear a solemn oath affirming that every Governor who shall neglect to disseminate the knowledge of our most holy faith shall be punished on his return to Portugal by a long term of imprisonment and by confiscation of his goods. . . . As long as the Viceroy and Governors are not forced by fear of disfavour to gain adherents to Christianity, your Majesty need not expect that any considerable success will attend the preaching of the Gospel in India."

QUEEN VICTORIA

There is no record of any nineteenth-century missionary having ever addressed Queen Victoria in this strain. Her

Majesty's own policy was proclaimed on the assumption
of the title " Empress of India " in 1858:—

> " Firmly relying ourselves on the truth of Christianity and
> acknowledging with gratitude the solace of religion, we disclaim
> alike the right and the desire to impose our convictions on any
> of our subjects. We declare it to be our Royal will and pleasure
> that none be in anywise favoured, none molested or disquieted
> by reason of their religious faith or observance, but that all alike
> shall enjoy the equal and impartial protection of the law; and
> We do strictly charge and enjoin all those who may be in authority
> under us that they abstain from all interference with the religious
> belief or worship of any of our subjects, on pain of our highest
> displeasure.
>
> " And it is our further will that, so far as may be, our subjects
> of whatever race or creed, be freely and impartially admitted to
> offices in our service, the duties of which they may be qualified
> by their education, ability and integrity to discharge. May the
> God of all power grant to Us and those in authority under Us
> strength to carry out these our wishes for the good of our people."

The Proclamation was welcomed first because, in its
opening and closing words, the Queen declared herself the
head of a nation that was not so indifferent to its religion
as her Indian subjects, not without good cause, had assumed
it to be. Lord William Bentinck had, it was true, suppressed Suttee, the immolation of widows on their husbands' funeral pyres, and waged war on Thuggee, both
of them associated with Hinduism in the popular mind,
but this had been on humanitarian rather than avowedly
Christian grounds. Lord Dalhousie had legalized the
remarriage of widows and in 1850 had established the
principle that no man's religion or change of religion
should operate to the loss of his civil rights, but these
measures were based on considerations of ethics rather
than religion. The official attitude of the Government
towards idolatry savoured of complete indifference to
religious principles. Government inherited the official
administration of Hindu Temples and the patronage of
religious ceremonies. So far from evincing any qualms,
the authorities publicly censured the aged Bishop Corrie,
when he presented a memorial against official patronage
of idolatry, signed by two hundred representatives of the
ecclesiastical, civil, and military departments, for " not

moderating the zeal of over-heated minds." The Commander-in-Chief of Madras was so shocked at the official attitude that he resigned, after refusing to punish a European soldier who would not take part in a ceremonial guard for the salutation of a heathen deity.[1] Queen Victoria had at least shown that religion was accounted of.

Secondly, the Queen had repudiated the Portuguese and Dutch policy of coercion and bribery. In this she was echoing a Memorial recently submitted to her by the C.M.S.: " Christian principles forbid the employment of fraud, bribery or coercion of any kind whatever, as the means of inducing men to profess the Christian faith."

Thirdly, it was understood that her Majesty had expressly declined to admit the word " Neutrality " into the Proclamation. It was a word which carried a suggestion of disloyalty to the Christian faith. Toleration there might and must be, with equal and impartial protection under the law for all, but not Neutrality. It was this which allayed anxiety aroused by the injunction to " abstain from all interference with religious belief." Was this a restriction on the private acts of Government servants ? This was a burning question at a time when many of the most distinguished were men of ardent religious conviction. " Christian things done in a Christian way will never alienate the heathen " was Sir John Lawrence's advice to his subordinates, and it was in this spirit that " interference " was interpreted. When Bishop Cotton protested to the Secretary of State (with the backing of the Governor of the Punjab, Sir Robert Montgomery, grandfather of the Field-Marshal) against an official censure of a Commissioner, Deputy-Commissioner and Colonel for attending the baptism of six converts, he secured a ruling which " empasised the private rights of all officers, military and civil, and gave to missionaries the right of access to Christian sepoys in their lines, as well as to non-Christian sepoys the right of receiving instruction outside their lines."[2]

It is a moot point whether Christianity did not lose more than it gained by being associated with the British

[1] *See* Arthur Mayhew: *Christianity and the Government of India*, passim.
[2] Ibid.

Raj in India. "No nation" said an Indian "can afford to adopt the religion of its conquerors." It is easy to retort that no nation can afford not to adopt the religion of its conquerors if it happens to be true. The fact remains that Christianity has had to live down the manner of its introduction to India as the religion of a Western ruler, as in China it has had to live down its association with the foreigner.

THE EMPEROR OF CHINA

It was in China that missionaries found themselves between two fires—the calumnies of the Chinese on the one hand, such as the story that the eyes and hearts of children were used by missionaries in the manufacture of drugs, and on the other hand the criticisms of Press and Parliament in London to the effect that missionaries were unwarrantable disturbers of the peace who were constantly getting themselves into trouble from which they expected to be extricated by Consuls and gunboats. " Parliament is not fond of missionaries, nor is the press, nor is general society," so ran a leading article in *The Times* in 1869. " Missionaries are people who are always provoking the men of the world. We occasionally meet them at home and find them very commonplace persons, not very well educated, not quite gentlemen, very much given to telling long stories. Some recent occurrences in China have tended to revive the prejudices against them." This had reference to a debate in the House of Lords in which the Duke of Somerset expressed himself anxious to know " what chance we have of reducing these missions? The further they go the more it will be prejudicial to the interests of Christianity: would the Government adopt some more efficient and stringent mode of dealing with these missionaries, either by sending them out of the country or by telling them that they should go no further and imperil our friendly relations with China by their proceedings? " Bishop Magee (afterward Archbishop of York) made a spirited reply. " The noble Duke had given a piece of advice to missionaries which he thought no missionary would accept—namely to leave particular parts of the world unconverted or flee from attempts to convert them, because forsooth these attempts might prejudice the interests of British trade, " that sacred opium trade." It was surely unworthy of a Christian nation to say that if its subjects engaged in any trade, however demoralising, they should be protected from the least infraction of their rights by all the might of Britain; but if they became missionaries and happened to displease the susceptibilities of the Chinese they should be left to their fate or saved from the mob by a forcible expatriation."

Here the distinction applies which we have already drawn. The missionaries took advantage of whatever rights of access and security were won by the Government, but there is no evidence of English missionaries taking advantage of their Government's power or prestige to enforce themselves or their doctrines upon recalcitrant Chinese. They consistently resented the pressure exerted by the French Government in support of their missionaries, and when the Germans exploited the murder of two missionaries as an excuse for demanding an indemnity, mining concessions and a 99 years' lease of Kiao-chow, it was felt to be a grave breach of principle. After the massacre of Tientsin the C.M.S. had protested against inflicting punishment; after the massacre of Ku-cheng the C.M.S. and C.E.Z.M.S. had refused to accept compensation which might have been regarded as an indemnity for the lives of the missionaries. " They deprecate any suggestion that evangelistic enterprise is to be dependent upon the possibility of protection being accorded to the missionaries either by the Government of the country in which they labour or by Great Britain." Lord Salisbury reported that the Chinese authorities were much impressed by the " high-minded attitude of the Societies."

4. *THE POWER OF INFLUENCE*

" For who can turn fierce heathen from their bent
By soft persuasion and sage argument ? "

Nineteenth-century missionaries did not share the scepticism of the Saxon annalist. They echoed King Alfred: " It is God's purpose which rules and not Fate." They believed in the universality of the Gospel. " I if I be lifted up . . . will draw all men unto Me." " Neither the missionaries nor those who sent them out " as we have already quoted from Archbishop Temple's Enthronement Sermon " were aiming at the creation of a world-wide fellowship. . . their aim was to preach the Gospel to as many individuals as could be reached so that those who were won to discipleship should be put in the way of eternal salvation." The figures given on page 224 are evidence that the faith of these early missionaries has been vindicated: in the light of the daunting odds—the violence of savage man, the virulence of tropical diseases, the entrenched systems of culture and religion, the cohesion of tribe and caste, the multiplicity of languages, the haphazardness of the whole enterprise, the failure of the Church to apply its mind to the strategy of expansion or the selection of the strongest available emissaries—the results may well appear miraculous. How, humanly speaking, have they been achieved?

(a) INDIVIDUAL CONVERSION

Bernard Lucas, writing at the time when the massive dome of the Victoria Memorial Hall in Calcutta was in course of construction, saw in it a parable: " Hidden from sight and doomed to remain for ever unseen, is an exact counterpart of the dome which shall one day rise to crown and glorify the edifice. The dome above is only rendered possible by the inverted dome below, upon which it is to be reared." The story of those who correspond to the inverted dome, doomed to remain for ever unseen, does not lend itself to historical summary. It has only been possible to record the names of a few pioneers, but they are representative of a great host of men and women, who, witnessing in bazaar, village market, zenana, from house to house, from kraal to kraal, by soft persuasion and sage argument, in spite of uncouth speech and foreign guise, elicited a first response to the Gospel from a solitary student or a single peasant. In course of time what was said or the way it was said or something in the character of the person who said it, took its effect. Antecedent to the witness of works, works of translation, of education, of medicine, was the witness of word. Opportunities of

Christian service opened up in many forms, but the primary service of the missionary was the proclamation of good news about God: it was by the revelation of a God of love, a God present in every place, accessible to the pure in heart of every race, promising pardon to every sinner, His ear ever open to every prayer, His peace stilling every storm, that the foundations of the underground dome were laid, " the exact counterpart of that which would one day rise to crown and glorify the edifice."

It was the old victory, won in earlier days for the Anglo-Saxons by Augustine, Columba, Cuthbert and Aidan, Boniface and Bede, the victory of God the Father over the gods of fear and fate. At this elementary stage there is little distinction to be drawn between what happened in India, China, Africa, or the Solomon Islands: there is little distinction to be drawn between missionary and missionary: each expressed himself in the theological language of the age, the idiom of his own experience, the accents of his own Church; much of their phraseology would jar on modern ears, sensitive to what would now be regarded as theological defects or distortions; but they kept close enough to their text, " God so loved the world that He gave . . . to the end that all that believe on Him should not perish but have everlasting life " to leave it imprinted on the minds of their converts long after their own commentary was forgotten.

(b) Mass Conversions: Mediæval and Modern

The individualism of the nineteenth-century missionary accorded with the prevailing temper and the dominant theology of the times; but it also accorded with circumstances. Cruel as was the spiritual and economic lot of converts, outcast by their own people and flung into dependence upon strangers, there was no escaping the initial cost of founding a Church; the disciple is not above his Master. But it is not only one by one that Christians have multiplied. In colonies of freed slaves such as were confided to the care of missionaries in Sierra Leone or Zanzibar, the growth of a Christian community could begin at an earlier stage. There have, moreover, been movements of the Spirit of God which have stirred whole communities; group conversion as well as individual conversion has been a factor in the expansion of the Church. Mass Movements have been a feature of Church History since the day of Pentecost when " there were added about three thousand souls."

> " Historically the mediaeval Church as distinct from the primitive was composed of societies. If we look at the history of the spread of Christianity from the days of Constantine, we find that Christianity spread by the addition of masses of men, not by the conversion of particular people. There were some striking exceptions, but, generally speaking, the acceptance of Christianity was, to use a modern phrase, an affair of state in which Kings and other leaders, moved no doubt by missionaries and as time went on acting under the influence of the Pope, carried their subjects with them or imposed their will upon alien social groups.
>
> " A religious system which originated in this way was, as in a more refined expression it has remained, a part of the social structure: its organisation was inextricably involved with that of the community. The powerful men who took a pride in their work fostered and endowed it; they regarded resistance to it as an affront not only to God but to society."[1]

Professor Powicke traces to these Mass Movements the blurring of " the border-line between the swamps and jungles of paganism and the sun-lit uplands of pure faith." A man remained a Christian because he was born a Christian, in " a state of acquiescence or merely professional activity, unaccompanied by sustained religious experience and inward discipline."

The emergence of pagan nations from paganism has seldom been accompanied by a clean cut. Professor Foakes-Jackson raises the question whether the Christianity of Gaul after the conversion of Clovis can be described as Christianity at all. " The Gaul of Gregory of Tours was profoundly pagan at heart. Defunct saints were very active especially in protecting their shrines and their property; their relics were marvellously efficacious. Charms, talismans, amulets abounded. The saints had replaced the ancient gods."[2]

In his life of St. Ambrose, Dr. Dudden sees in the veneration of Martyrs and their Relics a Christian development of pagan custom. " When after the conversion of

---

[1] F. M. Powicke: *The Legacy of the Middle Ages: The Christian Life.*
[2] F. J. Foakes-Jackson: *A History of Church History.*

Constantine multitudes of pagans flocked into the Church they brought with them the ideas and practices of the traditional hero-worship. Faustus not without reason maintained that the Christians had not abandoned pagan usage; they had merely substituted martyrs for idols and memorial feasts for sacrifices. Vigilantius, the Presbyter, denounced the cult as "virtually a heathen observance introduced into the Church under the cloak of religion."[1]

Mass Movements played their part in the making of our own Christian history. The Church in Kent and Northumbria owed much to Ethelbert and Edwin: but they were not alien conquerors as was Charlemagne in Saxony, nor did they impose the faith by force as did Olaf in Norway. No doubt the debacle of the Paulinus mission —when Cadwallon killed Edwin in 633 it was only eight years old—shows the weakness of a Mass Movement. "A day's preaching converted a hundred, a day's defeat swept the whole thing away," is Bishop Browne's rather drastic comment on six years of evangelization. But the Iona missionaries did not have to begin at the very beginning, and Aidan found in Oswald, who had learnt his Christianity in exile at Iona, a believer in soft persuasion and sage argument. "The King not only humbly and willingly in all things gave ear to his admonitions, but industriously applied himself to build up and extend the Church of Christ. When the Bishop, who was not perfectly skilled in the English tongue, preached the Gospel, it was a fair sight to see the King himself interpreting the Word of God to his Ealdormen and Thegns."[2]

These warnings from history are applicable wherever men in multitudes are added to the Church, but they are introduced here to point the contrast between Mass Movement mediæval and modern. Both in India and Africa, as Christianity gathered momentum, castes and tribes have been swept by a common impulse. Bishop Pickett estimates that this is "the path along which an overwhelming proportion of Indian Christians, including more than 80 per cent. of those affiliated with Protestant Churches, have come to profess faith in Christ Jesus." A hundred

[1] Dudden: *St. Ambrose.*
[2] Bede: III, p. 3.

years ago such a movement was in progress in Tinnevelly: the number of converts grew from 3,000 in 1835 to 6,000 in 1841, to 12,000 in 1848. In the reign of George V the Mass Movement in the Punjab raised the number of Christians from 40,000 to 400,000: and between these dates, Mass Movements have happened at intervals in other parts of India. In Dornakal in 1936, after very careful preparation, over 11,000 were baptized, 2,000 of them not outcastes but caste people.

In New Guinea it was the deliberate policy of German missionaries patiently to wait for years till the people themselves in their separate tribes came to a kind of national decision to banish the old gods, do away with sorcery, and transfer the allegiance of the whole community. The Mass Movements experienced within the Anglican Communion have not been the outcome of deliberate policy: there has been vigilant scrutiny of their spiritual validity and doubt whether they should be encouraged. The first movement of the kind stirred a community in Lower Bengal in the 1830's. Thirty of its members were baptized in face of much persecution: their numbers grew to three thousand. The C.M.S. insisted that time was necessary to ascertain the real character of the movement. " Experience (in West Africa) has taught the Committee to rejoice with trembling." Bishop Wilson of Calcutta visited the scene and baptized 500, but wrote a cautious report: " Popular movements draw in numbers of ill-informed followers. The habits of heathen society soon steal behind the Christian enquirer and entangle him in the old ambush." An open-eyed awareness of inherent perils is the first contrast between the mediæval and modern missionaries.

A second is a consequence of the first, namely, an appreciation both of the appropriateness of the Mass Movement to Indian life and of the positive safeguards which can ensure that a sound Christian Church shall arise out of a Mass Movement. On the one hand it has been recognized that by contrast with the individualistic West, India is group-conscious and has a deep-seated instinct for thinking in terms of the community rather than in terms of the individual. The individual through centuries of discipline has learnt to subordinate himself to his caste. " Ask the typical villager who he is and he will tell you not his own name but the name of his caste." This tradition may seem lowering to the dignity of individual personality, but it builds up what may be called a cor- porate personality, and makes family solidarity a potent force. The spiritual isolation of the convert disowned by his family is to that extent aggravated beyond what a member of a less closely-knit community would suffer. Cut off from his accustomed restraints and supports, he can only find compensation in fellowship with other Christians similarly outlawed, and a community of outlaws gathered round European missionaries is calculated to enhance the alien character of the Church in Indian eyes.

On the other hand, if Mass Movement Christians are not to breed a second generation who are Christians because they have been born Christians, exhibiting " a state of acquiescence unaccompanied by sustained religious experience and inward discipline " they must be inoculated with a measure of individualistic serum. There must be individual transformation of character, individual tuition in the fundamentals of the faith, individual training in worship and prayer.

The contrast between mediæval and modern is most marked when the origins of Mass Movements are compared. Neither in India nor Africa has the acceptance of Christi- anity been an " affair of state." It has not been imposed from above; it is a volcanic eruption from below. Mass Movements owe their origins not to Kings or Chiefs but to individuals or groups of individuals who have themselves been converted, and like Vedamanikam in Travancore or Ko Tha Bya among the Karens have infected their com- munities with their own devotion to their new-found Lord.

It is sometimes objected that these Movements have been confined to the Scheduled or Depressed Classes, whose desire to escape the wretchedness of their lot sufficiently explains their readiness to adopt Christianity. The Sudra movement in the Telugu country, with 15,000 conversions in five years, in widely separated areas, is evidence that Mass Movements extend beyond the Scheduled castes. The motive adduced for the caste movement sheds light on the genuineness of out-caste movements. A Government official belonging to one of the highest of the Sudra castes, when asked why he expected that entire village populations would soon become Christian, put first among his reasons the changed lives of the outcaste converts.

Bishop Trollope (p. 176) placed high among the qualifications of a missionary in Korea the capacity " to be very patient and very tender even with mixed motives." Missionaries in Mass Movement areas have no doubt had occasion to exercise this virtue. Their patience has been rewarded. Mass Movement Christians have exhibited what William James included among the symptoms of conversion. "What is attained is often an entirely new level of spiritual vitality, a relatively heroic level, in which impossible things have become possible and new energies and endurances shown. The personality is changed, the man is born anew." Among the endurances called for have been threats of eviction, concocted litigation, denial of employment, confiscation of wells, looting of crops. Among the energies evoked has been an impetus to bear witness corporately and individually. Mass Movement areas are renowned for their " Weeks of Witness " in which women as well as men set out to convince by soft persuasion and sage argument their non-Christian neighbours. The spirit in which the obligation to bear witness is honoured is shown by the popular titles for these weeks: " the Golden Week "; " the Queen of Weeks "; " the Joy-bringing Week "; " the Week that makes the Spirit burst into Flower ".

MISSIONARY SPECIALISTS

1. *LITERARY*

A distinction has been suggested between the witness of word and the witness of works—works of translation, of education, of medicine. It was drawn in order to give due precedence to evangelism as the first privilege and the *raison d'être* of the missionary, but not by any means to imply that the missionary scholar, teacher, doctor or nurse were otherwise engaged than in evangelism, or ranked lower among the makers of Christian history. They are men and women who have subordinated their special gifts to the primary purpose of the missionary.

The translation of the Scriptures has figured in all our references to the expansion of the Church. By way of summary it may be noted that the Bible has been translated into 181 languages, the New Testament into 220, and portions of Scripture into 665. Not only had these 1,066 tongues to be acquired, but many of them had to be reduced to writing for the first time, a Pentecostal achievement. They were usually deficient in theological terms; some of them lacked any equivalent for the metaphors, similes and parables of the Gospels; others could provide two or more renderings for one original, and which was to be selected became a matter of controversy involving delicate theological issues. The " Term Question " in China is a classic example. Archbishop Tait was asked to decide between three possible terms which might be used for the name of God; some favoured Shin, some Shang-ti, some T'ien Chu. The last was out of favour with some Protestants because it was used by Roman Catholics, but " why " asked Schereschewsky, who preferred it, " should we speak another language with reference to the Being Whom we adore in common ? "

Another great scholar, Dr. Legge, held strongly that Shang-ti was the proper equivalent, which was ruled out by Schereschewsky as being the name of the chief deity in the Chinese pantheon " and no more appropriate for the Christian God than Jupiter or Baal." Max Müller agreed with Legge. A similar problem, equally fundamental, arising in Africa, was later referred to Archbishop Davidson. What was the correct rendering of the name " Jesus Christ " in Swahili ? There were two in actual use in different sections of the African Church. Ultimately agreement was achieved on a version that met the views of Roman Catholic, Anglican and non-Anglican Missions.

There was also the problem of style: should it be the classical style such as is employed in the Chinese classics, or the colloquial which would be understood by the common people ? Morrison adopted a middle course. Moffat of Bechuanaland compromised between a free and a literal translation.

What the achievements of the British and Foreign Bible Society and its Scottish and American sisters have cost in courage and toil is beyond computation. It must be realized that to translate into any European language is a very different thing from translating into a language of which grammar, idiom, and mode of thought are entirely unlike one's own. Dr. Walter Miller gives a glimpse of the labours which went into the production of his Hausa Bible:—

> " A whole evening might well be spent with the Greek grammar and Testament, as well as the Arabic, and sometimes the French Testament, rightly to distinguish and fix the equivalents for such words as sin, offence, fault, transgression, trespass, wickedness, evil, wrong-doing, mischief. Constant revision was necessary to make sure of perfect symmetry and consistency in using the same word to express the same meaning. When the whole book was drafted it had to be typed, and the typed sheets sent to assessors. The first draft would come back with many sheets of notes and criticisms; all had to be carefully examined with the help of African friends. From all the emendations would have to be built up a new draft, and the process of circulation repeated. More notes and suggestions would come in. When after thirty years the work reached its last lap, and the whole draft was sent home, there still remained the drudgery of correcting three sets of proof sheets; every letter had to be fully examined and compared with the original text."

Several great translators of other communions have been mentioned. Of these Dr. Legge was an Aberdeen scholar of the highest distinction and afterwards as Professor of Chinese in the University of Oxford contributed six volumes to Max Müller's great series of the " Sacred Books of the East." Others were William Carey, the Kettering cobbler, Robert Moffat, the Scottish gardener; Robert Morrison, boot-tree maker's apprentice; all of them self-educated. In a bitter attack on the Bible Society and all its works, the *Quarterly Review* for 1827 ridiculed the translators employed by it, and the versions issued by " Directors in a hurry to dazzle their subscribers by an annual display of new translations." Carey had modestly admitted the necessity of revising his Bengalee Bible, because while the words were Bengalee the idiom was English: he was therefore accused of undertaking a work of sacred importance in schoolboy fashion, by way of an exercise while learning an Indian dialect. Morrison had modestly admitted that his was not a perfect translation and expressed the hope that work on his Chinese dictionary would mature his knowledge of the language. Here was another premature exercise. The critic waxes eloquent on the injury affected by the circulation of incorrect and unauthorized versions. Revision and alteration would shake the confidence of the ignorant and unlearned, who " distracted between two rival or dissimilar versions, the relative merits of which he is incapable of estimating, will attempt to escape from his dilemma by rejecting them both." " What might have descended to after ages as imperishable monuments of Christian benevolence and rational enterprise will only be remembered for the errors and blunders which disfigure them." Bishop Middleton is held up as the model whom the Bible Society should emulate instead of employing incompetent translators with little knowledge if any of Greek and Hebrew.

Morrison's comment on the article is restrained. " I wish the perfectionists all success—not in vituperation but in making perfect translations whenever they may condescend to undertake the work." Its criticism was misdirected; if the writer had rounded upon the Church of 1827 and rebuked its omission to enlist in this work of sacred importance its foremost scholars, he might have been the means of removing a reproach which the Anglican Church has still to live down. Its reputation in the sphere of scholarly Biblical translation still rests upon the achievements of the illustrious American Bishop Schereschewsky, who, though paralysed in hands and feet, insisted on returning to his former diocese of Shanghai to hammer out on a typewriter with his one finger a revised version of his Mandarin Bible and a complete translation into Easy Wenli. Much fine translation work has been done by Anglican missionaries in the midst of multifarious occupations, but the Church has never selected and commissioned scholars for this special work.

It is the same story in other branches of literary activity. Scholars have been few and far between who could bring first-rate ability to bear on the creation of a literature for the younger Churches, whether in English or the vernaculars.

The S.P.C.K. through its depots has been a stalwart distributor of Christian literature, and individual missionaries have hammered out commentaries and apologetic, but it is noticeable that the work of presenting Christ through the printed page has never taken rank as worthy of the greatest minds in the Church. Few Anglican students have produced work comparable to that of Farquhar, Macnicol and Hogg on the religions of India, or Legge and Soothill on the religions of China. Copleston's *Buddhism* stands out as an exception; it was published in 1892.

2. *THE EDUCATIONAL AND MEDICAL MEDIUMS*

It would need a volume to expound the role played by educational and medical missions in the expansion of the Anglican Communion, and another to do justice to their contribution to the culture and civilization of the communities they have served. A mere catalogue of the Church institutions, medical and educational, would be impressive, but unreadable. We can only here summarize their story.

Of the two services, between which there is much in common, the medical is the junior. In spite of Christopher Codrington's foresight in 1703 it was not till far on in the nineteenth century that Medical Missions were organized and hospitals built. In 1883 the C.M.S. established one in Persia, two in the Punjab, one in Kashmir and two in China: it had then seven qualified Doctors among its missionaries. The S.P.G. had founded a hospital in Nazareth (Palestine) in 1870, and two in India in 1874: St. Stephen's Zenana Hospital, Delhi, followed in 1884. It cannot therefore be claimed that medical missions had any decisive influence on the expansion of the nineteenth-century Church. Those who would attribute its growth to the ingenuity of missionaries in exploiting suffering, in taking advantage of their desperate anxiety to lure pagans into hospitals and baptize them in their beds, making conversion the price of cure, are refuted by history. Such a distortion of the facts does violence also to the motives of the missionary.

It was the missionary's first instinct on arriving among a people of unknown tongue and unfamiliar customs to find some point at which he could establish brotherly relations and perform some tangible service. Some found what they sought in teaching, some in healing. Both would aver that quite apart from any benefit conferred on mind or body of pupils or patients, mutual knowledge, understanding and affection had their chance of growing in the mutual relations thus established. It cannot be said that where there has been no medical mission the Church has failed to root itself and thrive in the soil of a people's heart, for the Church had succeeded in so doing long before the 1880's; but the accumulation of intimate relationships between patient and nurse or doctor has strengthened and established the Church's roots.

Secondly it is clear from the biographies of nineteenth-century missionaries that they were overwhelmed by the disclosure of the volume and virulence of tropical diseases, and the universal defiance of the most elementary laws of health and hygiene. Their instinct to do something, however amateurish, to alleviate suffering was reinforced by the remembrance that they were the apostles of One who in His brief earthly ministry had cared for bodies as well as souls: any appearance of indifference to physical miseries would be a glaring contradiction of the story they had to tell of the Incarnation. Doctor-Bishops—MacDougall in Borneo, Strachan in Burma, Hine in Central Africa, Calloway in Kaffraria, far from feeling any discrepancy between their medical and episcopal functions, regarded both as equally consonant with their calling as Fathers-in-God and successors of Christ's Apostles.

It is true that supporters at home were slow to recognize the significance of Medical Missions. They were prepared to acknowledge their use as a means of access to the inaccessible—to Afghan tribesmen, for example, who hailed from the mountains across the North West Frontier where no messengers of the Gospel could penetrate—but they asked in all seriousness " why should an expensive medical agency be employed in countries and districts where the ordinary missionary has free access to the people ? With the arrival of Doctors on the scene, many of them men of eminent attainments in medicine and surgery, new conceptions matured of the kind of equipment required, of the vocation of the medical missionary, and of the place of the medical mission in the life of the Church.

(*a*) The large Mission hospitals of to-day with their up-to-date equipment of wards, theatres and X-Rays, trace their genealogy to some humble refuge for lepers or opium addicts, to some modest ward containing a few maternity beds, or to some emergency provision for the victims of famine or plague. The doctors found themselves confronted with problems in the field of tropical research, with problems surgical and ophthalmic, which exacted every ounce of skill and energy. They could not rest content till the best possible apparatus had been made available, and the best possible system devised of subsidiary aid-posts, dispensaries and clinics linked up with well-equipped central hospitals, and adapted where necessary in everything but standards of efficiency to local habits and preferences. Each hospital thus became a centre not only for curative treatment and operations, but for the diffusion of education in the laws of health and hygiene. Preventive Medicine came into its own where so many diseases were preventable.

(*b*) The vocation of the medical missionary clarified. Doctors and Nurses found that they could not dichotomize themselves into missionary and professional compartments. They could not accept for themselves a dual standard; professional efficiency could not excuse failure in their spiritual ministry; evangelical zeal was no substitute for skill and science. A man's Christianity was at least as much a factor in his power to heal as his knowledge of medicine. No healing was worthy of the name which did not mediate the divine touch of the Master through simultaneous spiritual and physical influence. Patients were neither souls nor bodies but personalities. Religion and medicine must be fused in the medical missionary.

(*c*) " Medical work should always be subordinated to the spiritual." This was the clear-cut distinction in the minds of the earlier champions of Medical Missions. As the Church grew and Church-consciousness developed, the ministry of healing came to be recognized as an integral part of the Church's life and witness. It was a ministry that belonged primarily to the trained expert; no Church could bear a full-rounded witness till it was raising up its own trained experts and ceasing to rely on doctors and nurses from abroad. But it was also a ministry in which the Christian rank and file had a part, and the whole corporate Christian community a responsibility: particularly in the sphere of Preventive Medicine and Health education. The Tambaram Conference[1] registered the new conception. " No presentation of the Gospel is complete unless it includes the care of the body and the enlightening of the mind, for only thus will that new value be given to humanity, which came into the world through the Incarnation."

THE EDUCATIONAL MEDIUM

This coupling of the care of the body and the enlightenment of the mind underlines the suggestion that there is much in common between the Medical and the Educational Mission. Each in its own way attacked ignorance and superstition and promised relief from suffering and disability. Each provided a point of contact between the newly arrived missionary and the people, and an opportunity of tangible service. The teacher made friends by teaching, as the doctor or nurse by healing. Each calling opened the way for a deeper understanding of unfamiliar mentality. Both services became integral to the life and witness of the Church. Both are periodically exposed to the reproach of being " Institutional." It is the nature of both to be " institutions " for they require buildings and plant, but they are none the less personal for that: they are in fact complexes of co-operative human relationships in the service of Christ.

In two respects the medical had the advantage. Human anatomy the world over exhibits a higher degree of uniformity than the human mind: bones can be set according to the same technique in whatever continent they are broken: drugs have measurable effects: the element of the imponderable, and the necessity for adaptation loom larger for the teacher introducing as he does a new world

[1] Conference of International Missionary Council, December, 1938, at Tambaram, Madras.

of ideas. The medical sphere also has been accorded an autonomy denied to the educational. The history of Mission schools discloses that they were subject to constant control by those who would not have thought of interfering in the management of a hospital; though equally disqualified to guide educational policy they felt fully entitled to over-rule the expert, as being themselves experts. Instances could be multiplied of schoolmaster-missionaries being diverted to other missionary activities, and of their places being taken by men with no experience of schoolmastering. There is therefore an amateurish and precarious character about the educational enterprise which is not found in the medical.

The enterprise itself is best summarized under two aspects, according as it is facing inward, towards the Church, or outward towards the non-Christian. Histori-cally there are two functions which educational missions have set out to fulfil : the building up of the Church by lifting its intellectual level and raising up leaders of trained mind and balanced judgement; and the presentation of Christianity to students of other faiths, making them familiar with the Christian view of life, Christianizing their outlook and ideals, and sending them out as enlightened leaders of their country's life. These two functions are not always distinguishable: the same College may be performing both at the same time, or with the Church's growth may shift its emphasis and usefulness from " out-ward " to " inward."

But the functions are distinct enough to warrant different criterions of success: much controversy has raged over the respective merits of the two types of education, each being blamed for not producing the results appropriate to the other.

(i) It is not easy at this distance of time to appreciate the daring of Alexander Duff's educational experiments. Bishop Middleton had founded a College with the secon-dary purpose of " teaching the elements of youthful know-ledge and the English language to Mussulmans and Hin-doos, having no object in such attainments beyond secular advantage." But Duff's College in Calcutta, started in 1830, was primarily for Hindus; it bore no relation at all to the inward life of the Church; and so far from confining itself to elements of youthful knowledge aspired to carrying education to the highest level. He called it the " preparing of a mine, the setting up of a train which shall one day explode and tear up the whole from its lowest depths." He was strongly opposed by all the missionaries, with the exception of the aged William Carey who urged him to go forward. It was not only that he was a new arrival and only twenty-four, though that would explain and even excuse opposition. They did not believe in using higher education as a missionary instrument. He was also opposed by those who believed that not English but Sanskrit, Arabic or Persian should be the medium of higher education. There were still five years to go before Macaulay decided this issue, though by his own confession he had no knowledge of these languages: " I am quite ready to take Oriental learning at the valuation of the Orientalists themselves: I have never found one among them who could deny that a single shelf of a good European library was worth the whole native literature of India and Arabia." English then became the lingua franca of India.

Educational mines do not explode dramatically, but Anglican Colleges and Schools in China as well as India, founded by the S.P.G., the C.M.S., the Cambridge Mssioni to Delhi, owed much to Duff's inspiration. Both he and those who came after won the allegiance of individual students to the Christian faith, which they boldly taught even at the risk of wrecking their Colleges: Wilson's College at Bombay was threatened with extinction in 1839 when the baptism of a Parsee excited indignation. But Colleges, like Hospitals, have a right to be valued for the sake of the special service they render; both might yield a rich harvest of individual conversion and yet fail in making their distinctive contribution to the Kingdom of Christ. The same principles apply to the Secondary Boarding Schools of India, Ceylon, China, and Africa. These too have their direct fruits, but their indirect influence extends far beyond membership of the Church, through the character and integrity of men and women who, through their formative years, have shared a common life in which all communal and caste distinctions were transcended in a corporate unity transmuted by the Spirit of Christ.

(ii) Even if missionary education in the early nineteenth century had been wholly directed towards the inner life of the Church, it would have stood out against the contemporary background as a notable venture of faith. Education for the poorer people was still suspect. Would it not make them less industrious? Few answered so confidently as Dr. Johnson: "No, Sir, while learning to read and write is a distinction, the few who have that distinction may be the less inclined to work: but when everybody learns to read and write it is no longer a distinction. A man who has a laced waistcoat is too fine a man to work, but if everybody had laced waistcoats we should have people working in laced waistcoats."

Hannah More's Mendip schools in the first decade of the century exposed her to the petty persecution of farmers and pamphleteers who asserted that her "writings ought to be burned by the hands of the common hangman." Instruction would breed enthusiasts and Jacobins. "I do not vindicate enthusiasm. I dread it. But can the possibility that a few should become enthusiasts be justly pleaded as an argument for giving them all up to vice and barbarism? That the knowledge of the Bible should lay men more open to the delusion of fanaticism on the one hand or Jacobinism on the other, appears so unlikely that I should have thought the probability lay all on the other side."

If the education of English children was dangerous and absurd, how much more so the schooling of Maoris, Hindus and Hottentots. There was no reason to suppose them capable of assimilating learning. "A black man," wrote Mary Kingsley, "is no more an underdeveloped white man than a rabbit is an undeveloped hare."

Mary Kingsley was on stronger ground when she criticized the content and method of the missionary's teaching; but judged by contemporary, which are the only fair standards, the education given was enlightened, and became more so as the century advanced. There are Colleges, Training Colleges, and Secondary Schools which trace their genealogy to these early ventures. Long before

there were Government systems of education—there was
no Department of Education in Uganda till 1924—the
Missions had so far developed theirs that Governments
were glad enough to take them into partnership. " The
fact," writes Mr. Mayhew, " that in some of our dependencies 80 per cent. or even 90 per cent. of the educational
work is undertaken by Christian Missions may be attributed to the fact that, to their credit, they were first in the
field. But it is significant that they have not only been
allowed but encouraged by the Governments to continue
that work, assisted by financial grants and assured that they
are an integral part of the educational system. Annual
testimony is paid in education reports to the value of their
co-operation; their assistance and advice are claimed on
Advisory Boards and in the formulation of policy, and
Mission educational experience has more than once been
recognised as qualifying for high educational responsibility
in Government service." And Lord de La Warr's *Commission on Higher Education in East Africa* records that:
" It is impossible to praise too highly the devotion, courage,
zeal, charity and wisdom with which the missionaries
performed their task. We doubt whether in the whole
history of Christian enterprise there exists a finer chapter
than that which tells of the work of these ardent men
and women."

As we go to Press, the *Report of the Commission on Higher
Education in West Africa* clinches the argument (para. 56):
" When one looks for the root from which West African
education sprang, one comes back, everywhere and always,
to the missionaries. It was the Christian Missions who
first came out to the Coast, without desire for fee or reward.
It was the congregations in Britain and America who
provided the first development funds, the pennies of poor
people, expended without reckoning of capital or interest.
It was the Churches in both their African and European
memberships who first made Africanisation a working
creed, and produced the first, and still by far the greatest,
large-scale African organisation on the Western model.
Finally it was, and still is, the Churches who have made it
possible to talk of West African education, higher, middle
or lower, as a fact and not merely as an ideal. . . . The

Churches may rightly say that it was their work, long and patiently persisted in, through both Britain and West Africa, that has made co-operation between the two countries thinkable. This assertion, truly made, gives them the right to be heard on all these subjects, both now and in the future."

PART XI

ACCLIMATIZATION

I. CLIMATIC RIGOURS

1. The Climate of Primitive Society: (*a*) South America; (*b*) Melanesia; (*c*) Idolatry; (*d*) Customs; (*e*) Polygamy.
2. The Climate of Culture: (*a*) Alien Faiths; (*b*) Alien Cultures and Customs; (*c*) Caste; (*d*) Ancestor Worship.

II. TRANSPLANTATION PROBLEMS

1. The Local and the Universal: provincialism.
2. Debits and Credits: sectarianism.

III. TESTS OF ACCLIMATIZATION

1. Their limitations.
2. Self-existence.
3. Self-expression.
4. Self-expansion.

TO become acclimatized is to become " habituated or inured to a new climate, or to one not natural." No Christian can consistently admit that any climate is " not natural " to his religion, for he believes himself entrusted with a Gospel addressed to human nature as such by One Who is the Light of the World. No Westerner can pretend that Christianity is indigenous to Europe and would therefore find an Eastern climate " not natural." But there are climates in which Christianity has had its being for centuries, and climates to which it has been transplanted, as tea and rubber were transplanted to Ceylon. What climatic rigours have conditioned the process of acclimatization ? Has the Church succeeded in transplanting the essentials to the exclusion of the non-essential, the true Vine, to the exclusion of degenerate forms and parasitic growths ? Has acclimatization been achieved so completely that the transplanted roots are, in their new setting, proving hardy enough and at home enough to yield their appropriate fruits ? The expansion of the nineteenth-century Church must be reviewed in the light of these three questions.

I. CLIMATIC RIGOURS

Physically the Church has had to adapt itself to the extremes of heat and cold as it penetrated to the Tropics and the Arctic. Psychologically it has had to adapt itself to all degrees of civilization between the extremes of savage man and primitive superstition on the one hand, and on the other, highly developed cultures and philosophic religions. In his Bampton Lectures of 1843, Dr. Anthony Grant draws this distinction between those " whose minds are already moulded and fashioned by a definite creed and system of worship, and those whose religion consists of a blind and senseless superstition and rude idolatry." Bishop Barry in his Hulsean lectures of 1894 draws the same distinction in the titles of lectures on " Our Mission to India and the East " and " The Mission to the Barbarian Races," the latter a title which would hardly commend itself half a century later.

1. *THE CLIMATE OF PRIMITIVE SOCIETY*

Previous chapters have referred in passing, to some of the rigours of primitive Society in Africa: we may illustrate them more fully by visits to two regions hitherto neglected, South America and the South Seas.

South America

Allen Gardiner could be quoted as an early nineteenth-century witness to the climate of all three regions: his missionary career reproduced some of the characteristics of the naval career which he abandoned in 1834 at the age of forty; he still sailed the seven seas, conducting dashing raids into hostile territory, bearding the Zulu chieftain, Dingaan, face to face, landing in New Guinea and the Islands of the Archipelago, and finally founding a Pata-gonian Mission in 1844, based on the Falkland Islands, after daring exploration of South America from Buenos Aires to the Andes. His little launches, the *Pioneer* and the *Speedwell*, were the first Mission ships afloat, but the latter was misnamed for the expedition, and ended fatally. The South American Missionary Society was not dismayed and developed its Tierra del Fuego Mission to which

Charles Darwin paid tribute in words and cash: " The progress of Fuegians is wonderful, and had it not occurred would have been to me quite incredible. It is truly wonderful what you tell about their honesty and their language. I certainly should not have predicted it; I certainly should have predicted that not all the Missionaries of the world could have done what has been done." (1881).[1]

The thirty years' episcopate of Bishop Stirling, who went to the Tierra del Fuego Mission in 1862 and was consecrated first Bishop of the Falkland Islands in 1869, consolidated into a diocese both the missions and the British congregations scattered in all the ports of the vast coastlines of South America, East and West, where The Missions to Seamen were making homes for British sailors. But it is to the Missions of the S.A.M.S. that we must turn for a sample of primitive climatic conditions; in the great central plain of the Paraguay River known as the Gran Chaco, among the tribes of the Argentine Chaco and the Mapuche Indians of Chile. What kind of climate confronted Barbrooke Grubb when he took his life in his hand and went to live among the wild Lengua? No one can read *An Unknown People in an Unknown Land* without realizing that his life hung on a slender thread. " Had sickness broken out in a village through which I had passed I should have been held responsible, and if deaths resulted they would have felt justified by their laws in putting me to death. Their belief regarding dreams, as interpreted by wizards, would supply the basis for any number of accusations against me, and being a foreigner travelling alone and thus a mystery to them, I should naturally become the subject of many dreams. My habit of inquiring into their customs and rites and beliefs continually increased their danger." " The life of an Indian is not the free, thoughtless, unburdened and happy existence that he is often supposed to live: he is in a state of constant supernatural dread." South American missionaries staked their lives upon the conviction that the wildest and most wayward of the sons of men share mankind's high destiny to become the sons of God; and the Christian communities of the Chaco are their vindication.

[1] *Life and Letters of Charles Darwin*, iii, p. 128.

MELANESIA

Bishop Selwyn's Letters Patent invested him with the spiritual charge of 68 degrees of latitude more than was intended; his diocese was defined as stretching from the 50th degree of South latitude to the 34th degree of North, instead of (as was intended) South latitude. He set out to make it " the great missionary centre of the Southern Ocean." Year after year he contemplated no immediate results of his landing unarmed and alone on the shores of the Islands, generally among menacing crowds of savages and cannibals, beyond the establishing of a good under- standing, and the acquisition of some of the dialects." He had made seven Melanesian voyages and visited fifty Islands, from ten of which forty pupils speaking ten lan- guages had gone to school in New Zealand, before he returned home to enlist a fellow-Etonian, John Coleridge Patteson, as the first Melanesian missionary.

Patteson reached New Zealand in 1856 and five years later was consecrated first Bishop of Melanesia in Auck- land. Though the Bishop resented any insinuation that his islanders were savage, and believed in their essential kindness if kindly treated, he was exposed to tempestuous weather, psychological as well as physical. After a narrow escape from shipwreck on the reef at Guadalcanar, 450 natives swarmed on deck and in canoes. " If I had not been satisfied of their being quite friendly, I would not have put ourselves so entirely into their power; but it is of the greatest consequence to let them see you are not suspicious: perhaps Bishop Selwyn, being an older hand at it, will think I was rash." Kidnapping by whalers and deportation to the cotton plantations of Fiji " arouse all the worst suspicions and passions of the wild untaught man. Is it not difficult to find an answer to the question Who is the savage and who is the heathen man ? " There had been a tragedy in Santa Cruz in 1864, when the crowd opened fire on the Bishop's boat at fifteen yards range and two of his companions were transfixed with poisoned arrows and died of lock-jaw. It was a similar outburst provoked by similar grievance in the same neighbourhood which proved fatal to Bishop Patteson in 1871. He had landed alone. Allen and Taroniara waiting for him in the boat were also killed. Five men from Nukapu had been kidnapped and carried off to a doubtful fate: blood for blood was the Islanders' law, and vengeance their sacred duty.

IDOLATRY

As Boniface had hewed in pieces the sacred Thunderer's Oak with his own hands, so missionaries set about to blast idols with their own lips: the first step in acclimatization was to clear the soil for the transplanted sapling. History repeated itself. It was nothing new for Christians to be laying seige to idolatry, or for idol worshippers to be defending themselves against Christians. Tertullian (about 200 A.D.) had tolerated no taint of idols: Christians who earned a living by making idols—statuaries, painters, gilders—came under his lash: even the schoolmaster's living was gone, for he was bound to teach pagan literature, his holidays were heathen festivals, and his fees in part due to Minerva.[1] And as of old, the idols found defenders though they might not have been able to express themselves as well as Maximus of Tyre, the second-century Platonist: " It is because we are not able to apprehend the being of God that we lean upon words and names and animal forms, and representations of gold and ivory and silver. Craving for knowledge of Him in our weakness we give to earthly things the name of good and beautiful from His nature, as lovers delight in everything which wakens the memory of the loved."[2]

There was many a modern echo of the lament uttered by the golden-tongued Symmachus, Consul in 391, when Gratian disestablished the ancient religion: " We plead for a respite for the gods of our fathers; what matters it by what method each of us seeks the truth ? We cannot by a single road arrive at so great a secret. Where shall we swear to obey the laws and statutes ? By what sanction shall the deceitful be deterred from false attestation ? Our altar preserves the concord of all, and guarantees the faith of each."

[1] Cf. Glover: *The Conflict of Religions in the Early Roman Empire.*
[2] Quoted in W. R. Halliday: *The Pagan Background of Early Christianity.*

The missionaries had no Edicts to rely on such as were
issued by Theodosius decreeing the destruction of the
Serapeum at Alexandria, when even the Christians were
at first over-awed by the colossal idol and the memory of
a prophecy that if it fell the sky would fall. A soldier
heaved an axe, Serapis crashed, there scurried forth a
swarm of frightened mice, and the fear of the mob turned
to mirth: the secrets of the oracle stood exposed.[1] It was
not upon derision or force but upon soft persuasion and
sage (if sometimes strident) argument that nineteenth-
century missionaries relied to resolve what was for them
a simple and straightforward issue: the dethroning of
gods in the spirit of the 115th Psalm, and the substitution
of love for fear as motive of worship. This was a first
condition of acclimatization, and attended by obstacles
economic and patriotic as formidable in modern as in
ancient times.

SOCIAL CUSTOMS

As in England the Christmas Tree and Harvest Home
symbolize the fusion between religion and the social life
of folk and family, so were the sacred festivals and fasts of
paganism inextricably inter-woven with social and secular
custom. This is a deterrent to the " habituating or
inuring " of Christianity to a new climate that appeared
very early in our own history. Augustine propounded the
problem to Gregory: the Pope replied:—

> "Let the idols be destroyed, but let the temples be converted from
> the worship of devils to the service of the true God; let holy water
> be sprinkled in the said temples, let altars be erected and relics
> placed; and because they are used to slaughter many oxen in
> the sacrifices to devils, some solemnity must be exchanged for
> them, as that on festivals they may build themselves huts of the
> boughs of trees about those buildings which have been turned
> from temples into churches, and kill cattle to the praise of God
> in their eating, . . . to the end that whilst some gratifications are
> outwardly permitted them they may the more easily consent to
> the inward consolations of the grace of God, for there is no doubt
> that it is impossible to efface everything at once from their rude
> natures: because he who endeavours to ascend to the highest
> places rises by degrees or steps, and not by leaps."[2]

[1] Dr. Homes Dudden: *St. Ambrose.*   [2] Bede: I, p. 30.

Sprinkling with holy water has not always sufficed to exorcize superstition or magic, or to prevent lapses into witchcraft and sorcery; the twentieth-century missionary has, however, what was not accessible to his nineteenth-century predecessor, the aid of social anthropology in applying Pope Gregory's principle that care be taken to avoid any grave dislocation of a people's customs, which are to be modified, redirected and enriched.[1] He is in a better position to discriminate between what is capable of being baptized into Christ and what is not. Adult Christians, mature enough in the faith to form sound judgements on their pre-Christian heritage, may be even better advisers than anthropologists or missionaries on such questions as Initiation Rites, Marriage and Funeral Customs; they are the experts on acclimatization.

POLYGAMY

On the crucial problem of polygamy, which from the days of St. Paul has presented one of the most baffling hindrances to acclimatization, there is, for example, a special note of authority in the *Report of the Tambaram Conference of the International Missionary Council* held in 1938, where the majority of the delegates represented the younger Churches. The Africa Section weighed its words, in the knowledge that Africans professing Christianity had seceded from the Church on this issue.

"In most parts of Africa polygamy has been the custom, and insistence on monogamy is one of the great bars preventing the entrance of men into the Christian Church. Even within the Church there is a grave danger of serious hypocrisy in that men professedly monogamists are secretly carrying on illicit connexions. In some areas men brought up in a Christian atmosphere are reverting to polygamy and other social customs, and declare that these bring to them no sense of guilt, no pricking of conscience.

"The question is raised as to whether monogamy is essential to Christianity or is merely a factor in European civilisation—whether in the practice of polygamy there is something radically incompatible with a vital faith in Christ and the living of a true life in fellowship with Him. This is not a matter to be settled by the individual conscience; the criterion is the will of God for the

[1] See *Essays Catholic and Missionary*: Bishop Lucas of Masasi on *The Christian approach to non-Christian customs*.

people whom He has redeemed and purified in Christ. Monogamy is not a mere factor of civilisation; it is vital to the life of
the Church and its value has been realised in its own experience.
It was taught by the Lord Himself. . . . Both for men and for
women polygamy militates against the attainment of the fulness
of life which is in Christ.

"It is impossible to conceive of the full development of the
personality of the woman under the conditions which obtain in
polygamous life, nor indeed that of the man." (*The World Mission
of the Church. Tambaram Report:* Vol. IV, pp. 404 ff).

There follows positive teaching on the unique character
of the Christian home, and the incalculable value in the
life of the Church of the spiritual influence brought to
bear on the children in the Christian family to which has
been given by Christ Himself a spiritual significance
unattainable under the conditions of polygamy.

2. *THE CLIMATE OF CULTURE*

Some of the conditions of Christian acclimatization are
common both to primitive and advanced societies, both
to animistic and ethnic religions: polytheism and polygamy, for example, are not confined to the former: there
is no geographical boundary between the two extremes
of climate: the more elaborate religious systems have
grown out of or been imposed upon the simpler; the marks
of their origin are discernible in the cruder conceptions
which survive within them, and in periods of decadence
reassert themselves. St. Paul had to commend his revelation at Athens as well as at Lystra. The early Church
was confronted with Stoics as well as with those who
" worshipped devils and idols of gold and silver and brass
and stone and wood which can neither see, nor hear, nor
walk."[1] The nineteenth-century missionary met Buddhist,
Hindu, and Confucian systems as well as juju and taboo.

ALIEN FAITHS

It came natural to those who gloried in a unique revelation to speak of " the heathen " as promiscuously as the
Moslem speaks of Infidels and the Jew of Gentiles. In the
days before Max Müller they had too little knowledge of
Oriental religions to be able to discriminate. As know-

[1] Rev. ix. 20.

ledge grew by study of the Sacred Books of the East and by intimate intercourse with adherents of other religions, a more intelligent and a more reverent approach became possible. It became clear that it had been an over-simplification either to hold that all religions were equally good for those who belonged to them, and that it was fanatical interference to meddle with them; or to hold that all were equally bad and that it was a simple and obvious duty to go forth armed with Boniface's axe and lay it at their roots. The Edinburgh Conference of 1910 registered the change of outlook. Its volume on the *Missionary Message*, edited by Dr. Cairns, found room for each of the two more serious types of thought on the relation of the Gospel to other religions, exemplified long ago by Origen and Tertullian. Tertullian dwelt most on their evils and the newness of the Christian revelation; any parallel between Christian and pagan rites, the use of Baptism in the Isis cult, or of bread and cup in the mysteries of Mithras, was attributed to the strategy of " daemons who foresaw what the Christian rites would be, and forestalled them with all sorts of pagan parodies."[1]

Origen sought to show that all that was noblest in the old religions was fulfilled in Christ; in each was to be found a *praeparatio evangelica* in embryo. He wrote, in reply to Celsus, " When God sent Jesus to the human race it was not as though He had just awakened from a long sleep. Jesus had at all times been doing good to the human race. No noble deed amongst men has ever been done without the Divine Word visiting the souls of those who even for a brief space were able to receive its operations." Dr. Cairns insisted that " there is no real contradiction between them. There is no reason whatever for Christian propaganda unless the missionary has something new to proclaim; there is no basis whatever for the missionary's appeal unless he can say ' Whom therefore ye worship in ignorance, Him declare I unto you.' "

Von Hügel and Kraemer may be taken as modern exponents of two acclimatization policies. Von Hügel saw in the Buddhist longing for Nirvana, in their sense of the sickening character of all mere slush of change, in their dim inarticulate sense of what the Abiding means, a quite

[1] Glover: op. cit., pp. 159 ff.

magnificent prolegomenon of all religion—one of the most
striking effects of the Real Presence of God in their minds.
He revelled in the teaching of a Spanish Jesuit Cardinal
that some light and some help everywhere proceeds from
God for the salvation of those who have never heard the
Name of Christ.   There was no touch of levelling down,
he said, in the Cardinal's teaching, no pretence that to
have been a Jew was not a great advantage over and
above the help to be found in ancient Greek and Roman
paganism, no obscuring of " the great surplusage of light
and help in the Christian Church as compared with the
Jewish Community," but the Cardinal saw a most real
use in Hindu Temple or Buddhist Monastery " in bringing
home to many a simple unsophisticated soul certain truths
which are not the less truth because they are mixed with
many an error, nor which again are less truths because
compared with the full orb of Christian verity they do
indeed seem small."

Dr. Kraemer would dismiss Origen as "emotionally a
Christian, intellectually more than half a pagan."   Though
he grants that " God, shining revealingly through the
work of His creation, through the thirst and quest for
truth and beauty, through conscience and the thirst and
quest for goodness, is continuously wrestling with man in
all ages and with all peoples," he insists that the entering
of Christianity into the non-Christian world means and
must mean a new chapter.   " Biblical realism " demands
an " austerity towards ' all religions ' the so-called ' higher '
as well as the so-called ' lower ' ; all are but products of
the human mind, the various efforts of man to apprehend
the totality of existence, often stirring in their sublimity
and as often pathetic or revolting in their ineffectiveness."

The issue has sometimes been focussed on the Old
Testament: some have suggested that a Church that has
sprung out of Hindu or Buddhist soil or antecedents
should discard the Old Testament and substitute Oriental
sacred books as the proper *praeparatio evangelica* for eastern
peoples, as being their forefathers' " schoolmasters to bring
them unto Christ."   Others claim that, apart from the
Old Testament being necessary to an understanding of the
New Testament, the divergencies between the two are as

nothing to the contrast between the religion of Christ and a religion based on the law of Karma, with its ethic of detachment, its appeal to the motives of merit, its goal of absorption in the Absolute " as the dewdrop slips into the shining sea "; between a religion based on history and a religiòn contemptuous of history, a religion glorifying and a religion belittling human personality and the life of human relationships.

It is not in order to attempt a synthesis between these views, still less to embark on a study of comparative theology, that the relation between Christianity and other faiths is here introduced, but to illustrate the complexity of the process of acclimatization.

ALIEN CULTURES

There was, as we have seen, a clash of cultures, Celtic and Continental, in the early English Church. The nineteenth-century missionary found himself compelled to emulate the example of St. Aldhelm, first Bishop of Sherborne, as reconciler and interpreter of each to each. Saxon enough to be able to win the ear of passing peasants by singing on the roadside like a professional minstrel their own Saxon songs, Aldhelm had at Malmesbury sat at the feet of Maeldubh, an Irish anchorite, product of the great monastic schools which made Ireland the leader of Western culture in the sixth century: he had at Canterbury sat at the feet of Theodore and Hadrian, representatives of another culture. But the missionary in the East soon discovered that the highly developed cultures were as inextricably interwoven with religion as the primitive: the whole social life of India and China respectively was bound up with the religious conceptions embodied in caste and ancestor worship. Both presented baffling impediments to acclimatization.

CASTE

The Caste controversy dated back to the early seventeenth century when Robert de Nobili consistently countenanced Caste in the Christian Church. He lived himself as a Brahmin among Brahmins, wearing the robe of a Sanyasi, a sacred thread round his neck, and caste-mark on forehead. Dr. Grant in an appendix to his *Bampton Lectures* quoting from Father Jouvenci's *History of the Jesuits*, tells how de Nobili, to establish his Brahmin status, produced an old parchment on which he had forged a deed " showing that the Brachmans of Rome were of much older date than those of India, and that the Jesuits of Rome descended in a direct line from the god Brahma ": when its authenticity was questioned he declared upon oath that he really and truly derived his origin from Brahma. Voltaire regarded the work as genuine, pounced upon it as a proof that the doctrines of Christianity were borrowed from the heathen, and pronounced it a work of immense antiquity. De Nobili dissociated himself, except in secret, from his fellow-Jesuits who were working among out-caste Christians. These were definitely degraded to the position of second-rank Christians in a second-rank Church.

Müllbauer, a Roman Catholic historian, condemns such segregation. " The thoughtful student will not fail to observe the contradiction to the all-reconciling love of Christ, Christian concord cannot but be broken when a Christian Brahmin deems himself unclean through his having in the same Church at the same holy board knelt side-by-side with a Pariah and with him received under the form of Bread, his Saviour to whom no respect of persons is known." But a Papal decree of 1623 approved the accommodating policy of the Jesuits, and the double system of priests continued to exist in India till the suppression of the Order in 1759, fourteen years after Benedict XIV had declared against their brahmanizing policy. Professor Latourette records that in the twentieth century, when a new Church was opened in Pondicherry with one half assigned to Pariahs, one half to Sudras, so great a tumult arose that the building had to be closed and could only be re-opened after all distinction had been removed. Caste still interposes a barrier to the Roman Catholic priesthood for the fisher caste in Cochin.[1]

The Abbé Dubois published in 1917 what was regarded as the standard *Description of the Character, Manners and Customs of the People of India*, which contains a vigorous defence of caste. " I consider the institution of

[1] Latourette: Vol. VI, p. 91.

castes amongst the Hindu nations as the happiest effort of their legislation. . . . If when all Europe was plunged in that dreary gulf (of war) India kept her head, preserved and extended the sciences, the arts and civilisation, it is wholly to the distinction of castes that she is indebted for that high celebrity." It was an institution of which Moses had availed himself for managing an intractable and rebellious race, Cecrops and Solon for civilizing Athens, Numa Pompilius for composing the animosities of Romans and Sabines.[1]

Such precedents offered no very helpful guidance to the early missionaries called to cope with a social phenomenon entirely outside their experience. It has generally been supposed that the Danish Mission (pp. 71–74) dealt over-leniently with caste. Macaulay arrived in India in June 1834 and spent August in the Nilgiris. As a member of the Council of India he was beset by petitioners from Tanjore, begging for his championship in their quarrel with the missionaries. The missionaries, he wrote home, "refused to recognise the distinction of caste in the administration of the Sacrament and the Bishop supported them in their refusal. I do not pretend to judge whether this was right or wrong. Schwartz and Bishop Heber conceived that the distinction of caste, however objectionable politically, was only a distinction of rank, and that as in English Churches the gentlefolk generally take the Sacrament apart from the poor of the parish, so the high-caste natives might be allowed to communicate apart from the Pariah, I believe that nobody on either side of the controversy found out a text so much to the purpose as one which I cited to the Council of India, when we were discussing the business. ' If this be a question of words and names and of your law, look ye to it: for I will be no judge of such matters.' But though like Gallio I drove them from my judgment seat, I could not help saying to one of the missionaries that I thought it a pity to break up the Church of Tanjore on account of a matter which such men as Schwartz and Heber had not been inclined to regard as essential."

Whether Macaulay was fair to Schwartz is doubtful. When a Brahmin asked, " Mr. Schwartz, do you not think

[1] Op. cit., pp. 13–23.

it a very bad thing to touch a Pariah ? " he had replied,
" Yes, very bad." But when the Brahmin went on to ask,
" What do you mean by a Pariah ? " Schwartz added,
" I mean a thief, a liar, a slanderer, a drunkard, an adul-
terer, a proud man." Whereupon the Brahmin went away
sorrowfully, murmuring " Then we are all Pariahs." It
is possible that such treatment of the subject led to misunderstanding. The true nature of what was a real
dilemma must not be forgotten. A rigorist policy may well
have seemed to involve precisely those evils against which
Bishop Pickett had waged war in India, Dr. Gutmann of
Kilimanjaro among the Chagga and Professor Freytag
in the Solomon Islands: namely the detachment of the
convert from his group, his dependence on the Mission,
his resulting isolation, denationalization, loss of self-
respect and incapacity to influence his own people. How
much sounder, we are told, the approach to the group,
the conversion of the whole group and its continuance in
its original environment and occupation. The individualist
structure of the West fits ill a collectivist Society in the
East and experiment and error were part of the cost of
adaptation.

It is no doubt probable that if the Danish Mission had
grasped the nettle more firmly, later scandal would not
have occurred, as when a worthy catechist was refused
ordination; he was a Pariah, and it was not to be expected
that a Sudra would receive the Sacrament at his hands.
Schwartz cannot bear the whole blame for what happened
thirty-six years after his death. Macaulay's citation of
the authority of Bishop Heber certainly did him an injustice. The fact is that the Bishop died before he had time
to complete his tour in the South and to make up his mind.
Within a fortnight of his death he wrote: " I am most
anxious to learn from every quarter the real truth of the
case. I have some fears that recent missionaries have
been more scrupulous in these matters than need requires,
and than was thought fit by Schwartz and his companions.
God forbid that we should wink at sin ! But God forbid
also that we should make the narrow gate of life narrower
than Christ has made it, or deal less favourably with the
prejudices of this people than St. Paul and the primitive

Church dealt with the almost similar prejudices of the Jewish converts.

It was Heber's successor, Bishop Wilson, who grasped the nettle Danger. He was shocked by what he found: " approach to the Lord's Table in common forbidden, separate divisions in the burial grounds imposed, the impassable barriers of Brahmanical caste erected again, condemning the one class of mankind to perpetual debasement and elevating the other to disproportionate pride, by which all the inter-community of the Body of Christ is violated and destroyed." Bishop Wilson saw in caste the very stronghold of heathenism. " The distinction of Caste must be abandoned, decidedly, immediately and finally." Uproar arose in the South Indian Church; the majority of Indian preachers preferred to be dismissed rather than at the Bishop's orders to take part in a Communion Service in which Sudras, Pariahs and Englishmen were to join. It was this commotion which disturbed Macaulay in the Nilgiri Hills. The nineteenth-century missionary had to make up his mind for or against Robert de Nobili's seventeenth-century policy for acclimatizing Christianity in India. He came to the conclusion that caste was not a social distinction to be winked at and gradually lived down, but was rooted in false religion, existing as it did, not like class distinctions in spite of religion but because of it.

ANCESTOR WORSHIP

He had also to make up his mind for or against Matteo Ricci's seventeenth-century policy for acclimatizing Christianity in China. This Italian Jesuit who reached China in 1582 and assumed the garb of a Chinese scholar, was fully prepared to tolerate the ceremonies of Ancestor Worship and the devotions paid to Confucius: they were merely social and national in character and not incompatible with Christianity. His attitude led to a century of controversy between Jesuits and Dominicans, the latter sharing the Franciscan view that the compromises tolerated were dangerous to immature Christians, and offered almost fatal facilities for men to become Christians and yet remain non-Christian at heart. Christians should not be permitted to render cultus to Confucius and to the dead, by profound obeisances, and worse still by oblations, sacrifices, prayers, and prostrations before tablets in which the Chinese believed that the Spirit of Confucius or the Ancestor was present. The problem once more became acute in the 1930's when the Japanese Government insisted on all students in College or School taking part in Shinto rites. Such are the problems of acclimatization.

II. TRANSPLANTATION PROBLEMS

The greater the odds against successful acclimatization, the more important it becomes that what is transplanted shall be worth transplanting, and possesses survival value. It will be wasted effort if the imported plant proves to have been too dependent on its native habitat to thrive in alien soil, or produces fruits which, however much appreciated in the country of their origin, meet with no acceptance in the country of their adoption. Even the power to survive is not by itself the equivalent of survival value: flora and fauna may become acclimatized rather to the detriment than to the benefit of a country. A flowering shrub, Lantana, was introduced into Ceylon to adorn a lady's garden; it soon swallowed up thousands of acres of good pasture. Rabbits soon became a pest in Australia. Did the nineteenth-century missionaries transplant the essentials? Did they introduce any parasitic weeds? Many of their contemporary critics would have replied that they were too narrow-minded to discriminate between what was of local and what of universal significance, and too sectarian to take due precautions against a harvest of transplanted divisions.

1. *THE LOCAL AND THE UNIVERSAL*

Missionaries no doubt share the idiosyncracies of their nineteenth-century fellow-countrymen. Among these was a prejudice in favour of reproducing overseas the familiar conditions of home life, with as little change as possible in diet, drink, dress and other domestic habits. Troops fought under tropical suns in busbies and scarlet regimentals: climate was not allowed to interfere with the normal consumption of alcohol, and carnivorous meals. Lawns must be green where no grass had been known to grow. There must of course be a race-course. In the religious sphere there were similar symptoms of nostalgia. The Church must look as like as possible to Churches at home: a city Church must look like a City Church, and a village Church like a village Church. Chants, hymns, and the Prayer Book liturgy must recall as far as possible the atmosphere of home worship.

William Carey's delight over an English daisy explains a great deal: botany was his great hobby and the destruction of his gardens by flood a major tragedy. He had asked a friend to send him all kinds of British seeds and bulbs: " That I might be sure not to lose any part of your valuable present, I shook the bag over a patch of earth in a shady place: on visiting it a few days afterwards I found springing up to my inexpressible delight a *Bellis perennis* of our English pastures. I know not that I ever enjoyed since leaving Europe a simple pleasure so exquisite as the sight of this English daisy afforded me—not having seen one for upwards of thirty years, and never expecting to see one again."

Many missionary biographies contain stories of the same kind, which show that missionaries were very human and therefore very homesick. Even in the wireless era residence abroad involves the breaking of many ties and loss of touch with the background of public opinion; exile is still exile. But distance was magnified for the nineteenth century. Families were large, and parents were separated from their growing children for years at a time. Incongruous Churchwarden Gothic disfigured oriental landscapes not because it was the only valid type of architecture, but because it accorded best with sentiment and custom. Other anomalies can be explained on the same lines.

Instinctive custom and sentiment were reinforced by reasoned conviction. Men and women would not have found their way to distant climes in the name of the Lord if they had not possessed very definite and articulate convictions. Their faith was none the less personal for reflecting the environment in which it had been nurtured: the company which he keeps, the confessions and watchwords of that company, their theological emphasis and terminology, cannot but affect, consciously and subconsciously, the believer's experience and the expression of his belief. The missionary could only proclaim his faith in the language and liturgy which meant everything to himself. It may be thought that it would have saved many complications if the Gospel could have been exported in dehydrated packets, from which all transient and provincial fluids had been eliminated, and only the spiritual vitamins retained. But that is an impossible demand. The Gospel can only be mediated through the impact of personality on personality; the Spirit works through very ordinary men and women, in spite of all their limitations of outlook and experience. The missionary could not be expected to leap over his own shadow—the shadow of a man or women belonging to a particular epoch, a particular race, and a particular ecclesiastical home. He cannot be blamed for not discriminating nicely between the elements in his message which were universal and essential, and those which were local and variable; or for not analysing his personality neatly into its component elements, Christian, British, Victorian, Tractarian or Evangelical.

Further, the effect of a century of ecclesiastical debate was to sharpen the edge of controversy; the missionary inevitably tended to stress not only what distinguished Christianity from other religions, but what distinguished his own interpretation of Christianity from others which he held to be defective or erroneous.

As the century advanced a fuller understanding of the problems and perils of acclimatization developed. Bishops and missionaries became sensitive to the dangers of perpetuating a foreign guise, at once repellent to the unbeliever and unsuited to the believer's mentality and self-expression. Archbishop Benson bade the Bishops assembled for the Lambeth Conference of 1888 remember the pregnant words of Gregory to Augustine, " Non pro locis res, sed pro bonis rebus loca amanda sunt." Augustine had asked " The Faith being one, are there different customs in different Churches ? " To which Pope Gregory replied: " It pleases me that if you have found anything, either in the Roman or the Gallican, or any other Church, which may be more acceptable to Almighty God, you carefully make choice of the same, and sedulously teach the Church of the English, which as yet is new in the faith, whatsoever you can gather from the several Churches. For things are not to be loved for the sake of places, but places for the sake of good things."

Ten years before, the Bishops had drawn attention, though cautiously, to *Article XXXIV*: " It is not necessary that Traditions and Ceremonies be in all places one, or utterly like; for at all times they have been divers and may be changed according to the diversities of countries, times and mens' manners, so that nothing be ordained against God's Word. . . . Every particular or national Church hath authority to ordain, change and abolish ceremonies or rites of the Church ordained only by man's authority, so that all things be done to edifying."

A later section will show how this principle, inherited from the earliest makers of Christian History in England, was applied in terms of constitutions and canons to the expanding Church overseas. Resolutions 18 and 19 of the Lambcth Conference of 1897 register what may be taken to have by then commanded general assent: " It is of the utmost importance that from the very beginning the idea that the Church is their own and not a foreign Church should be impressed upon converts. . . . It is important that, so far as possible, the Church should be adapted to local circumstances, and the people brought to feel in all ways that no burdens in the way of foreign customs are laid upon them, and nothing is required of them but what is of the essence of the Faith and belongs to the due order of the Catholic Church."

There is often a long interval between the enunciation of principles and their application. It cannot be maintained that the expansion of the Anglican Communion has been accompanied by a smooth and uninterrupted progress towards that just freedom of its several parts, that freedom of local development which the Lambeth Encyclical of 1908 commended as a " characteristic element in the in-heritance which the Anglican Communion has received, and in the tradition of the English-speaking race, which belongs of right to the native Churches which we have fostered." But it may be claimed that there has been progress: what checks there have been may be debited to tendencies and temperaments that are confined to no single race, the tendency of an older generation to withhold responsibility from a younger, or of a younger to resent the conservatism of an older, the temperament which instinctively domineers, or instinctively rebels.

2. *DEBITS AND CREDITS*

SECTARIANISM

Bishop Edward Talbot, towards the end of his life, addressed a Ministers' Fraternal on Unity. " It was not difficult," he writes, " to give a fairly interesting account of the change in my time from the old ' cat and dog ' aloofness of ' Church and Chapel ' in England, with the controversies over the Universities, Burials Bill, Education Acts—to the new period, where by a reflex action from the Mission-field, ' Edinburgh 1910 ' inaugurated a new epoch of inter-denominational action, which has leavened and sweetened relations, though, alas, unity is far enough off still."

No one can study the expansion of the nineteenth century without being aware of the background of " cat and dog " aloofness of which the Bishop speaks. Happily it is incomprehensible to the present generation that the Burials Bill of 1880, for example, to which Bishop Talbot refers, should have excited such alarm and animosity. Sixteen thousand clergy signed a petition against an Act for the martyrdom of the National Church, for the burial of the Church of England herself. The Lower House of Convocation delivered itself by solemn protest " of all responsibility as to any dishonour which may be done to Almighty God by the character of the worship which hereafter may be offered in our Churchyards." Rather than allow the " desecration " of Nonconformist prayers at the graveside, it would be preferable, though an " enormous sacrifice " to adopt a rule of silence for all. The Act was " an artful, treacherous and insidious blow at Episcopacy, abolishing the consecration of the Bishops, the Holy Orders of the Clergy, and the authority of the Book of Common Prayer."

Panics and pogroms had inevitable repercussions overseas. The Secession from the Church of Scotland in 1843 cost Duff and Wilson their Colleges in Calcutta and Bombay; they had to begin all over again. Mutual suspicion dictated extreme caution in any *rapprochement* between Anglicans and their fellow-missionaries of other communions. Bishop Heber felt it necessary to address several thousand words to Ceylon missionaries who desired to engage in solemn conference on topics connected with their work. He welcomed their brotherly and tolerant spirit, but there was " the risk of levelling, in the eyes of others and even in your own, the peculiar claims to attention and peculiar hopes of grace and blessing which are possessed by the holders of an apostolic commission, over those whose call to the ministry is less regular, though their labours are no less sincere. . . . Prayer-meetings are apt to degenerate into enthusiastic excitement or irreverent familiarity, each labouring to excel his brother in the choice of his expressions and the outward earnestness of his address."

Yet, as Bishop Talbot testifies, it was by reflex action from the Mission-field that a new era began. He alludes to the Edinburgh Conference of 1910, out of which sprang the International Missionary Council, and branching National Christian Councils. This was the first of a series of œcumenical conferences, and the product of the hundred years which we have been reviewing. It was a notable Anglican landmark, for nobody expected thirty-six years ago to see the Archbishops of Canterbury and York, or Bishops Talbot, Gore and Montgomery appearing on an interdenominational platform; they themselves felt that they were doing something epoch-making in accepting invitations to take part, and hesitated long. It was a notable landmark in missionary history, not only because it was a new beginning; it was itself the climax of a long ascent.

Four definitions from the *Oxford English Dictionary* will help to particularize the stages of that ascent. *Contiguity*: the condition of living in contact; proximity in time or place. *Comity*: the courteous and friendly understanding by which each respects the laws and usages of every other, so far as may be, without prejudice to its own rights and interests. *Coalition* : an alliance for combined action of distinct parties, persons or states, without permanent incorporation into one body. *Coalescence*: the growing together of separate parts; fusion.

It had been found impossible to acclimatize Christianity in the valley of Contiguity, where the vapours of competition smothered the young plantations in a miasma fatal to their growth. The first ascent was to the foothills of Comity; here by mutual agreement between all but the Roman Church and the Salvation Army, an area was allotted to each community within which it might grow without interference, and with room to stretch itself; there were friendly understandings by which members of one community were not accepted into another without consultation as to the motives for transfer. The next stage was exploration of the upper slopes of Coalition by all the extra-Roman Churches in alliance for combined thinking and action; joint conferences, joint campaigns, and some joint institutions are characteristic of this stage. The younger are now spurring on their elders to an assault on the higher peaks of Coalescence, where the separate parts, having grown together, may achieve fusion. " Visible and organic union must be our goal " was the message of the Younger Churches at the Tambaram Conference. " We appeal with all the fervour we possess to the responsible authorities of the older Churches to take this matter seriously to heart, to support and encourage us in all our efforts to put an end to the scandalous effects of our divisions."

It is not unnatural that the Younger Churches should deplore the introduction, together with the precious plants of the Church, of what they would describe, and their language is no stronger than St. Paul's—as weeds choking its growth and parasites corrupting its life as doth a canker: of what Moffatt's translation of Galatians, v. 20, calls " quarrels, dissensions, jealousy, rivalry, factions, party-spirit." To them the magnitude of the treasure which they hold in common far outweighs their differences: the magnitude of the task which they share transcends all lesser loyalties; the history which lies behind the tensions of the West is not their history, though theirs is the discredit which division earns in the eyes of their non-Christian neighbours: they find themselves handicapped thereby from winning the allegiance of non-Christians to Christ: they feel their Lord dishonoured.

The Lambeth Conference of 1908 " could not but believe that the Foreign Mission Field is likely to react upon the Church at home by teaching a truer proportion, widening the outlook and strengthening the spiritual vision." Those on the circumference are more conscious that the centre reacts upon the Church overseas and that no schemes of union overseas can hope to avoid the creation of embarrassing anomalies as long as there are no schemes of union in operation at the headquarters of the Mother Church.

Historically the Anglican Communion began to play a part in the Reunion movement with the promulgation of the Lambeth Quadrilateral in 1888, as a basis of Reunion. The Conference of 1897, summing up the experiences of the century, reported that " the day is passed in which men could speak of the Church of God as if it were an aggregate of trading establishments, as if our divisions promoted a generous rivalry, and saved us from apathy and indolence. Men of all schools of thought are realizing the grievous injury which has been done to Christianity by the separations." The 1908 Conference noted that " essentials and non-essentials are not always wisely discriminated . . . the aspiration after a deeper unity will not be in vain: as in the West a time of disintegration is being followed by a time of consolidation, so in the East Christianity may take root without the perpetuation from generation to generation of the divisions of the West." In 1920 the " Appeal to all Christian People" for a new approach to Reunion rang out to all the world. At the 1930 Lambeth Conference, the Bishops " rejoiced that one part of the Anglican Communion should be found ready to make this (South Indian) venture for a corporate reunion with certain non-episcopal Churches. We feel that in a sense our brethren in South India are making this experiment on behalf of the whole body of the Anglican Churches. They are our pioneers in the direction of the movement for unity." It cannot therefore be said that the

Anglican Communion has been unmoved by the disquiet which moved the delegates of the Younger Churches at Tambaram. War has been declared on the weeds and parasites; it is only the measured pace of the older Churches which leads the younger, in face of what appears to them to be a situation of extreme urgency, to ask whether it is a war which anyone really expects to win.

In what we have called the " upper slopes of Coalition " the Anglican Communion has been increasingly active in spite of inhibitions, at times timidly acquiescing in co-operation as a necessary evil, at times greeting with a cheer the opening of gates long locked. The scope of co-denominational activity has extended. In their partnership with Governments in educational, medical, and social welfare plans, the Churches have acted as one. In the production of literature, in evangelistic surveys, in attacks on such social evils as race-discrimination, illiteracy, and the opium traffic, in services to the German Missions orphaned by the war, in the approach to students, the Churches have accomplished together what they could not have attempted singly. Universities, Theological Colleges, and Medical Schools have been founded on a scale that no single Church could have achieved. In India, for example, the distribution of places in medical schools on a communal quota would have extinguished all opportunity for Christian students of medicine if the Churches had not combined in a co-denominational Medical College at Vellore. In India also it has been found possible to survey the whole field of theological education, and to produce a joint scheme for Theological Colleges in all language areas which all the representatives of the Churches on the National Christian Council could adopt unanimously.

III.   TESTS OF ACCLIMATIZATION

1.   *THEIR LIMITATIONS*

A Christianity which proves robust enough to smother weeds and resist pests, to counteract and quell divisive influences, may be said to have passed one of the tests of a quasi-indigenous Church. Such fruits imply firm roots.

But like all other tests of acclimatization, only the passage of years can establish its permanent validity. Many a plant, like coffee in Ceylon, has had the appearance of permanent settlement—the hills were white with its blossom and its berries went forth into all the world, till the passage of years revealed a susceptibility to a fatal blight, and the place thereof knew it no more. Doubtless the Churches of Asia Minor and North Africa had all the appearance of permanence till their stars were eclipsed and their candlesticks removed. The question, therefore, is not whether acclimatization has been achieved—that must be left to posterity to answer—but whether the process is advancing to the degree that might reasonably be expected after taking into account the age of the Church, the special circumstances of its birth and infancy, and any peculiarities of its environment which might retard normal growth.

One very relevant subject for examination will be the extent to which a Church is self-governing or advancing towards self-government. Does it possess, and is it exercising, organs of corporate self-administration which contain within themselves the capacity for growth in conformity with the increase of the body? If the Church were a machine, new parts could be inserted and elaborated as occasion demanded. If the Church is a body, the organs must be there from the beginning. This raises constitutional questions which will be more appropriately dealt with in a chapter on Consolidation.

It is not difficult to identify at once three symptoms which would immediately provoke anxiety if their presence was proved. If a Church showed signs of growing up permanently dependent on external aid, if a Church continued in adolescence to exhibit the imitativeness of childhood, if a Church stayed stationary, serious doubts might well be entertained as to the genuiness of its acclimatization. Self-existence, Self-expression, Self-extension, are the positive principles which, if exemplified in the life of a Church, would betoken healthy naturalization. But it must be understood that the prefix " Self " is used as in " self-respect," with no suggestion of a life that is independent of God and His grace. These tests can only be applied with any confidence on the hypothesis that the Promises of the Gospel stand. " He that abideth in Me and I in him, the same bringeth forth much fruit. If ye abide in Me and My words abide in you, ye shall ask what ye will, and it shall be done unto you." It is assumed, too, that these tests only remain valid as long as the normal processes of spiritual cultivation are assiduously maintained from generation to generation. " You can inherit everything in this world except experience."[1]

2.   *SELF-EXISTENCE*

Self-existence is defined as " the existence of a being by virtue of his inherent nature independently of any other being : having a primary or independent existence." No Church is self-existent which depends for its ministry on foreign missionaries, for its finance on foreign funds, for its education on foreign teachers, for its medicine on foreign doctors and nurses. Such dependence may be a necessary stage, but until it is out-grown it is too soon to speak of complete acclimatization.

(a) FINANCIAL SELF-EXISTENCE

" Strictly speaking," wrote Bishop Azariah, " the word ' self-support ' ought to be applied to a Church only when all its legitimate needs and activities, pastoral, evangelistic, educational and philanthropic, are supported by itself without any outside help." Judged by this standard, few Churches can claim " self-existence ", and the Church of England with its ancient endowments is not one of them. The standard is justly applied more leniently to Churches which originated in communities of rescued slaves, or of peasants wresting a bare living from the soil, or of converts who, by the fact of their conversion, have suffered the economic effects of ostracism. Between 80 and 90 per cent of the Christians in India, China and Korea are villagers : in Africa an even larger percentage is directly dependent on the soil: Churches so composed must be peculiarly sensitive to bad harvest, droughts and slumps. Pre-war statistics show that the income raised locally was in India over three-eighths, in Tropical Africa nearly three-

[1] Dr. A. C. Welch: *Deuteronomy.*

quarters, in China one-seventh, in the West Indies six-sevenths, of that which came from England. In nine areas which received help the total of local contributions approximately balanced the total sent from England, namely £1,150,000. The deduction may be drawn that the principle of self-help has been honoured, and progress made towards financial self-existence.

Our survey of the past shows that missionaries have been from early days alive to the danger of perpetuating traditions of dependence. Griffith John in China, in the '80's, threw the whole burden of building churches upon the congregations and insisted on their obligation to maintain the ministry. Bishop Tucker in Uganda desired to exclude to the utmost English money from the normal work of the Church: England was to provide the missionaries but the native clergy and teachers were to be maintained and the Churches built by the Baganda themselves. It was the damaging effect of dependence upon the recipients that the early missionaries had mainly in mind. It was bad for their people to be provided with what they should provide for themselves: the legend of a bottomless British purse was easily propagated by the difference in European standards of living, and exerted a pauperizing influence. As the century advanced, it was the damaging effect on the missionaries and their supporters of being depended upon that came to be realized. Missionaries found their relation with their people embarrassed by their possession of the power of the purse: it was spiritually detrimental to be regarded as the dispensers of what to their peasants appeared to be riches. Supporters of missions began to realize that " He who pays the piper calls the tune " may, as Bishop Azariah used to say, be a good slogan in mundane affairs, but is unworthy as between Christians. The attitude of the Lady Bountiful had outlived its usefulness in England; charity tainted with patronage and the assertion of power had been recognized for the little it was worth ; could it be that the power of the purse vested in nineteenth-century middle-class pockets was making for estrangement between benefactor and beneficiary ? How could the lot of the poorer Churches be lightened without offence to the self-respect of the recipient, without infringing the principles of self-help, and without trespassing on the rights of a local Church to unfettered freedom in the direction of its work and worship?

Three answers were worked out to this question:—

(i) A distinction was drawn between expenditure which should normally fall on local budgets, and expenditure to which the home subscriber could contribute without misgivings. It was, for example, obvious that the missionaries could not be a charge on the Church of their adoption, but must be supported by their Church of origin. Again, there were institutions, medical and educational, vital to the life of a young Church but beyond its means to build and maintain. It was the privilege of an older Church to fill the role played by William of Wykeham and Henry the Sixth, Rahere, Thomas Guy, and the Prior of St. Mary Overy in founding Colleges and Hospitals. It was the obvious duty of an episcopal Church to make provision for the Episcopate. Younger Churches might properly be assisted in the erection of Cathedrals and other places of worship, of a beauty and dignity beyond their own means, provided that discretion was shown in the type of architecture selected. There were types of endowment corresponding to the dowry of a daughter, and no more objectionable. The line was not always wisely drawn, as when it demarcated the pastoral sphere as the special responsibility of the local Church and reserved the evangelistic for missionary support, thus introducing a fatal division of function; but the drawing of a line was in itself an advance.

(ii) Subsidies were, at least in principle, dissociated from control. The China Centenary Conference of 1907 reported that " Happily the control of the purse as the basis of authority is passing away. If any man thinks he can rule in the Church because when his judgment is threatened he has the power to withhold a salary, he has yet to learn what are the first principles of the government of the House of God." In practice the principle has not always been easy to apply. Human nature being what it is, donors are stirred to greater generosity if they know that their gifts will be used to support their distinctive tenets and administered by those who share their views: if the representatives of the donor have no voice in the distribution of funds there may be no funds to distribute. It is natural and legitimate that individuals should wish to support the work and workers of their choice, prompted by affection of personal association. But as his children grow up, a parent feels less and less entitled to dictate to them how his cheque should be spent, and is content to leave it to their judgement to decide, without any diminution of his own instinctive desire to help them. Similarly there has been a growing acceptance of the necessity of consulting an adolescent Church as to the form in which help would be most acceptable and accord best with its order of priorities.

(iii) Dependence, Independence, and Interdependence established their separate identities. Each was robbed of its sting when related to the conception of a Family Budget. The budget of the Anglican Communion is not the budget of a limited liability company which each shareholder studies to make sure that he secures his fair dividend : it is not a Government budget which the tax-payer studies to make sure that no more than his due proportion of his country's burden is being extracted from him. Members of a family approach their domestic budget in a different spirit, each anxious to reduce his claim on the common resources and to increase his contribution, so that the resources of the whole may be expended to the best advantage of each, and especially of the younger, though they can contribute little if anything themselves.

In this context dependence degrades none, and becomes an incentive instead of a deterrent to effort. Independence loses all taint of assertive self-sufficiency and acquires instead the stamp of manly strength and self-respect. Inter-dependence comes into its own—the original authentic interdependence of the New Testament Church. It happened in the nineteenth century that it was the Macedonians who were poor and Jerusalem rich: complications arose because relations were thus reversed and the Mother Church was no longer the beneficiary but the benefactor. But St. Paul's principle of inter-dependence still applies. Within the family there could still be the bestowal of gifts without conditions, without affront to self-respect, without detriment to the harmony and unity of the whole fellowship.

It is in this spirit, but not without trial and error, that the movement towards financial self-existence has been progressing.

(b) SELF-EXISTENCE AND MAN-POWER

" The euthanasia of a Mission " wrote Henry Venn, Secretary of the Church Missionary Society, in 1851, " takes place when a missionary, surrounded by well-trained Native congregations under Native Pastors, is able to resign all pastoral work into their hands.". This seemed a far-off ideal. Writing at the turn of the century, Bishop Montgomery, Secretary of the Society for the Propagation of the Gospel, regarded the foundation of a stable Indian Christianity as still to be laid. " Able as some of the native clergy are, they seem to look at the faith through Western eyes. The nineteenth century has given us four or five African Bishops. The twentieth century should give us Indian, Chinese and, we suppose, Japanese Bishops."

Nothing would astonish Allen Gardiner more, if he retraced his voyages to-day, than to find five Papuan priests in New Guinea, thirty Zulu clergy in South Africa, and several Mapuche Indians in the ranks of the South American Ministry. Bishop Patteson, shortly before his death, foretold that " in some quite unexpected way, or at all events in some way brought about independently of our efforts, a work will be begun here some day, in the day when God sees fit." By 1941 there were forty Melanesian priests and twenty-six deacons, and 720 lay workers. In 1925, Ini, a Melanesian of twenty-two, mission scholar, police boy, sergeant of police, Chief Constable, saw from his hospital bed a vision of a Brotherhood that should go forth in poverty, chastity, and obedience to evangelize the Islands. The revival of the Religious Life was in its infancy when Bishop Patteson died, and though the Cowley Society of St. John the Evangelist and the Clewer and Wantage Sisterhoods had come into being, none of the great Communities had yet begun their missions overseas: nor had their later expansion brought them within reach of Melanesia. Ini's was certainly a " quite unexpected way " and no one would have been more surprised and rejoiced than Bishop Patteson to find over a hundred Melanesian Brothers forming spontaneously a striking force of incomparable value and penetrating to the wildest tribes in the most remote islands.

Other Bishops whose acquaintance we have made in earlier chapters would find similar cause for astonishment— Bishop Selwyn to find a Maori Bishop, Heber to find an Indian Bishop with an English Suffragan, Macdougall to find Dyak priests, Feild to find ordained Eskimos. The Chinese ministry which had reached the hundred-mark by the begining of the first world-war, was reaching 300 by the beginning of the second, with 9 Chinese Bishops; by the end of the 1930's India had raised up approximately 600 Anglican clergy, Burma 50, and Ceylon 100. 500 out of the 700 in Tropical Africa, East and West, were African. There has thus become indigenous a calling wholly foreign in character and ideal, for in no other religion was there anything corresponding to the pastoral ministry.

As this acclimatization advanced, three consequential problems can be identified, universal in range though treated variously by different Churches:—

(i) *Training*. It was soon realized that the English model could not be followed slavishly; training must be simplified but must be thorough. Precautions, almost morbidly scrupulous, were taken against any subordination of quality to quantity. As a rule a prolonged apprenticeship as catechist was the avenue to ordination; or a course of private tuition by the missionary. Divinity Schools were the next stage. As long as the ideal of a peasant priesthood satisfied the needs of the Church, teaching was in the vernacular. As the standard of education rose the standard required of educated ordinands had to be raised: Theological schools were supplemented by Theological Colleges: English was superimposed upon the vernacular. Gradually the experience derived from haphazard and sectional experiments had to be reviewed and revised, and an agreed system evolved, which would guarantee the maintenance by all Churches of standards appropriate to different degrees of training.

(ii) *Finance.* In the delimitation of boundaries between what properly was the responsibility of the local Church, and what could rightly be contributed from external resources, we noted that the maintenance of the ministry fell in the former category. It was not felt to be consonant with the self-respect of a Church to shirk the full expense of supporting its own clergy. Self-existence was at stake. In most areas the principle holds hard and fast. In others doubts have emerged; its rigid application has been felt to bind burdens too grievous to be borne upon poor congregations, diverting too much attention and energy into monetary channels. While no-one would tolerate a return to the system which put the missionary in the position of employer of ordained employees, there would not be the same objection to the clergy being paid out of a Diocesan fund to which Missionary Societies had contributed. An actively evangelistic ministry might occasionally be more numerous than a local Church could afford: the fewer the Christians the greater the need of a strong striking force: the weaker the Christians the greater their need for intensive pastoral care.

It is where the need for a better educated clergy is most conspicuous that local resources are often found to be inadequate. There were Churches from which educated Christians held aloof because the clergy were not qualified to understand their difficulties or speak to their condition. However self-sacrificing the better educated clergy may be, and however willing to live on a salary far below what their College friends would regard as a minimum, they cannot avoid some expenses unknown to their illiterate neighbours: the advantages of having been educated will evaporate if they can never buy a book, and if their standard of living cuts them off from all access to their more educated neighbours to whom they are specially qualified to minister. It may therefore be argued that one of the privileges of an older Church may be to come to the assistance of a younger at this point, without doing violence to its self-existence.

(iii) The contrast between the earlier days when missionaries were the only ordained servants of the Church, and the later when the native ministry had become the majority, implies an adjustment of relationship between the two. It would be too much to claim that the missionary's transformation from being monarch of all he surveyed to the standing of partner, colleague and even subordinate has everywhere been effected with ease. The patriarchal tradition took an unconscionable time to die: the patriarchal missionary, jealously watchful over a charge too sacred to be exposed to risks, was genuinely unaware that his authority could be felt repressive, or cramping, or his relations with his beloved people lacking in reciprocity: he transmitted to younger missionaries paternal assumptions which a younger generation of Christians was beginning to resent. The dilemma is as familiar in the political as in the ecclesiastical field; how can responsibility be handed over till men have shown a capacity for carrying responsibility? How can men show such a capacity till they have had the chance of developing what only the experience of carrying responsibility can give?

The Rev. V. S. Azariah startled us at the Edinburgh Conference of 1910 by the urgency of his plea for the adjustment of both personal and official relationships between missionaries and their Indian colleagues: " The foreign missionary should exhibit unmistakably that he is not afraid to give up positions of leadership and authority into the hands of his Indian fellow-workers, and that his joy is fulfilled when he decreases and the Indian brother increases." " You have given your goods to feed the poor. You have given your bodies to be burned. We also ask for *love*. Give us *friends*." As Bishop of Dornakal, almost up to the day of his death thirty-five years later, he still felt it more than ever necessary to reiterate the same plea. It is as the servant of the indigenous Church that the missionary will be welcome in post-war India, " as a friend and co-worker of the Indian head, functioning if need be in a subsidiary capacity under indigenous leaders. It may hurt the pride of both young and old. But post-war India will demand this, and the sooner we adjust ourselves to the new day the better. The Church must increase, the Mission must decrease." Much had been done in the interval between these utterances to break the vicious circle. By the date of the Tambaram Conference, at which the delegates of the younger Churches were in the majority, it had become possible to discuss with perfect frankness the role of the modern missionary as "colleague and friendly helper in the up-building of the life of the younger Churches, by enriching their spiritual life and by helping to train leaders for the varied ministry of the Churches."

The fact that the ordained Ministry has become so universal and omni-racial a brotherhood crowns the achievement of the pioneers, and points to foundations well and truly laid.

The Teaching and Medical Professions supply corroborating evidence of acclimatization. How are the Church's educational and medical institutions staffed? In the Anglican areas of Tropical Africa, India, Burma, and Ceylon, and China, there are over 15,000 men and women serving their respective countries, with less than 500 reinforcements from outside; more than 3,000 of the 15,000 are women. In the medical missions of all (extra-Roman) Churches in India and China, out of a total of 1,500 Doctors, only 500 come from overseas. Of the 1,500, 500 are Women Doctors, in the proportion of two foreigners to three native. Only ten per cent. of the 13,000 nurses in mission hospitals are foreign. It is clear that mountains of prejudice and convention have been successfully removed and cast into the sea.

3.   SELF-EXPRESSION

To carry on into adolescence the imitativeness of childhood has been noted as a second symptom of arrested development. Something has been said under the heading " The Local and the Universal " (p. 276) in extenuation of the charge sometimes levelled against the early missionaries, that they transplanted too much. It is easy after the event to blame them for a negative and unsympathetic attitude to traditional customs and culture. Robert Moffat excused himself on the ground that they would be " neither a very instructive nor a very edifying " subject of study: they were in fact " a mass of rubbish " and corrupted by taint of heathen superstition. Nurtured in this tradition the early converts instinctively dissociated themselves from

national and tribal antecedents, and modelled themselves
and their worship on what they were taught to regard as
the authentic Christian pattern. Nobody knew better
than they that many of the missionaries' strictures were
well-founded.   Sacred associations gathered round the
new patterns: familiar forms enshrined memories of
missionary heroes and early converts. At first it was only
in minor details that there was a departure from custom,
for example, in the presentation of a congregation's alms.
It would puzzle an English sidesman to cope with the
offering of bushels of rice or bunches of bananas, of eggs
or hens.

The imitative period lingered so long under these
influences that when the reaction came it set in with some
vehemence. As missionaries in Africa fell under the
anthropological spell, and in India and China entered more
fully into their cultural inheritance, they became more
sensitive to the dangers of superficial acclimatization. As
converts became more sure of themselves they cast a more
discriminating eye upon their pre-Christian heritage. As
the spirit of nationalism and racial self-respect extended
its sway Christians became acutely conscious of all that
was repellent, because foreign or occidental, in the presentation of their religion to their fellow-countrymen. The
revitalizing effect of Christianity itself stirred creative
instincts. As Spanish artists expressed themselves in one
idiom because they were Spanish, and Dutch in another
because they were Dutch, so Indian, Chinese or African
Christians expressed their creative instincts in their own
vernacular of art, architecture, music, and liturgy.

It is not always easy to discriminate between what was a
matter of instinct and what a matter of policy in the process
of adaptation. Where the latter preponderated the voice
of the iconoclast sometimes made itself heard. Condemnation of the foreign because it was foreign has sometimes gone further than the domestic experience of the
Anglican Church would seem to justify. Many of the most
English of our treasures owe most to foreign enrichment
of the native tradition: Canterbury Cathedral to William
of Sens: Westminster Abbey to Master Henry's familiarity
with Rheims; the Abbey's central shrine of the Confessor

was Italian workmanship and it owes the glories of its
Tudor tombs to Pietro Torregiano. It was inevitable that
reaction to the stimulus of a dominant nationalism should
sometimes appear as inept as Queen Victoria's assertion of
her Stuart ancestry in the tartan upholstery of Balmoral.
It has sometimes sounded strident: adolescence is often
strident, and stridency a sign that childhood is being left
behind.

But the growth in self-expression is a symptom of genuine
acclimatization where it is neither agressively self-conscious
nor predominantly the outcome of calculated policy.   No
one could accuse the Bhajanas (metrical versions of the
Gospel narrative for community singing) and Lyrics of
South Indian Christians, of being anything but the spontaneous expression of deep-seated instincts of worship and
evangelism.   Chinese artists portray the Gospel story with
authentic originality.   Bantus in South Africa have shown
a true genius for religious sculpture.   The Sea Dyaks of
Borneo decorate their Churches with paintings and carv-
ings that owe nothing to external suggestion.   The Chapel
at Trinity College, Kandy, may be taken as one example
of the experiments that are being made all over the world
to revive and adapt to the purpose of Christian worship
ancient architectural traditions.   " It was unthinkable
that the designers of a modern Chapel in Ceylon should
fall back upon architecture of an exotic type, Gothic,
Classic or Byzantine, turning their backs on the inspiration
to be derived from the sacred buildings of the past.   Our
Christianity would have stood condemned as an alien
growth if Trinity builders had shown themselves insensible
to the majestic traditions of Sinhalese builders of two
thousand years ago."

The festivals and fasts of paganism presented, as we have
seen, as puzzling a problem to the early missionaries as
they did to St. Augustine (p. 5). The sacred and the
social were so intimately fused that it needed the judgement
of mature Christians both to decide how far they should or
should not take part, and to devise equivalent community
festivals, processions, pilgrimages, which would stand
comparison with the pre-Christian in attractiveness, pic-
turesqueness and indigenous character, and at the same

time embody the distinctive witness of a community rejoicing in its Christianity.

4. SELF-EXPANSION

Our section on Mass Movements (p. 243) showed how large a share in the process of the Church's expansion must be attributed to the spontaneous evangelistic energy of its members. Weeks of Witness and their like are the most convincing evidence that can be offered of progressive acclimatization. Conversely, Churches which in the past have died of spiritual inertia, or capitulated tamely to external influences, showing no power of aggression or resistance, owe their failure to defective acclimatization. As Dr. Cash notes, the collapse of Christianity in the Near East before the Mohammedan onrush may be attributed to the fact that it had never become indigenous, tied as it was to the Byzantine state. " The authority and control of all church affairs was in the hands of Greek nationals, and the ' young Churches ' of the day had little or no voice in ecclesiastical matters. . . . There is no evidence to show that either liturgy or Bible was ever translated into the vernacular in pre-Islamic days."[1]

There is, however, a second aspect of this question. Whatever its success in presenting its Gospel persuasively to the individual, can a Church be regarded as on the road to acclimatization which is not bringing to bear a corporate impact upon its environment ? There must be an element of speculation in assessing such corporate influence. Christianity cannot always be insulated from all other civilizing factors; it is impossible to assign to Church and State their respective share of credit. Where some would hold that there was discredit to be shared, as in the break-up of tribal life, and the breakdown of tribal sanctions and economy, it would be equally difficult to apportion blame, if blame there be, between merchant, missionary, and miner.

It is in the more primitive societies that advance may be most definitely accredited to the Church. Allen Gardiner, for example, if he were to revisit Zululand, New Guinea, and South America, would have no difficulty in tracing a

[1] Dr. Cash: *The Missionary Church*, pp. 199, 200.

miraculous transformation to Christian influence. As in
other African dependencies, *Pax Britannica* among the
Zulus depended for its foundation upon *Pax Christiana*.
It was through Barbrooke Grubb and the South American
Missionary Society that the Indians of the Paraguayan
and Argentine Chaco reached the stability of an attractive
community life. Australian and American soldiers bear
no uncertain testimony to the qualities of Papuan and
Melanesian Christians :—

> " Bringing back the badly wounded, just as steady as a hearse,
> Using leaves to keep the rain off, and as careful as a Nurse;
> Slow and careful in bad places, on that awful mountain-track;
> And the look upon their faces makes you think that Christ
>   was black;
> Not a move to hurt the wounded and they treat him like a saint,
> It's a picture worth recording that an artist's yet to paint."[1]

Of the more diffused influence of Christianity upon the
world of Oriental culture it is more difficult to speak
definitely. The Bishop of Kunming, Bishop Y. Y. Tsu,
when he was in England in 1944, constantly established
the point that in China it was out of all proportion to
numerical strength. Even a minority movement may bring
to bear a massive weight of influence when all its members
act as one. The Christian Churches may be small in comparison with the total population, but through National
Christian Councils they count for much: their special
circumstances impel and indeed compel them to such
united action, and render such united action efficacious.

(*a*) A minority Church in a non-Christian environment
cannot but be more aware of its separation and distinctive-
ness than where Christianity is diffused and outlines are
blurred. The Christian community stands out more
starkly, exposed to the observant inspection of hostile eyes.
This induces a corporate solidarity. The Church discovers
what Dr. Quick missed in mediæval theology, " the notion
of the Church with all its members as a whole Community
living in the world but not of it, carrying on all the secular
activity necessary to a temporal society, yet transforming
all by the new relation to God attained through Christ,
that glorious picture of which we get glimpses in the New

---

[1] Written by an American naval man : quoted on p. 20 of *So lives the Church*, by
E. C. Rust.

Testament and the primitive Church, and which rises before our minds once more as soon as we take seriously that the Church here and now is meant to be not only the society which suffers with the Crucified, but also the society which in its own life anticipates the new heaven and the new earth of the world to come."[1]   The sense of common obligation to bear witness for Christ by word and work and worship, and the consciousness of mutual inter-dependence between all servants of Christ whatever their occupation, welds all into a more closely integrated Christian community than any to which the average Christian teacher or doctor in England is conscious of belonging.

(b) The Christian community could not, if it would, remain indifferent to its economic environment.   Its pro-blems of financial self-existence have been touched upon. The necessity of discovering an economic basis stable and substantial enough to support the social structure of a self-existent Church, has operated increasingly as an incen-tive to social and economic studies and experiments. Every impediment to social welfare has been attacked in a crusading spirit: improved methods of village husbandry, preventive medicine and hygiene, co-operative societies as a cure for chronic insolvency, these have ceased to be secular subjects: they affect too closely the spiritual destiny of the Christian community and all its individual members.   So it comes about that the Church, once a loosely-knit society of individualists, has become a corporate community increasingly competent by its example and its exertions to make an appreciable impact upon its environ-ment.

(c) Despite its ecclesiastical sub-divisions and occasional racial tensions, the Church has accumulated a rich experi-ence of unity in diversity.   " Christians," as Sir Alfred Zimmern has recognized, " are members of an œcumenical body, the members of which are scattered throughout the world.   This is, or should be, a much closer bond than internationalism.   It is not a bond between two indepen-dent groups; it is membership in a single group."[2]   It is

[1] O. C. Quick: *The Gospel of the New World*, p. 78.
[2] Sir A. Zimmern: *Spiritual Values and World Affairs*.

this unique privilege which should qualify the Universal Church to make an impact upon the problem of universal community. But the local Churches are microcosms of the universal Church: they comprise members of many races, nations, and castes: they have their own experience of victory over divisive forces which have yielded only to the unifying power of Christ: they know by experience that there are no limits to that power: however far they themselves fall short of the ideal, they know that it is not utopian. It is a secret destined to transform their country's life.

(*d*) In the earlier days the Church was alone in the field of social welfare: its educational and medical services had no rivals. If any impact was to be made upon environment it was the Church alone that could make it. In recent years in China, in India, in the Colonies, the State has assumed the initiative in many spheres. How has the Church reacted to Colonial Development and other forms of Government enterprise? Some have resented what they would call an " encroachment "; others have hailed as long overdue the application of all the resources of Government to the solution of problems beyond the capacity of voluntary agencies to solve.

How have the Governments concerned reacted to the Church? So far from regarding it as superseded or redundant they have in no ambiguous terms protested that their plans depend upon the dynamic which only the Church can supply. This is independent testimony to the validity of the belief of the nineteenth-century pioneers, that Christianity could become " habituated and inured " to every variety of climate. They had transplanted, watered and cherished, shoots of the Vine. God gave the increase. As we look back to the modest beginnings, we may say with the Psalmist: " Thou preparedst room before it, And it took deep root, and filled the land. The mountains were covered with the shadow of it, and the boughs thereof were like cedars of God."[1]

---

[1] Psalm lxxx. 9, 10 (R.V.).

PART XII

CONSOLIDATION

Introduction: *Parable of the Stained-Glass Window*.

1. The Diocese : (*a*) Contrasts between Home and Overseas Dioceses; (*b*) The Beginnings of Synods; (*c*) Diocesanization.

2. The Province.

3. The " National " or " Regional " Church.

4. *Ecclesia Anglicana*: (i) Lambeth Conference Questions: (*a*) The Lambeth Conference; (*b*) The Consultative Body ; (*c*) Standards of Worship and Doctrine; (*d*) The Archbishop of Canterbury; (*e*) Isolated Dioceses; (*f*) The Basis of Anglican Unity. (ii) The Role of the Mother Church: (*a*) The Lambeth Conference of 1897; (*b*) 1908; (*c*) 1920; (*d*) 1930; (*e*) The Logic of Events.

WHEN a stained-glass window, under construction or repair, is spread upon the studio table, the uninitiated visitor may be excused misgivings about its future beauty. The pattern is difficult to decipher: the colours of contiguous fragments clash; the leadwork obtrudes itself upon the eye. But stained-glass windows are meant to be seen erect, when the light shining through sets aflame " the giant windows' blazoned fires." The artist himself will have no misgivings, for he has made allowance for the transforming effect of light. Then the design will show its coherence, the colours will blend and the lead fulfil its function unnoticed.

Thereby hangs a three-pronged parable. The Church is meant to be seen and can only be understood when the Light shines through; when it is fulfilling its window function of letting in the light in full radiance. Then only in the first place can be discerned the pattern of the great design, which remains confused and inarticulate when spread out flat in text-book fashion. Secondly, it is only then that what seemed to be jarring and discordant colours are found to harmonize. Thirdly, only then does all that

corresponds to the leading, all that gives to the Church the
stability which lead gives to the window, win due recognition of its importance and at the same time fall incon-
spicuously into its place.   Having in previous chapters
studied the pattern and noted the diverse hues of the
fragments which compose it, we must now turn our attention to the stanchions, crossbars, mullions, transoms, lead,
which guarantee stability against all weathers.

As in the window, these must be calculated to withstand
the maximum of pressure from the elements.   The beauty
of the design and the glowing colours of its mosaic will not
save the window from disaster unless its stability is guaranteed by such calculations.   When what is at stake is the
holding together not of a few fragments of glass but of an
immense society of human beings drawn from all races
and nations, universal and diverse beyond precedent, the
problems of the tracery and leadwork assume an absorbing
interest.   It becomes obvious that Councils, Canons and
Constitutions are not to be reckoned as belonging to the
external machinery of the Church, still less as archaic or
obsolete machinery.   They are the very human devices by
which even a divine Society must ensure its continuity and
cohesion against all that threatens them.

Parables must not be pressed in every detail, and the
stained-glass window has its obvious limitations as a figure
of the Church.   Metaphors from the earthly can be so
used as to distort the spiritual moral;   the mechanical
metaphor may obscure the essential flexibility of human
relationships;   no metaphor based on the static can do
justice to the truth that the Church exists for attack as well
as defence, for the service as well as the worship of God.
When we begin to calculate the maximum pressure of the
elements to be withstood, the parable exhausts its applicabi-
lity.   A church window has to contend with destructive
forces from without, a Church with divisive forces from
within as well as destructive forces from without—"grievous
wolves entering in not sparing the flock," and also " of
your own selves shall men arise, speaking perverse things."

The nineteenth-century Church, as we have seen, had
to face foes from without, the physical violence of savage
man, the intellectual assault of infidelity, the infiltration

of sub-Christian elements from a pagan environment. Had it been an army lacking officers and N.C.O.'s, lacking an articulate faith, untrained, unorganized, undisciplined, it must have succumbed. Creeds and Constitutions, Doctrine and Discipline, contributed to its survival. The Church was able not only to resist but to attack destructive forces from without, because and in so far as it had learnt how to counteract the divisive forces which threatened its unity from within. This was a lesson which had to be learnt again and again, by process of trial and error, by patience and bold experiment. As expansion grew, temptations to disruption and occasions of stumbling multiplied, the problem of maintaining unity became more complex, and the elements to be assimilated became more heterogeneous and incompatible.

It must be remembered that at no time within the century was the sending Church free from controversy; it was an age when religious men allowed themselves considerable latitude in the use of invective: passions ran high; panics were easily provoked. Some of the issues raised were fundamental; some appear trivial to a later generation which stands aghast at the acrimony they aroused, at the weapons employed, the vast diversion of energy from tasks of spiritual magnitude, and the heritage of bitterness bequeathed. Such was the Church which was expanding across the world. It is idle to speculate what might have happened if this expansion had coincided with a period when the corporate life of the Church was strongly welded in a unanimity of conviction and purpose. It did not. How then is it to be explained that the Anglican Communion stands where it does? The lead must have been good lead.

I. THE DIOCESE

We have traced the formation of the original dioceses of the Anglican Communion, from which daughters and grand-daughters have sprung. The diocese is the primary unit in the Church's organization and we must inquire what amount of constitutional lead-work was found necessary to withstand what amount of divisive influence.

These early dioceses were expected to rely for their stability upon a somewhat Erastian principle. (Erastus was a Heidelberg doctor of the sixteenth century credited with extreme views on State authority in ecclesiastical affairs). The control of the State in ecclesiastical affairs had a long history and had been taken for granted by such dissimilar characters as Philip the Second, Queen Elizabeth, Luther, Calvin, the Stuart Kings, and their Hanoverian successors. It was without precedent in England that until what is known as the Jerusalem Bishopric Act of 1841 (see p. 205), Bishops should be appointed without control and intervention on the part of the Crown. It was a matter of course (except in the case of the second and third Bishops of the United States who were consecrated at Lambeth under special legislation) that all Colonial Bishops were appointed under Royal Mandate; the reading of the Royal Mandate was an integral part of the Prayer Book's Consecration Service; their jurisdictions were defined by Letters Patent. These granted full power and authority " to confer the order of deacon and priest, to confirm . . . and to perform all the other functions peculiar and appropriate to the office of a bishop . . . and to exercise jurisdiction spiritual and ecclesiastical in and throughout the said diocese." The Bishop was constituted a " Body Corporate " with perpetual succession. He was to be " subject and subordinate to the archiepiscopal see of Canterbury . . . in the same manner as any bishop of any see within that Province." It will be recalled that Bishop Selwyn registered a protest against the Erastian expression, " the Queen giving him power to ordain." " I think it right in expressing my readiness to accept the Patent as now framed, to state to your Lordship that whatever meaning the words of it may be construed to bear, I conceive that those functions which are merely spiritual are conveyed to a bishop by the act of consecration alone."

(a) CONTRASTS BETWEEN HOME AND OVERSEAS DIOCESES

The assumption that a diocese overseas was on all fours with any See in the province of Canterbury proved an over-simplification. It could only apply to countries in which the Queen's writ ran. Only the accident that there were minute but convenient islands off the coast of Borneo and China under the British flag made possible the sees of Labuan and Sarawak, and Victoria, Hong Kong. The difficulty had been evaded in the case of Bishop Sea-bury by recourse to the Bishops of the Episcopal Church in Scotland, to whom also Archbishop Tait turned to consecrate Bishops for George and Madagascar: but it was not a practice that could become habitual without scandal. The time was not far distant when British Colonies would set up constitutional governments, as happened in 1850 in Cape Town, where its Parliament had " authority to make laws for the peace, welfare and good government of the Settlement." Henceforward the Crown's power of conferring by Letters Patent coercial jurisdiction, ecclesiastical and civil, was ruled to have lapsed; though the same lawyers who gave the ruling issued fresh Letters Patent to Bishop Gray three years later conferring these lapsed powers. Henceforward there could be no subjection or appeal to the Ecclesiastical Courts of another country.

(i) There were other factors invalidating the assumption that dioceses at home and overseas could be treated as equivalent. In the first place the powers conferred by Letters Patent on distant Bishops invested them with a degree of autocracy such as no bishop of an English diocese enjoyed in practice. Distance alone lent immunity from archiepiscopal oversight, and the check imposed by brother-Bishops and public opinion. *Ex hypothesi*, overseas Bishops were selected as being men of virile independence and strong leadership, and there were circumstances calculated to enhance both these qualities and their defects. A bishop's control of his clergy is magnified if for reasons of race and language they are debarred from escape into another diocese: the bishop's prestige as a member of the ruling race, as a representative of an older Church, as a precursor of a new and dominant civilization, may combine with his personal powers to win him unhealthy deference. " A missionary Bishop stands so much by himself that if in course of time he happens to be a man of eccentric mode of proceeding he might upon his own responsibility compromise the Church both at home and in the Colonies."[1]

[1] Randall Davidson : *Life and Letters of Archbishop Tait*, Vol. I, chap. 13.

X

(ii) Secondly there was the fact which we have seen illustrated in many countries, that missionaries had more often than not been in the field long before the founding of a see and the arrival of a Bishop. Gregory had sent Augustine to Kent while still in Priest's orders: as soon as converts multiplied, Augustine was consecrated. The first half of the precedent had been very generally observed, the second long overlooked. What was to be the relation between Bishop and Missionary? The missionaries, like the Bishops, would not have uprooted themselves and faced the adventure of exile upon the frontiers of the Church if they had not been endowed with a spark of independence beyond their fellows. A tropical climate and the stress of life did not always make for equability. Some missionaries were indisposed to accord to bishops any greater dignity than they had been accorded in the early Irish monasteries, which denied their jurisdiction while recognizing that they were necessary for the performance of such episcopal functions as confirming and ordaining. Behind the missionaries were Committees in London exercising exclusive power to select, support, locate, remove or dismiss them. Behind them was the power of the purse. Bishops found themselves confronted with an *imperium in imperio*; it was not in fact always clear which was *imperium* and which *in imperio*. Even where Bishop and Missionary Society saw eye to eye on ecclesiastical questions, relations could become strained, as between Bishop Wilson of Calcutta and the C.M.S.; and it was only after three arbitrators at home had been asked to intervene that a concordat between them was hammered out.

Nearly fifty years later Archbishop Davidson still spoke with bated breath of the troubles of the 1870's, when as Archbishop Tait's Chaplain, he was involved in the perplexities of arbitration between the youthful Bishop Copleston of Colombo and the C.M.S. missionaries whose licence he had cancelled because they dissociated themselves from his policy and disapproved his practices; nor were these the only countries in which friction threatened to develop, reminiscent of that which existed in the Middle Ages between the Friars and the regular Clergy.

There is nothing to be gained by stirring the embers of these *causes célèbres* except in so far as the solution arrived at marked a stage in the development of the Church's constitutional leadwork. The Lambeth Conference of 1878 established the validity of the principles for which each party stood. Bishops had contested principles which threatened to extinguish their office; they wished to safeguard the unity of the Church, its just order and discipline, the rightful authority of the Episcopate, and the recognition of the Bishop's ultimate responsibility for the superintendence and control in spiritual things over all persons licensed by them to perform spiritual functions. The Society wished to safeguard their missions from the danger of extinction by episcopal caprice. As Sir Charles Trevelyan wrote to Mr. Venn in 1839: " the possession of unlimited power by the Bishop would place the Society's operations on an extremely precarious footing . . . one Bishop might object to High Church missionaries, another to Low Church missionaries, another to zealous evangelical missionaries; the very existence of the Society in India would by the acknowledgement of an arbitrary absolute veto on the appointment of missionaries, become dependent on the will of the Bishop for the time being."

As Calcutta had had six Bishops in twenty-five years this was a formidable prospect: and as we have seen, the Bishops did hold autocratic power. It is one of the curiosities of missionary history that the C.M.S. should have claimed independence of the Bishop on the ground that theirs was the status of perpetual patrons and church-wardens of all the missionary Churches;[1] perpetual because whereas the patron of an English living had for the time being exhausted his function once he had discharged his responsibility of nominating a new incumbent, " as we are to pay the salary our patronal office is in a sense perpetuated." This had been fastened on as an anomaly by Bishop Wilson. It was an unfortunate analogy characteristic of an age when without aspersion of simony, money could purchase the power of imposing for ever the tenets of a party upon unconsulted parishioners. It was an analogy which squared ill with Henry Venn's principle

[1] Knight : *Memoir of Henry Venn*, p. 153.

that a " foreign mission " must always be treated as " a transition state " and " gradually and silently removed as the nascent community advances towards completion: the mission is the scaffolding, the National Church the building it leaves behind when the scaffolding is removed."

(iii) Yet a third distinction must be drawn between dioceses at home and overseas. The latter were more often than not what Mr. Furnivall in his study of the Netherlands East Indies calls " Plural Societies." He defines them as " Societies comprising two or more elements or social orders which live side by side, yet without mingling, in one political unit." Indian dioceses, for example, were ecclesiastical units in which British and Indian elements lived side by side without mingling and the Indian elements in themselves were not singular but plural.

By the 1870's, each of the three Indian dioceses, Calcutta, Madras, and Bombay, had outgrown the administrative capacity of any single Bishop. Sub-division and the creation of new dioceses was the obvious course, but this required an Act of Parliament, which was for the time being unobtainable. Bishop Milman, the Metropolitan, learned to his surprise that without any consultation with himself a solution had been devised by the S.P.G. and C.M.S. and sanctioned by Archbishop Tait. Coadjutor Bishops were to be consecrated in England and sent out as " episcopal commissaries, one to minister to S.P.G. missions, the other to C.M.S. missions in an intermingling territory." It happened that for only the second time in history the three Bishops were in conference together at Nagpur, and they determined to resist a solution which would have been a sad capitulation to racial and ecclesiastical plurality—the appointment of " sectional bishops, i.e. bishops who should govern one portion of the clergy in a certain district, but not another portion." " A missionary bishop in another Bishop's diocese seems to me an anomaly. His existence might lead to dangerous pursuits. . . . I cannot approve of a bishop nominated by a Society, or of making his endowment or rather salary dependent on the will of the committee of a Society. . . . The natives dislike the idea of a Bishop who would be over them and not over Europeans. It would have a tendency to make the native Christians a caste, which idea is even now dangerously at work, preventing the extension of Christianity."[1]

The three Bishops registered their objection to coadjutor Bishops on three grounds: (a) They would lack the freedom and independence essential to the due exercise of their office. (b) Their position as mere Curates in subordination to the Bishop they assist and only as long as he pleases, would render them in public estimation an inferior class of Bishops: whereas the work of missions should be treated as the noblest and most honourable in the service of the Church. (c) They would be so closely connected with the respective societies to which they had belonged that they would tend to separate, by party distinctions, those who are cordially united under one Bishop.

The episode was reflected in the Lambeth Conference of 1878, when it was laid down that " there are manifest objections to the appointment of a Bishop to minister to certain congregations within the diocese of another Bishop and wholly independent of him." In 1897 and again in 1908 the principle is reiterated: " two Bishops of the Anglican Communion may not exercise jurisdiction in the same place." The principle of one Bishop for one area is the ideal to be aimed at as the best means of securing the unity of all races and nations in the Holy Catholic Church. All races and peoples, whatever their language or conditions, must be welded into one Body and the organization of different races living side by side into separate or independent Churches, on the basis of race or colour, is inconsistent with the vital and essential principle of the unity of Christ's Church."

(b) The Beginnings of Synods

In the case of these problems, the autocracy of Bishops, the relation of Mission and Diocese, the plural character of the growing Churches, no appeal could be made to Anglican precedent; the modern application of ancient principle presented novel and distinctive features. Dioceses

[1] *Memoir of Bishop Milman.*

set about their solution along very similar lines, though at different rates of advance, by experiments in Synodical Government and constitutional Episcopacy. It was natural that the first moves should be made where there were most Churchmen of British descent. The pace was indeed forced as the connexion with the State was snapped by disestablishment or loosened by the development of the Colonies towards Dominion status. The Church had to replace its Erastian lead and follow Mr. Gladstone's advice " to organise themselves on that basis of voluntary consensual compact which was the basis on which the Church of Christ rested from the first." The Church was compelled to adjust itself to Lord Westbury's ruling: " The Church of England, in places where there is no Church established by Law, is in the same position as any other religious body, in no better but no worse position, and the members may adopt rules for enforcing discipline within their body."

But the pace was also accelerated by the Bishops' own discovery that, in Mr. Gladstone's words " in their very power lay their weakness," for purposes of government. The first Bishop of Melbourne complained that " the government of the Church of England in this colony is a pure autocracy. While the Colonial clergy justly complain of the insecurity of their tenure, men of high standing and ability in England, such as we especially require, are for the most part unwilling to accept employment where they would be subject to the will of a single individual." Simultaneously Selwyn in Auckland, Broughton in Sydney, Gray in Cape Town, Mountain in Quebec, undeterred by Mr. Gladstone's failure to pass through the House of Commons the Colonial Churches Regulation Bill of 1853 (which was based on the recommendations of a conference of English and Colonial Bishops) launched out in the direction of unfettered self-government and fettered Bishops. The fetters were what they themselves desired, for these Bishops would cordially have approved the Report of the Lambeth Conference of 1908 which affirmed that the authority of the Diocesan Bishops, as the Minister of the Church, is not absolute but constitutional, being limited on the one hand by the Canons applicable to Province and Diocese, and on the other by the analogy of the ancient principle that he should act after taking counsel with his clergy and his people. They set up a Synod in every diocese. Their example was followed by the West Indies, by India, Burma and Ceylon, by China, Japan, Korea and by African dioceses.

Bishop Trollope, as we have seen, strongly deprecated the inclusion of the laity in Synod as a departure from ancient custom, and there were loud echoes of his view in British Guiana; but their admission was accepted by the Conference of English and Colonial Bishops and has been generally adopted. A Canadian Bishop quotes the authority of John Keble in defence of the innovation. " The voice of the laity in one form or another has always been a most essential part of the voice of the whole Church. Even in the most vital case of fundamental doctrine the Church diffusive in which the laity are included has a kind of veto, as I understand it, on the decision of a General Council. . . . Now if they, the laity, have a negative voice, it is not *prima facie* essential at what stage in the discussion that voice is permitted to be heard." After quoting this august authority the Canadian Bishop claims that Membership of Synod, " gives the laity in a modern method an opportunity of exercising the right of concurrence which has always been their privilege as members of the whole Body of Christ. We believe therefore that it is not inconsistent with Catholic principle."

The very first report of the first Lambeth Conference endorsed and formulated the policy of Diocesan Synods as the primary and simplest form of Synodical organization. " By the Diocesan Synod the co-operation of all members of the body is obtained in Church action: and that acceptance of Church rules is secured, which in the absence of other law, usage or enactment, gives to these rules the force of laws " binding on those who, expressly or by implication, have consented to them. . . . It is not at variance with the ancient principles of the Church, that both clergy and laity should attend the Diocesan Synod." The Constitution may be locally determined, but it is recommended that the Bishop, Clergy, and Laity should sit together, the Bishop presiding; that votes should be taken by orders, whenever demanded; that the concurrent assent of Bishop, Clergy, and Laity should be necessary to the validity of all acts of the Synod.

The last Lambeth Conference, in 1930, reaffirmed " the ancient Catholic principle that the fundamental unit of Church organization is the territorial Diocese under the jurisdiction of one Bishop. A duly organized diocese under its Bishop has the right, subject always to its duty to the whole fellowship of the Church, to decide and act for itself in its own affairs." The principle of autonomy is further corroborated by the recommendation that " no act of a provincial Synod is operative in a Diocese until it has been accepted by the proper authority in that Diocese." This is balanced by the proviso that " any enactment of the Diocesan Synod which affects other Dioceses in the Province is properly subject to revision or rejection by the Provincial Synod."[1]

A 1930 Resolution (56) assumes that the right to elect its Bishop belongs to a Diocesan Synod: it would be cumbersome to detail the technical differences in Synodical usage in this matter, but the universal enjoyment of this right must be noted. The principle and the procedure of its application were approved as long ago as 1867 by the first of the Lambeth Conferences.[2]

(c) DIOCESANIZATION

The 1920 Lambeth Conference dealt with the relations between the Missionary Societies and the Church, which as we have seen had not always run smoothly. " We consider that the Societies should not stand outside the one organization, but should be elements in it, co-ordinated, whether by a central advisory council or otherwise, under the supreme Synodical Authority, but retaining severally such degrees of independence as the conditions of their efficiency demanded. . . . Their work should centre from the first in the Church rather than in the mission organization, and in particular

> (i) By the establishment of Councils fully representative of the congregations, having real responsibility of government;

[1] *Lambeth Conference*, 1930.
[2] *The Six Lambeth Conferences*, pp. 67, 68.

(ii) By substituting for committees and councils representative chiefly of the mission and its subscribers, Diocesan Boards and Committees, and in general associating all their work with the Diocesan organisation;

(iii) By entrusting to these local bodies a real share in the financial control and general direction of the work of the mission;

(iv) By giving the widest freedom to indigenous workers to develop their work on lines in accordance with their national character."[1]

These principles find expression in the system known by the awkward if descriptive name, "Diocesanization." We may turn to the same Tinnevelly, which so narrowly escaped the infliction of "Episcopal Commissaries" in Bishop Milman's day, for an example of its working:

"The main development in Tinnevelly since 1900 is simply this—and it is enough—that what were two groups of congregations under the two foreign Missionary Societies have become one Church, a Church which is truly such and realises itself to be so; a Church, which under the guidance of a Bishop, and with the help of a very few English clergy, administers its own affairs; a Church which is beginning to take up its responsibility for evangelising non-Christians amongst whom it lives.

"The work of the Societies had been quietly tending in this direction for many years, but the critical point came when:—
(i) Organisation of Church work was definitely transferred from the two Societies to the one diocese;
(ii) The number of missionaries had been so far reduced, that Indians did in fact become the leaders in the Church's organisation and life.

"As regards administration, the two Societies had their separate councils and committees, largely Indian in personnel, but dominated by the missionaries, and these councils in Tinnevelly were themselves fully controlled by missionary committees in Madras. Now a Diocesan Executive Committee, a Finance Committee and a Standing Committee of the Diocesan Council for pastoral, educational and other branches of work have full and final control of diocesan administration and policy.

"In each of these committees the Bishop has a strong position of leadership, and individual missionaries have considerable personal influence, but not even the Bishop can dominate the proceedings, and the control of administration and policy is very largely Indian. The very important post of Diocesan Treasurer was in 1937 given to an Indian."[2]

[1] *The Six Lambeth Conferences*, 1920, pp. 55, 56 ; Resolutions 33, 34.
[2] *Partners*, p. 77.

2.   THE PROVINCE

" It is not good that the Diocese should be alone " is the recurring theme of Lambeth Conferences from 1867 onwards.   Dioceses must be clustered in the larger unit of the Province.   The constitutional machinery devised for holding together the whole is so similar to that which held together the component dioceses that it will not be necessary to describe it in detail.   The single Bishop becomes a House of Bishops and the presiding officer becomes a Metropolitan; but the Houses of the Clergy and the Laity are constituted as in a Diocesan Synod, and the rules for voting by Orders, concurrent assent, etc., hold good.   The Provincial Synod " not only provides a method for securing unity amongst the associated Dioceses, but also forms the link between these dioceses and other Churches of the Anglican Communion."[1]   Its agenda should cover " questions of common interest to the whole Province, and those which affect the communion of the Dioceses with one another and with the rest of the Church."[2]   " If the Anglican Communion is to render that service to the varied needs of mankind to which the Church of our day is specially called, regard must be had both to the just freedom of its several parts, and to the just claims of the whole Communion upon its every part."[3]

The 1920 and 1930 Lambeth Conferences showed a certain impatience over the existence of so many dioceses still unattached to Provinces.   " Each newly-founded Diocese should as soon as possible find its place as a constituent member in a neighbouring Province."[4]   This would " tend to the health and strength not only of those dioceses immediately concerned but of the Church in general.   Whenever and wherever possible new Provinces should be created, and Dioceses now working in isolation encouraged to attach themselves."[5]   New Metropolitans should be elected, to whom the Bishops should take an oath of canonical obedience.   Again in 1930 " the diffi-

[1] *The Six Lambeth Conferences*, 1867, p. 60.

[2] Ibid., 1867, p. 60.

[3] Ibid., 1908, Encyclical Letter.

[4] Ibid., 1920, Resolution 43.

[5] Ibid., p. 79.

culties and dangers of isolation " are emphasized; " An Isolated Diocese may fail to realise its proper relationship to the whole Church. Isolated action may be weak and ineffective; an isolated Diocese may so emphasise certain elements of the faith, the order or the worship of the Catholic Church as practically to exclude others equally valuable and necessary."[1]

Provincial organization gives practical expression to the Church's fundamental principle of fellowship; it offers opportunities for mutual consultation on any question which cannot be satisfactorily dealt with by a single Bishop or diocese; it facilitates common action in regard to other Provinces or to Governments and the formation of new dioceses, the fixing of common standards, the promotion of union with other Christian communions.[2]

To encourage and expedite the process, emphasis was laid upon the minimum required for the initiation of a Province. There need not be more than four dioceses: there must not be less because it would be unseemly if two out of three Bishops had to sit in judgement on the third. There need not be at the start the full paraphernalia of three Houses. " The only thing essential to provincial life in its initial stages is that the Bishops should act corporately in dealing with questions concerning the faith, order and discipline of the Church." This proviso reduces the formidable obstacle of distance. The Province of the West Indies, where it would be difficult to assemble clergy and laity across many miles of ocean, remains at this stage; its sole organ is a House of Bishops. The Church of India had to wait for its new Constitution in 1930 before it could outgrow this stage.

It will be of interest to see how far these recommendations have succeeded in reducing the number of unattached dioceses. The hopes expressed in 1920 that China and Japan would assume provincial status had been fulfilled by 1930, when the Conference noted with thankfulness that they had now become organized Provinces, each with its own College of Bishops, and its General Synod of Bishops, Clergy, and Laity. On the other hand the expectation

[1] *The Six Lambeth Conferences*, 1930, p. 158.
[2] Ibid., abbreviated.

that the five dioceses (now eight) of East Africa and the four dioceses of West Africa (now six) under the jurisdiction of the Archbishop of Canterbury, would coalesce in new East and West African Provinces, has not yet been fulfilled, though it is known that the project was engaging the attention of Archbishop Temple. Political as well as ecclesiastical differences affect the issue. There were those who dreaded that the growth of autonomous Churches in Canada and Australia would estrange the colonies from the Mother Country and tend to the break-up of Empire. A converse fear has militated against the realization of an Eastern African Province, lest it should lead to a political unification of Uganda, Kenya and Tanganyika which they do not all desire, especially if, as is feared, it would enhance the European influence which is suspected of being unduly dominant in the diocese of Mombasa.

3. THE "NATIONAL" OR "REGIONAL" CHURCH

It is characteristic of the Anglican Communion and the manner of its evolution that new names should introduce themselves unannounced and undefined even into its official phraseology. The Report of the 1920 Lambeth Conference refers in passing to each National or Regional Church or Province. A 1930 Resolution (54) refers " to the constitution adopted by any Province or Regional Church ": Resolution 57 rejoices to welcome the Nippon Sei Kokwai and the Chung Hua Sheng Kung Hui as " constituent Churches of the Anglican Communion," another new phrase. "National Churches" attain the dignity of a paragraph to themselves. " It is consistent with the past history of the Church, and may be of real advantage, that Provinces or Dioceses within the borders of one national territory should be associated in one organization sometimes spoken of as a " National Church."

The authority of such a " National Church " is in theory derived from that of the Provinces or Dioceses which constitute it, and on whose behalf it acts. The peculiar function of a " National Church " is two-fold. On the one hand (to quote from the Constitution of the Church of India, Burma, and Ceylon) " the liberty of a regional Church has enabled and may in any place enable the God-given genius of great nations to find its appropriate expression in the worship and work of the Church." On the other hand, a "National Church" by its intimate connection with the nation as a whole can effectively influence its national life. The warning is added that a "National Church" should not overdo its nationalism.

Some new terminology was certainly required to correspond to the facts. The Protestant Episcopal Church of the United States comprised eight Provinces, Canada and Australia four each. New constitutional machinery had to be improvised to encircle Provinces in a super-provincial unit. Regional or national Synods took the title in the United States of "General Convention", in Canada and Australia of "General Synod." Again, the machinery varied in scale, not in type, and needs no further description. There is, however, a distinction to be drawn between Canadian and Australian developments. In Australia a General Synod came into being in 1872 with the Bishop of Sydney Primate of Australia while it was still a single Province: it was not till 1905 that Victoria and Queensland were erected into Provinces: West Australia not till 1914.

In Canada on the other hand the Provinces came first. The Bishop of Montreal had been appointed Metropolitan of the Province of Canada in 1861, the first Provincial Synod of Rupert's Land had been held in 1875. It was not till 1893 that the General Synod came into being. The consolidation of the Church of Canada owes much to a great Aberdonian, Robert Machray, Bishop, afterwards Archbishop, of Rupert's Land from 1865 till his death in 1904. He had himself built up the Province of Rupert's Land and valued provincial independence too highly to countenance the merging into one of Provincial Synods. "No one advocated the extinguishing of the Provinces of Canterbury and York; such an idea would be at once scouted: the two Provinces had their different characteristics." Similarly there was a community of interest and feeling among the people of the North West different from that in Eastern Canada. "In our first days we were nursed by the C.M.S. and as our missions under their devoted missionaries have penetrated into and through the vast solitudes of the country we have been helped by that Society with no niggard hand, in a Churchly manner." Machray carried the day against Bishop Anson of Qu'Appelle. Provincial Synods were by-passed and pre-served their *status quo*. Delegates to the General Synod were chosen on a proportional basis from the clergy and laity by the Diocesan Synods: none of its Canons were to be operative until accepted by the Provincial Synods.

Machray became the Primate of All Canada and Arch-bishop of Rupert's Land, for the Provincial Metropolitans were henceforward to assume boldly the title of Archbishop. " How this will be received in England by the Archbishop of Canterbury we do not know; two or three Bishops suggested caution but the House would not hear of this. So whatever opinion may be entertained in England this resolution is irrevocably passed."[1] It was certainly not such as would commend itself to Archbishop Benson, who was by no means pleased at getting the first news " on a half-sheet of foreign note-paper " from a mere Canon. " Lightly done ! The Church of Canada is not a very courteous body." Benson was inclined to attribute the step to jealousy of Rome, who could always out-trump an Archbishop by creating a Cardinal. Archbishoprics he thought should not be created " in a sporadic manner by local Synods without any reference to the vast Anglican Communion."[2] The precedent was accepted by the Lambeth Conference of 1897: " recognising the almost universal custom in the Western Church of attaching the title of Archbishop to the rank of Metropolitan, we are of opinion that the revival and extension of this custom among ourselves is justifiable and desirable. It is advisable that the proposed adoption of such a title should be formally announced to the Bishops of the various Churches and Provinces of the Communion with a view to its general recognition."

4. " ECCLESIA ANGLICANA "

The constitutional consolidation of Diocese and Province, of " National," " Regional," " Constituent " Churches,

---

[1] Mackray: *Life of Archbishop Machray.*
[2] A. C. Benson: *Life of Archbishop Benson.*

affords impressive evidence of the statesmanship of nine-teenth-century makers of Christian history; but it posed problems of formidable magnitude for their twentieth-century successors. The former were more prescient than is always acknowledged. They gave full rein to the principles of autonomy with their eyes open. Successive Lambeth Conferences repaired, replaced, adapted and extended the lead-work of the window on the scale that seemed from time to time adequate to withstand the weather of the day. As the century advanced the centre of gravity shifted. Colonial Churches of British origin, and their relation with the British Parliament and the See of Canterbury, ceased to monopolize attention. The problem of acclimatization in alien soils dealt with in the last chapter, loomed on the horizon. It may be claimed that the ecclesiastical statesmen were before rather than behind imperial statesmen in their thinking and constitution-mongering. What Mr. G. M. Young says in his history of Early Victorian England in relation to the South Seas is even more true of other and larger areas. "Just as the work of Theodore of Tarsus in seventh-century Britain preceded the work of political unification, so in the South Seas the missionaries from their bases in Australia and New Zealand were planning the extension of Church organisa-tion and the creation of Bishoprics long before the British Government had begun to recognise that it would have to make itself responsible for law and order." Long before the States of the Australian Commonwealth were federa-lized, the Church had its federal constitution. Long before the Statute of Westminster was heard of, the regional branches of the Anglican Communion had attained what may be called Dominion status. The first Lambeth Con-ference was held in 1867, the first Colonial Conference in 1887, the first Imperial Conference in 1911. In India the new constitution of the Church long antedated the promises of Sir Stafford Cripps. In the Far East the Church trans-lated its respect and regard for Chinese nationalism into constitutional terms before the powers of Europe had begun to adjust themselves to the fact of the new China.

It cannot be claimed that progress was consistently tranquil and smooth, or that brakes were never applied jerkily and in panic. Even in ecclesiastical circles there were those who were slow to shed the tone of condescending patronage towards Colonial Churches and Bishops which in British statesmen exacerbated the Colonies.

" I vow and declare," wrote a future Archbishop in 1874, " that if any friend of mine is made a Colonial Bishop, and doesn't eschew buckles, tights and aprons, I won't speak to him. It's the Buckles that ruin the Colonial Churches, *and* the Loops of the Hats. Think of it. Men taking Shepherdships for Buckles and Loops. Walking about town and sauntering into Clubs, as half-occupied men, dressed like our Bishops (who certainly *work* whether they think or not) and getting called by the horrible word ' Colonials ': their station in Society is unlike what it ought to be, and is generally lowering in men's eyes to the clerical body."

This gross if playful caricature of a Colonial Bishop is hardly a caricature of an attitude towards Churches and Missions overseas by no means rare. At the same time, in the ecclesiastical as in the political sphere there was genuine anxiety lest Churches and Colonies should be cut adrift before they were old enough or strong enough to stand alone.

The fact remains that the Anglican Communion in the twentieth century inherited problems of consolidation beyond anything that the most prescient of the nineteenth-century prophets could have foreseen. " Can anything short of a Moses," asked Archbishop Benson, " codify or unite our duty and ourselves ? Will there be a Cyprian of the latter days ? How is the solidarity of a Society so vast geographically, and both ecclesiastically and racially so heterogeneous, to be guaranteed against divisive forces which accumulate strength with every advance in size and variety ? What amount of welding can secure the cohesion and stability of a Society which to the Provinces of Canterbury and York, Armagh and Dublin, the Episcopal Church of Scotland and the Church in Wales, has added great autonomous Churches in the United States, Canada, Australia and South Africa; equally autonomous Churches drawn from nations in the throes of nationalistic ferment, India, China, Japan; dioceses within the jurisdiction of Foreign Governments, South American or European; Lebombo in the Portuguese sphere, Madagascar and

Mauritius in the French, Ruanda in the Belgian; dioceses such as Egypt, Iran and to some extent Jerusalem, within the jurisdiction of Mohammedan powers; dioceses in which peoples of other races and colours predominate; the West Indies, West Africa, East Africa, and the Islands of the South Seas.

The subject bifurcates. It must be examined from two points of view: (1) from the standpoint of the whole Communion; what provision has been made to enable all these Provinces and Dioceses to maintain and deepen their fellowship not only with the Mother Church but with one another? (2) From the standpoint of the Mother Church. This is a domestic question and must be dealt with separately. What provision has the Mother Church made to adjust its relations with its children as they grow up to adolescence and maturity?

(i) *LAMBETH CONFERENCE QUESTIONS*

THE LAMBETH CONFERENCE

It was perhaps natural that the original impetus towards the holding of general Conferences of Bishops derived not from the centre but the circumference. It was a Canadian Synod in 1865 which urged the Archbishop of Canterbury to devise means " by which the members of the Anglican Communion in all quarters of the world should have a share in the deliberations for her welfare and be permitted to have a representative in one General Council of her members gathered from every land." It was with some timidity that Archbishop Longley committed himself to the project, discouraged as he well might be by the refusal of the Archbishop of York and the Bishops of his Province to take part. It was an unpropitious moment for the experiment. The Bishop of Natal had recently made it known that he could no longer accept Moses as the author of the Pentateuch, that he could therefore no longer ordain men to the ministry ; and that at the same time he felt himself conscientiously precluded from vacating his See. The 1867 Conference met in the vortex of controversy, and it was known that while the Archbishop was determined to rule the subject out of order, confining the

Conference to "brotherly consultations," some of the Bishops
were equally determined to extract from it a verdict on
Bishop Colenso. Neither party had its way.

The controversy is obsolete, but it is clear that from the
first there were those who expected and desired the Lambeth
Conference to become an œcumenical Synod, superimposed on Provincial Synods as they had been superimposed on Diocesan Synods: it appeared to them to be
the logical climax of synodical reform. It is equally clear
that this is what the Lambeth Conference never became.
Even Bishop Selwyn's Committee had to report to the 1867
Conference that united action was impossible between
those Churches which were free to act independently and
others whose Constitution was fixed not only by ancient
usages but by the law of the State. No Assembly that
might be convened would be competent to enact binding
canons or frame obligatory definitions of faith. It would
be better to adopt an innocuous name for the meeting,
such as " Congress." Its decisions could only possess such
authority as might be derived from the moral weight of
such united counsels and judgements, and the voluntary
acceptance of its conclusions by any of the Churches
represented. It should be attended by both Clerical and
Lay Representatives of the several Churches, with the
Archbishop of Canterbury in the Chair, and the proceedings should at least in part be public.

The Conference of 1878 decided that " the assembling
of a Synod of all the Anglican Churches presented difficulties too great to allow of its being recommended for
present adoption." The question was never raised again.
It is not for any legal or constitutional prerogative, but
for its moral authority that the decennial meetings of
Bishops have won their place in the Church and the
world. " In case any risk of divergence to the point even
of disruption should arise, it is clear that the Lambeth
Conference as such could not take any disciplinary action.
Formal action would belong to the several Churches of
the Anglican Communion individually; but the advice
of the Lambeth Conference, sought before executive action
is taken by the constituent Churches, would carry very
great moral weight." (*L.C.* 1930, *p.* 154).

THE CONSULTATIVE BODY

It was hoped from the first that the Lambeth Conference would at least set up a central Tribunal for the whole Anglican Communion, to which questions of doctrine might be carried by appeal from Provincial Tribunals. It was urged that such a Voluntary Spiritual Tribunal would " tend to secure unity in matters of Faith and uniformity in matters of Discipline, where Doctrine may be involved "; no appeal was allowed from the Colonial Churches to any of the ordinary Ecclesiastical Courts of England, and there was a gap to be filled. The Tribunal project reappears in Conference after Conference under varying titles, Voluntary Arbitration Board, Council of Reference, Council of Advice, Central Consultative Body, Consultative Committee, Continuation Committee. Bishop Wordsworth of Salisbury's Committee reported in favour of a Tribunal of Reference in 1897, but the Conference rejected his proposals, preferring a Central Consultative Body " for supplying information and advice." " This body must win its way to general recognition by the services which it may be able to render to the working of the Church. It can have no other than a moral authority, which will be developed out of its actions." The Conference of 1898 revised its name and constitution, and a Central Consultative Committee actually met for the first time in July 1901: all Provinces were represented in a membership of eighteen; it was instructed to meet at least once a year. It was necessary to re-assert in 1920 " that it was a purely advisory body, neither possessing nor claiming any executive or administrative power." " The Consultative Body " was more fully defined in 1930 as " of the nature of a Continuation Committee of the Lambeth Conference", prepared to advise on any questions of faith, order, policy, or administration referred to it by any Bishop or groups of Bishops, calling in expert advisers at discretion, and reserving the right to decline to entertain any particular question. It was to carry on the work left by the preceding Conference, and assist the Archbishop in the preparation for the next. An Appellate Tribunal was held to be inconsistent with the spirit of the Anglican Communion: final Courts of

Appeal should be left to the decision of local and regional Churches. The long story of evolution behind this organ of centralization illustrates the difficulties experienced in devising an appropriate constitutional framework for the whole Anglican Communion. Second only to the Lambeth Conference itself, the Consultative Body has the important function of contributing to stability and cohesion.

Standards of Worship and Doctrine

As long as the Thirty-Nine Articles and the Book of Common Prayer held undisputed authority, the maintenance of fellowship in doctrine and worship caused no anxiety. When the question arose of providing Prayer Books " suitable to the needs of native congregations in heathen countries", it was laid down that the principles embodied in them must be identical with those embodied in the Book of Common Prayer, and deviations in point of form should only be such as are required by the circumstances of particular Churches. Some alarm arose in 1888 from " the danger of important divergencies with regard to doctrine being introduced by the possible assumption on the part of each Province or Diocese of the power of revising the Prayer Book."

Of course the Conference could not dictate, least of all to the Episcopal Church in America, but it must be understood that " the Book of Common Prayer is not the possession of one Diocese or Province, but of all; that a revision in one portion of the Anglican Communion must therefore be extensively felt; that it is not just that any particular portion should undertake revision without consulting with other portions and especially with the Church at home." Again in 1897, " the Book of Common Prayer next to the Bible itself is the authoritative standard of the doctrine of the Anglican Communion. We hold that it would be most dangerous to tamper with its teaching either by narrowing the breadth of its comprehension, or by disturbing the balance of its doctrine." Nevertheless the *jus liturgicum* of Bishops is asserted, " Since no Book can supply every possible need of worshippers in every variation of circumstance " and it is the Bishop's prerogative to

sanction additional services and adapt the Prayers already
in the Book.

The emphasis alters in 1908. " While the educative
value of the Book of Common Prayer and the importance
of retaining it as a bond of union and standard of devotion
should be fully recognised, every effort should be made,
under due authority, to render the form of worship more
intelligible to uneducated congregations, and better suited
to the widely diverse needs of the various races within the
Anglican Communion." Native forms of marriage are
to be consecrated to Christian use. By 1920 the position
of the Prayer Book is no longer what it was: *Resolution
36*: " While maintaining the authority of the Book of
Common Prayer as the Anglican standard of doctrine and
practice, we consider that liturgical uniformity should not
be required as a necessity throughout the Churches of the
Anglican Communion. The condition of the Church in
many parts of the Mission Field renders inapplicable the
retention of that Book as the one fixed liturgical model."
The Report asked that in the exercise of liberty care should
be taken to maintain a Scriptural and Catholic balance of
Truth, to give due consideration to the precedents of the
early Church, and to remember with brotherly consideration the possible effect on other Provinces.

We have seen that the Thirty-Nine Articles had not
been included in Bishop Bickersteth's formularies for
the Church of Japan: nor were they included in the 1930
constitution of the Province of India, Burma, and Ceylon.
The omission has the authority of Archbishop Benson's
Conference of 1888: " A certain liberty of treatment must
be extended to the cases of native or growing Churches, on
which it would be unreasonable to impose, as conditions
of communion, the whole of the Thirty-Nine Articles,
coloured as they are in language and form by the peculiar
circumstances under which they were originally drawn up.
On the other hand it would be impossible for us to share
with them in the matter of Holy Orders, as in complete
intercommunion, without satisfactory evidence that they
hold substantially the same form of doctrine as ourselves.
It ought not to be difficult, much less impossible, to formu-
late articles in accordance with our own standards of

doctrine and worship, the acceptance of which would be required of all ordained in such Churches.

THE ARCHBISHOP OF CANTERBURY

It has often been discussed whether the Anglican Communion, which has in the Lambeth Conference a parallel to the Imperial Conference, and in its system of devolution something analogous to Dominion Status, possesses in the Archbishop of Canterbury an impersonation of authority corresponding in the ecclesiastical sphere to that which is vested in the Crown. Archbishop Davidson would have had no hesitation in replying unambiguously. As Bishop of Winchester he wrote: " the Authority of the Archbishop of Canterbury, if we can call it so, is almost universally recognised but undefined: moral, not legal: its effective exercise depends upon the personal weight, tact and courtesy of the Primate." An American Bishop wrote to him in alarm lest a proposal to create a Canterbury Patriarchate should appear on the agenda of the Lambeth Conference of 1897, urging that it would be most unwise to attempt and absolutely impossible to create if National Christians were to be expected to defer to it. Randall Davidson replied: " that anything in the nature of a Canterbury Patriarchate will receive the support of the Conference, I do not for a moment believe."[1]

As long as all Bishops on their consecration took an Oath of Canonical Obedience to the Archbishop of Canterbury, the succession of St. Augustine constituted an outward and visible sign of inward and spiritual unity. But Bishop Gray saw in it an acknowledgement of suzerainty such as no self-respecting Bishop of an autonomous Province could make without casting a slur on his own Metropolitan. Archbishop Tait did not feel at liberty to delete what was prescribed in the Ordinal as integral to the Consecration Service, but he conceded to a South African Bishop the opportunity of making an interpretative declaration reserving the rights of his own Metropolitan. Archbishop Benson found it " Totally impossible to conceive that any Church is united in communion with the Church of

[1] Bell: *Randall Davidson*, I, p. 300.

England, if you are not consecrated here, and your oath taken to the See of Canterbury." The oath preserves the constitutional nexus; if abolished, clergy would come to England without having taken an oath to any prelate within the nexus. He was indignant at having been asked as Archbishop of Canterbury to consecrate a Bishop " to keep up " the union of the Churches; while asked at the same time not to claim an oath of allegiance. Consecration to a diocese meant Mission, and there could be no Mission where there was no jurisdiction. " It'll never do that while they decline to be an integral part of the Church of England we should in a mere colour or figure present them to the world as if they were." The 1897 Conference decided that " it would be for the further consolidation of all provincial action that every Bishop at his consecration should take the oath of allegiance to his own Metropolitan, and that every Bishop consecrated in England for service abroad should make a solemn declaration that he will pay all due honour and deference to the Archbishop of Canterbury, and will respect and maintain the spiritual rights and privileges of the Church of England and of all Churches in communion with her." " No supremacy of the See of Canterbury over Primatial or Metropolitan Sees outside England is either practicable or desirable", but there is " universal recognition in the Anglican Communion of the ancient precedence of the See of Canterbury."

ISOLATED DIOCESES

We have already reported (p. 315) the anxiety of the Lambeth Conference of 1930 lest isolated dioceses not enjoying the opportunities of cross-fertilization afforded by sharing membership in a Province with dioceses representing various schools of thought " should so emphasise certain elements of the faith or order or the worship of the Catholic Church as practically to exclude others equally valuable and necessary." No estimate of the strength or weakness of the ties which bind together the units of the Anglican Communion would be complete which left out of account what Archbishop Lang has called the " monochrome " dioceses. We have noted that Bishop Trollope of Korea believed, and Bishop Tucker of Uganda would probably have agreed with him, that missionaries in a non-Christian land are very seriously handicapped unless they can agree to a substantially unanimous presentment of the faith which is in them." He believed that he owed it to his simple Korean Christians to shelter them from disturbing dissimilarities in worship or discipline. Trollope in Korea and Tucker in Uganda imparted the faith in the fullness of those systems which corresponded to their own convictions and experience. Yet no one would claim that either combined in his own person the whole ethos of the Anglican heritage. The fact must be faced that, to return to our metaphor, the Anglican stained-glass window is not a mosaic of many-coloured fragments blended into a harmonious whole by the radiance of the divine sun shining through them; it would be nearer the truth to say that it is composed of separate lights, each of a prevailing hue, not necessarily blending harmoniously with the colour of its neighbouring light.

In a fictitious account of an imaginary conference, the Chairman, an aged African Bishop, is reported to have expressed himself as follows :—

> " He himself owed everything to the traditions of the Missionary Society which had brought Christianity to his country: he was a grateful and fervent upholder of those traditions. But a wider knowledge of the Anglican Communion throughout the world had forced him to recognise that those traditions represented only one aspect of the Anglican Communion. He could not but covet for his Church a knowledge and appropriation of other aspects of truth: he could not but feel anxiety lest one aspect developed in isolation from all others might breed error: he was not content that his country should be presented with an incomplete and fractional interpretation of the whole truth as it is in Christ. He attributed the limitations he had in mind to the organisation of the Home Church; they were the reflection of its partial loyalties—to Cephos, to Apollos, to Paul; and he begged that the danger of rivetting such limitations upon the Church of Africa and the necessity of counteracting any harm they may have inflicted in the past, should be borne in mind."

The old African Bishop is certainly entitled to a hearing. It is not easy in England to recognize how much we are enriched by rubbing shoulders with those whose experience and convictions differ from our own: cross-fertilization, however unobserved, tempers our bigotries. Nor is it easy to realize that it is the African, Indian or Chinese Church which pays the price of our segregation into the parties which are complacently assumed to be of the nature of things. If we place ourselves in the position of the Korean who crosses the Straits of Tsushima into Kyushu, of a soldier catechumen in Tanga who returns to his home in Kauirondo, of a Nigerian transferring to the neighbouring diocese of Accra, it becomes obvious that the disturbance of the converts' mind by dissimilarities in worship and discipline has only been postponed. He will not find it easy to recognize his own Church. This painful feature in the expansion of the Anglican Communion is no subject for praise or blame—it may be nobody's fault or everybody's—but it cannot be omitted from notice in any faithful presentation of all the facts relevant to the consolidation of the Anglican Communion as it is.

The Basis of Anglican Unity

So many of the safeguards on which, at one time or another, men pinned their hopes for the consolidation of the Anglican Communion have one after another been discarded that little seems left. The State connexion went first, unmourned. The vision of a Super-Synod dissolved. The central Tribunal was chivied from the stage. The Articles were dethroned. The Prayer-Book lost its pre-eminence. The notion of a Patriarch of Canterbury was still-born.

It can hardly be an accident that there is so close a correspondence between the Church which looks to Canterbury as the Mother Church and the Commonwealth which looks to Great Britain as the Mother Country. Common to both is an inherited distrust of written constitutions, a faith in life rather than logic, a refusal to be disturbed by incompleteness of organization, a confidence that in time of crisis the dynamic of a deep-seated common purpose will leap into operation. " We in England," wrote Dean Church, " with a kind of gallant contempt for the protection of a theory, shaped our measure as well as we could, to suit the emergencies which at the moment most compelled the attention of the steersman at the helm. The English Reformation ventured on its tremendous undertaking with what seems the most slender outfit of appliances. Principles it had, but they were very partially explored, applied, followed out to consequences, harmonised, limited . . . Laws, all but the most indispensable, Canons, Synods, tribunals, the adjustment of the differing elements of its constitution, were adjourned to a more convenient season, which in fact has never arrived."

Mulberry, Pluto, Fido, and other marvels of war-time organization have perhaps dethroned Muddle for ever from its pedestal as the symbol of the nation's faith in itself. It has proved as expensive an object of worship for the Church as for the Nation, and the price is paid by the innocent and distant. It may be questioned whether so massive a Society as the Anglican Communion ought to expect to maintain its solidarity if it adjourns indefinitely " the adjustment of the different elements of its constitution," and the development of organs of consolidation. But that is for the future and beyond the province of this book.

We may sum up the past in a quotation from the Lambeth Conference Report of 1897 : " Each decade as it passes brings out more clearly our duty to maintain and develop the coherence of the Anglican Communion. We have to realize more and more explicitly the value of the unique combination of respect for authority and consciousness of freedom in the truth which distinguishes the great body in which God has called us to minister."

We may find guidance for the future in the Lambeth Conference of 1920 : " Because our Church has spread over the world, and still more because we desire to enter into the world-wide fellowship of a reunited universal Church, we must begin now to clear ourselves of local, sectional and temporary prepossessions, and cultivate a sense of what is universal and genuinely Catholic in truth and in life."

As for the present, it is summarized in the Report of the last Lambeth Conference, held in 1930 : " There are two prevailing types of ecclesiastical organisation : that of centralised government and that of regional autonomy within one fellowship. Of the former the Church of Rome is the great historical example. It is upon the latter principle that the Anglican Communion is founded. It is a fellowship of Churches directly associated with the British Isles. While these Churches preserve apostolic doctrine and order, they are independent in their self-government, and are growing up freely on their own soil and in their own environment as integral parts of the Church Universal. It is after this fashion that the characteristic endowment of each family of the human race may be consecrated, and so make its special contribution to the Kingdom of God. The bond which holds us together is spiritual. . . . The Anglican Communion includes not merely those who are racially connected with England, but many others whose faith has been founded on the doctrine and ideals for which the Church of England has always stood.

What are these doctrines ? We hold the Catholic faith in its entirety: that is to say, the truth of Christ, contained in Holy Scripture; stated in the Apostles' and Nicene Creeds; expressed in the Sacraments of the Gospel and the rites of the Primitive Church as set forth in the Book of Common Prayer with its various local adaptations; and safeguarded by the historic three-fold order of the Ministry.

What are these ideals ? They are the ideals of the Church of Christ. Prominent among them are an open Bible, a pastoral Priesthood, a common worship, and a fearless love of truth. We acknowledge thankfully as the fruits of these ideals, the sanctity of mystics, the learning of scholars, the courage of missionaries, the uprightness of civil administrators and the devotion of many servants of God in Church and State."

THE RÔLE OF THE MOTHER CHURCH

Child psychologists are never tired of warning parents that unless they periodically submit their relations with their offspring to ruthless scrutiny, they run the risk of forfeiting their affection and exposing them to neuroses which will ruin their lives. " Woe betide the parents who delay too long the giving of their children sufficient liberty, even though they use their liberty to make mistakes. There comes a time when advice is more valuable than command."

The Church of England in her relation with her daughters has not been unmindful of these pitfalls. Latch-keys have been conceded. Allowances appropriate to age and responsibility have been continued as long as they were needed. Interference has been scrupulously avoided. At family gatherings a becoming reticence has been observed and no questions have been admitted that savoured of indiscreet curiosity. Relations of the children with their parent, and with one another, though occasionally strained, have been on the whole conducted with decorum and family affection. "How sharper than a serpent's tooth it is, to have a thankless child!" "Idle old man, that still would manage those authorities that he hath given away!" There has been no such exchange of pleasantries between the generations within the Anglican Communion.

It is a natural outcome of this mutual respect, or when need be, mutual forbearance, that the Lambeth Conferences, so prolific in discussions on the machinery of constitutional consolidation, have been economical in the time and attention bestowed upon what was the domestic affair of each Church, namely its method of discharging its missionary obligations. More than one of the systems summarized in Chapter IV were represented at the Conferences: it was delicate ground to tread, and only three times has it been trodden.

(a) In 1897, it was noted that the General Convention of the Episcopal Church in the U.S.A., the representative body of the whole Church, was also its Board of Missions, in contrast with the English habit of entrusting its Missions to the special care of Societies within the Church. "In the failure of the Church as a whole to realize the bounden duty to be the great Missionary Society of the world, the work could only be done by some of her members forming themselves into societies within the Great Society to do what is the work of the entire Church. . . . These Societies have supplied a Providential stage in leading the whole Church to a higher conception, which has never yet been adequately worked out in Church history." "The Societies do not profess to do more than form or found Churches, retiring from the work when the missions pass on to the stage of organised Church life."

(*b*) The Conference of 1908 waxed bolder. It talked of the " overlapping of missionary agencies, each with its committee, secretaries, organising secretaries, deputations and staff, and the placing of missionary effort on a wrong footing in the estimates of too many, as though it were simply a matter of choice, and a response to the efforts of rival agencies."

> " As the Church rises to a higher spiritual level and insists on doing its own work . . . the drawbacks will be removed. The whole deputation system in England will give way, we hope, to a sounder system, in which the clergy will not wait for deputations to visit their parishes, but will regard their Mission work as on precisely the same footing as the care of the sick and the young, glad enough to obtain from time to time the services of those who have been abroad and can testify of the work from personal experience, but not dependent on such visits; studying themselves the increasing literature that illustrates the work, and informing their people as to the progress of the Church of Christ as a regular part of their pastoral work, and not only when collections are made.
>
> " When the Church at home rises to this higher level, much of the present overlapping of agencies will be avoided, the home expenditure of the Societies will be much reduced, the missionary vocation will be brought into greater prominence, and the essential unity of the work at home and abroad far better realised."

The Report welcomed the formation of Diocesan Boards of Missions as the means of co-ordinating missionary agencies and enabling supporters of the various Societies to realize their essential unity.

(*c*) It was however reserved for the 1920 Conference, with Bishop Westcott, Metropolitan of India, presiding over the " Missionary Problems " Committee to provide a classic exposition of the system of Home Organization. A section headed " Missionary Societies still indispensable " at first sight suggests that the British system had come into its own again, but on closer examination it proves to have no relevance to dual systems. It is indeed what may for convenience be called the American system which is twice dubbed " the normal." It is described as:—

> " the one which the newer Churches have almost universally adopted, as in itself the normal way, and arising out of the nature of the Church; " the method by which " the whole Body is so ' organised for missions ' that one current of enthusiasm and

activity flows through and out of every member, every group, and every individual. .... Great decisions are made in full Synod, and the executive is in the hands of a Board over which the Synod is supreme. . . . This organisation for Missions, to which the large English-speaking Churches have come completely or in part, is being adopted spontaneously and, so to speak, instinctively, by the indigenous Churches of other races; in the dioceses, for example, of Uganda, of Nigeria, of Dornakal; in the Nippon Sei Ko Kwai and the Chung Hua Sheng Kung Hui. Sometimes the diocese, sometimes the Province, is the unit, but in all such cases the initiative and the control are synodical." "The system which we have called the normal method is probably admitted on hands to be in itself the better."

Where, however, the method of Society organization prevails (to which the Report applies the term used in Chapter IV, great "chartered" Societies, acting as specialized channels through which the energy of the Body has found itself flowing), "it should be used to the full." "We believe that it can be used to the full within a Church which is itself, as a Church, conscious of its own corporate Mission."

The subject of the co-ordination of missionary agencies receives fuller treatment than in 1908. "A central Advisory Council may guide, or wisely influence, all the agencies by which zeal is aroused, funds collected, and workers recruited, and may direct their associated energies to the needs of the enterprise which from time to time are seen to be most urgent or most hopeful."

This leads on to the first official mention of the Central Board of Missions, which " aims, but on a small scale and tentatively, at some such co-ordination of agencies " and " exists in order to represent and express the mind of the Church in respect to its work overseas." " The creation of the National Assembly of the Church of England with statutory powers, able to give expression to the voice of the Church, has produced a new condition. It is desirable that the Central Board of Missions should be under its control. . . . The National Assembly must make itself responsible for expressing the mind of the Church in all that belongs to its overseas work; it should claim from the first and as a whole, to be the supreme missionary authority, superseding none but embracing and co-ordinating all."

It is a quarter of a century since this important Committee framed its recommendations and it is worth while asking why they never proved acceptable enough to be implemented. The expectation that the National Assembly would " claim from the first and as a whole to be the supreme missionary authority " has not been fulfilled.

(a) The composition of Bishop Westcott's Committee provides one clue. Out of its fifty-two members only four represented home dioceses; only two could speak from first-hand knowledge of Missionary Society Headquarters; eleven were from the Far East, four from India, seven from Africa, while the fifteen who represented the U.S.A., Canada, Australia and New Zealand could only speak from experience of what the Conference called the " normal method " of missionary administration.

A Committee thus composed could not but be inhibited by motives of delicacy from drastic comment on the Church of England's domestic arrangements for conducting its missionary operations. Most of the dioceses represented on the Committee owed too much to the Missionary Societies for their Bishops to feel free to criticize their organization. Their unfamiliarity with the actual workings of the English system deprived their recommendations of the authority which only belongs to the rulings of a body intimately conversant with the nuances of the situation.

The rôle of the Mother Church is not in fact a Lambeth Conference question in the first instance. The formulation of proposals for adjusting its home-base organization is primarily a domestic concern of each local Church. This is not to deny that at a later stage the criticism and ratification of such proposals by a Lambeth Conference would be valuable and even necessary, for only the Bishops could say authoritatively whether they were likely to imperil or ensure the security of their dioceses, to soothe or shock the susceptibilities of the Churches they represent.

(b) The date of the Conference provides a second clue. The atmosphere of 1920 was charged with optimism inspired by the infant League of Nations. The phrase " supreme authority, superseding none but embracing and co-ordinating all " had a certain topicality. As the authors of the Covenant thought to circumvent the sovereign rights of States, so the authors of the 1920 Report thought to circumvent the sovereign rights of the Missionary Societies. Did their respective policies founder on analogous rocks ? Had the authors of either fully realized the extent and implications of the autonomous powers enjoyed and guarded by the corporate units which they wished to see incorporated in a larger whole ?

(c) A third clue is provided by the fact that the phrase " supreme authority, superseding none but embracing and co-ordinating all " could not be expanded because " our limits do not allow us to deal with those essential parts of the Home Church's work, for the sake of which the organization we have been treating of exists." But it contained elements difficult to reconcile, if not contradictory of one another. It would be impossible for the National Assembly to assume supreme authority without superseding the existing authority of autonomous Societies—without some curtailment of their powers. These powers were not in excess of the responsibilities which, as we have seen, had been carried by the Societies with accumulating weight throughout the nineteenth century. But they were too extensive to be compatible with the supreme authority which it was desired to superimpose, without some measure of re-distribution of power; and it was not to be expected that the new Assembly would venture on any such measure without a more definite directive from the Lambeth Conference than had been forthcoming.

The Missionary Societies

As the " officially recognised agencies of the Church for its overseas work " the Societies between them hold a monopoly of the Church's missionary funds: they are, speaking broadly, the sole channel through which a parish or individual can contribute to the Church overseas; if one or other wishes to bestow a gift on the Church in Uganda, Zanzibar, or Jamaica, it must pass through the books of the C.M.S., the U.M.C.A. or the S.P.G. respectively, whether or no the donor desires to be identified with their distinctive characteristics. This gives the Societies the power of the purse: it leaves them free to decide in what proportions grants shall be allocated to what Churches or dioceses. Society Committees therefore have it in their power, by transferring their grants from the Church of X to the Church of Y, to affect fundamentally the relations between the Church of England and the Churches of X and Y. Questions of higher policy can be debated and decided behind closed doors by those who, however qualified to bring an expert judgement to bear upon them, are not necessarily in touch with the mind of other Societies, or of the Church as a whole.

No authority which allows such extensive powers to elude its control can be the " supreme missionary authority " anticipated by the Lambeth Conference of 1920. Such an authority, to be worthy of the name, would at least retain the possibility of working out a united strategy, of securing, for example, in consultation with the Churches of X, Y and Z that the whole of its resources are brought to bear in the place and manner most likely to be effective. A " supreme authority " should have some control over the selection, training and allocation of its emissaries, but the Church as such has acquired no right to a voice in these matters. It has ruled out all possibility of a world-strategy in its overseas relations by leaving supreme authority in the hands of its several Missionary Societies, independent of one another and autonomous.

We have said enough to show that the efforts of the Lambeth Conference of 1920 failed to mature, but they were not entirely fruitless. One of the first Acts of the Church Assembly in the following year was, in partial conformity with the 1920 recommendation, to create the Missionary Council in place of the Central Board of Missions. Forty of its members were nominated to form this Council with thirty representatives of the Missionary Societies and six co-opted members; its function was to be " to stimulate the sense of corporate responsibility in the Church, in such a way as to increase the volume and effectiveness of the service rendered by the Missionary Societies as officially recognised agencies of the Church for its overseas work." The last words of the Lambeth recommendation, " embracing and co-ordinating all " were rescued from the oblivion which enveloped the first.

z

The Missionary Council

Dr. Cash in *The Missionary Church* may be quoted as an authority on the merits and limitations of the Missionary Council. He welcomes its formation as " the most outstanding event in the recent history of the Church. By its constitution the Council is not a super-missionary society. It administers no overseas work, and is pledged not to raise funds but to function as a co-ordinating body ... its main function is to strengthen and support the Societies, ever seeking through missionary education and other means to increase their incomes and to further the work they have undertaken on behalf of the Church. The Societies still maintain their separate existence and the Missionary Council draws them all into co-operation and fellowship. All the Societies in co-operation in the Missionary Council recognise its place and position in the life of the Church to-day, and that position is secure so long as the Council does not ... administer and control work overseas. If once it did this, it would lose its distinctive character and thereby much of its support and co-operation accorded to it by the Societies."

The Missionary Council during its twenty-five years of life has witnessed and taken its part in a substantial advance in the spirit and practice of co-operation, especially at Headquarters. In Area Committees of the Council, preparing annually a Unified Statement of the main events and problems within their respective spheres, representatives of all the Anglican agencies concerned have found an opportunity for common counsel. Team work between the officers of the Societies and the Council has been characteristic of the missionary education movement, the missionary approach to Youth, and the campaign for enlisting recruits. It is symptomatic of the prevailing mood that when plans were set on foot for a Younger Clergy Missionary Fellowship it was taken for granted that this must be, not as formerly on a Society basis, but on a comprehensive Church foundation.

Dr. Cash is on impregnable ground when he states that " The Church has no machinery of its own by which it could be its own missionary society." This does not of course settle the academic question whether in the past the Church could or should have developed such machinery or the practical question whether it could or should develop it in the future. It is not a case of the Church having tried and failed to bring such machinery into existence: the reader will search our survey of the nineteenth century in vain for any vestige of such an endeavour. The Church was throughout content to leave missionary policy and propaganda in the hands of Societies. The position may be compared to that of a miller who abandons as unnecessary and impracticable any expansion of his plant in a down-stream town because he is content that his up-stream branches should divert the water to work mills on either bank.

Dean Church has been quoted as saying that " we in England with a kind of gallant contempt for the protection of a theory, shaped our measures as well as we could, to suit the emergencies which at the moment compelled the attention of the steersman." The story of the Church's expansion, as we have seen, reflects this national characteristic. Optimists assume that the Church's missionary institutions will prove to resemble other national institutions which look unworkable on paper but work well enough in practice. But the parallel of the British Empire suggests that the world would have been a very different place and the war a very different war if there had been no deliberate adjustment of its institutions; if there had been no Statute of Westminster: if the Chartered Companies had survived to block the path of Colonial government; if the Colonial Office had not given birth to the Dominions Office. " New occasions teach new duties: time makes ancient good uncouth; they must upward still and onward who would keep abreast of Truth." To keep abreast of growth equally demands the upward and onward spirit: the growth of a Church, like the growth of an Empire, involves the bold adaptation of institutions.

It does not follow that the parallel of the British Empire can be pressed to the point of detail: there are too many discrepancies between the Kingdoms of this world and the Kingdom of Christ. The parallel of the Chartered Company and the Missionary Society, for example, must be handled with caution. Readers of Trevelyan's *Social History of England* will recall that "There came an age when the powers and privileges of Chartered Companies could no longer be wisely entrusted to a private group of the Queen's subjects." We saw this happening in India and Uganda. Even Goldie's great work in Nigeria, just because it was great, had to be subordinated to a Minister responsible to Parliament: no private group of the Queen's subjects could be conceded permanent control of the relations between people and people, nation and nation. To assume that the analogy necessarily implies a parallel change in the relations between the Missionary Societies and the Church would be to overlook one fundamental contrast between Church and State. The Church has not the coercive power of the State: it does not impose rates and taxes: its revenue is drawn from free-will offerings; it shares with the Missionary Society the character of a voluntary and democratic association, and neither is more likely or less likely than the other to become impersonal or bureaucratic in its dealings. None the less the analogy of the Chartered Companies has its use as suggesting the dimensions of the problem of adaptation; it raises exactly the type of searching question which needs to be asked if an examination of the Mother Church's role is to probe below the surface to the deeper and more fundamental levels.

THE CASE FOR CONSULTATION

No one can foretell whether such an examination would establish a case for major or for minor adjustments in the Church's missionary organization. It could not fail to confer one far-reaching benefit, namely the reassurance of those who believe that in the world-wide Christian fellowship lies the greatest hope of the future of the world, and that within that fellowship the *Ecclesia Anglicana* has been allotted a special vocation. There are many of these who care deeply that the Church's visible organization should be such as in everything to make manifest and in nothing to obscure the character and destiny of the Church. If the whole ground were to be surveyed officially or unofficially by those best qualified to advise, there would be an end to any misgiving that this organization retains its nineteenth-century characteristics because nobody cares or dares to bring it up to date. The assurance that it had been searchingly scrutinized by the leaders of the Church, and adapted by them to the role of the Mother Church in changed and changing days, would liberate spiritual energy.

(i) Confidence would be restored in the resolve of the Church to conserve the harvest of the nineteenth century by adapting its methods realistically to the scale and circumstances of the twentieth-century enterprise.

(ii) The rank and file of the Church would be given the clear and comprehensive view of their obligation to the Church as a whole, which is necessary if their latent energy and interest are to be engaged.

(iii) The younger Churches would rest assured that their relationship with the Mother Church was understood and appreciated, as being not static but progressing.

(iv) Missionaries would be enheartened by the sense that the whole Church was behind them.

(v) The Missionary Societies would have everything to gain from a redefinition of their mandate.

(i) " On such a full sea are we now afloat, and we must take the current when it serves, or lose our venture." No reader can have followed the story sketched in these pages without realizing the scale and costliness of our forefathers' ventures. This legacy is a great trust. To lose their ventures would be the supreme tragedy. It would be a mistaken compliment to assume that we must necessarily take the current in vessels rigged as theirs were rigged. Their experiences and their achievements must be taken into account as having themselves created the occasion for adaptation, if we in our turn are to catch

> " the tide in the affairs of men,
> Which, taken at the flood, leads on to fortune;
> Omitted, all the voyage of their life
> Is bound in shallows, and in miseries."

(ii) The present which we have inherited from our forebears makes its own demand for a re-examination of missionary institutions. The growth of Church-consciousness stands out as a dominant characteristic of the twentieth-century Church. The Home Church has its share of it, and this has its bearing on the present discussion.

Archbishop William Temple used to urge the need for intermediary groupings between individuals and so vast a whole as the State. "The State is too large; the individual feels impotent and unimportant over against it; in his local or functional association he may count for something in the State and influence it. There must be groupings (the family, the school, the guild, the trade union, the village, the city, the county) small enough to enable the individual to feel (not only to think) that he can influence the quality of the larger group, and that it needs his contribution, so that he can develop a sense of responsibility towards it." The Archbishop went on to apply the same principle to the Church as being also too vast and world-wide to evoke a living allegiance without intermediary groupings: parish, diocese, national Church, these were the traditional nurseries of ascending loyalties.

With the growth of Church-consciousness many are finding in the parish and its subsidiary associations, in the Diocese and Church Assembly and their subsidiary associations, the satisfaction of their need for intermediate units: Parochial and Diocesan Groups, Committees, Conferences, Schools of Study, elicit the enthusiastic loyalty and evoke the self-sacrificing and prayerful service which has in the past been specially associated with membership of sectional Societies within the Church. In connection with the overseas work of the Church its members find that they must range themselves with one or another section of the Church, since no Missionary Society is co-terminous with the whole Church, either ecclesiastically or geographically. The fact that the missionary organizations of the Church are thus sectional and cut across those on a more comprehensive Church basis, obscures the total view of the task and character of the Church, and alienates the sympathy of those who kindle more readily to an appeal based on the mutal relationship and interdependence of Churches than to one based on the needs of Societies.

(iii) Of the growth of Church-consciousness in the Church overseas we have noted the evidence in Part XI. This too has its bearing on missionary organization at the home base. Lambeth Conferences were mainly concerned with two aspects of the subject: (i) the relations between the younger Churches and the Missionary Societies, with a view to their closer integration on the field; (ii) the relations between the Church and the Missionary Societies at home with a view to removing the reproach that the Church of England, to its spiritual impoverishment, had lost sight of its corporate missionary obligations. Much has happened in the intervening years to bring to the fore a third aspect of the question. The coming of age of overseas Churches, and their growth in Church-consciousness, inspire and entitle them to entertain views as to the type of missionary organization with which they would prefer to deal. There is even a certain restlessness because the euthanasia of the Missions in the Church has not been accompanied by any corresponding euthanasia of the Missionary Society: because Churches which have achieved a corporate voice through which to express themselves find corresponding voices at the English end with which they cannot converse as Church with Church, but only as Church with Missionary Society.

Some may think it regrettable but nobody need be surprised, that the Church of India, Burma, and Ceylon, or the Chung Hua Sheng Kung Hui, should feel it more consonant with its dignity, and with the facts, to deal as Church with Church on mutual terms of equality, rather than with Missionary Societies. Much has happened since 1920. The repudiation, for example, of foreign missionaries and foreign subsidies by the Church of Japan in 1940 would then have been unthinkable and constitute a warning. There is a new and healthy sensitivity to whatever brands Christianity and the Church with the stigma of foreign-ness, and dependence on the foreigner. The Tambaram Conference with its title " The World Mission of the Church " exhibited and expedited a general determination to think in terms of the Church. The term " Missionary Society " which would have passed muster twenty-five years ago now suggests to many an inferior status in the recipients of its bounty. It is pointed out by way of contrast that from New Testament days, Church has always stood by Church, to the enrichment of mutual respect and fellowship.

(iv) If volunteers for overseas service are to be forth-coming and if having entered the service of the Churches overseas they are to maintain their energies at the maximum, they must have unshaken confidence that their assigned tasks are well and truly co-ordinated, and are subordinated to the long-term strategy of the whole Church which they serve. Nothing dims the joy or dulls the lustre of Christian service so disastrously as the misgiving that the will of the Lord is being thwarted by the survival of obsolete equipment or outmoded tactics, or by short-sighted and unrealistic strategy.

(v) The Missionary Societies need no better insurance against rash reform or superficial criticism than the reverence which knowledge of their past history must inspire. Nobody who has followed this story of the expansion of the Anglican Communion can fail to be impressed by the magnitude of the debt which it owes to the Missionary Societies and to the unnumbered hosts of their supporters. The Anglican Communion owes its existence, humanly speaking, to the men of faith and vision who founded these voluntary associations, and to all who at great personal sacrifice financed their ventures. They hold between them the title-deeds of all the Anglican Churches throughout the world: their annals embody great traditions; their Rolls of Honour are inscribed with noble names; they possess that rich sense of family continuity which famous regiments derive from their common heritage of heroes and their corporate history of adventure and achievement. Of the Societies it may reverently be said that they bear in their bodies the marks of the Lord Jesus.

No misgiving or impatience for adaptation must be allowed to eclipse that debt. No pre-occupation with long-term policy can excuse any failure to meet the urgent situations which confront the Societies at the moment, or to extract every ounce of benefit and inspiration from their missionary leadership; any failure at this critical moment in world history to stand by the Hosts of the Lord on all the frontiers of His Kingdom, or to press on with them into the regions beyond, where the good news of God in Christ is still unheralded. Christian history is still in the making.

EPILOGUE

A.D. 2000

O God! Thy arm was here;
And not to us, but to Thy arm alone,
Ascribe we all.
Come, go we in procession to the village:
And be it death proclaimed through our host
To boast of this or take the praise from God
Which is His only.
Do we all holy rites:
Let there be sung " Non nobis " and " Te Deum "

Henry V, Act iv. Scene viii.

" Holy is the True Light and passing wonderful, lending radiance to them that endured in the heat of the conflict; from Christ they inherit a home of unfading splendour, wherein they rejoice with gladness evermore."

(Words from the old *Church Service Book* selected by Sir Herbert Baker to encircle the dome of the Assembly Hall in his new Church House.)

"AS though in preparation for such a time as this, God has been building up a Christian fellowship which now extends into almost every nation, and binds citizens of them all together in true unity and godly love; almost incidentally the great world-fellowship has arisen; it is the great new fact of our era." It was with these words from Archbishop William Temple's Enthronement Sermon that our survey began. In outline the story of nineteenth-century expansion has now been told. Great stories carry their own moral within them. It is not the part of the annalist to preach or prophesy. But there are three notes which a musician would be expected to strike if called upon to improvise an appropriate Finale. It should open with a paean of praise.

" Non nobis and Te Deum." " They gat not the land in possession through their own sword; neither was it their own arm that helped them; But thy right hand and thine arm and the light of thy countenance; because thou hadst a favour unto them." Our story has been full of human endeavours and heroisms, but it will have gone awry if it is not the Eternal Purpose of God which shines out through its pages. In preparation for such a time as this God was working His purpose out. It is with the joy and confidence of membership in a God-created fellowship that Christians are called to face and fashion the future.

Thanksgiving to God would certainly be the motif which all who endured in the heat of the conflict would approve, to the exclusion of all thought of themselves. But we have no right to exclude from our thanksgiving those who have bequeathed so rich a legacy of memories and traditions. Any review of the holy Catholic Church throughout the world must lend radiance to the conception of the Communion of Saints and set aglow the sense of unity in continuity with the glorious company of the Apostles, the goodly fellowship of the Prophets, the noble army of Martyrs.

The Finale should then soar to the heights of resolve, but not without an intermezzo in a different key. Our story would have misled if it had not honestly recorded what is matter for humiliation rather than exultation. It is clear that at no time within the century could those who endured in the heat of the conflict look confidently for the reinforcements they needed. Nor could they depend on their home Church to give its whole mind to the strategy or its whole will to the execution of what they believed to be the divine design. The Church had too many preoccupations; some of these were strengthening and healthy —preoccupation with the revival of its own life and worship, with crying social evils on their own doorstep; some of them weakening and pathological—preoccupation with partisan contentions, as though St. Paul in his letter to the Corinthians had been too naïve to be taken seriously. So far from setting a model to the world of politics of how men should behave one towards another when they differed on vital issues, the Church itself accepted the parliamentary model as its own, acquiescing in the system and to some extent the spirit of party as normal and necessary concomitants of Church life. The Celtic and Continental strands in the Anglican genealogy have often failed to intertwine. Division of function has taken precedence of the co-ordination of functions, and where no nerve system connects limbs and brain, the body is inevitably smitten with lassitude. Human infirmities cast their shadows on the nineteenth-century record.

But it is on the note of dedication and resolve that the Finale should reach its climax. It is for this reason that the date A.D. 2000 is prefixed to these concluding words. It is remote enough to see most of the over-thirties into their graves, not too remote to see many of the under-thirties still in their prime: remote enough to cool the polemical temperature, yet near enough to set the present in perspective. All aim to build a structure which will still be standing in A.D. 2000 and beyond. It should be possible to debate objectively whether what is in process of construction will go to the making of that structure, or will need to be altered or undone to make room for the architecture of the future. Abbot Haimon's account of the Cathedral Builders of Chartres suggests the spirit of discipline and dedication in which the Church of A.D. 2000 should be raised aloft:—

" Who has ever seen or who heard in all the ages of the past that Kings, princes and lords, mighty in their generation, have bowed their haughty necks to the yoke and harnessed themselves to carts like beasts of burden, and drawn them laden with all things needful for the construction of the Church, even to the doors of the asylum of Christ ?

" But what is even more astonishing is that, although sometimes a thousand or more of men and women are attached to one cart, so vast is the mass, so heavy the load—yet so deep a silence reigns that not a voice, not a whisper even can be heard. And when there is a halt called on the way there is no sound save that of the confession of sins and suppliant prayer to God for pardon.

" There whilst the priests are preaching peace all hatred is lulled to sleep and quarrels are banished, debts forgiven and the union of hearts re-established. Forward they press, unchecked by rivers, unhindered by mountains."[1]

" Construction is not the dull subject that some would have it to be," wrote Sir Thomas Jackson in *Reason in Architecture*. " It only needs to be understood to become interesting."

" It would surprise many people as they stand in the silence of some great Gothic minster, whose ancient stones seem to have grown old in peaceful calm and slumberous quiet, if they were to

[1] Cecil Headlam : *The Story of Chartres*.

realize the truth that so far from everything being at rest around them they were surrounded by mighty unseen forces engaged in active combat, thrusting and counter-thrusting one another in fierce encounter, a never-ending conflict that never slackens between antagonists that never tire; the high vaults striving to push the walls outwards but rebuffed by the flying buttresses which try to push them inwards; the aisle vaults doing their best to push the nave columns inwards but unable to move them under the dead-weight of the superstructure of triforium and clerestory which holds them down; the whole fabric struggling to burst asunder, but manfully resisted by the system of counter-vailing forces, which only bargains as a condition of success, that their great parent buttresses outside shall stand like a rock and give them a firm footing from which to get a purchase—buttresses loaded with heavy pinnacles whose weight helps them to assimilate the force which attacks them obliquely.''

Sir Thomas Jackson's analysis of forces in active combat and fierce encounter might be interpreted by the cynic as applicable to Minsters not made with hands, but that would be to distort the two-fold moral of the parable. Whoso stands in silent contemplation of the Church of A.D. 2000 must not underrate the incalculable potency of the forces which menace its stability and equilibrium. A Society so omni-national and omni-racial as the Church is exposed to the thrust and counterthrust of the most powerful and most divisive motives which move mankind. It will not survive by accident or automatically; the whole fabric will burst asunder without active and acknowledged mutual interdependence. Sir Thomas happens to interpret Interdependence in terms of mutual combat and bargain: it is equally legitimate to interpret Interdependence in terms of mutual support and sacrifice, and this is the appropriate language to apply to the architecture of the Church of A.D. 2000, the condition of all great building. Pinnacles, buttresses, columns, walls and vaults must conspire, as countervailing forces, to neutralize one another's weaknesses, and grip the whole fabric together, that it may be worthy in beauty and majesty, in solidarity and unity, to be offered to Him for whose worship and service it has been called into existence.

SOME BOOKS FOR FURTHER REFERENCE

IT is inevitable that a bibliography of nineteenth-century literature should contain the names of many books which have gone out of circulation. Those mentioned here can, however, be obtained at the Lending Libraries of the Missionary Societies.

I. HISTORIES

" The study of history is the best cordial for drooping spirits."—BISHOP LIGHTFOOT.

ADDISON, J. T. **The Mediæval Missionary :** A Study of the Conversion of Northern Europe A.D. **500–1300.**

ALLEN AND McLURE. **Two Hundred Years :** the History of the S.P.C.K. **1698–1898.**

ARNOLD, T. W. **The Preaching of Islam.**

BARKER, Professor ERNEST. **The Legacy of Islam :** The Crusades.

BEDE, The Venerable. **Ecclesiastical History.**

BRIGHT, W. **Early Chapters in English Church History.**

BROWNE, L. E. **The Eclipse of Christianity in Asia.**

BROWNE, Bishop G. F. **The Conversion of the Heptarchy.**

BUCHANAN, CLAUDIUS. **Christian Researches in Asia.**

BUCHANAN, CLAUDIUS. **An Apology for Promoting Christianity in Asia.**

Cambridge History of the British Empire. Vol. II.

CAMPBELL, T. S. **The Jesuits 1534–1921.**

CARPENTER, S. C. **Church and People, 1789–1889.**

CASH, Bishop W. **The Missionary Church.**

CASH, Bishop W. **The Expansion of Islam.**

CASH, Bishop W. **Christendom and Islam.**

CHATTERTON, Bishop EYRE. **A History of the Church of England in India.**

CHURCH, R. W. **History of the Oxford Movement.**

COOPER-MARSDIN, A. C. **History of the Islands of the Lérins.**

COULTON, G. G. **Mediæval Panorama :** The English Scene from the Conquest to the Reformation.

COUPLAND, R. **East Africa and its Invaders.**

COUPLAND, R. **Exploitation of Africa, 1856–1890.**

DAWSON, C. **The Making of Europe.**

DUKE, J. A. **The Columban Church.**

EATON, A. W. **The Church in Nova Scotia.**

ELTON, Lord. **Imperial Commonwealth.**

FENGER, J. F. **History of the Tranquebar Mission** (translated).

FINDLAY AND HOLDSWORTH. **History of the Wesleyan Methodist Missionary Society, 5** Vols.

FOAKES-JACKSON, F. J. **A History of Church History.**

FURNIVALL, J. S. **Netherlands India :** A Study of Plural Economy.

GARLICK, P. **The Wholeness of Man :** A Study of Medical Missions.

GIDNEY, W. T. **History of the London Society for Promoting Christianity among the Jews.**

GOUGAD, DOM LOUIS. **Christianity in Celtic Lands** (translated).

HAILEY, Lord. **African Survey.**

HANCOCK, W. K. **Survey of British Commonwealth Affairs,** Part II.

HERTZ, F. **Nationality in History and Politics.**

HODGKIN, R. H. **History of the Anglo-Saxons, 2** Vols.

HUTTON, J. E. **History of the Moravian Missions.**

JENKINS AND MACKENZIE. **Episcopacy Ancient and Modern** (composite).

KNOWLES, DOM DAVID. **The Monastic Order in England.**

KOSMALA AND SMITH. **The Jew in the Christian World.**

LAMBETH CONFERENCES. **The Six Lambeth Conferences 1867–1930.**

LATOURETTE, K. S. **A History of the Expansion of Christianity.**

LATOURETTE, K. S. **A History of Missions in China.**

LINDSAY, A. D. **Report of Commission on Christian Higher Education in India.**

LOVETT, R. **History of the London Missionary Society, 1795–1895, 2** Vols.

LOWTHER CLARKE, H. **Constitutional Church Government** (in the Dominions).

LUGARD, Lord. **Dual Mandate in British Tropical Africa.**

MacDONELL, S. D. **A History of the American Episcopal Church.**

MacMILLAN, W. M. **The Cape Colour Question.**

MacMILLAN, W. M. **Bantu, Boer, and Briton.**

MacMILLAN, W. M. **Africa Emergent.**

MacNICOL, NICOL. **The Religion of India.**

MANNA, PAOLO. **Conversion of the Pagan World.** Translated by FATHER J. F. McGLINCHEY.

MANROSS, N. W. **A History of the American Episcopal Church.**

MAYHEW, ARTHUR. **Christianity and the Government of India.**

MOORMAN, J. R. H. **Church Life in England in the Thirteenth Century.**

MUNRO, D. C. **The Kingdom of the Crusaders.**

MURRAY, A. V. **The School in the Bush.**

OLDHAM, J. H. **Christianity and the Race Problem.**

OMAN, Professor C. **England before the Norman Conquest.**

OPPERMAN, C. J. A. **English Missionaries in Sweden and Finland.**

ORR, C. W. J. **The Making of Modern Nigeria.**

PARKES, J. W. **The Jew in the Mediæval Community.**

PARKES, J. W. **The Conflict of the Church and the Synagogue.**

PASCOE, C. F. **Two Hundred Years of the S.P.G., 1701–1900,** 2 Vols.

PENNY, F. **The Church in Madras.**

PERHAM AND SIMMONS. **African Discovery.**

PICKETT, Bishop J. W. **Mass Movements in India.**

POWICKE, F. M. **Legacy of the Middle Ages :** The Christian Life.

ROBINSON, C. H. **The Conversion of Europe.**

SMEATON, D. M. (I.C.S.). **The Loyal Karens of Burma.**

SMITH, A. L. **Church and State in the Middle Ages.**

SOOTHILL, W. E. **China and the West.**

SOOTHILL, W. E. **The Religions of China.**

STENTON, F. M. **Anglo-Saxon England.**

STEPHEN, Sir JAMES. **Essays in Ecclesiastical Biography.**

STOCK, EUGENE. **History of the Church Missionary Society, 4** Vols.

SYKES, Professor N. **The Church in the Eighteenth Century.**

THOMAS AND SCOTT. **Uganda.**

TREVELYAN, G. M. **British History in the Nineteenth Century.**

TREVELYAN, G. M. **English Social History.**

TUCKER, Bishop H. ST. G. **History of the Episcopal Church in Japan.**

VERNON, C. W. **The Old Church in the New Dominion** (Canada).

WALKER, E. A. **The British Empire :** Its Structure and Spirit.

WAND, Bishop. **A History of the Modern Church from 1500.**

WARNECK, GUSTAV. **History of Protestant Missions.**

WILLSON, T. B. **History of Church and State in Norway.**

WILSON, G. H. **History of the Universities' Mission to Central Africa.**

II. BIOGRAPHIES

" History is the essence of innumerable biographies."—T. CARLYLE

Alcuin. G. F. BROWNE.

Aldhelm. G. F. BROWNE.

Alfred, His Life and Times. C. PLUMMER.

Augustine of Canterbury. E. L. CUTTS.

Augustine and his Companions. G. F. BROWNE.

Bede, The Venerable. His Life and Writings. G. F. BROWNE.

Bede, Life, Times and Writings. Ed. by A. H. THOMPSON.

Benson, Archbishop. A. C. BENSON.

Bickersteth, Bishop Edward. SAMUEL BICKERSTETH.

Bompas, Bishop. The Apostle of the North. H. A. CODY.

Brooke, Rajah Sir James. SPENSER ST. JOHN.

Broughton, Bishop. F. T. WHITINGTON.

Buchanan, Claudius, 2 Vols. H. PEARSON.

Carey, William : in Everyman's Library. G. SMITH.

Carey, William, Missionary Pioneer and Statesman. F. DEAVILLE WALKER (S.C.M.).

Carey, William : Life and Times of Carey, Marshman and Ward. MARSHMAN, J. C.

Cassels, Bishop W. W. MARSHALL BROOMHALL.

Charlemagne. H. W. C. DAVIS.

Columba, St. Adamnan's Life of, ed. WILLIAM REEVES.

Corfe, Bishop. Bishop TROLLOPE.

Corrie, Bishop Daniel, Life of.

Cotton, Bishop G. E. L. Memoir of. Mrs. COTTON.

Crowther, Bishop Samuel. The Black Bishop. PAGE.

Davidson, Archbishop Randall. 2 Vols. G. K. A. BELL.

Duff, Alexander, 2 Vols. G. SMITH.

Duff, Alexander. W. PATON (S.C.M.).

Feild, Bishop. Memoir of Life and Episcopate. H. W. TUCKER.

Francis Xavier, St. E. A. ROBERTSON (S.C.M.).

French, Bishop Thomas Valpy : Life of. H. BIRKS. 2 Vols.

French, Bishop T. V.: Life of: H. BIRKS. 2 Vols.

French, Bishop Thomas Valpy : An Heroic Bishop. EUGENE STOCK.

Gairdner, Temple. C. PADWICK (S.C.M.).

Gobat, Bishop Samuel : His Life and Work.

Grant, Charles. HENRY MORRIS.

Gray, Bishop, 2 Vols. C. N. GRAY.

Gregory the Great : His place in History, 2 Vols. F. HOMES DUDDEN.

Grubb, W. Barbrooke : An Unknown People in an Unknown Land (autobiography).

Hannington, Bishop. E. C. DAWSON.

Heber, Bishop. G. SMITH.

Heber, Bishop, Journals, 3 Vols.

Hudson Taylor, and the China Inland Mission. Dr. and Mrs. H. TAYLOR.

Inglis, Charles : Life and Letters. C. LYDEKKER.

John, Griffiths : The Story of Fifty Years in China. R. WARDLAW-THOMPSON.

Johnson, W. P. My African Reminiscences 1875–1895 (U.M.C.A.).

Judson, Adoniram. Memoirs, 2 Vols. F. WAYLAND.

Kirk, Sir John. Kirk on the Zambesi. R. COUPLAND.

Krapf's Journals.

Leaders of the Northern Church : Bishop LIGHTFOOT.

Lefroy, Bishop : Life and Letters. Bishop MONTGOMERY.

Legge : James Legge, Missionary and Scholar. H. E. LEGGE.

Livingstone, David. Life. R. J. CAMPBELL.

Livingstone, David : Some Letters from. Ed. D. CHAMBERLIN.

McDougall, Bishop: Memoir of. C. J. BUNYON.

Machray, Archbishop of Rupertsland. R. MACHRAY.

Mackay, Alexander Murdoch : by his Sister.

Marks, John Ebenezer : Forty Years in Burma. PURSER.

Marsden, Samuel : Marsden and the Missions. E. RAMSDEN.

Marsden, Samuel : Letters and Journals, 1765–1858. J. R. ELDER.

Marsden, Samuel : Marsden's Lieutenants. J. R. ELDER.

Martyn, Henry. G. SMITH.

Martyn, Henry. C. PADWICK (S.C.M.).

Middleton, Bishop, 2 Vols. LE BAS.

Miller, W. R. S.: Reflections of a Pioneer (in Northern Nigeria).

Milman, Bishop. Memoir of. F. M. MILMAN.

Moffat, Robert: Letters recently discovered.

Morgan, E. R.: Ed. by. Essays Catholic and Missionary.

Morrison, Robert. MARSHALL BROOMHALL (S.C.M.).

Patteson, Bishop John Coleridge, 2 Vols. C. M. YONGE.

Pratt, Rev. Josiah: Memoir.

Raffles, Sir Stamford. H. E. EGERTON.

Raffles, Sir Stamford. R. COUPLAND.

Richard, Timothy. W. E. SOOTHILL.

Richard, Timothy: Forty-Five Years in China (Autobiography).

Schereschewsky, Bishop. J. A. MULLER.

Schwartz, Christian Frederick: Schwartz of Tanjore. J. PAGE.

Seabury, Bishop: Mission of. W. J. SEABURY.

Selwyn, Bishop George Augustus: Memoirs of Life and Episcopate. H. W. TUCKER.

Simeon, Charles: Simeon and Church Order. C. SMYTH.

Six Great Missionaries of the Sixteenth and Seventeenth Centuries. D. JENKS.

Smythies, Bishop, of Zanzibar. Memoirs. C. ALLAN.

Steere, Bishop, of Zanzibar. Memoirs. E HANBURY.

Stern, Aaron. A. A. ISAACS.

Tait, Archbishop: Life and Letters, 2 Vols. RANDALL DAVIDSON.

Talbot, John: Apostle of New Jersey, 1645-1727. E. L. PENNINGTON.

Theodore of Tarsus: Theodore and Wilfred. G. W. BROWNE.

Thornton, Douglas M. TEMPLE GAIRDNER.

Trollope, Bishop Mark Napier: Memoir.

Tucker, Bishop A. R. Eighteen Years in Uganda. Autobiography.

Tucker, Bishop A. R.: Tucker of Uganda, A. P. SHEPHERD (S.C.M.).

Venn, Rev. H.: Memoir. W. KNIGHT.

Watson, Joshua: Memoir, 2 Vols. E. CHURTON.

White, Bishop William: Life and Letters. W. H. STOWE.

Wilberforce, William. R. COUPLAND.

Williams, N. P. Northern Catholicism: The Theology of the Catholic Revival. Ed. by. (N.P.W.).

Wilson, Bishop Daniel, 2 Vols. J. BATEMAN.

Wolff, Joseph: Travels and Adventures, 3 Vols.

Ziegenbalg, Bartholomew: Lives of Missionaries. S.P.C.K.

INDEX

Printed in Great Britain at The Church Army Press, Cowley, Oxford.

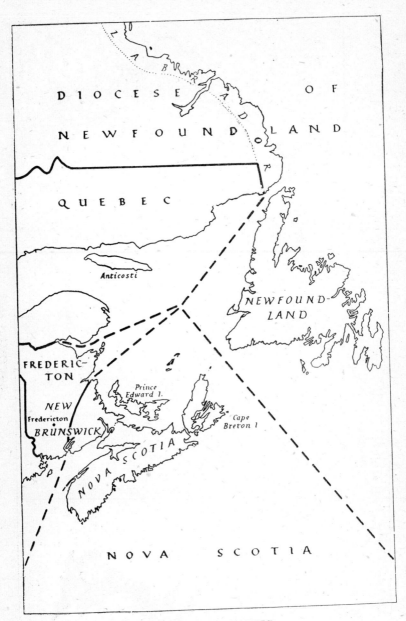

THE NORTH ATLANTIC

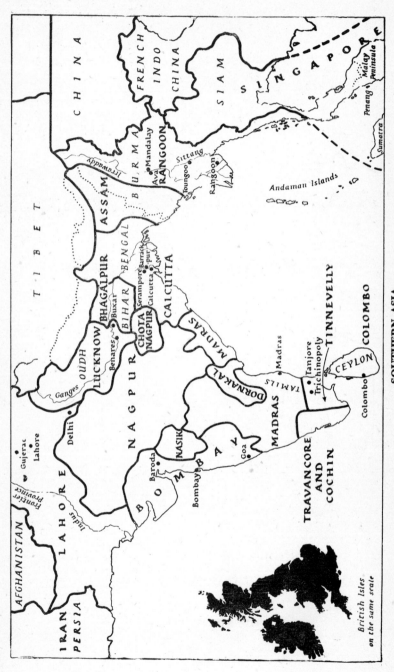

SOUTHERN ASIA

British Isles
on the same scale

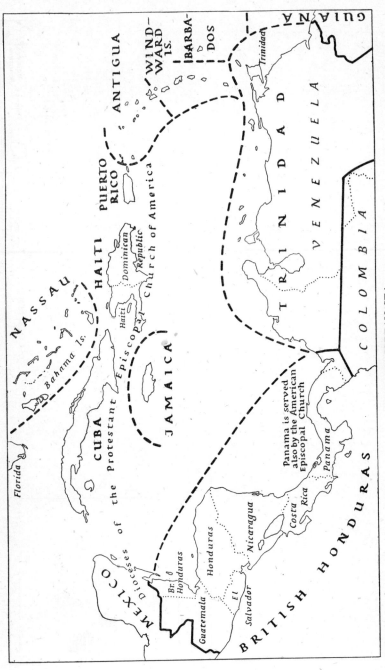

THE CARIBBEAN SEA

363

THE SOUTH PACIFIC

DIOCESES IN VICTORIA
& NEW SOUTH WALES

1 Melbourne   7 Goulburn
2 Ballarat   8 Sydney
3 St. Arnaud   9 Newcastle
4 Bendigo   10 Grafton
5 Wangaratta   11 Armidale
6 Gippsland   12 Bathurst
              13 Riverina

PROVINCE OF
NEW ZEALAND

1 Auckland   4 Wellington
2 Waikato   5 Nelson
3 Waiapu   6 Christchurch
              7 Dunedin

POLYNESIA

(MISSIONARY DIOCESES OF THE
PROVINCE OF NEW ZEALAND)

Society Is.
Tahiti
Samoa
Fiji

MELANESIA

NEW
GUINEA
(MISS. DIOCESE
OF THE PROVINCE
OF QUEENSLAND)

Santa Cruz
Is.
Guadalcanal

Norfolk I.

NORTH WEST
AUSTRALIA
CARPENTARIA
NORTH
QUEENSLAND
ROCKHAMPTON
BRISBANE · Brisbane
PERTH
KAL-
GOORLIE
BUNBURY
WILLOCHRA
ADELAIDE
AUSTRALIA

TASMANIA
(VAN DIEMAN'S
LAND)

Durham
Parramatta
Sydney
Botany Bay
Melbourne

NEW ZEALAND

NORTH I.
Bay of Islands
Auckland Waiapu
Wellington

SOUTH
I.

British Isles
on the same scale

364

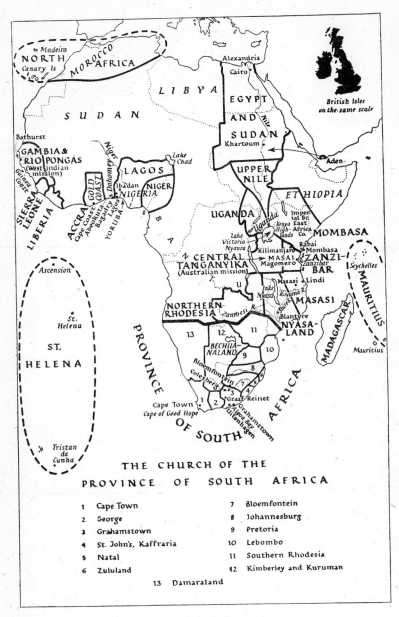

THE CHURCH OF THE
PROVINCE OF SOUTH AFRICA

1	Cape Town	7	Bloemfontein
2	George	8	Johannesburg
3	Grahamstown	9	Pretoria
4	St. John's, Kaffraria	10	Lebombo
5	Natal	11	Southern Rhodesia
6	Zululand	12	Kimberley and Kuruman
		13	Damaraland

AFRICA

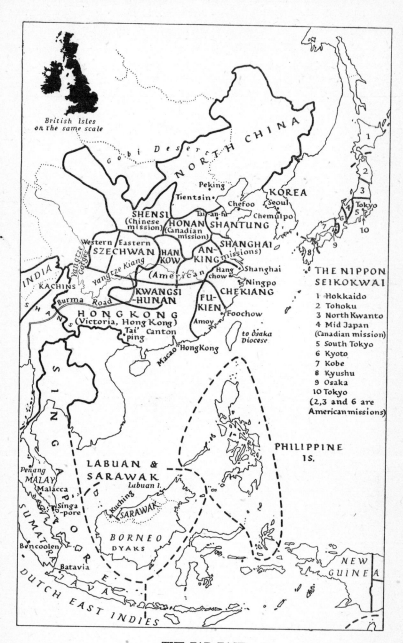

Labels on map:

British Isles on the same scale

Gobi Desert

NORTH CHINA

KOREA

Peking
Tientsin
Chefoo
Seoul
Chemulpo
Lu-an-fu

SHENSI (Chinese mission)
HONAN (Canadian mission)
SHANTUNG

Western   Eastern
SZECHWAN
HAN-KOW
AN-KING
SHANGHAI (missions)

Yangtze Gorges
Yangtze Kiang
(American)

Hang-chow
Shanghai
Ningpo

INDIA
KACHINS
Burma Road
KWANGSI -HUNAN
FU-KIEN
CHEKIANG

Foochow

HONG KONG (Victoria, Hong Kong)
Tai'ping
Canton
Amoy

to Osaka Diocese

Macao   HongKong

THE NIPPON SEIKOKWAI

1 Hokkaido
2 Tohoku
3 North Kwanto
4 Mid Japan (Canadian mission)
5 South Tokyo
6 Kyoto
7 Kobe
8 Kyushu
9 Osaka
10 Tokyo
(2,3 and 6 are American missions)

1 Tokyo
5 6
7
8
9
10

PHILIPPINE IS.

LABUAN & SARAWAK
Lubuan I.
Kuching
SARAWAK
BORNEO
DYAKS

Penang
MALAY
Malacca
Singa-pore
SUMATRA
Bencoolen
Batavia
JAVA
DUTCH EAST INDIES

NEW GUINEA

THE FAR EAST

366

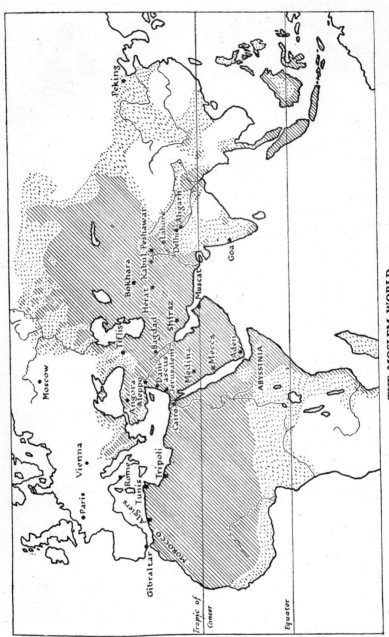

Peking

Moscow

Paris

Vienna

Rome
Tunis
Algiers
Gibraltar

Tripoli

MOROCCO

Angora
Aleppo
Damascus
Jerusalem
Cairo

Tiflis

Bokhara

Bagdad
Shiraz

Herat Kabul Peshawar
Lahore
Delhi Aligarh

Muscat

Medina
Mecca
Aden

Goa

ABYSSINIA

Tropic of Cancer

Equator

THE MOSLEM WORLD

PROVINCE OF THE WEST INDIES

British Isles
on the same scale

TRINIDAD

VENEZUELA

GUIANA

Br. Du. Fr.

COLOMBIA

ECUADOR

B R A Z I L

PERU

DIOCESE OF THE FALKLAND IS.

B O L I V I A

PARAGUAY

Gran Chaco

served also by
the American
Episcopal
Church

DIOCESE OF ARGENTINA AND EASTERN SOUTH AMERICA

Lengua

C H I L E

Andes

A R G E N T I N A

Patagonia

Buenos
Aires

FORMER

FORMER ARGENTINA SOUTH AMERICA

Falkland Is.

Terra
del Fuego

N O T E :
The two Dioceses covering most
of South America were combined
in January 1946 to form the
Diocese of the Falkland Is, Argentina, and Eastern South America

SOUTH AMERICA

368

89 Dioceses of the Protestant Episcopal Church of America

19